To professor Joseph Raz,
with my best wishes
for the future.

Madrid 27-I-2007

Punishment and Culture

Punishment and Culture:
A Right to Punish?

by

María José Falcón y Tella

Professor, Department of Legal Philosophy,
Ethics and Politics
Director of the Institute of Human Rights
Universidad Complutense, Madrid

Fernando Falcón y Tella

Doctor in Law
Assistant Professor, Department of Legal Philosophy,
Ethics and Politics
Universidad Complutense, Madrid

Translation into English by Dr. Peter Muckley

from

Fundamento y finalidad del castigo:
¿Un derecho a castigar?

Madrid, Marcial Pons

Martinus Nijhoff
Leiden • Boston

A C.I.P. Catalogue record for this book is available from the Library of Congress.

Printed on acid-free paper.

ISBN 90 04 15149 4

Koninklijke Brill NV incorporates the imprints Brill Academic Publishers, Martinus Nijhoff Publishers and VSP.

http://www.brill.nl

Printed and bound in The Netherlands.

To Carlos

Table of Contents

Preface

María José Falcón y Tella has asked me to pen some lines of presentation for this book, which she is publishing together with her brother, and I agree most happily because of the great satisfaction it gives me to do so. This is as much from a personal viewpoint as it is from the academic, both for the quality of the investigation, and because the person who asked me to write it is who she is.

I know, and consider most highly, María José Falcón y Tella, Professor of Legal Philosophy, Director of the "Instituto de Derechos Humanos de la Universidad Complutense", and disciple of Professor José Iturmendi Morales, Chair of the Discipline, and Dean of the Faculty of Law. I also know Fernando Falcón y Tella well, Doctor in Law, and Professor of the Department of Philosophy of Law who, doubtless, will follow in the footsteps, and the brilliant academic path, of his sister.

However, before speaking of the work to which this is prologue, allow me but a few words about María José Falcón y Tella because, with her, I have had a closer academic relationship, thanks to her post-graduate courses, her Masters, and the rest. She has organized these courses for some time now at the Institute of Human Rights, as well as lectures by illustrious colleagues (Jürgen Habermas, Ronald Dworkin, Michael Walzer or Joseph Raz, amongst others), given under the aegis of the Centre, which this disciple of Professor Iturmendi's directs, and which I have had the pleasure to attend.

I can say, straightaway – and with no exaggeration, because in the university community we are all well aware – that Professor Falcón y Tella has earned, through her intellectual rigour and tenacity, day by day, the prestige which all her colleagues recognize. Despite her youth, the investigative work and teaching of María José Falcón y Tella reveal, as in few cases happens, a scientific maturity rare for her age. She is, above all, a serious and rigorous intellectual, with an extraordinarily well-rounded intellectual background, restless, and always open to the analysis of reality, and to honest debate, free from dogma and prejudice.

Those who know her better point to the intellectual excellence, and great capacity for study, of Professor Iturmendi Morales' disciple, her discipline and total commitment to university tasks; and, above all, her sincere, personal attitude of unbribeable dedication to the search for truth, and to the "fight for law", proper to those who recognize in science a "social" and a "practical" vocation, at the service of mankind, which transcends the range of the merely theoretical-academic.

María José Falcón y Tella's scientific production, tenacious, brilliant and fruitful investigating, of course, has already reaped publishing success hardly common in the legal discipline. Some of her publications, I am aware, have been translated into various languages, and not a few, published in Spain, have seen various editions.

Still, if it were possible, I should emphasize even more than the above, her teaching skills. Students consider her a great professor. Moreover, a professor who delights in teaching, who feels passion for learning, and who communicates this. Probably because she thinks – quite rightly – that the end function of the scientist does not consist solely in treasuring up knowledge for herself, in warehousing discoveries, but rather in transmitting all these things to others.

The work I present here, dense and rigorous from the theoretical-conceptual point of view, but very clear and instructive, with masterly touch, tackles the complex problem of punishment; a classic, though always present, problem, a faithful indicator of humanity's evolution – of its lights and its shades, of its progress and its barbarism – which, as jurists and criminologists know, has traditionally pitted against one another two worlds difficult to reconcile: "white coats" and "black togas" (or, if you prefer, in a different fashion, two antagonistic methods: the empiricist, of the Natural Sciences, and the abstract, formal and deductive, of the normative disciplines).

The bibliographic section, the authors have attached, is rich and balanced, without any unnecessary parade of erudition, nor any concession to the latest demands of fashion. Personally, I must confess that what strikingly caught my attention was the objective selection of sources, and the precise and careful citing of the classics in the original languages. And, above all else, the expository and argumentative clarity of the work, which reconciles, in an admirable way, the precision proper to the delicate thought, abstract and categorical, on the one side, and, on the other, the teaching demands, which allow the reader access to the world of theoretical concepts. The authors make what is difficult, easy, but without simplifying or rendering banal, in the slightest.

In this excellent, prologued monograph, the reader will find objective, well-documented information on the problems relating to punishment which will be of interest to the most diverse of disciplines: to Philosophy and Ethics, to Social Pedagogy, to Psychology, Law, Sociology, and many more. To my way of thinking, the analysis of punishment, and its conceptual requisites in the Legal Sciences, carried out in the first chapter, is of particular interest. Further, the revising of the classic debate between free-willers and determinists; or between retributionists and deterrent advocates is spot on. I believe the authors are right to underline the reciprocal approximation which is today observed between the two, basic legal consequences, of Criminal Law (punishment and deprivation of liberty deterrents); likewise the dogmatic, categorical crisis of "guilt" in its classic sense, that is, bound to retributive schemes of deep moralizing and axiomatic connotations, difficult to empirically entertain, of "*anders handeln können*".

From a methodological viewpoint, I find their investigative premise unobjectionable: that only an interdisciplinary analysis may allow a scientific approximation to the total reality of punishment, as an Institution. That, therefore, the normative examination of the basis and ends of punishment (that is, the "ideal" foundation and goals "assigned" punishment) must be completed with another type of examination, one of an empirical and interdisciplinary character, that might verify the true functions which punishment really fulfils in today's society, considering the historical-political framework, and the State model, into which the social institution of punishment is inserted.

On another plane, the authors have known how to highlight the permanent dialectic tension found in the "being" and the "ought-to-be" of punishment, the framework or "factual", "real" support of this, and its normative covering. And, doubtless, they are right. Because, let us not fool ourselves: every day we appeal to "guilt" and to the "just deserts" of the offender to legitimate punishment, the punishment is "just", but, what do humans know of justice? "Legal" punishment really has little to do, in its pure state, with "just" punishment. I suspect that if punishment were legitimated solely, and exclusively, by reasons of justice, based on the objective deserts of the guilty man, the ironic words of Judge Chesterton to the accused would merit some serene consideration: "I sentence you to three years in prison, because the law so decrees, but God knows full well that what you need is three weeks on the beach". Between the ideal aims of punishment and prison reality a great abyss yawns. Legal academics, and legislation alike, attribute to punishment, without blushing, a "resocialization" aim, for instance, when daily reality mocks such sublime *desideratum*, and empirical experience bears witness that quite the contrary is true: that punishment does not resocialize the prisoner, rather it stigmatizes him, sparking off so-called "secondary deviation", or other psycho-social mechanisms (*i.e.* "*self-fulfilling prophecy*") and degrading ceremonies that irreversibly cut short the expectations and the life horizons of the inmate.

Delving into the aforementioned dialectic tension between "being" and the "ought-to-be" of punishment, can anyone doubt that, very much despite the Kantian prohibition against making a means of the prisoner, for utilitarian ends, so often appealed to, the State turns to public punishment for strictly deterrent reasons, to prevent others from committing crimes, seeking in legal sentences the same dissuasive effect which, following the well-known critique of Hegel, "the master" looks for "who raises his stick against his dog"?

Here I come to a close. The "conclusions" of this work simply breathe forth sensitivity and sound sense. I share the "critical consensualism" (or, to put it another way: the moderate "conflictual" thesis) which the authors of the monograph here present when reconciling consensual legitimation of the social order with the recognition of a certain conflict functionality. They thereby place themselves within the confines of a realist position, equidistant from both radical, conflictual models and idyllic, conflictual positions. The last mentioned, as a sector of modern Sociology complains, offers a bucolic and unrealistic image of society, forgetting that – even in democratic countries – the daily endorsement of the citizens rests upon an ignorance (or, on a limited and only partial knowledge) of the true values of the system and its specific workings and the effect of such things.

I also celebrate their questioning of the condemned's "emancipatory utopia", which, during the last century, was lead by the fervent advocates of resocializing "treatment", so much in crisis today. It appears to me very positive that, in any case, they try to trace the axiological patterns and criteria of a legal prison intervention as regards the inmate, rather than hiding behind the "*nothing works*", and other well-known catchphrases. For, whoever, from anthropological pessimism or revolutionary utopianism, denies the possibility of a well-doing intervention in the prisoner's life, plunges the prison population into desperation, turning their back on the conquests made by Psychology, Pedagogy, and the behavioural sciences, until the desired structural changes should arrive which, it is true, usually arrive too late.

I congratulate, then, María José and Fernando Falcón y Tella most sincerely. A serene and clarifying reflection such as that fashioned in this monograph faithfully synthesizes, together with the rationalizing and humanizing process of punishment, the scientific demystifying of the true variables of punishment's ability to dissuade; and the subjection of State "*ius puniendi*" to effective, material limits. A hopeful future, of course, awaits! Still, within the framework of that rationalizing and humanizing process, any realist program, to be any good, must, at least, meet that minimum requirement, laid down by François Marie Arouet (Voltaire):

> We ask that Justice should not be dumb, as she is blind, that she make man aware of the blood of other men... Punish, but punish usefully. If Justice is pictured with a blindfold over her eyes, it is most needful that reason should be her guide.

Antonio García-Pablos
Professor of Criminal Law
Universidad Complutense de Madrid

Chapter I

Scope of the Work

1 From the Most Abstract to the Most Concrete

The main object of this investigation is that of the basis and the goal of punishment considered from a critical standpoint *vis-à-vis* the right to punish. Studies and works dedicated to punishment are scarce when we compare them to those dedicated to crime theory or some aspect thereof. The idea of punishment presents itself to us at first sight as a something we could not do without in a society which wishes to maintain order.[1] That it fulfils a basic social function is an undeniable fact.[2] What we set ourselves in this study is the why and what-for of punishment, and, likewise, the limits of the right to punish.[3] Simply put, not everything goes. To this end, we pass in review the main doctrines that have dealt with the theme from Antiquity to the present. We shall not limit ourselves to the legal-philosophical sphere but shall also analyze the contributions of other of the Social Sciences. Together with theoretical approaches to the basis and goal of punishment – the focal point of our study – we shall, in the final part of the book, touch upon how these are reflected in the sphere of Positive Law.

When deciding upon the plan of the book, it seemed to us useful to carry out the study process by moving from the most abstract and general to the most concrete and specific. Thus we distinguish between various subjects relating to the concept which are not exactly equivalent

1 David Garland, *Punishment and Modern Society. A Study in Social Theory*, Chicago, The University of Chicago Press, 1990, pp. 3 ff.

2 *Cf.* Borja Mapelli Caffarena, Juan Terradillos Basoco, *Las consecuencias jurídicas del delito*, 3rd ed, Madrid, Civitas, 1996, p. 19. Gerardo Landrove Díaz, *Las consecuencias jurídicas del delito*, 5th ed. reviewed by María Dolores Fernández Rodríguez, Madrid, Tecnos, 2002, p. 15.

3 On the subject of the limits of the right to punish, *cf.* Herbert L. Packer, *The Limits of Criminal Sanction*, Standford, Calif., Standford University Press, 1968. There is a translation into Italian, *I limiti della sanzione penale*, Milano, 1978.

and that, nevertheless, are often terminologically confused with one another. These thematic blocks are:

- Punishment, as the widest concept, called *châtiment* in French, *castigo*, in Spanish. It is not exclusively used in the legal world, but also in the worlds of Pedagogy, Medicine, Psychology, Sociology, Literature, and the like. All these spheres will be taken up in the first part of the book.
- Punitive Practice – *sanction pénale, sanción penal* – touches upon a more concrete sphere, the legal world already mentioned and the law, one of whose prime characteristics is precisely coercion.
- Sentence – *peine, pena* – constitutes the third subject of our analysis. Here, the least generic concept is dealt with, having to do with that patch of law which is basically made up of Criminal Law. This constitutes the central part of our work and also the most extensive. There, via a dual structuration, we distinguish between punishments and deterrents, as the prime types of punitive practice, with a distinct historical tradition, diverse bases and functions, around which different sorts of theories and schools have developed: absolutist-retributive; and relativist-preventive, both general and special, in all their different forms – under the aegis of the State, also differently conceived.
- Penalty – *pénalité, punición*. This theme is analyzed in the final part of the work which closes with a series of critical conclusions as to what, in our opinion, should be a correct conception of punishment. This is true especially where penalty appears in other disciplines outside Criminal Law, mainly, though not exclusively, administrative sanctions.

2 An Interdisciplinary Approach

The subject of punishment has been one of the matters which has given rise to more philosophical reflection than any other since the Classical World. It has attracted thinkers from the most diverse schools and tendencies, from Plato or Aristotle, through Saint Thomas Aquinas, Thomas Hobbes, John Locke, Immanuel Kant, Georg Wilhelm Friedrich Hegel, Jeremy Bentham or John Stuart Mill, to the current legal-philosophical doctrines, especially the Anglo-Saxon.[4]

4 Saint Thomas Aquinas, *Suma de Teología*, Madrid, Biblioteca de Autores Cristianos, 1989. Thomas Hobbes, *Leviathan*, London, J.M. Dent, origi-

In spite of the fact that this subject has been studied since Antiquity, this antiquity does not convert the subject into one which is out-of-fashion. Quite the contrary. From the 40's on, theoretical studies on punishment have multiplied, a good indication of the inexhaustible nature of the subject, always open to new approaches. We need only recall the works of some of the most important English-speaking moral philosophers of our times; amongst them we might highlight Herbert Lionel Adolphus Hart, for many years Professor at the University of Oxford, or the recently deceased University of Harvard scholar, John Rawls, likewise a large "and so on" of authors to be referred to in this book.[5]

---

nary *Leviatan*, 1rst ed. 1651; Madrid, Editora Nacional, 1979, translation into Spanish by Escotado. John Locke, *Two Treatises on Civil Government* (1690), there is a Spanish translation by Lázaro Ros, *Ensayo sobre el gobierno*, Madrid, Aguilar, 1969. Immanuel Kant, *Die Metaphisik der Sitten*, Königsberg, 1797; ed. by W. Weischedel, Frankfurt am Main, Suhrkamp Verlag, 1982. *Eine Vorlesung Kants über Ethik*, Berlin, 1924; translation into English, *Lectures on Ethics*, by L. Infield, London, Methuen and Co. (new ed. 1979); translation into Spanish, *Lecciones de Ética*, by R. Rodríguez Aramayo and C. Roldán Panadero, with introduction and notes of the former, Barcelona, Crítica, 1988. Georg Wilhelm Friedrich Hegel (1770-1831), *Grundlinien der Philosophie des Rechts*, Berlin, 1821; Frankfurt am Main, Suhrkamp Verlag, 1978. Translation into Spanish by A. Mendoza de Montero, México, Juna Pablos ed., 1980. Also in México, UNAM, 1975. There is a translation into English by T.M. Knox, Oxford, Oxford University Press, 1962. Jeremy Bentham, "El Panóptico", "Memoria", in Francisco Ferrer y Valls (ed.), *Principios de Legislación y de Codificación*, Madrid, Imprenta de D. Tomás Jordán, 1834. Madrid, Ediciones La Piqueta, 1979. *An Introduction to the Principles of Morals and Legislation*, 1st. ed. London, 1789; Oxford, Clarendon Press, 1823; ed. by H.L.A. Hart, J.H. Burns, London, The Athlone Press, 1970. *The Rationale of Punishment*, London, Robert Howard, 1830. John Stuart Mill, *On Liberty*, Everyman's Edition, London, Dent, 1910 ed. *Cf.*, also, D. Loftsgordon, "Present-day British Philosophers on Punishment", in *Journal of Philosophy*, 63, 1966, pp. 341-353.

5 H.L.A. (Herbert Lionel Adolphus) Hart, *Punishment and Responsibility: Essays in the Philosophy of Law*, Oxford, Clarendon Press, 1968; New York, Oxford University Press, 1982, reviewed edition. "Punishment and the Elimination of Responsibility", London, 1962. Included in H.L.A. Hart, *Punishment and Responsibility, op. cit.*; *The Morality of Criminal Law*, Jerusalem, Hebrew University Magnes Press, 1964. John Rawls, "Two Concepts of Rules", in *The Philosophical Review*, 64, 1955, pp. 3-32. *A Theory of*

To this exemplary array, one would have to add another long list of names from all branches of knowledge, from Psychology and Psychoanalysis, Sociology, Educational Theory, Political Economy or Pedagogy to the fields of Literature, Theology or Fine Arts, without mentioning, of course, other of the Social Sciences and, more especially, the Legal Sciences around which this analysis centers. In turn, however, in the world of law, the subject has not been exclusively tackled by Legal Theory, while the very important contributions made by Legal Anthropology and Criminology are by no means to be slighted. On the other hand, punishment and sanction are not only studied in Criminal Law but also in Administrative and International Law, and the like.

Given the depth and diversity of approaches from which to reflect on the topic of our investigation, we here adopt an *interdisciplinary* perspective, more especially in Chapter II – when dealing with punishment in general – and in Chapter V – whilst developing punishment in spheres distinct from Criminal Law.

We must remember that what befits an interdisciplinary study, and not a mere multidisciplinary one, is the piecing together of the results achieved in each of the disciplines, in the service of a global result which will yield us a concept of the phenomenon in question in all its complexity, and will not simply juxtapose data and conclusions from the different branches of knowledge, as if one were working with isolated and rigid compartmentalization.[6] We do not attempt to exhaust the topic of punishment, but we do wish to offer the widest and most complete vision of it possible.

Justice, Oxford, Clarendon Press, 1962. Oxford, Oxford University Press, 1971. Cambridge, Massachusetts, The Belknap Press of Harvard University Press, 1971; there is a Spanish translation by María Dolores González Soler, México, F.C.E, 1978. *La justicia como equidad. Una reformulación*. Edited by Erin Kelly, Barcelona, Paidos, 2002.

6 *Cf.* José Iturmendi Morales, Preface to the Spanish translation by Isabel Hoyo Sierra of the book by François Ost, *El sistema jurídico entre orden y desorden*, Madrid, Servicio de Publicaciones de la Facultad de Derecho, Universidad Complutense de Madrid, 1997, pp. 11-33, esp. pp. 14 and 15. Nicola Lacey, "Penal Practices and Political Theory: An Agenda for Dialogue", in Matt Matravers (ed.), *Punishment and Political Theory*, Oxford, Hart Publishing, 1999, pp. 152 and 153. Antonio Beristain, *La pena-retribución y las actuales concepciones criminológicas*, Buenos Aires, Depalma, 1982, pp. 4 and 94-95. Fausto Costa, *Delitto e pena nella storia del pensiero umano*, Torino, Fratelli Bocca, 1928, Preface, p. V.

The need for a multidimensional focus on the punishment topic stems from the theme's very depth and complexity. In the future, punishment should be seen as something to view not solely from a criminological or legal perspective, but rather as a complex, social institution in both its function and its meaning, which, studied with sufficient care and attention reflects a form of life that brings with it a clarity of analysis as to the type of society in which it is imposed and as to the people which compose it.[7]

7 David Garland, *Punishment and Modern Society, op. cit.*, p. 2.

Chapter II

Punishment in General

I Punishment in Legal Science

1.1 Definition of Punishment. Elements[1]

In 1954, Anthony Flew set out a series of requirements for the definition of punishment: punishment must be an evil or something unpleasant for the victim, inflicted – at least supposedly – from motives of an offence having been committed, inflicted on the presumed offender, in virtue of an authority conferred by institutions against whose norms the offence has been committed. Five years after Flew's work, Stanley I. Benn added a rider to the aforementioned requirements: the suffering should be an essential part of the punishment and not just something incidental to it.[2] Also in 1959, H.L.A. Hart, in his *Prolegomenon to the Principles of Punishment*, drawing heavily upon Flew and Benn, introduced some nuances into the concept of punishment. These would restrict it to legal punishment or to punishment which should be inflicted by human beings other than the one offended.[3] Below, we analyze some of the characteristics of punishment mentioned.

1 Herbert Lionel Adolphus Hart, "Prolegomenon to the Principles of Punishment", in *Proceedings of the Aristotelian Society*, LX, 1959-1960, pp. 1-26. Reedited in P. Laslett, W.G. Ruciman (eds.), *Philosophy, Politics and Society*, 2nd. Series, Oxford, Blackwell, 1962, pp. 158-182. Re-edited with notes by H.L.A. Hart, *Punishment and Responsibility*, Oxford, Clarendon Press, 1968, pp. 1-27. There is a translation into Spanish by Jerónimo Betegón –"Introducción a los principios de la pena", in Jerónimo Betegón, Juan Ramón de Páramo (comps.), *Derecho y Moral. Ensayos Analíticos*, Barcelona, Ariel, 1990.

2 Stanley I. Benn, "An Approach to the Problems of Punishment", in *Philosophy*, 1958.

3 *Cf.* H.L.A. Hart, "Prolegomenon to the Principles of Punishment", *op. cit.*, pp. 4-6. Jerónimo Betegón, *La justificación del castigo*, Madrid, Centro de Estudios Constitucionales, 1992, pp. 139-205. Eduardo A. Rabossi, *La justificación moral del castigo*, Buenos Aires, Astrea, 1976, pp. 68-69.

I.I.I Existence of Suffering, Displeasure, Pain or Evil

If we should come to discover that prison was experienced by its occupants as a pleasant way of life, the prison would cease to figure as a punishment. This characteristic feature of punishment differentiates it from other coercive measures which the state may adopt and which might, though not easily, be confused with it. The state intentionally causes some suffering, unpleasantness, pain or evil to the offender with a specific end in view, or as a means to that end. This distinguishes it from other coercive state measures such as quarantine where the suffering caused is not intentional, but rather a by-product, a necessary consequence of an unlooked-for deprivation.

The idea of manipulated pain is not exclusively covered by physical pain or suffering but spreads to all imaginable situations involving the *frustration of personal desires* of whatever kind. We might rather speak of *evil* rather than of pain, insofar as the privation of a good is concerned. This is clearly seen in the evolution of punishment from Antiquity to present day societies. The gamut runs from the death penalty, as the ruling punishment, passes through prison and, from there, to pecuniary punishments as a deprivation of the basic goods of life, liberty and property. In each case, the suffering is increasingly less physical and more of a psychological or even an economic nature.

Not all deprivation of a good, however, falls within the category of punishment. A *desired good* may be involved. Hence, one might propose the substitution of the words "not desired" or "disliked" for the word *evil*. This sets certain problems for individuals who fall outside the common pattern. Think of the fanatic who does not mind suffering the evil which the punishment consists in since what he seeks is simply publicity for his cause; of the tramp who commits small, legal infractions in order to assure himself of the shelter and sustenance to be found in prison; or, even, the extreme case, of the person of masochistic tendencies who finds pleasure in corporal punishment. In all these cases, what is in principle an evil is experienced as something desired and wished for, already in itself at the service of the end sought.[4]

In such cases can we still speak of punishment? To answer this question, it will prove useful to distinguish between *objectively* considered punishment and the *subjective*, individual representation of how the punishment might affect its addressees. Actions which objectively

4 S. Guendin, "The Meaning of Punishment", in *Philosophy and Phenomenological Research*, XXVIII, 1967-1968, pp. 236-237.

fulfil all the requirements of punishment may not be lived and experienced as such by the specific person to whom they are applied, in a definite case.

Another interesting question is that of how we legitimate inflicting evil on others, even should it be done in the name of the State. To admit that there exists an *authority* within the legal system *for the infliction of evil* would seem incompatible with the very idea of law. A crime has been committed. By this action an evil has been produced in three senses: as concerns the victim – physical pain; as concerns society – a breach of order; and, even, as concerns the soul of the offender – a moral evil. Still, will the situation be improved by the addition of a fourth evil, that is, causing harm or pain to the offender? This fourth evil, in principle, leads to no good effect either for society or for the offended, since evil is only overriden by a good counteracting the evil, not by the infliction of another evil.

We might claim that evil is never justified, it is never a good. What evil might be is legally excused. The distinction between the *justification* – on the moral plain – and the *excuse* – on the legal – rests in the fact that the justified is morally good, while excused conduct is merely not reprehensible at a legal level, even though ethically it might be objectionable. In other words, the evil punishment brings in its wake is a 50% evil. It does not represent an *unqualified evil*, but neither does it constitute an absolute good. It is an evil in the service of good, always so long as it meets certain requirements and demands. It must be a necessary measure; it must be proportional; imposed by a legitimate authority; there must be no desire for vengeance; and it must achieve some end. It must not be an end in itself. While it might not achieve the goal according to theological postulates, that is, the moral improvement or expiation of the offender, it should at least try to help in his re-education and social reinsertion, and ensure that his outward behaviour does no harm to the social order.

I.1.2 Existence of a Previous Legal Offence

A second requirement for the definitions of punishment considered is that there should exist a prior harmful action or omission. Such action or omission might be owing to two causes: either because a breach of a rule of conduct has taken place, no matter what the moral motives for the conduct in question – an *objective* focus on the illicit; or, because a moral flaw on the part of the agent is present because he has failed to live up to his own convictions and principles, irrespective of whether or not a breach of conduct has taken place – a *subjective* focus on the illicit.

According to J. D. Mabbott, the first focus should be foremost. One would have to give value to an objective and legal concept of punishment, independently of moral motives. *The criminal would be a man who breaks the law and not the bad man; the innocent is he who has not broken the law and is not necessarily a good man.* A person may be innocent of an offence in spite of being a bad person or even have broken other laws. Therefore, for Mabbott, punishment would be restricted to offences going *exclusively against legal norms.* This would allow the denial of any punishments based on retroactive laws, in contradistinction to moral offences, which must be punished both before and after they are entered on the books as crimes, always given that such offences exist. Along similar lines, of not punishing individuals for their wickedness, but rather for their specific transgressions of the law, are to be found the ideas of H.L.A. Hart, A. Ross, J. Rawls and S.I. Benn.[5]

There is the danger of *circularity* in any definition of punishment whose meaning is made to depend upon the definition of crime or offence. The problem arises when we wish to define the concept of *offence,* since it would be difficult to give a definition of the latter which would not require as some necessary element a reference to the definition of punishment. It is difficult to account for the concept of punishment without connecting it with the definition of crime and, likewise, to define crime without alluding to punishment.To overcome the danger of circularity, some authors have suggested characterizing *offences against legal norms* as *transgressions of legal duties,* rather than as presuppositions of punishment. The trouble is not every breach of a legal duty constitutes a crime. Crime is a subclass of types of behaviour which constitute the antecedent of punishments. A second solution to the problem might be the abandonment of legal criteria to characterize crime and their substitution by moral criteria.[6]

The concept of *penalty* would have to be separated from that of *punishment.* The former embraces all kinds of disparate coercive measures, such as fines, disqualifications, sports penalties. The latter would have moral connotations. Penalization of a person who infringes some

5 *Cf.* Jerónimo Betegón, *La justificación del castigo, op. cit.,* pp. 159-163.

6 Richard Wasserstrom, "Some Problems in the Definition and Justification of Punishment", in A. Goldman, J. Kim (eds.), *Values and Morals,* Dordrecht, Reidel, 1978.

legal norm would then constitute a crime only when the said person is considered morally guilty. Being punished would bear with it a *stigma*, stemming from the moral condemnation of the offender, something lacking when one is merely penalized.

For others, the difference between the foregoing concepts would lie in the fact that penalization would be the form or *formal expression* of the punishment. Finally, there is not lacking those who distinguish between penalties, usually in reference to less serious offences, and punishments which represent a greater *degree of seriousness*.

I.I.3 Punishment Must Be Inflicted Upon the Author of the Offence. Punishment of the Innocent as a Form of Victimization

The controversy surrounding the possibility of *punishing the innocent* has occupied a great deal of the literature dealing with the moral justification of punishment. Here, an important distinction should be highlighted. The problem basically arises when, *being conscious* of their innocence, innocent people are punished. If those who punish the innocent do so because they consider them guilty, we should be faced with a supposed *error*. However, when we knowingly inflict a punishment upon someone who does not deserve it, then we can speak of *victimization* in the strict sense of the term. The idea that we may only refer to punishment when this is directed at the person guilty of an offence has been studied in-depth by A.M. Quinton, and accepted by S.I. Benn, amongst others.[7]

Guilt through the commission of an offence figures as a *logical* prerequisite for punishment to *exist*, for us *to be able to punish*, according to the retributive vision; and, as a *moral* prerequisite for punishment to be *justified*, that we *should punish*, according to utilitarianism. In our opinion, here we are treating of a theoretician's position over the greater

7 From the point of view of the victim, *cf.* also James Morden Hough, "The Impact of Victimization: Findings from the British Crime Survey", Paper prepared for the *Third International Institute of Victimology*, Lisbon, 1984. James Morden Hough, Path Mayhew, *Taking Account of Crime: Key Findings from the Second British Crime Survey*, London, Her Majesty's Stationery Office, 1985. James Morden Hough, D. Moxon, "Dealing with Offenders: Popular Opinions and the Views of Victims", in *Howard Journal*, 24, 3, 1985, pp. 160-175. James Morden Hough, Julian Roberts, *Attitudes to Punishment: Findings from the British 1996 Crime Survey*, London, Home Office, 1998. Andrew Karmen, *Crime Victims. An Introduction to Victimology*, Belmont, California, Wadsworth, 1984.

or lesser importance to award the prerequisite of guilt. Either guilt is essential, a *conditio per quam*, of punishment, a sufficient reason for the said punishment, or else, though not a sufficient reason, it is a necessary one, a *conditio sine qua non*. For some, punishing the innocent is not punishment nor can it receive the name of punishment, it is, at maximum, victimization. We are confronted with an essential problem of logical, conceptual definition. Unjust punishment would not be punishment, but victimization. For others, even if only conceptually, there is room for the distinction between just and unjust punishments, according as punishment is applied to the guilty or the innocent, although, at the moral level, only punishment of the guilty would be justified. It is not that we *cannot* punish the innocent, that to do so would represent a *contradictio in terminis*, but rather that we must not do so. This is because not everything that we can do, on the factual plane, we should do, on the ethical plane. The best solution would be to accept a *wide* definition of punishment, which would include punishment of the innocent, even if only gnoseologically and conceptually, though it might well be excluded from the moral point of view, not being ethically justified. The desert of punishment does not so much affect its quality as it affects its just application to a particular individual.

This would appear a more correct approach than that which consists of proposing an eclectic approach, *quantitative* rather than qualitative, in line with which punishment of the innocent would be explained as happening in isolated and *exceptional* cases. The eclectic approach does not seem adequate to us, not even taking into account the idea of the *exceptional* as a *qualitative* discriminatory criterion – as the exceptionally justified – not to mention using it as a mere statistic and quantitative datum – as the unusual, infrequent or rare. The punishment of the innocent would never be justified, even though it may exceptionally take place in reality.

Another possible way of solving the problem of the, in principle, implicit contradiction which exists in the expression "punishing the innocent" might stem from the distinction between concepts in a *weak* sense and concepts in a *strong* sense, according to the degree of propriety with which we handle them. A concept in the *weak* sense is when it is used in a somewhat improper or inexact fashion, as opposed to the technical, proper or *strong* sense of the concept. For instance, after a long day of training, an athlete may exclaim: "I'm half dead". In any strong sense, this would be untrue, since life is a legal good not open to grading. One cannot speak of a percentage of life. A person is either alive or dead. It is another thing when a very old person may have a lesser quality of life. Nevertheless, in a weak sense there is room for the "half dead" expression to denote tiredness. In a similar way, to speak of the punishment of innocents is like speaking of "*punishing someone for something he has not done*". In any strict sense, this would be a contradiction. In a weak sense, its existence could be conceived of as arising in miscarriages of justice or when, deliberately, a flagrant injustice is committed. Though erroneous or unjust, punishment of the innocent can, in fact, take place in reality. When it does, we use the expression "punishment" in the weak, not in the strong, sense.

I.I.4 Punishment Must Be Intentionally Inflicted (In Contrast to Repentance) by Human Beings (In Contrast to Divine Punishment) Who Are Distinct From the Offender (In Contrast to Self-punishment) and By The Institutionalized Authority to Punish (In Contradistinction to Private Vengeance)

Punishment is imposed upon the offender as a consequence of human action. We do not speak of punishment where there is no mediation by a punitive authority exercising its will, but of *repentance*, whenever there is voluntary restitution of the benefit unrightfully obtained, or when there is compensation or satisfaction for the evil derived from the offence. Punishments are not only imposed against our will but must also be imposed by a will alien to ours, by other human beings. It is not enough that they appear unexpectedly – just happening like the pain caused us when the dentist does not anesthetize us properly – nor that they be inevitable though intentionally inflicted, as would be the case of the surgeon who, for some reason, cannot give us analgesics against the pain. On the contrary, punishments must be impositions deliberately carried out on the part of the agent or authority applying them.[8]

Natural disasters or accidental damage cannot be considered punishments, other than from a *religious* point of view. We might think of the god of the *Old Testament* who sent plagues and punishments upon mortals. Theory tends to coincide on the demand that punishment must be inflicted by human beings, in contradistinction to religious punishment, of *divine* origin. The contrary premise would require assuming the existence of an afterlife which is a profession of faith, something not everyone is willing to admit. In that hypothetical future life, rewards

8 J. Kleinig, *Punishment and Desert*, The Hague, Martinus Nijhoff, 1973, p. 23.

and punishments would be distributed. Another feature of Divine Punishment would be the lack of institutionalization, both in the sense that specific rules are not necessary when determining which *actions* should count as offensive, and with regard to the way the *authority* to inflict punishment arises.

On the other hand, what Divine Punishment seeks would not be *efficacy* or obedience to a system of rules and norms – as is the way with earthly punishment – since such would follow as a postponed reaction in the hypothetical context of an afterlife. What Divine Punishment would have in advantage is that it is infallible, with no place for error, it corresponds to the real and effective guilt of he who has committed the offence, given that the one inflicting the punishment has direct and absolute knowledge of the degree of guilt of he who is to suffer. God never punishes an innocent man. The possibility of collective Divine Punishment would be another question.

Again, those who apply punishment must be individuals distinct from the offender, hence *self-punishment,* which one imposes upon oneself, is excluded from the standard definition of punishment. There must be nothing of unintentional punishments, nothing of punishments imposed by fate, no Divine Punishments. Nor can there be punishments that we might inflict upon ourselves.[9]

Finally, a characteristic feature of punishment to be noted is that it must be imposed by people who have been *institutionally* awarded the faculty to punish – for example, a judge – as against the idea that just anyone may take justice into his own hands. The latter case is more properly considered personal vengeance which is typical of the pre-social state before the constitution of the State.[10] What does not appear necessary is the restriction of the idea of punishment to some state organization or to the judges; the existence of any *authority* able to elaborate rules, together with *agents* to apply them is enough.

9 Th. McPherson, "Punishment: Definition and Justification", in *Analysis,* 28, 1967-1968, pp. 21-27, esp. p. 22.

10 E.L. Ayers., *Vengeance and Justice: Crime and Punishment in the Nineteenth Century American South*, New York, 1984.

I.I.5 Desert as an All-encompassing Concept of Merit – Positive – and Its Negative Version – Demerit – as a Justification for Punishment. Can We Speak of Punishment as Reward?

When considering punishment as just and legitimate, a central idea is that of deserving.[11] The absence of certain typical or defining qualities of punishment may cause it to be characterized as unjust or undeserved punishment. Nevertheless, the subject of desert has usually been studied in relation to questions of social justice or distributive justice,[12] rather than in relation to studies and research into the justification of punishment.[13] This does not prevent us from applying some characteristic features attributed to the idea of desert – or not deserving, in its negative guise – to see what their relevance might be in relation to punishment.

The terms "deserve" or "desert" almost always reflect deeply rooted feelings or our intuitions concerning what is just, vestiges of a primitive tendency which drives us to desire good to our benefactors and ill to our detractors. Whoever has made some effort to achieve some task has merit and we consider their effort should be crowned with success

11 On the subject, *cf.* Ted Honderich, *Punishment. The Supposed Justification*, Harmondsworth, Baltimore, Maryland, Penguin Books, 1969, pp. 26-47.

12 *Cf.* on the subject, among others, Robert Nozick, *Anarchy, State and Utopia*, Oxford, Basil Blackwell, 1974; and Michael Sandel, *Liberalism and the Limits of Justice*, Cambridge, Cambridge University Press, 1982.

13 *Cf.* on desert, Joel Feinberg, *Doing and Deserving*, New Jersey, Princeton University Press, 1970; Wojciech Sadurski, *Giving Desert its Due*, Dordrecht, D. Reidel Pub. Co., 1985; George Sher, *Desert*, New Jersey, Princeton University Press, 1987. John Braithwaite, Philip Pettit, *Not Just Deserts. A Republican Theory of Criminal Justice*, Oxford, Clarendon Press, 1990. R. Burgh, "Do the Guilty Deserve Punishment?", in *The Journal of Philosophy*, vol. 79, n. 4, 1982, pp. 193-210. D. Husak, "Why Punish the Deserving?", in *Nous*, 26, 1992, pp. 447-464. F. Hussey, "Just Deserts and Determinate Sentencing: Impact on the Rehabilitation Ideal", in *The Prison Journal*, LIX, 2, fall-winter 1980, pp. 36-47. Richard G. Singer, *Just Deserts: Sentencing Based on Equality and Desert*, Cambridge, Massachusetts, Ballinger, 1979. Martin Wasik, Andrew von Hirsch, "Non-Custodial Penalties and the Principles of Desert", in *Criminal Law Review*, 1988, pp. 555-572. L. Stern, "Deserved Punishment, Deserved Harm, Deserved Blame", in *Philosophy*, 45, 1970, pp. 317-329. Andrew von Hirsch, A. Ashworth, "Not Just Deserts: A Response to Braithwaite and Pettit", in *Oxford Journal of Legal Studies*, 13, 1992, pp. 83-96. Jerónimo Betegón, *La justificación del castigo, op. cit.*, pp. 205-321.

and, contrariwise, whoever has acted badly morally does not deserve any triumph in his undertakings.

Judgements of desert are characterized by: their reference to the past;[14] their apparent tie to the idea of obligation; and their being judgements about people.

To deserve something is not equivalent to *having a right to* that something.[15] When dealing with rights, the personal circumstances of the subject are completely irrelevant. One might be an owner in spite of being lazy and not deserve to have that property right at all. One must distinguish between *deserving X* (a moral concept), *having a title to X* (a legal concept), and *affirming the necessity of X* (a factual concept). Each one of these three criteria are conceptually independent.

A deterministic vision of the world and of the individual in society, where the individual is compelled, by factors external to his will, to commit crimes is apparently incompatible with the idea of deserving and undeserving. If the offender is not free to commit the offence, if he is determined thereto, he does not deserve a prize (since he does commit it), but neither does he deserve a punishment (since his action escapes the control of the human will, in part denying the role played by intelligence, talent, will-power, self-control, and so on). There, one would have to give up the retributive idea of punishment as a deserved and just consequence of a moral offence committed by a free subject. There, the existence of the illicit or of an offence would be enough to immediately set the blind punishing mechanism of the State in motion. It would be enough to commit the forbidden to acquire a right to be treated after a pre-determined fashion – a normative consequence.[16] The imposition of a punishment would be a function of what an individual does and not of what he is.[17] We shall return to this topic when discussing social determinism or Free Will as presuppositions of the utilitarian bases and of the retributive bases of penal sanctions, respectively.[18]

14 *Cf.* Sadurski, *Giving Desert its Due, op. cit.*, p. 118,

15 *Cf.* on the subject, J. Deigh, "On the Right to Be Punished: Some Doubts", in *Ethics*, 94, 1984, pp. 191-211.

16 J. Betegón, *La justificación del castigo, op. cit.*, pp. 236 ff.

17 Wojciech Sadurski, "Distributive Justice and the Theory of Punishment", in *Oxford Journal of Legal Studies*, 5, 1, 1985, p. 47. *Giving Desert its Due*, Dordrecht, Reidel, 1985, p. 225.

18 Chapters IV.3.2.1. A; and IV. 3.2.2. A.

Already in his *L'éducation morale*, Émile Durkheim distinguished between two large groups of punishments: *negative* sanctions and *positive* sanctions. Negative sanctions are *punishments* and positive sanctions are *rewards*. What they have in common is that they reinforce the fulfilling of norms. They do this antagonistically: in the case of negative sanctions, by punishing the malefactor; in the case of the positive, they reward those who fulfil their duties. Within negative sanctions are included both *repressive* or criminal punishments and *restitutive*, civil or administrative sanctions. Positive sanctions are, for instance, those existing in schools when better marks or distinctions are awarded the most outstanding pupils. The same also occurs in morally healthy societies. Nevertheless, the number of punishments is always much greater in comparison with the much lesser importance of the prizes. Hence, when speaking of legal sanctions, we think of punishments first and foremost. In fact, there is no Prize Code which would parallel the Criminal Code. Positive sanctions rather deserve the name of *incentives* or *advantages* than sanctions properly speaking, even though there are those who use the not very common, and even at first sight contradictory, term "*sanction as reward.*"[19]

1.2 *Criminology's Contribution to the Theory of Punishment. The Criminal as Patient. Punishment as Intervention*

The legal treatment of punishment has not been exclusively the enclave of Criminal Law Theory, it has also, and increasingly, been the subject of Criminology, especially correctional Criminology.[20] For Criminology,

19 *Cf.* on the subject Gregorio Robles, *Crimen y castigo (Ensayo sobre Durkheim)*, Madrid, Civitas, 2001, pp. 61-63. Mario Alberto Copello, *La sanción y el premio en el Derecho*, Buenos Aires, Losada, 1945. Luis Jiménez de Asúa, "La recompensa como prevención general – El derecho premial", in *Revista General de Legislación y Jurisprudencia*, t. 125, pp. 5-32 and 353-394. Angelo de Mattia, "Merito e ricompensa", in *Rivista Internazionale di Filosofia del Diritto*, XVII, VI, pp. 608-624. Jeremy Bentham, *Tratados de Legislación penal y civil*, I, pp. 66-95, and IV, pp. 311-314, Villalpando, Madrid, 1821. Jacinto Dragonetti, *Tratado de las virtudes y de los premios*, in Beccaria, *Dei Delitti e delle pene*, Villamil, Madrid, 1836. F. Holbach, *Justice Laudative*, Larcier, Pedone, Brussels-Paris, 1904.

20 *Cf.* Enrique Gimbernat, "¿Tiene un futuro la dogmática jurídico-penal?", in *Estudios de Derecho Penal*, Madrid, 1967. "El sistema del Derecho Penal en la actualidad", in *Anuario de Ciencia Jurídica*, I, 1971, pp. 278 ff. Gaston Ste-

the delinquent is seen as someone with abnormalities and, hence, someone susceptible to treatment or intervention.[21] The idea of intervention is difficult to explain from exclusively normative postulates. It is for this reason that Criminology, in its various branches, is necessary. This does not represent a step backwards in the law or in legality, as some suggest, it is rather that crime has ceased to be a purely legal notion and the exclusive domain of the specialists in law, subject to legal criteria and parameters alone. Here, one must speak of penal sanction as intervention, an idea over which Criminal Law and Criminology might join hands. Punishment as intervention attempts to find preventive efficacy, as a means of social protection in the face of future crimes. It is not that Criminal Law is without worth but rather that it should be complemented by Criminology, and vice versa. In effect, there can be no treatment or intervention other than that within a system of legality, that is, when treatment is determined by law. Further, intervention, insofar as it is a type of punishment, will be determined at a trial, after a crime has been committed and, likewise, will be legally controlled in its execution, the which presupposes respecting the rights of the criminal throughout it.[22] Individualization of treatment, as proposed by correctional Criminology, is radically different from legislative or legal individualization as

fani, G. Levasseur, R. Jambu-Merlin, *Criminologie et science pénitentiaire*, 5th ed, Paris, Dalloz, 1982. Ian Taylor, Paul Walton, Jock Young, *Critical Criminology*, London, Routledge & Kegan Paul, 1975; Spanish translation, *Criminología Crítica*, México, Siglo XXI, 1977. *The New Criminology: For a Social Theory of Deviance*, London, Routledge & Kegan Paul, 1975. Spanish translation, *La nueva Criminología. Contribución a una teoría de la conducta desviada*, Buenos Aires, Amorrortu, 1975.

21 *Cf.* on the subject José Luis Peset (coord.), *Enfermedad y castigo*, Madrid, Consejo Superior de Investigaciones Científicas, Instituto "Arnau de Vilanova", 1984. Jeffrie G. Murphy, *Punishment and Rehabilitation*, Belmont, California, Wadsworth, 1973. *Retribution, Justice and Therapy: Essays in the Philosophy of Law*, Dordrecht, Holland – Boston, D. Reidel Pub. Co., 1979.

22 *Cf.* on the subject, from a different perspective, Alessandro Baratta, "Criminologia liberale e ideología della difesa sociale", in *La Questione Criminale*, 1975. "Sistema penale e marginazione sociale", in *La Questione Criminale*, 1976. "Criminologia critica e politica criminale alternativa", in *Revue Internationale de Droit Penal*, 1978. "Integración-prevención: una 'nueva' fundamentación de la pena dentro de la teoría sistémica", in *Cuadernos de Política Criminal*, 1984. Ignacio Muñagorri Laguía, *Sanción penal*

conceived in the 19th century. The personality of the offender is now of fundamental importance when determining the treatment to employ, and this demands its systematic study via scientific procedures and perspectives.[23]

The theory of punishment has always been portrayed as a substitute for the theory of crime. The subject was interesting insofar as he was the author of a crime, on the normative plane, but not interesting insofar as he was the passive subject of punishment, except in certain cases, of a philanthropic nature. The development of Sociology, Criminology and the critical sciences of Criminal Law has slowly meant that the lawyer has come down from his ivory tower and attends to practical reality, seeking harmony between legal appraisals and real life situations.[24]

On the subject of treatment or intervention, the question arises as to whether it is a right in itself or an imposition, and whether there exists a right or not to be rehabilitated. Indeed, it might be thought that the criminal may refuse the option to be treated and resocialized. In that case, it would be very difficult, even if imposed, to make any such treatment produce any lasting effect. Given that punishment is an undesired imposition, the doubt arises as to whether there is room for allowing the refusal of the one punished to submit to a further imposition; that of his being changed. The idea of treatment stems from a disquiet about punishment, it tries to humanize and to rationalize the imposition of punishment. It does not come from the desire to impose new demands upon the infractor, new systems of repression, via coercive State mechanisms. Therefore, that treatment becomes an inefficient form of coercion should be avoided. In this sense, the right to not be rehabilitated, in principle, seems as legitimate as the rights of free thought and self-determination which are recognized at both national and international levels by Constitutions and Treaties. These rights are of a general character and are not only relevant in cases of political prisoners and conscientious objectors.[25]

y política criminal. Confrontación con la nueva defensa social, Madrid, Reus, 1977, pp. 134-136.

23 Ignacio Muñagorri Laguía, *Sanción penal y política criminal…*, *op. cit.*, p. 138.

24 *Ibid.*, p. 195.

25 *Ibid.*, pp. 178 and 179.

1.3 Legal Anthropology

One of the most troublesome spectres of modern legal obscurantism is the positivist-anthropological idea of the "natural criminal", the Nazi doctrine of "criminal punishment of the Will" or "the criminal type" (*Tätertyp)* and the Stalinist "Enemy of the People". Along the same lines, we might cite pre-offence deterrents, which anticipate the committing of crime, based on purely subjective criteria, as the mere suspicion of having committed crimes or, worse yet, the presumption of the danger to society of the individual, derived from the person's social *status*; the "lazy", the "tramp", the "criminally inclined", the "recidivist", the "habitual criminal", the "professional criminal", "having criminal tendencies", and the like. In brief, this is the punishing not *quia prohibitum* but *quia peccatum*; and, in consequence, not so much punishing someone for *what he has done* as punishing someone, above all, for *what he is.*[26]

2 Punishment in Psychiatry and Psychology

The subject of punishment has been broadly studied by Psychiatrists and Psychologists.[27] Are criminals, or at least some of them, sick people?[28] The answer to this question depends on the concept of illness which we employ.[29]

---

26 Luigi Ferrajoli, *Derecho y razón. Teoría del garantismo penal.* Preface by Norberto Bobbio, Madrid, Trotta, 1rst ed. 1995, 2nd ed. 1997, 3rd ed. 1998, translation into Spanish by Perfecto Andrés Ibáñez, Alfonso Ruiz Miguel, Juan Carlos Bayón Mohino, Juan Terradillos Basoco and Rocío Cantarero Bandrés, p. 42.

27 *Cf.* Gregory Zilboorg (1890-1959), *The Psychology of the Criminal Act and Punishment,* New York, Harcourt, Brace, 1954; London, Hogarth Press, 1955; New York, Greenwood Press, 1968.

28 José María Rodríguez Devesa, "Tratamiento psiquiátrico en la delincuencia", in *R. E. P.,* 1970, pp. 1121 ff. Günter Stratenwerth, "Strafrecht und Sozialtheraphie", in *Festschrift für Bockelmann,* 1979.

29 D. Abrahamsem, *The Psychology of Crime,* New York, Columbia University Press, 1960. Gibbens, "Les problemes posés par le traitement psychiatrique des delinquants", in *Revue de Science Criminelle,* 1958. Peter Robert Hofstatter (1913-), "Pena y reprochabilidad desde el punto de vista social-psicológico", in *Sexualidad y crimen,* translation into Spanish by Enrique Gimbernat, Madrid, Reus, 1969. Nicholas N. Kittrie, *The Right to Be Dif-*

2.1 Crime as Deviant Conduct

In English Law, from 1843 to 1957, McNaghten's Rules specified, in an irrefutable fashion, when we were confronted with a mental abnormality, as a means of defence against criminal imputations. For someone to be considered abnormal to this effect, with respect to a specific act, at that moment, he must have been suffering a mental aberration which prevented him from realizing the nature of the act he was performing, and that the act in question should be a wrong one. The mental aberrations referred to are madness or mental incapacity.

Mental aberrations, though they come in many forms, may be grouped together in two main categories, according to whether they are more of a physical or a psychological nature. Amongst *physical* disorders, we find dementia. Confusion, delirium, loss of mental faculties, all typical of dementia, may stem from a physical illness, a stoke, some types of intoxication, genetic inheritance, and so on. Within the category of the physical are also encompassed defects such as imbecility or idiocy.

The second group, of a *psychological* sort, can be divided into subgroups. The first of these are emotional disorders like anxiety, depression or mania. A second subgroup is made up of schizoid states, characterized by disordered thought or strange behaviour. A third subgroup would include compulsive or obsessive states, various forms of hysterical disorders, together with psychopathologies. Psychopaths are indeed a very common type amongst criminals, more especially amongst recidivists.

If that is the spectrum of illnesses, not all criminals are sick. This is the opinion of many doctors. For these, an offender only enters into the category of "mentally ill" if his case is covered by something appearing in psychiatric books and manuals. Another way of approaching the problem is the *Freudian* one. This speaks of the unconscious, basic, instinctive impulses, sublimation and repression, the Oedipus Complex, the Pleasure Principle and the Reality Principle, Super-Ego formation, and the rest.[30] Following the Freudians, criminal actions

ferent: Deviance and Enforced Therapy, Baltimore-London, The John Hopkins Press, 1971.

30 Jacques Lacan, "La metáfora del sujeto", in *Introducción teórica a las funciones del psicoanálisis en criminología*, Buenos Aires, Homo Sapiens, 1978.

could be mapped out as a consequence of aberrant, emotional states with respect to normal conduct. Criminals, they hold, are individuals who suffer from character flaws, stemming from an incorrect relationship between *Id, Ego,* and *Super-Ego.* As a consequence of an unsatisfactory emotional background or of traumas, especially in childhood, one may develop an inadequate Super-Ego. From this perspective, criminals are like big babies whose basic instincts are not under control, or who have an Oedipus Complex unsatisfactorily resolved, which leads to a pathological response when faced with authority. There are also cases where someone may commit a crime because they desire punishment. The sense of guilt underlying these examples might have its origin in early, sexual experiences. Further, an individual may have a fixation with the infantile stage or the family and may steal for this reason.[31]

There exist other similar theories which have a general application. Thus, many people relate criminal instincts to a *lack of affection in childhood* – for instance, separation from the mother, suffering rejection or a lack of love. Any one or various of these factors might unleash a psychological malfunction or could produce criminal behaviour at some later date.

There are other theories which locate the answers to aberrant behaviour in the physical make-up of a person. In this regard, we might cite the *theory of reflex actions* as responses to external stimuli. When an external stimulus impinges upon our senses, for example a current of air on the open eye, the sensorial excitation reaches the brain and produces a response, in this case, blinking. There also exists inhibition which is a defence mechanism against excitation. Both processes – excitation and inhibition – are two sides of one single coin. If, in the example given, I were to hear an explosion each time my eye received a current of air, there would come a time when I would instinctively associate both phenomena and would blink on hearing the noise, though no wind were present. As in the case of blinking, something similar happens in general human behaviour and crime. If a child is punished every time he commits a bad action, there will come the time when he will associate the evil caused with the punishment, feel it as an unpleasant experience, and will attempt not to be subject to the latter by avoiding the former. He will become accustomed to feeling pain and fear at the offence and, unconsciously, try to avoid it. Should we not receive such

31 Diego-Manuel Luzón Peña, "Prevención general y Psicoanálisis", in *Derecho Penal y Ciencias Sociales*, Barcelona, Ed. Mir, 1982, pp. 149 ff.

reprobation from childhood on, we would not associate the bad action with the punishment.

Other factors which influence deviant behaviour might be mentioned: *genetic inheritance* and the *environment*, for instance. Both determine our behaviour and diminish the degree of freedom granted our responses to stimuli. A case in point might be if someone is neurotic or has acquired bad behaviour patterns and a proclivity towards crime, because of inheritance or because of environmental factors, having been brought up in a marginalized environment or in one surrounded by crime, then this will influence his behaviour. When someone becomes a criminal, it is normally because he has been in contact with criminal patterns of behaviour and because he has not lived in conformity with the normal canons of conduct expected by the law.

Often such individual and social factors act in a mixed fashion, interacting with one another. Criminals are what they are due to *personal* as much as to *social* factors. This could be explained as easily in Freudian terms as in the social idea of *anomie*. If the delinquent suffers Freudian disorders, the Psychoanalyst and psychotherapy are called for. If the crime is a consequence of social factors, however, behavioural therapy would be proper.[32]

Medico-Psychiatric explanations of crime refer to crime as deviant conduct, using labels such as "hyperactivity" and "socio-pathology", employing measurements like the *Minnesota Multiple Personality Inventory* (MMPI) in the United States, and causal explanations based on the theory of deprivation in Great Britain. In both these countries, and in many others, it is held that there are factors related to education in a subculture, or lack of affection and maternal care in the early years of life which predispose individuals to commit crimes. Children who do not attend school, single-parent homes or homes where the mother spends a long time absent, or the fact that the father is in prison makes it likely that the young – children and adolescents – will be more vulnerable and more inclined to criminal behaviour.[33]

32 Ted Honderich, *Punishment. The Supposed Justification, op. cit.*, pp. 96-103.

33 Barbara Hudson, *Justice Through Punishment. A Critique to the 'Justice' Model of Corrections*, London, MacMillan, 1987, p. 135.

2.2 Punishment as the Deliberate Imposition of Pain

Miguel de Unamuno, in his *The Tragic Sense of Life in Men and Nations* (1913), said:[34]

> Pain is the way of conscience and it is through it that living beings come to have knowledge of themselves. Because to be aware of oneself, to have a personality, is to know oneself and feel oneself distinct from other beings, and to feel this distinction can only come about by the shock, by the greater or lesser pain, by the feeling of one's own limits ...[35]

The imposition of punishment, within the framework of the law, means causing pain, a *deliberate pain*. This goes directly against our predominant value system which includes forgiveness and mercy. How can these two incompatibles be made compatible: compensating for one bad deed by imposing another one, which involves deliberate pain? What sort of reasons are given for this intentional imposition of punishment?[36]

In what follows, we shall deal with pain, even though it is difficult to know exactly what it consists of and how to measure it. Literature is jam-packed with heroes who stoically put up with pain and with cowards who flee it. We might approach the physiology of pain from a medical point of view, by studying the nervous system of the body, and we may thus be able to work out what is most painful for specific persons. That is a possibility. However, in the measurement of pain, we must also take into account psychological, moral, religious, and social factors. All these may neutralize what should have been an acute pain or may aggravate what should have been a pain of little importance. That is why we do not bother to measure pain, in order to see if certain pains are

34 Citation in Antonio Beristain, *La pena-retribución y las actuales concepciones criminológicas, op. cit.*, p. 121, n. 13.

35 J. Lasso de la Vega, *El dolor y la condición humana en el teatro de Sófocles*, Barcelona, 1971, pp. 65-66.

36 *Cf.* C.S. Lewis, *The Problem of Pain*, Great Britain, 1940, Fontana Books, 1980. Of the same author see also "The Humanitarian Theory of Punishment", in *Res Judicatae*, 6, 1953; and in Leon Radzinowicz, M. Wolfgang (eds.), *Crime and Punishment*, vol. 2, New York, Basic Books, 1971. Ulf Lindblom, "Smärtbehandling under omprövning", in *Nordisk Medisin*, 95, 1980, p. 75.

worse than others nor do we analyze if pain has increased or decreased in the world.

Some of us might say that pain makes a man grow, brings him closer to the Transcendental, makes him more mature, lets him be reborn and have a more profound outlook on reality. In certain cases, this is doubtless true. Others of us have perhaps indeed experienced such benefits. Nevertheless, we have also experienced the opposite effects: the pain which paralyzes, the pain which creates bitterness, which impedes inner growth, which brutalizes.

A conclusion could then be: *when in doubt, you should not inflict pain or, at the least, you should inflict the minimum amount of pain possible.* This applies to punishment. *We should look for alternatives to punishment, and not different types of punishment.* While affliction is inevitable, a man-made Hell is not.

In modern societies, there is a *a taboo surrounding expressing pain,* affliction and acute grief. The expression of suffering should be controlled in both time and intensity. This is the case with mourning the loss of loved ones. Similarly, it is recognized that punishment is an evil, still, the analysis of the pain caused by it, the suffering and the agony which accompanies it, is usually omitted. It is the hidden side of punishment, but it is the most vital and real side for the one suffering. In legal texts, they talk of "punishment", but it would cause no end of scandal if the Criminal Codes were to call them "laws of pain", if we were to say that Professors of Criminal Law should explain "the Law of Pain". Neither would judges thank us should we attribute to them the task of "sentencing to pain", nor would prison institutions like to be considered as "places for inflicting pain". It would simply be taken as "politically incorrect" to set out the subject in this light. Pain and suffering have disappeared from the textbooks, but they have not disappeared from the experience of the penalized, the frightened, the shamed and the miserable. It is taken for granted that whoever experiences punishment suffers. If it were discovered that they enjoy it, the method would have to be changed.

Pain is equally implicit in the idea of treatment. Treatment also causes pain, in the same way that it effects cures and rehabilitations after an accident or an illness. The latter, however, does not have pain as its final aim, but rather it seeks to find a cure. The prisons are full of people who need treatment, care and cure, people with nervous breakdowns and a lack of education and who find themselves "warehoused" there, awaiting the right kind of treatment. Prisons should not confine themselves to being places where punishment is carried out and pain is administered, but also and primarily establishments which help to alleviate pain, as much the pain caused by the crime for which the prisoner was punished as the pain stemming from that very punishment.

It is no good saying that it is not us, not those who have the power, who have cast the first stone, and thus salve our consciences. We cannot simply allege that the criminal is the one who acted first and hence set in motion the repressive State apparatus. That is indeed true, but: What made these people break the law? Is it conceivable that Society has nothing to do with social ostracism, with drug dependency, and with all the other circumstances that lead to crime? *We distance ourselves from the suffering of others and, at a safe distance from suffering, we answer with more pain.*[37]

2.3 Guilt as a Symptom of Depression. Anti-psychiatry

There is a school of anti-psychiatry, born in England with Cooper, Laing, and Esterson, which sets out a kind of rehabilitation of the mentally ill. Here, the individual is not considered an abnormal being one tries to change by way of some sort of "brainwashing", be it for his own good or as a reply to a social demand. On the contrary, he is seen as an innocent victim of an often abusive society, a pathological system, full of self-contradictions which, in some way, "induces madness as a form of defence". This school considers the guilt feeling a symptom of depression and holds that we should help the subject find his true self again and not simply re-adapt him to an environment he does not understand and that does not understand him.[38]

---

37 Nils Christie, *Limits to Pain*, Oxford, Martin Robertson, 1982. We use the Spanish translation by Mariluz Caso, *Los límites del dolor*, México, Fondo de Cultura Económica, 1984, pp. 7-124.

38 Norberto Álvarez González, *La tendencia a sufrir el castigo: una contribución a la teoría de la culpa*, Alcalá, Universidad de Alcalá de Henares, Servicio de Publicaciones, 1996. Ignacio Muñagorri Laguía, *Sanción penal y política criminal…, op. cit.*, pp. 155-156.

2.4 *Passions and Psychological Mechanisms Fuelling Punishment*

2.4.1 Psychological Ambivalence Surrounding the Punishment of Others. The Contributions of Norbert Elias and Petrus Cornelis Spierenburg

In Elias' work, the concept of *civilization* refers to a specific transformation in human conduct in the long run, as a *process* of change, which has affected Western cultural behaviour and emotional life from the Middle Ages to the Present. The most interesting aspects of Elias' work, from the viewpoint of our investigation, are not so much his sociological as his psychological arguments, which are, in a novel way, an attempt to blend history with Freud's theory of the Psyche. Elias holds that human beings interiorize their fears, anxieties and the *inhibitions* imposed upon them by their parents and by their social surroundings to develop a *super-ego* that, with greater or lesser efficacy, inhibits the expression of the instincts, making them conform to the demands of cultural life. This produces changes in the structure of the individual's personality, especially in the development of self-control and inhibition mechanisms such as shame, fear or sensitivity.

An important point insofar as punishment is concerned, and which Elias highlights in his work, is that dealing with the *privatization of disturbing and bothersome events.* Certain aspects of everyday life are hidden from public notice and remain outside the social scene, confined to the sphere of the intimate. Sex, violence, bodily functions, illness, suffering or death gradually become a source of embarrassment and, increasingly, are shifted to the private domain, to the domestic environment of the nuclear family, to the bedrooms, prison cells and hospitals. Though Elias does not put it so clearly, this cultural tendency to hide the embarrassing behind the scenes is nothing but a corollary to the mental process of repression of instinctive desires *which are sent to the unconscious there to be enjoyed privately, and guiltily, in dreams and fantasies.*

Spierenburg, in his book *The Spectacle of Suffering,* offers a specific thesis of Elias' which has much to do with the decrease in public executions as social sensibility was transformed in the long run.[39] The argument is that, during the XVlth and XVllth centuries, when public security was scarce, individuals normally went armed and there were still traces of the feudal codes of honour, violence was not seen as something repugnant, though, of course, there were the varying feelings of

39 Petrus Cornelis Spierenburg, *The Spectacle of Suffering: Executions and the Evolution of Repression,* Cambridge, Cambridge University Press, 1984.

pity, sympathy, anger and disgust towards certain victims about to be executed. However, from the XVIIth century on, in a process lasting several centuries, attitudes toward violence began slowly to change. According to Spierenburg, as repugnance at the sight of violence amongst the governing classes developed, bit by bit, these classes began to privatize punishment and to not exhibit suffering. By the beginning of the XIXth century, many of the old atrocities had disappeared.

The clearest example of this process of civilization in the criminal justice system is the *extension of sympathy* – or inter-subjective identification with the victim. Deviant individuals and offenders are taken from the sphere of normal social life, they are removed *off-stage*. Similarly, the process of civilization shows itself in the *humanization of punishments*. These are no longer so brutal and do not consist of physical and corporal punishments, but rather of deprivation of liberty or the removal of financial resources.[40]

Throughout the civilization process – as much at the individual as at the social level – human beings tend to *repress*, or *sublimate*, their instincts and, especially, their aggressions. Nevertheless, this process of repression does not imply the total disappearance of such instincts – as is shown by the Holocaust and the wars of the 20th century. What happens is that these instincts are removed from the conscious sphere and relegated to the unconscious. Both Freud and Elias insist that repressed instincts and unconscious desires continue to exist and to express themselves – either as dreams and fantasies or as pathological and aggressive behaviour. Civilization brings with it a conflict in the individual between instinctive desires and *super-ego* control, a conflict with deep psychological and social repercussions. Thus, although a social renunciation of what constitute, for some, certain instinctive pleasures (aggression or sadism) is imposed upon us, it is only a partial renunciation; the unconscious desire remains.

Elias describes the suppression of these instincts as a source of anxiety. Civilization makes hypocrites of us all and many attitudes have their roots in unconscious conflicts rather than in rational deliberations. One indication of civilization's emotional repression is that found in the *aggressive tone frequently accompanying a moral reproach*. This is clearly evidenced, for instance, in the adult's response to a child who has done something against "good taste" and which can be seen as paralleled by the response of the "good citizen" when faced with the criminal.

---

40 David Garland, *Punishment and Modern Society*..., *op. cit.*, pp. 193-238.

The threat posed by the criminal – and the fear and hostility he provokes – have a much deeper unconscious dimension than the real risk to safety which the crime represents. "Fear of crime" has its, sometimes out of all proportion, irrational roots, and even phobias. Ironically, the paradox arises *whereby we detest the crime yet enjoy hearing the reports and stories* which the media transmit to us of the most horrendous and vicious cases. These often cause a fascination and a terror in the general public which are nothing more than warped emotions. The disproportion in the resentful reaction and the hostility toward the criminal are nought but a demonstration of the *psychological ambivalence as regards the punishment of others.* We are pleased that the crime is punished because thus we make up for the energy and efforts we ourselves make in renouncing criminal activity. That is why the punishment of others often produces a certain feeling of gratification and secret pleasure in those individuals who have subjected their own instincts to suppression and repression. According to Freud, however, this creates a *guilt feeling* in the individual since his instincts clash with what is socially correct. This feeling of guilt is a form of sadomasochism, resulting from *the tension produced between the super-ego and the ego.* Freud himself transferred psychoanalysis to the world of crime when, in 1915, he said that there were *criminals created by their sense of guilt.* He was referring to those *people who feel the need to be punished* as a result of the inner conflict they experience between their unconscious desires and an excessively severe super-ego. It is precisely the tendency of civilized societies to lock away offenders, far from our sight and memory, which may be interpreted as a desire to forget that psychological ambivalence we feel towards the punishment of others.[41]

41 David Garland, *Punishment and Modern Society..., op. cit.,* pp. 238-241. *Cf.* on the subject, also by David Garland, "Durkheim's Theory of Punishment: A Critique", in *id.* and Peter Young (eds.), *The Power to Punish,* London, 1983. *Punishment and Welfare: A History of Penal Strategies,* Aldershot, Gower, 1985. "The Criminal and his Science", in *British Journal of Criminology,* 25, 2, 1985, pp. 109-135. "The Punitive Mentality: Its Socio-Historical Development and Decline", in *Contemporary Crises,* 10, 1986, pp. 305-320. "British Criminology Before 1935", in *British Journal of Criminology,* 28, 1988, pp. 131-147. "Criminological Knowledge and its Relation to Power: Foucault's Genealogy and Criminology Today", in *British Journal of Criminology,* 32, 4, 1992, pp. 403-422. "Penal Modernism and Postmodernism", in T. Blomberg, S. Cohen (eds.), *Punishment and Social Control,* New York, Aldine de Gruyter, 1995. "The Limits of the Sovereign State:

2.4.2 Émile Durkheim and Adam Smith: Resentment

In his classic work, *The Division of Labour in Society* (1893), in "Deux lois de l'evolution pénale" (1902) and in many later lectures collected in *Moral Education* (1902-1903),[42] Émile Durkheim views punishment as the representation of society's moral order and of how this order sustains itself. Durkheim's thought concerning punishment has more to do with *primitive* than with modern societies. Many of the references he makes are to ancient societies or to small-scale groups – aborigines, the ancient Hebrews – and he deals with ceremonial rituals of a religious content and background.

For Durkheim, crimes are violations of a society's sacred moral code and that is why they bring punishment in their wake. It is precisely because criminal acts breach the sacred norms of the *collective conscience* that penal reaction takes place. Why should crimes be punished instead of us acting in some other way? Durkheim believes the answer lies in the fact that the crime violates feelings and emotions deeply rooted in the

---

Strategies of Crime Control in Contemporary Society", in *British Journal of Criminology*, 36, 4, 1996, pp. 445-471. "Governmentality and the Problem of Crime: Foucault, Criminology, Sociology", in *Theoretical Criminology*, 1, 2, 1997, pp. 173-214. *The Culture of Control. Crime and Social Order in Contemporary Society*, Chicago, The University of Chicago Press, 2001. David Garland – Peter Young, *The Power to Punish: Contemporary Penalty and Social Analysis*, London, Heinemann Educational Books, Atlantic Highlands, N.J., Humanities Press, 1983.

42 *Cf.* Émile Durkheim, *De la division du travail social*, Paris, Alcan, 1893; Paris, Presses Universitaires de France, 5th ed., 1998. *Les règles de la méthode sociologique*, Paris, Alcan, 1895 ; Paris, Presses Universitaires de France, 10th ed., 1999. "Deux lois de l'évolution pénale", in *L'Année Sociologique*, 4, 1902, pp. 65-95; also in *Émile Durkheim on Institutional Analysis*, ed., translation and introduction by Mark Traugott, Chicago, The University of Chicago Press, 1978, pp. 153-180 : "Two Laws of Penal Evolution"; reedited as Chapter 4, "The Evolution of Punishment", in Steven Lukes, Andrew Scull (eds.), *Durkheim and the Law*, Oxford, 1983. *Les formes elementaires de la vie religieuse (Le système totémique en Australie)*, Paris, Alcan, 1912 ; Paris, Librairie Générale Française, 1991, preface by Michel Maffesoli. *L'éducation morale*, Paris, Alcan, 1924; translation into English, *Moral Education*, New York, 1973; translation into Spanish by M.L. Navarro, Buenos Aires, 1947. On this author, *cf.*, Anthony Giddens, *Durkheim*, Hassocks, Sussex, 1978. London, Fontana, 1986. Gregorio Robles, "Émile Durkheim (1858-1917)", in *Juristas universales*, comp. by R. Domingo, Madrid, Marcial Pons, 2002.

majority of society's members. It impacts upon their healthy consciences. This attack sparks psychological reactions, even amongst those not directly affected. It provokes rage, anger, indignation and a passionate desire for *vengeance*. As opposed to abstract *ideas*, which we cling to in a superficial way, and where we tolerate contradictions, these deep moral *feelings* have such an importance and strength that they admit of no disagreement. For Durkheim, *passion* is the soul of punishments. This may be clearly seen in less developed societies which *punish for the sake of punishment*. In modern societies, this spirit of vengeance is less in evidence and, nevertheless, it also exists. It is kept within certain limits and absurd violence is frowned upon, still, irrational vengeance continues to live on in the soul of punishment.

Hence, according to Durkheim, the function of punishment, both in primitive and modern societies, is not something rational seeking control of crime, it is rather an *irrational force, passions and emotional reactions* that arise when deep-seated social feelings are attacked. It is an authentic act of vengeance. While the majority of legalists consider punishment has only two agents involved, the controllers and those controlled, Durkheim insists on the role played by a third element, *the observers*, whose feeling of rage underlies the mechanism of punishment. Therefore, it could be maintained that, for him, punishment has a psychological and emotive dimension above all else, a field of social values and an explosion of psychic energy. Punishment has no objective goal, it is not a means to an end. It is simply something in the nature of things, like the sparks which fly when someone touches an electric current, a spontaneous reaction of the individuals who make up society, an occasion for the collective, shared, moral passions, an occasion which reinforces these very passions.

The moral order of society – and society's *solidarity* – rest completely upon society's capacity to punish. Though he highlights the emotional, expressive and non-utilitarian nature of punishment, Durkheim does, after all, award an objective function to it. It is there to cement solidarity in an automatic fashion, to spontaneously reaffirm mutual beliefs and the social relations of solidarity. While punishment is produced as an impassioned, irreflective, mechanical reaction, it does have a role to play. This role, however, is not the one usually thought of, to punish the guilty or to intimidate possible imitators. From such a perspective, its effectiveness is debatable and even mediocre. Its true function is a double one. On the one hand, it is an *individual* emotion and, on the other and at the same time, a *collective* reinforcing of morality.

Both aspects mutually interact to achieve social cohesion and they do so in both primitive and modern societies. Besides punishment, other social cohesive factors come into play. They are religious rites, family life, education and, in modern societies, the division of labour.[43]

Durkheim points out *two laws for the evolution of punishment*, one is quantitative, the other qualitative. Types of punishment have differed over time, mainly because the *intensity* of punishment has been reduced as to *quantity* and, as to the nature or quality of punishment, there has been a substitution of deprivation of liberty for capital or corporal punishment. The most primitive societies had recourse to draconian punishments, since the collective conscience and ruling morality in these societies was severe and rigid. These took the form of transcendental religious laws, authorized by the gods. Crimes were considered as *committed against the very gods*, not, as was later thought, against men themselves. Hence they were punished in the most severe way possible. The offence of one man against another cannot be decked out with the same gravity as that committed by one man against God. Other factors aggravating punishment must be added: the rise of *absolutist political regimes*, ready to use exemplary punishments, for instance. As Durkheim shows, the high point of absolute monarchies coincides with the period of great repression. When punishing crimes, absolutism plays a similar role to that of the lust for vengeance.

Together with the above, which deals with the intensity or quantity of punishment, Durkheim refers to the *quality* of punishment and the giving up of such practices as execution with torture or mutilation and their substitution by the prison. This fits in with what he thinks should be the type of *moral modern education*. It should be secular, rational and the school should socialize children with a new collective conscience. It should be free of mysticisms and blind religiosity while open to rational debate. With the new conscience, punishment no longer plays the role of revenge but takes on the role of *communication* with an audience. The audience must feel the force and meaning of punishment and, therefore, punishment must adapt itself to the sensibility of that audience, the which is nothing but society as a whole.

Certain aspects underlying Durkheim's idea might be *critically analyzed*. For example, whether talking of a *collective conscience* is worthwhile when what is most evident in the contemporary world is precisely the opposite: intra-societal group, class, race, sex, religious,

43 David Garland, *Punishment and Modern Society...*, *op. cit.*, pp. 23-35.

ideological *conflicts*. Though it is true that a consensus may be arrived at, a minimum of social agreement. We should perhaps talk of the *ruling ideology* rather than the collective conscience, since, at least according to the Marxists, we are dealing with the ethic of the ruling class, the class in power, which has *hegemony* over the rest. It is open to question whether the criminal laws which dictate punishment are an expression of a collective conscience when, often, the laws do not reflect collective sensibilities but are indeed opposed to them. More, the interaction also plays the other way round: it is not only social feelings which influence what laws to pass, but also the existing laws which mould such feelings. Again, the idea of the existence of a sacred social order might better be substituted by what Max Weber dubbed "charisma".

Something should also be said about the social need to punish. Durkheim treats it more as a question of *governance* than of *management*. The difference between these concepts lies in that the latter suggests efficiency, the fulfilment of objectives at all costs, and is found in the preponderance of the *administrative*. Governance, however, is not pure management, it has more to do with the domain of *political* decisions, not administrative. It does not limit itself to effectiveness. It has a much wider and much more complex application; the upkeep of the whole social order. Governance relates to ends chosen and the means selected to attain them.

Here, punishment is only resorted to as the final recourse, when obedience cannot be obtained in any other way. Where authority is weak, what should be sought is respect for that authority rather than punishment, given that *punishment does not produce authority, no matter how severe it might be, the moral order can only be reaffirmed where authority already exists*. Punishment is more ineffective whenever authority is either weak or non-existent. The more authority, the less need for punishment and the show of force. This is without falling into the Nietzschean extreme of conceiving a society so strong that it could afford not to punish criminals.[44]

Like Durkheim, Adam Smith alludes to the anger, aversion and lust for vengeance which the criminal act produces in the hearts of other society members as causes of punishment. However, he makes his description more pointed by identifying but one type of sentiment as the key to punitive action: resentment.[45]

44 *Ibid.*, pp. 47-61.

45 *Ibid.*, pp. 62 and 63.

According to Smith, resentment is the sensation of pleasure which the *impartial spectator* experiences when he sees the suffering inflicted upon the one who causes a bad act. Resentment may be distinguished from other sentiments like hatred or aversion, since it is a *more active* emotion than the others. It is *fueled by the conviction that something should be done to offset the injustice.* With Durkheim, Smith endows resentment with a moral standing. This sets it apart from simple vengeance or individual aggression. Smith denies that resentment might be the most hateful of passions, always so long as it be *proportionate* to the suffering of the victim. Any punishment *exceeding* this moderate desire for justice would be objectionable. For Smith, though the majority of society may be incapable of the required moderation, in civilized societies, those in charge of imposing punishments can indeed grade resentment.[55]

2.4.3 Friedrich Wilhelm Nietzsche, George Herbert Mead and Sigmund Freud. The Contribution of Psychoanalysis

Friedrich Wilhelm Nietzsche offers a dark interpretation of the feelings which motivate punishment.[46] For him, rather than a moral sentiment lying in the duty to punish, there exists a positive pleasure in imposing punishment. Punishing another is a way of satisfying the *sadism* and the *cruelty* which the feeling of power over another produces in the human mind. *Making another suffer leads to pleasure.* It is an archaic human instinct. Following Nietzsche, the most ignoble feelings are to be found amongst the popular classes. This is owing to the fact that *the pleasure is greater, the less frequently the feeling of power has been experienced.* When it comes to punishing, the least powerful are gripped by a glorious feeling, not usual for them, that of treating another human being as inferior to themselves. Or so Nietzsche believes. Even though in modern societies it is the State which punishes, the people share the indirect enjoyment of power. Nietzsche insists that these passions continue to exist, below the cloak of hypocrisy – perhaps what Freud would call the unconscious. Even today, the pleasure of being cruel has not been extinguished, for the most part, it has been sublimated and draped in the robe of delicacy. One criticism of Nietzsche's theory might argue

46 Friedrich Wilhelm Nietzsche (1844-1900), "The Genealogy of Morals" (in *The Birth of Tragedy and the Genealogy of Morals),* New York, 1956; original edition in German, 1887. J. Minson, *The Genealogy of Morals: Nietzsche, Foucault, Donzelot and the Eccentricity of Ethics,* London, 1985.

as to the error involved in having a partial and unilateral vision when announcing which emotions and feelings are stored up in the punitive spirit when punishment is administered. Here, as in many other spheres, we should have to speak of ambivalence, of the coexistence of contradictory impulses and emotions.

George Herbert Mead also explores the complex world of the psychological dimension of the public response to criminal offences.[47] Like Durkheim, Mead considers that hostility to criminals helps cement mutual *solidarity* and *love* among non-criminal citizens. Unlike him, however, Mead considers that, at basis, we find the psychic forces of *mutual hostility* and *self-affirmation*.

This same ambivalence underlies Freud's analysis.[48] For Psychoanalysis, the *instinctive mechanisms, inhibition, repression* and the rest, are seen as following Mead's line.[49] From this point of view, punishment represents a compensation for the restrictions one places on one's own sadism. Freud assures us that this can be observed when viewing the morbidity and avidity with which the public devours news of crimes. For him, this is nothing but *gratification for desired but repressed aggressions* and for the repressed sexual desires which continue within the civilized citizen.[50] Crime and punishment bring together a series of contradictory feelings: fascination, intense curiosity, the pleasure of guilt… Sublimated desires and some civilized sentiments such as charity, or philanthropic works, which arise around penal institutions and express sympathy, love, pity, and which give rise to benevolence, pardon and generosity. In short, *there is a complex amalgam of sensations and passions rather than any one uniform, collective passion.*

---

47 George Herbert Mead (1863-1931), "The Psychology of Punitive Justice", in *American Journal of Sociology*, 23, 1918, pp. 577-602.

48 Sigmund Freud (1856-1939), *Civilization and Its Discontents*; first edited in London, 1930; New York, 1962. "Criminality from a Sense of Guilt", in "Some Character-Types Met with in Psycho-Analytical Work", in *id., Collected Papers*, IV, ed. by J. Riviere, New York, 1959; first edited in *Imago*, 4, 1915-1916.

49 Guglielmo Gulotta, *Psicoanalisi e responsabilità penale*, Milano, Giuffrè, 1972. J. Gunn, A. Maden, M. Swinton *Mentally Disordered Prisoners*, London, Institute of Psychiatry, 1991. Jäger, "Strafrecht und psychoanalistische Theorie", in *Fest. Henkel*, 1974, pp. 125 ff.

50 *Cf.* Philip Rieff (1922-), *The Triumph of the Therapeutic: Uses of Faith After Freud*, Chicago, University of Chicago Press, 1966.

It is undeniable that these feelings exist. In the press, in the daily treatment which the media gives to news relating to crime and punishment, in the effects that slogans like "law and order" inspire in the voters, in the crowds of the curious or the furious who flock to trials, in each and every one of these cases, such emotions clamour aloud. These emotions are, in truth, sweetened and disguised by culture: for instance, the lust for vengeance today is frowned upon as a motor force behind the inflicting of punishment. *Courtesy, the politically correct and the feeling of shame force these "unhealthy" emotions to drape themselves beneath the garb something more "acceptable"*. They are there nevertheless.[51]

2.5 The Power of Punitive Rituals as Creators and Manipulators of Emotions

The rituals of penal justice – the trial, the sentence and the carrying out of the punishment – are the external forms which make up the body of punishment. Punishment rituals not only express emotion but, at the same time, allow these emotions to bloom and say to the public at large what they should feel and how they should act. They manipulate the emotions and act as a kind of sentimental education, generating a particular mentality and sensibility. In some cases, we might come to speak of show-cases and of high drama which symbolically reaffirm order and authority. They aid in linking punishment with accompanying feelings of breathlessness, insecurity or create a disorder which so often leads to criminal acts. Being direct or indirect witnesses of punishing rituals, citizens go through a species of *catharsis*. At the same time, the rituals are symbolic forms, educating and reaffirming the audience's public and private sensibilities, offering a moral guide, patterns of behaviour to follow, a common language. Through the rituals in the court, the public confirm two twin, but contradictory, emotions: *respect for the law* and *hatred of the aggressor*. It is as if the government and the state proclaim themselves *champions* in this kind of legal battle between criminality and public order. This fight, this *public performance*, is clearly evident in cases where the death penalty is imposed, where the condemned is played upon like the gladiator in the Roman circus or the bull in the ring. The role of execution rituals is highlighted in the works, amongst

51 David Garland, *Punishment and Modern Society...*, *op. cit.*, pp. 65-66.

others, of Spierenburg for Amsterdam, Foucault for France, Masur for the U.S.A., in general, or Zeman for Puritan Massachusetts.

Michel Foucault considers that, today, punishment rituals consist more of *management* than of *governance*. They are more a system of *surveillance* than a spectacle, being a question of *private regimes* of sentence execution than *public ceremonies*. David Garland considers this opinion perhaps excessive and that public rituals continue to play an important role at the present time, as anyone might prove for himself when watching American Presidential elections or a coronation in Great Britain. For Garland, what today might be considered a private matter would be the execution of sentences. However, the public nature of punishing rituals is most clearly seen in the openly public character of the sentencing declaration. This situation contrasts with that of older times when the public phase of punishment was most in evidence in executions. In our times, the courtroom is a public forum of debate to which the audience's attention is directed, while the later execution of punishment is reduced to a technical process. It has become more a matter of management than of governance. We appreciate this with especial clarity in the case of trial by jury where it is precisely members of the public who decide the verdict.[52]

2.6 Stanley Milgram's Experiment

Stanley Milgram made painfully obvious that the intentional infliction of suffering was much easier as the recipient or subject of the pain was set further and further away.[53] How many times have we seen deeds done where we could have helped prevent the harm by sending humanitarian aid or by protesting and we have simply kept quiet and obeyed the system because we considered the situation was a little too far off, that alone we could do nothing to fight the evils of humanity or – a psychological distance – that these things were not going to affect us?

52 Michel Foucault, *Surveiller et punir: naissance de la prison*, Paris, Gallimard, 1975; translation into English by Alan Sheridan, *Discipline and Punish: The Birth of the Prison*, New York, Vintage Books, 1979; translation into Spanish, *Vigilar y castigar*, México, Siglo XXI, 1966. By the same author, cf. "La pussière et le nuage", in *L'impossible prison*, Paris, Du Seuil, 1980. David Garland, *Punishment and Modern Society...*, *op. cit.*, pp. 67-74.

53 Stanley Milgram, "Some Conditions of Obedience and Disobedience to Authority", in *Human Relations*, 18, 1965, pp. 57-75.

Likewise, in the process of inflicting punishment, no-one need feel responsible in a personal fashion, one is a mere agent in a chain of command which begins with the legislator who created the criminal law, the judge who applies it, the police who capture the offender and the Prison Administration that executes the punishment imposed. Nevertheless, there are times when the individual should attempt to stop the machine, breaking the chain carrying out punishment, a chain which is impossible to perpetuate if its links are not kept united.

Stanley Milgram proved all this by a simple experiment. There, various volunteers were called to an elegant laboratory at Yale to effect a simulacrum in which one tried to see the influence of fear of punishment in people when getting the answers to a test right or wrong. Every time the subject made a mistake, another individual had to inflict pain, in the form of an electric discharge whose intensity was graded from minimum to maximum.[54] In truth, the real end of the experiment was to see how far the volunteers were able to administer up to the final electrical charge, of great intensity, causing intense pain, simply because the "experimenter" told them they should obey in the interests of scientific progress.[55] Through his experiment, Milgram tried to explain – not justify – phenomena as barbaric as those which took place in the Nazi death camps during the Second World War. How could people collaborate *en masse* to cause pain to innocent beings just because they were ordered to do so?

Erich Fromm's contributions to the subject are also noteworthy. Fromm holds that from earliest childhood, in schools, the family, the army or the workplace, the idea that obedience is a virtue and disobedience a vice has been inculcated into us.[56] We accept it because it is often much easier to not swim against the current which risks our losing

54 *Cf.* on pain, Jonathan Miller (1934-), *The Uses of Pain,* introduction by Peter Cadogan, London, South Place Ethical Society, 1973.

55 Stanley Milgram, *Obedience to Authority,* New York, Harper and Row, 1974. José Félix Tezanos, "Los límites de la obediencia. Consideraciones sobre el experimento de Stanley Milgram", in *Sistema,* 12, 1976, pp. 99-114. María José Falcón y Tella, *La desobediencia civil,* Preface by Fernando Garrido Falla, Madrid, Marcial Pons, 2000, pp. 29-34. There is a translation into English by Peter Muckley, *Civil Disobedience,* preface by Martti Koskenniemi, Boston-Leiden, Martinus Nijhoff, 2004.

56 Erich Fromm, *On Disobedience and Other Essays,* London, Routledge & Kegan Paul, 1984, pp. 3-8.

the support of the group. This is Fromm's Fear of Freedom. Freedom, in this psychoanalysis, is embodied in the death of the authoritarian conscience, as represented by paternal mandates and imperatives – the Super-ego – and its substitution by the humanitarian conscience – our own inner voice. Therefore, we should make the following principles our own: *sapere aude* (dare to know), and *omnibus est dubitandum* (everything is open to doubt). It is not that doubt in itself should be the aim, the goal. It is rather a means to allow us to escape prejudices and ingrained "truths". It is the critical spirit which questions conventional wisdom that often needs to be questioned and improved. It is that methodological doubt of which Descartes spoke.

All this is clearly applicable to the subject of punishment, where its necessity and social convenience is often taken for granted and, what is worse, where the current means employed to inflict punishment are considered to be the best possible. We must ask ourselves, with a certain degree of empathy and solidarity with those who suffer: to what extent is punishment inexorable and to what extent is society, that is all of us, to blame for allowing infra-human life situations where crime becomes unavoidable and the rare thing is that there is not more committed?

3 Punishment in Sociology

Deviant conduct might be the sociological parallel to the illegal act, in legal terms, or, the other way about, deviation of conduct.[57] Again, Sociology thinks more in terms of crime rather than offences, the latter being wider in scope and more neutral than the former.[58] The sociology of punishment, in its widest sense, would be the exploration of the relations existing between punishment and society, how the sentence is a social phenomenon and what its role is in social life. In some way, sociology of punishment resembles Criminology, but, as distinct from the latter, which analyzes punishment from the *inside* (Hart's "internal point of view"), sociology offers an *external* critique – the external point of view of the criminal system. Montesquieu, in *The Spirit of the Laws*,

57 T. Fai Erikson, "Notas sobre sociología de la desviación", in *Estigmatización y conducta desviada,* comp. by R. del Olmo, Centro de Investigaciones Criminológicas, Venezuela, Universidad de Zulia, Maracaibo. Norman Johnston, Leonard Savitz, Marvin E. Wolfgang (eds.), *The Sociology of Punishment and Correction*, New York, Wiley, 1962.

58 Gregorio Robles, *Crimen y castigo...*, *op. cit.*, pp. 125 and 126.

had already shown that, in all or nearly all European governments, punishment increases or decreases in proportion to how far the government favoured or disapproved of liberty. Severe punishments were associated with despotic governments, based on terror, more than with monarchies or democracies, based on honour and virtue. Almost one century later, Alexis de Tocqueville affirmed that *"although the United States of America is a paradigmatic example of liberty, the prisons of that country offer a most despotic panorama."*[59] The facts to which Montesquieu and De Tocqueville addressed themselves continue to be debated even now.

However, despite these early, suggestive texts, the sociology of punishment does not represent a fully-developed science. One finds a series of disconnected texts, written from different perspectives. Outstanding studies have been made by Émile Durkheim, Michel Foucault or George Herbert Mead, further important contributions have been made by writers like Rusche, Kirchheimer, Michael Ignatieff and Douglas Hay. In part, the reason for the disparate points of view of these investigations stems from the fact that they are tackling a complex subject, but it also resides in their treating of punishment in isolated parts of their works rather than as the centrepiece. Although the distinct tendencies are usually considered as perspectives in complete conflict, nevertheless, it is possible to mark out at least four lines of thought within the sociology of punishment. Three are already established, the fourth is emerging:[60]

– The Durkheimean tradition, which studies the moral and socio-psychological roots, together with the effects of punishment which produce solidarity.[61]
– Marxist studies which emphasize the role of punishment in the class struggle, and its socio-economic base.[62]

59 Gustav de Beaumont, Alexis de Tocqueville, *On the Penitentiary System in the United States*, Philadelphia, 1833, p. 47.

60 David Garland, *Punishment and Modern Society…*, *op. cit.*, pp. 10-16.

61 Werner Gephart, "Die non-rationalen Elemente der strafrechtlichen Rationalisierung. Die Lehre Émile Durkheims" , in Brun-Otto Bride, Wofl-gang Hoffmann-Riem (eds.), *Rechtsproduktion und Rechtsbewusstsein*, Baden-Baden, Nomosgesellschaft, 1988, pp. 177-194. S. Spitzer, "Punishment and Social Organisation: A Study of Durkheim's Theory of Evolution", in *Law and Society Review*, 9, 1975, pp. 613-637.

62 *Cf.* C. Adamson, "Punishment After Slavery: Southern State Penal Systems, 1865-1890", in *Social Problems*, 30, 1983, pp. 555-569. "Toward a

- The work of Michel Foucault, which views punishment as a power-domination strategy.[63]
- The work of Norbert Elias.

All these theories are an attempt to answer the questions: What is the essence of punishment? And, what are its causes?

3. 1 Crime as a Normal and Positive Phenomenon in Sociology

Durkheim places great emphasis on marking the limits *between Psychology and Sociology* as concerns punishment. From the psychological viewpoint, punishment may be a *pathological* phenomenon. Nevertheless, for Durkheimean Sociology, it is a *normal* social phenomenon.[64] Here, we find a concept of normality which is not usual, as far as common sense is concerned. In Sociology, normality is a fact determined by its being present *generally* in societies of a certain sort at a given phase of their evolution. Crimes being a phenomenon present in societies of all times and places, one which does not decline with civilization, but increases with it, it can be concluded, from the sociological point of view, that crime is a normal fact in every society. There is but one limit to the consideration of crime as normal. That is that crime should not produce a breakdown in *social balance*, wherein, according to Durkheim, the health of society resides. The idea of social equilibrium, which is considered essential, rests like a pillar on *flexibility*: a system must be sufficiently flexible for it to permit a certain level of criminality. When the number of crimes *is not too great*, society runs no grave risks, it does not become unbalanced. Besides, deviant behaviour has the hallmark of

Marxian Penology: Captive Criminal Populations as Economic Threats and Resources", in *Social Problems*, 31, 1984, pp. 435-458.

63 *Cf.* Carlos Fernández Liria, *Sin vigilancia y sin castigo: una discusión con Michel Foucault,* Madrid, Libertarias/Prodhufi, 1992.

64 Hans Haferkamp, *Kriminalität ist normal – Zur gesellschaftlichen Produktion abweichenden Handelns,* Stuttgart, Ferdinand Enke Verlag, 1972. *Cf.* of the same author "Zur Notwendigkeit handlungstheoretischer Analysen der Kriminalität und der Kriminalisierung", in Arbeitskreis Junger Kriminologen (Hrsg.), *Kritische Kriminologie,* 1974. Bernhard Haffe, "Hat emanzipierende Sozialtherapie noch eine Chance?", in *Seminar: Abweichendes Verhalten. III.* Ed. by Lüdersen and Sack, *Die Gesellschaft Reaktion auf Kriminalität,* Frankfurt am Main, 1977.

the personal, of the *original* and, in this sense, it may appear a creative or heroic act. For heroism and creativity to flourish in society, a certain degree of freedom must be in place, a certain breaking-away from the rule. The other side of the coin of liberty is crime. The ideal would be a *midpoint* between obedience and rule on the one side, dissent and originality on the other. It would be best to not break out of the normal, to not destroy the balance, neither by defect nor by excess.

Similarly, Durkheim makes a distinction between the moral and the sociological when considering crime, beyond its being a normal social fact and a *positive* social fact. While Psychology might see crime as an indication of a pathology, and the moralist see it as deserving of *reproach*, for Sociology, so long as no social imbalance is produced –that is, while crime is kept within reasonable figures – criminality fulfils a *positive social function* since it expresses the health of a society, being the expression of freedom and creativity, albeit their negative expression. Durkheim's thesis is a reformulation of the *theological problem of good and evil*, put in sociological terms, wherein *the good is only possible if evil is also possible*. The reason is simple, good and evil both presuppose freedom. Without freedom, no-one can do evil, but neither can they do good. They are the two sides of the same coin. Together with this *indirect* social utility, crime, in certain cases, also has a *direct* use: crime may be useful in *directly preparing social changes, anticipating the morality of the future*. Such was the case with Socrates. He was ahead of his times, defending freedom of thought, even though this brought upon himself the death sentence, in conformity with Athenian law. The same is true of Jesus Christ who died upon the cross, condemned as a common criminal by the laws of the time, but who sowed the message of brotherly love for posterity.[65]

3.2 Punishment and the Family

Families who fail when it comes to socializing their adolescents, who fail to adapt to their social surroundings, families which do not take sufficient care of their children and those that have ties with criminality, all these are *criminogenic* families. They incite their members, especially the youngest, to commit crimes. Further, their members probably feel attracted to crime. This situation presents a challenge to the public authorities, these must act at the pre-criminal stage or with new criminals

65 Gregorio Robles, *Crimen y castigo...*, *op.cit.*, pp. 73-83.

before it is too late, and eliminate criminal tendencies while remedying the flawed social situation within the family environment. They should concentrate most on the youngest individuals or on those who have committed their first offence.[66]

3.3 Punishment as a Bureaucratized and Rationalized Process (Michel Foucault and Max Weber) as Opposed to Its Being Conceived as a "Passionate for Vengeance" Phenomenon (Émile Durkheim)

Foucault is a philosopher and sociologist in the tradition of Nietzsche and Weber. From Nietzsche, he adopts a sceptical method and a vision of punishment as a means of constructing individuals with self-discipline, subject to a higher power. From Weber, he takes his vision of modernity as an organization of ever-increasing powers and capabilities. Although there exists no particular theory of punishment in Weber, one may be extracted from the elements of his work. What is interesting about Foucault's, partly Weberian, analysis is to see how the rationalization process has transformed punishment, going from an institution, heavy with moral and emotive overtones, of practices and rituals, to become a dispassionate, rationalized and bureaucratized process, dispassionate and professionalized. This process which punishment has followed has been the most important change effected in penal sanctions in the XIXth and XXth centuries.

From the XVIIIth century on, the capacity to punish has been increasingly monopolized by government and state agencies, producing a tendency to centralization. A group of professionals is thereby created – prison governors, guards, medical personnel, criminologists, psychiatrists and psychologists. All these have their own jurisdictions and competencies, careers, interests, ideologies, salaries and training. One characteristic of the bureaucrat is precisely that he acts in a routine and dispassionate fashion, without anger or enthusiasm – *sine ira ac studio* – with a studied neutrality and objectivity, in a deliberately dehumanized way, eliminating all love, hatred, or any other irrational emotion from the profession. This intermediation of the bureaucrat between the emotional reactions of society and the real punishment of the offender is an indication of refinement and civic manners, of social distance and

66 Barbara Hudson, *Justice Through Punishment. A Critique of the 'Justice' Model of Corrections,* London, MacMillan, 1987, pp. 15 and 16.

professional objectivity, of scientificism and the lack of emotional involvement.

One ironic consequence of this lack of moral and emotional involvement in the execution of punishment has been that the rehabilitatory *ethos* has been somewhat pushed aside in favour of a more "technical" spirit. With the professionalization and bureaucratization of the criminal process, within modern societies, an institutional punishment has been created that is much less accessible to the general public, much more socially invisible and secret than it was in prior regimes. The social task of punishment has been delegated to specialized bodies on the margins of social life, bodies that, to a certain degree, remain hidden. Punishment quits the sphere of daily life. A powerful penal bureaucracy arises which does not limit itself to being the executor of legal decisions and collective sentiments. It has its own power and influence within the punishment system.

Here, we have highlighted the importance of rationalization in certain sectors of the penal system and noted its effects. It is now necessary to make clear the *limits* of such rationalization, to show the continuing existence of non rational forces in the rituals of punishment. In this sense, there is room for Durkheim's analysis which insists that punishment today continues to be a passionate and vengeful reaction, motivated by feelings of rage, far removed from that neutral, dispassionate response which it pretends it is.

These two interpretations of punishment, however, are not so mutually incompatible as they might appear at first sight. Durkheim himself recognizes that punishment increasingly tends to impose less cruel, hard and passionate sentences in favour of the more rational. On the other hand, Foucault's analysis, as opposed to that of Durkheim, is not based on the entire social process of punishment, from courtroom through sentencing to the prison, but rather details the practices carried out in prisons and penal institutions. The *courtroom* is the main place where punitive rituals are enacted and where moral sentiments are expressed, while modern penitenciaries are more and more technocratically and instrumentally managed, in brief, more dispassionate. The courts, the politicians and a great part of the general public go on treating the subject of punishment in a passionate and moral way. They call upon substantive values, adopt emotional attitudes of condemnation and clamour for retributive punishment.[67]

67 David Garland, *Punishment and Modern Society..., op. cit.*, pp. 177-193

3.4 Punishment and Culture: Mentality and Sensitivity influence the Penal System and Are Influenced by It

We now wish to concentrate on the values that influence the criminal process and, in general, on how cultural mentality and the sensibility of a specific society influence penal institutions. In part, the argument comes to the conclusion that culture determines the type of punishment and, at the same time, the type of punishment helps determine the type of culture.

Still, what is culture? The idea of culture broaches such phenomena as *mentalities*, of a cognitive nature, and also *sensibilities*, of an emotional cast. In truth, it covers all kinds of mental manifestations, from the highest to the lowest levels, from the fully developed to the inarticulate, thus it includes everything from Philosophy, Science, Technology, *Weltanschaung* to social prejudices and common sense. What we are trying to show here is that these mentalities and sensibilities have far-reaching effects on the way in which we punish offenders. Cultural patterns structure the way we see criminals, establishing the intellectual framework through which we judge these individuals and attempt to understand their motives. This framework may be scientific or religious or of another kind. One writer who has done much to explain the interaction between social relations and Psychology is Norbert Elias. He considers punishment a complex cultural instrument containing symbolic codes and cultural signs in its very practice.

The penal practices a given society adopts tend to imitate or reflect the cultural forms dominant in that society, in the widest sense. The similarity, parallelism and affinity that unite punishment and culture, in this wide sense, *change over time* as do cultural patterns. Cultural change tends to exercise a direct influence on the forms of punishment. We shall look at some examples of this.

Sexual differences play an important part in penal practices. Some historians, like Spierenburg, show how, in the XVIIth and XVIIIth centuries, women offenders were treated differently from men. Not so long ago, in the XVIIIth and XIXth centuries, differences of rank and status, within the social hierarchy, were reflected in differences of punishment, nobles were considered distinct from the ordinary people. When historians talk of the influence of culture on penal practice, they are usually thinking of *religion* or *humanitarianism*. This may be seen most clearly regarding the Criminal Law reformists of the XVIIIth and XIXth centuries, when a crucial role in the process of change is given to religious and humanitarian motives. Indeed the medieval Roman Catholic Church inspired humanitarian practices which later had a great effect and were taken over by the secular State tradition. One important example as to how much culture altered with the passage of time is the different historical conceptions that have existed of justice, of the criminal and of the very nature of criminality.

Above, we have mainly considered the cognitive aspects of culture, centering on intellectual forms and systems of belief through which distinct modes of punishment were formulated and understood. Still, as noted earlier, culture does not only refer to things of the mind and forms of thought. It also covers so-called sensibilities and ways of feeling. Cultures differ not only as to the mental apparatus and ideologies but also as to emotions, sensibilities and affective dispositions. These emotions play an important and a direct role *vis-à-vis* punishment. Here, we concentrate on how crime and punishment provoke a moral response in public opinion. Feelings such as fear, hostility, aggression and hatred coexist with pity, compassion and forgiveness, by way of being reactions towards the offender. What is more, to the extent that punishment implies the use of violence or the production of pain and suffering, it too will see itself affected by the prevailing sentiments of society when it comes to deciding the permissible and the forbidden, the tolerable and intolerable violence. There is an entire range of possible punishments – torture, physical punishment, and the like – that are considered by the majority of society unthinkable and inadmissible. They appear to us cruel and barbaric. This repugnance is felt as a visceral judgment, as an emotional rejection and repulsion rather than as a rational objection. As Winston Churchill pointed out, a society's methods of punishments are an indication and measure of its degree of civilization or, as Dostoyevsky had it, a nation's standards of civilization can by judged by opening the doors to its prisons.[68]

4 The Philosophy of Punishment

Punishment has concerned many philosophers both ancient and modern with a persistence which usually passes unnoticed. Plato, Aristotle, Saint Thomas, Hobbes, Spinoza, Hegel, Bentham and Mill are but some

68 *Cf.* Norbert Elias, *The Civilizing Process*, edited in 1939. N. Elias, *The Civilizing Process, i. The History of Manners* , Oxford, 1978;v. ii. *State Formation and Civilization,* Oxford, 1982.

in a list too long to tabulate. Contemporary philosophers have not been indifferent to this concern. They have made important contributions to the development of traditional approaches to punishment and have influenced the analysis of the subject in a noteworthy way.[69]

Two moments might be distinguished as regards the modern treatment of the subject, it would be too much to talk here of stages.[70] The first reached up to the beginnings of the Second World War, and contained, amongst others, contributions by A.C. Ewing[71] and W.D. Ross[72], culminating in J.D. Mabbott's excellent work, "Punishment."[73] The second moment began at the end of the war and one of its points of departure was a debate over Mabbott's work. The 1950s were particularly fruitful. In 1953, it was discussed by A. Flew[74] and C.W.K. Mundle[75] in the "Scots Philosophical Club". Their findings were published in 1954.

69 H.B. Acton (ed.), *The Philosophy of Punishment*, London, Macmillan, 1969. Robert M. Baird, Stuart E. Rosenbaum (eds.), *Philosophy of Punishment*, Buffalo, N.Y., Prometeus Books, 1988. Philip Bean, *Punishment: A Philosophical and Criminological Inquiry*, Oxford, M. Robertson, 1981. Gertrude Ezorsky (ed.), *Philosophical Perspectives on Punishment*, Albany, NY, State University of New York Press, 1972.

70 Eduardo A. Rabossi, *La justificación moral del castigo*, Buenos Aires, Astrea, Colección Filosofía y Derecho, 5, 1976, pp. 15-18.

71 A.C. (Alfred Cyril) Ewing (1899-), *The Morality of Punishment with Some Suggestions for a General Theory of Ethics*, Preface by W.D. Ross, Montclair, N.J., Patterson Smith, 1970. "Punishment as a Moral Agency: An Attempt to Reconcile the Retributive and Utilitarian View", in *Mind*, 36, 1927, pp. 292-305. "Armstrong on the Retributive Theory", in Mind, 72, 1963, pp. 121-124.

72 W. D. Ross, "The Ethics of Punishment", in *Journal of Philosophical Studies*, 4, 1929, pp. 205-211.

73 J.D Mabbott, "Punishment", in *Mind*, 48, 1939, pp. 152-167, re-ed. in H.B. Acton (ed.), *The Philosophy of Punishment, op. cit.*, pp. 39-54. "Professor Flew on Punishment", in *Philosophy*, 30, 1955, pp. 256-265. "Freewill and Punishment", in *Contemporary British Philosophy*, Third Series, London, Allen and Unwin, 1956, pp. 289-309.

74 A.G.N. Flew, "The Justification of Punishment", in *Philosophy*, 29, 1954, pp. 291-307. Re-ed. in H.B. Acton, *The Philosophy of Punishment, op. cit.*, pp. 83-104.

75 C.W.K. Mundle, "Punishment and Desert", in *Philosophical Quarterly*, 4, 1954, pp. 216-228; re-ed. in H.B. Acton, *The Philosophy of Punishment, op. cit.*, pp. 105-114.

That same year saw an important work by A. Quinton and, in the years that followed, others by K. Baier,[76] J.D. Mabbott, J.Rawls,[77] S.I. Benn[78] and H.L.A. Hart,[79] among others. They all made important contributions to the debate and, together with the older school, to a large extent, shaped the future course of the discussion. From then on, the bibliography experiences a quantum leap. So numerous are works dedicated to punishment now that it would not be an exaggeration to say that it constitutes of one the central chapters of contemporary Moral Philosophy.

4.1 *Justification of Punishment*

How might we morally justify punishing anyone?[80] Why can and must the selfsame act – for instance, hitting another person – in certain situations deserve an absolute moral reprobation while, in others (at least, for some people), when as punishment, it can produce assent and approbation or, at least, a refraining from moral judgment? Because in the first case, the act constitute an *offence*, while, in the second, it consists in the *punishing of an offender*. This is what marks out the difference between the two. Thus, it is said that, while the action of striking another *is never justified*, in the case where it is a punishment, and so long as it is proportionate, it may be *excused*. Though morally, in a philosophical sense, the action of striking another would be an evil act and, from another angle, it does not seem reasonable to provoke a further evil just because one evil has already taken place. Ontologically, evil is only re-

76 K. Baier, "Is Punishment Retributive?", in *Analysis*, 16, 1955, pp. 25-32; re-ed. in H.B. Acton, *The Philosophy of Punishment*, London, MacMillan, 1969, pp. 130-137.

77 John Rawls, "Two Concepts of Rules", *cit.*, pp. 3-32. *A Theory of Justice, op. cit. La justicia como equidad. Una reformulación*. Edited by Erin Kelly, Barcelona, Paidos, 2002.

78 S.I. Benn, "An Approach to the Problems of Punishment", in *Philosophy*, 1958; "Punishment", in P. Edwards (ed.), *The Encyclopedia of Philosophy*, New York, Macmillan and the Free Press, 1967, vol. VII, pp. 29-36.

79 H.L.A. (Herbert Lionel Adolphus) Hart, "Prolegomenon to the Principles of Punishment", *cit., Punishment and Responsibility: Essays in the Philosophy of Law, op. cit. The Morality of Criminal Law*, Jerusalem, Hebrew University Magnes Press, 1964.

80 J. Lisle, "The Justification of Punishment", in *International Journal of Ethics*, 25, 1914, pp. 346-359.

solved by good never by another evil. Quite the contrary. The question of the moral justification of punishment can be subsumed under the wider problem of the moral justification for actions (in general).

4.2 *The Goal of Punishment*

According to the *retributionists*, punishment inflicted upon an individual is morally justified by dint of the fact that the said individual deserves to be punished, and he only deserves to be so when he is guilty of having committed an offence.

For the *utilitarians*, punishment, all punishment, is harmful. If this is true, how can one morally justify something which is an evil in itself, by relating it to a past action which was also bad and undesireable? From the utilitarian viewpoint, punishment may only be morally justified by taking into consideration the valuable consequences which might be produced from its carrying-out. For utilitarians, the "what-for" is more important than the "why". Looking to the future is more important than looking to the past.[81]

A great part of what follows will be concerned with these questions: the justification and the ends of punishment and the penal sanction, as a prototype of punishment.

5 Punishment and Its Basis in Political Economy Following the Neo-Marxist Tradition

In the two sections which follow, we wish to delve into the possible influence the economic infrastructure, and the class struggle deriving from that, might have on Criminal Law. We shall consider the influence as much on the symbolic as on the material plane. The theme is present in the work of Foucault, Weber, or even Elias, but it is the Marxist tradition, in its diverse manifestations, which has best articulated it. This is especially true of Neo-Marxist studies, particularly those of Rusche

81 H.J. McCloskey, "The Complexity of the Concepts of Punishment", in *Philosophy*, 37, 1962, pp. 307-325. "A Note on Utilitarian Punishment", in *Mind*, 72, 1963, p. 599. "A Non-Utilitarian Approach to Punishment", in *Inquiry*, 8, 1965, pp. 249-263. "Utilitarian and Retributive Punishment", in *Journal of Philosophy*, 64, 1967, pp. 91-110. Eduardo A. Rabossi, *La justificación moral del castigo*, *op. cit.*, p. 90. *Cf.* also, Daniel Gilling, *Crime Prevention: Theory, Policy and Politics*, London, UCL Press, 1997.

and Kirchheimer who, while not being included in Orthodox Marxism, are within the Marxist Tradition taken in its widest sense. That is, the doctrine which could be called Neo-Marxism. In the latter, we find the greatest contributions of Marxism to the topic of punishment. Neo-Marxists approach the theme from different perspectives and with varying emphases, given the lack of a clear and unified position on sanctions in the classic works of Marx and Engels.

5.1 Marxist Theory in General

According to Marxism, the *Economy* is the true *infrastructure* from which all other reality derives. Aspects of society such as the Law, Philosophy, Religion or Art, make up the *superstructure.* Whoever dominates production relations will be those who attempt to keep themselves in power through a manipulative and intentionally deformed vision of reality, the which, in Marxist tradition, is known as *ideology.* On the other side, the dominated and economically exploited classes – for example, the proletariat – will be oppressed, in capitalist society, by bourgeois superstructures. Both spheres, economic infrastructure and superstructures, inter-react with one another, the former having an especially determining influence on the latter, though, the causal relation will not be unidirectional. The capitalist model of production gives rise to the class struggle, this is a dynamic key to social evolution and to History as a dialectic process. The main classes are the exploited – slaves, serfs or the proletariat – and the exploiter – citizens, feudal lords or the bourgeoisie, according to whether we are exploring ancient domination, feudal or capitalist domination. The dominated classes *acquire consciousness* of their being exploited and organize themselves to oppose this. The law, political structures and ideologies – in the realms of education, religion, ethics, and the like – reaffirm the *status quo* and legitimate social inequalities, justifying them as necessary and inevitable. This occurs with Criminal Law and, within the law, with the sanction. From the end of the Second World War on, the nucleus of Marxist analysis shifted from the narrow framework of means of production to questions regarding elements of the superstructure – power, law, culture or ideologies.[82]

82 *Cf.* Karl Marx (1838-1883), Frederick Engels, *The Communist Manifesto*, New York, Verso, 1998; New York, Penguin, 2002; original edition 1848.

5.2 Neo-Marxist Theory, especially that of Georg Rusche, Kirchheimer, Eugenii Bronislavovich Pashukanis, Douglas Hay and Michael Ignatieff

The emergence of the subject of punishment in Criminal Law is, however, rather the work of modern neo-Marxism. The first studies along these lines are those of the Frankfurt School. Later, in the seventies of the XXth century, we find the writings of Hay, Linebaugh and Thompson. Within the neo-Marxist tradition, one first line of thought belongs to those who, like Rusche, Kirchheimer, Melossi and Pavarini, underline the relationship between the penal sanction and the *means of production*, with the economic phenomenon. There are others, such as Pashukanis, Hay or Ignatieff, who prefer to emphasize the role of the repressive state apparatus in punishment, as an element in the *class struggle*. Both perspectives are not at all incompatible but rather different versions within Marxist thought which share the features of punishment outlined above. That is, it is a phenomenon linked to the means of production and to the subordination of the proletariat with respect to the dominant classes.

The most well-known and representative neo-Marxist doctrine concerning punishment is that shared by Rusche and Kirchheimer, in the tradition of the Frankfurt School – a school also formed by such outstanding writers as Adorno, Benjamin, Marcuse or Horkheimer. The doctrine referred to appears as much in the jointly-written text of 1939, *Punishment and Social Structure*, as in the earlier essay by Georg Rusche "Labor Market and Sanction" (1933). In the 1939 work, we find the story of penal methods from the Middle Ages to the middle of the XXth century, from an historical rather than a theoretical perspective. Still, from there, we might highlight certain, theoretical propositions in the neo-Marxist tradition. They would include the following:

- Criminal punishment is a specific, historical phenomenon which only appears in determinate, concrete historical settings and not, as Durkheim supposed, something immutable and universal.
- Each system of production tends to discover the type of criminal sanction best suited to that system.
- Punishment has a meaning independent of the crime-control aims usually attributed to it. This is never the only goal of punishment, rather, the priority given it is made up of a complex of social forces. Criminal punishment is, then, *a social, and not simply a legal, phenomenon*.

- Penal policy is one *strategy* amongst others to *control* the poor and it is aimed at those who, because of their lack of means, of training, of education or because of their demoralization, have a tendency to commit crimes.
- Punishment must be looked at, not as a social answer to the delinquency of specific individuals, but, above all, as a *mechanism in the class struggle*, between the bourgeoisie and the proletariat, within a market system, with its fundamental basis in the *economic* sphere, rather than in the political or the ideological spheres.
- Therefore, it is necessary to *rip away the ideological and legal veil* which enshrouds social institutions that impose punishment in order to bring its true nature into the light.

Following Rusche and Kirchheimer, the true nature of punishment is rooted in the relations of production.[83] During times when there is an *abundance of manual labour*, such as the *Middle Ages*, penal policy could allow itself to punish with *death* or to inflict *corporal punishment*. Nevertheless, in the mercantilist stage, when such excess of manual labour ceased to exist, and workers were needed to man the factories, *prisons* and the depriving of liberty became more useful, though always given certain conditions (discipline, work, diet, and so on) which served to dissuade the less wealthy classes, in such a way that there would appear nothing appealing about being in prison – this is the notion of *less eligibility*. All the while, modern sanctions *train* the worker-convict in the skills which will be necessary in order for him to adapt to the workplace. It is a way of acquiring new workers. They are taught to submit to authority and to get used to a monotonous, regular and productive working life. At the same time, out of economic motives, in order to meet Prison Administration expenses, in the XXth century, property sanctions are imposed.

Rusche and Kirchheimer take us through the history of punishment. Their first stage is the Middle Ages, before the emergence of capitalist relations and centralized state power. Therein, we find pri-

83 Georg Rusche, "Labor Market and Penal Sanctions: Thoughts on the Sociology of Punishment" (original edition 1933), translation into English in Tony Platt, Paul Takagi (eds.), *Punishment and Penal Discipline*, Berkeley, California, 1980. Georg Rusche, Kirchheimer, *Punishment and Social Structure*, Preface by Thorsten Sellin, New York, Russell & Russell, 1968; original edition in New York, Columbia University Press, 1939.

vate revenge or a revenge which must be settled between the parties directly involved. It was in the XIVth and XVth centuries when a series of changes took place which transformed the private nature of Medieval Criminal Law into an instrument of domination, especially with the emergence of centralized powers. These changes lead to the transference of the power to punish from local communities to a central authority. Monetary compensation ceased to be a means of settlement between the parties. It was converted into a measure of income and of State enrichment, reserved for the wealthy, while corporal punishment, brutal forms of mutilation, execution and the display of bodies were the lot of the poor. These were terrible punishments, with an admixture of sadism, which allowed the public to indulge its desires for cruelty. Rusche and Kirchheimer explain the facts by reference to the existence of a great reservoir of manual labour, especially with the appearance of cities, that served to devalue human life.

Towards the end of the XVIth century, the situation began to change. Wars, plagues, and famines produced a decrease in population and, hence, the supply of manual labour. Rather than humanitarian motives, it was this economic cause which produced a progressive abandonment of capital punishment and of corporal punishment. They were substituted by new penal methods, with the rise of *Capitalism*. Rusche and Kirchheimer point to three new forms of punishment, introduced at the beginning of the modern era. These were: *the galleys*, deportation, and a series of forced labour measures. The first of these was used in Europe, especially in France and Spain, from the end of the XVth century to the XVIIIth century. It was a punishment for grave offences and for vagabonds. As it was difficult to recruit free men for the job, convicts were condemned to a life sentence in this terrible work. Only with technological advances in ship design, which made the oar obsolete, in the first half of the XVIIIth century, was this punishment abolished and its place taken by forced labour in the *bagnes* (work camps) in ports such as Toulon and Marseille.

Something similar happened with *deportation*. Colonial powers like Spain and Portugal used the work of convicts in their overseas colonies and their military settlements in the XVth century. Deportation to America and later to Australia was a central axis of the English XVIth century penal system. It lasted until the middle of the XIXth century. The American colonies began to consider the practice a humiliating obligation. Moreover, they obtained black, manual, slave labour at a lower price. Deportation to America ended in 1770, with the American Revolution and the War of Independence. It might then be thought that its end was due more to political motives than to economic ones. Rusche and Kirchheimer do not see things this way and consider the economic element – the inability to absorb any more convict labour – as the essential thing. In this period of Capitalism, the idea of *the house of correction* was developed. It combined the principle of the *poorhouse* with those of the *workhouse*. Its main aim was to convert the capacity for work of "undesirables" into a socially productive force thanks to vigilance, discipline and order. These same values are the basis for the modern prison. At first, only minor delinquents, tramps, orphans, and children in need of reform, were condemned to this institution but, with the passage of time, dangerous criminals were also sent there. It began to assume the role of a penal institution.[84]

A third stage of punishment's evolution is that *following the Industrial Revolution*, at the opening of the XIXth century, with its demands for a free market and *laissez-faire*. Now, the introduction of industrial machinery and mass production made the convict work of these penal institutions less profitable. There followed a collapse and the new prisons became obsolete in terms of the reforming ends for which they had been created, almost at the same time as their birth. Ironically, this was precisely when they were most necessary, given the massive increase in the crime rate, produced by unemployment and the harsh conditions of life brought on by industrialization at the start of the XIXth century. Some sectors of society responded by trying to reintroduce the bloody methods of the XVIth century and ignoring all the most recent experience. Though it was claimed that torture and the physical destruction of the criminal might be the best solution, yet the Enlightenment and its criticism of corporal punishment caused political prudence to prevail and the authorities were obliged to remodel the prisons rather than return to earlier methods. Prisoners were held in silence and solitary confinement for long periods of time. While this did not serve to reform nor improve the morals of the delinquent, it did succeed in producing great terror at what a prison sentence represented – general deprivation. The new prisons were conceived of in this fashion, as time wasted

84 *Cf.* Dario Melossi, Mássimo Pavarini, *Cárcel y fábrica*, México, Siglo XXI, Nueva Criminología, 1980. Translation into English, *The Prison and the Factory: Origins of the Penitentiary System*, London, Macmillan, 1981. McCorkle, Korn, "Resocialization within Walls", *Readings in Criminology and Penology* (Dressler, ed.), 2nd ed, New York-London, 1972.

and burdensome work, even if all were coated in a reforming rhetoric. In the U.S.A., the work of convicts was only restricted at the end of the XIXth century, when the labour unions began to voice opposition to competition from prison workers. Even then, prison production continued to exist, even if only to supply the prison itself or the government, rather than the free market, where it was no longer competitive.[85] Compared to the profits from property confiscation and the low cost of corporal punishment and executions, prison was never an attractive option from the economic point of view.

Marxism need not be interpreted as a form of economic determinism nor as social reductionism. As a good part of modern Marxist literature shows, the tradition admits of a more complex and sophisticated reading. As interpreted from this non-reductionist angle, Marxist thought has produced theories and works which do not treat solely of punishment but have tackled punishment within a wider Theory of Law. Below, we shall investigate various examples of this approach to punishment, found in the works of authors such as Eugenii Bronislavovich Pashukanis, Douglas Hay or Michael Ignatieff. These will be used in more general contexts.

The Russian jurist E.B. Pashukanis considers that the essential thing is that punishment be *equivalent* to the offence, when handing down sentences. In this way, justice would consist, to a certain extent, in the equity, or just interchange, of a harmful action for another, equivalent action.[86] This idea of equivalence converts punishment itself into an *interchange*, into a transaction, where the offender would *pay back his debt* and where the offence would be converted into an *involuntary contract*. From this viewpoint, the Courts aid in regenerating the basic cultural forms of capitalist society when faced with inequality, lack of freedom, destitution, and the like which otherwise would have a disturbing influence. Thus are repeated the truths of the market system, criminal law perpetuates the system.

Pashukanis holds that the reality behind crime and punishment is very different to that which its legal form and ideology reflect. Criminal

85 *Cf.* M.G. Yeager, "Unemployment and Imprisonment", in *Journal of Criminal Law and Criminology*, 70, 1979, pp. 585-588. J. Young, "Working-class Criminology", in Ian Taylor *et al.* (eds.), *Critical Criminology*, London, Routledge & Kegan Paul, 1975.

86 *Cf.* Eugenii Bronislavovich Pashukanis (1891-1938?), *General Theory of Law and Marxism*, London, Ink Links, 1978.

Law is, like all law, an instrument of class domination and, occasionally, of *class terror*. It protects the ruling class' property, social structures and ethics, which it sustains, and it directs itself against those who represent a political danger to itself. For the Russian jurist, a rational criminal system should not limit itself to retribution, it should also contribute to rehabilitation. However, to do this, the absurd and irrational legal element conceiving of punishment as interchange would have to be demystified. That element is but a projection of bourgeois ideology which dwells at the heart of the penal system. The existing contradiction between the social goal of punishment and its legal form is not only found in books and theories, but in life itself, in legal practice, in the very structure of society. Hence, only a social revolution could produce the necessary conditions for the change required.

Nevertheless, as the facts show, Pashukanis overestimated the fixity of the legal-penal framework. During the XXth century, in Europe and America, capitalist societies changed legal forms as regards punishments, introducing non-fixed sentences, irresponsibility as offence, and criminal psychology, categories which notably differ from traditional ideas concerning the subject. None of these changes has completely taken the place of ancient legal forms of penal practice, rather they have introduced modifications, and they have done so without any fundamental economic revolution whatever.

It might also be pointed out that Pashukanis presents a rather simplistic picture of punishment, that is, as a function of class struggle. If, for Durkheim, punishment expresses societal interests as a whole, for Pashukanis, penal practice only serves the ruling class, the bourgeois, interests. It is they who impose penal terror. Neither position can be upheld. Criminal Law offers protection, as well as terror, to the working classes and also there is a social function to punishment insofar as it prohibits violence. Penal sanctions protect perceived interests as if they were universal, rather than specific, interests. It is exactly the legal form which punishment adopts that simultaneously proportions a certain equality of protection for all, even if, at the same time, it contributes to inequality and class domination. Via Criminal Law, individuals can legally demand protection of their persons and property, as victim or as accused, on the plane of *equality before the law*, independent of their social class. However, precisely because the law considers all equal before it, it often silences *real inequalities*, the power and liberty quotas which separate the rich from the poor, and the owners of the means of production from those who are not owners. Criminal Law, therefore, protects people against crime and criminals, but not against social inequalities and class domination.

Douglas Hay carries out an analysis into XVIIIth century, English Criminal Law from a largely different perspective from that of Pashukanis.[87] Both theoreticians conceive of sanctions as an ideological mode of class coercion, but, while Pashukanis emphasizes the often external and unconscious cultural and structural forces, Hay puts the accent on the *deliberate* nature of human actions and on the strategic calculations of those in power. In effect, historians tend to treat of the human processes of manipulation rather than of the relationship between the cultural patterns resulting from such processes. They tend to deal with things such as the taking of penal decisions when passing laws or sentences, penal ritual organization and the mind-sets which lie behind these processes. This is clearly seen in the paradox of maintaining the Death Penalty throughout various English governments, in spite of the manifest promise by those governments to abolish it.

So far, we have set forth certain interpretations concerning criminal punishment from the points of view of economic relations, legal-ideological forms or political manipulation. Still, there exists another, even more Marxist, approach. This consists in considering penal policy and institutions as the result of a *complex of converging forces* in a specific setting, rather than as a monolithic process. Punishment is thus the result of a conjunction of interconnected and conflicting forces. What makes this analytic perspective Marxist or neo-Marxist rather than multidisciplinary is its insistence on the fact that these forces act within a wider structure. This is the production system and the class hierarchy. That is to say, religious, humanitarian or scientific factors are inserted into the dominant class culture. A good example of this mode of analysis is the work of Michael Ignatieff, *A Just Measure of Pain*. Here, the criminal system's success was its capacity to not merely fit the crime but also to provide an answer to the social crisis of the period and to appeal to wider interests.[88]

87 *Cf.* Douglas Hay, "Property, Authority and the Criminal Law", in *id. et al., Albions Fatal Tree: Crime and Society in Eighteenth-Century England,* Harmondsworth, 1975.

88 Michael Ignatieff, *A Just Measure of Pain: The Penitentiary in the Industrial Revolution 1750-1850*, London, Macmillan, 1978. "Class Interests and the Penitentiary: A Reply to Rothman", in *The Canadian Criminology Forum*, 5, 1982, p. 66. "State, Civil Society and Total Institutions: A Critique of

6 Punishment in Pedagogy, Punishment and Education

A.C. Ewing morally justifies punishment basing his argument on the educational function which it fulfils.[89] Punishment is educational to the extent that it makes people abstain from carrying out bad actions not simply because they consider them bad. That is, beyond the cases where they do not do them merely from fear of the reprisals they might be subject to in the form of punishment for realizing them.[90]

7 Punishment and the Theory of Communication

Normally, within the Theory of Criminal Law and of Criminology, it is recognized that punishment and penal sanctions make sense and are a means of communicating with the population in general – who are potential offenders, or else who constitute the public in a broad sense. This communication takes place not only through conduct or actions, but also through symbols, signs, declarations and rhetorical mechanisms. In what follows, we attempt to offer some brushstrokes to trace the function of punishment as a communicative and didactic institution.[91]

The sanction is an institution which aids in constructing and keeping up the social world, when it produces common categories, shared by the majority of people, and which allow individuals to understand one another. The routine activity of imposing sanctions teaches, clarifies and dramatizes some of the basic, moral-political categories, creating

Recent Histories of Punishment", in S. Cohen, A. Scull (eds.), *Social Control and the State*, Oxford, 1983. David Garland, *Punishment and Modern Society, op. cit.*, pp. 96-130, esp. p. 126. Cf. also F. Alexander, H. Staub, *The Criminal, the Judge and the Public: A Psychological Analysis*, London, 1931; Glencoe, Free Press, 1956. And Thomas Baldwin, "Punishment, Communication, and Resentment", in Matt Matravers (ed.), *Punishment and Political Theory, op. cit.*, pp. 124-133.

89 Alfred Cyril Ewing, The *Morality of Punishment with Some Suggestions for a General Theory of Ethics*, preface by W.D. Ross, Montclair, N.J., Patterson Smith, 1970, p. 104.

90 Jean Hampton, "The Moral Education Theory of Punishment", in *Philosophy and Public Affairs*, 13, 3, 1984, pp. 208-238. Jean Hampton, "Correcting Harms versus Righting Wrongs: the Goal of Retribution", in *UCLA Law Review*, 39, 1992, pp. 201-244.

91 Robert Ervin Gahringer, "Punishment as Language", in *Ethics*, 76, 1960, pp. 46-48.

a symbolic universe, communicating information not only about crime and punishment, but also about power, authority, legitimacy, normality, morality, the person, social relations, and a long so on of tangential matters. The signs and symbols of penal discourse are part of authority's institutional discourse which tries to organize and educate the Great Public's moral and political mentality, its feelings and sensibility. It proportions continuous and repetitive information with a series of instructions on what we should think, what is good or bad, what is normal or pathological, legitimate or illegitimate, politically correct or incorrect. Through its judgments, condemnations and classifications of all kinds, punishment-language teaches us – and persuades us – how to judge, what to condemn and how to classify individuals according to the law and it does this by way of a specific language and vocabulary.

When we try to delve into the complex punishment world, our attention is inevitably drawn to institutional practices that have a public and declaratory form. These, however, change over time. In the past, these public practices were particularly evident in the shape of *public executions*, before a vast expectant crowd. Likewise, they were evident in the rituals of *public confessions* – we may think here of medieval torture as a means of extracting evidence. Today, the situation is very different. Criminal punishments are rarely carried out in public, even if, in practice, certain elements exist which are deliberately aimed at public consumption, and which are communicated to a wide audience. Think of what happens with the legal act of *passing sentence* which is addressed not only to the offender, but also, via the press, to the victims, potential offenders, and to the public in general. Other occasions and forms also exist by which penal institutions direct themselves at the great public. Ministry of Justice annual reports or government declarations regarding their policy on crime are clear instances of this. Equally, though with less authority, we find the work of criminal reformers, critics, and of criminal and criminological *scientific doctrine*, all of whom elaborate their discourse around punishment.

However, all of this is still not enough. We cannot reduce our analysis to *speech acts*. We must further include practices in equal measure, whatever the type, for these also imply communication. Otherwise we perpetuate the artificial distinction between *language and action, the mental and the physical, the ideal and the real, theory and praxis*. These day-to-day practices are *symbolic activities*. Such is the case with the activity of handing down a sentence which activates a whole legal process and puts into effect a mechanism, in many cases, leading to imprisonment, a practical effect. Another example of symbolic effect may be seen in the outer aspect of the modern prison and its architectural iconography, as also in the appearance of prison staff.[92]

It can be claimed that punishment has a communicative function. It is more correct to speak of "communication" rather than of "expression". Communication implies the idea of "reciprocity" and "rationality", while expression merely requires someone to express himself. If there is someone who receives what is expressed, he may do so as simply a passive addressee. Further, the effect produced on the passive addressee might take place where the expression is totally irrational, without need for any mediation through ratiocination or understanding of the message. Contrariwise, in communication, the receiver plays an active role in the process, receives and responds to the message communicated. He must do this in a rational fashion for there to be understanding between both parties.

When punishing, the State addresses its citizens to establish communication and treats them as rational, responsible citizens. For instance, retributive sentences communicate a message of dissuasion to the population at large (general prevention) and make that population take the threat of punishment seriously, while warning potential offenders. The message, however, is primarily aimed at the offender being punished, without bearing this in mind, we fall victim to that defect, which Kant pointed out, of using the said offender as but a means – to warn off other offenders – and not as an end in himself. From the retributive viewpoint, the message would consist in the condemnation or censure of a past offence and the acceptance of the offender's repentance, the which reconciles him with his fellow citizens and restores his proper belonging to the community from which his offence has excluded him. All of this is only how the system "should" ideally operate, not how it actually works. The latter implies that the penal sanction is fallible, that it may fail in its attempt to elicit the offender's repentance. He is free to follow his own inclination. Even should it not achieve its persuasive effect, still communication takes place, in the same way as we might have a discussion which finally reaches no conclusion. However, what is necessary for there to be communication is the existence of a com-

92 David Garland, *Punishment and Modern Society…, op. cit.*, p. 250.

munity model with a common language, with some shared values and forms of life.[93]

Criminal Law and trial, insofar as they are a moral critique, are communicative tasks given that they seek the assent and agreement of those to whom they are addressed. The law seeks the citizen's approval insofar as he is a rational, moral agent. The trial looks to bind the parties in a rational dialogue concerning the justice of the accusations, persuading the accused – if finally found guilty – that he should accept, and make his own, the censure which the sentence implies.[94]

No less than the rest of us, judges are subject to the devastating, psychological consequences of scepticism. The institutional character of their function may even increase this state, in that judges not only make value judgments, but, what is more, they impose them upon the rest of us. If the daily task of a judge consists in imposing values upon others, doubtless, it can be very hard to do so should he consider that those values are but his own subjective values. In effect, this has produced a tendency towards a lack of confidence in the ability to discern the difference between what is good and what is bad. This is in part due to the existence of a great variety of opinions as to what is good and what is evil. The problem is especially difficult when positions in this regard are taken by one person or several persons who then impose them on others who do not share their beliefs. This makes communication difficult. It is crucial that the law and the judge be the mouth through which the community speaks. That is, they should be the voice of "shared" values and their language must be understandable so that it might be understood by the defendant being tried. It is important that the accused "understand" what is being said.[95] Because, only if this rational communication takes place between State and criminal regarding the sanction, can we say that the sanction is justified.[96] It would hardly

93 Robin Antony Duff, "Punishment, Communication and Community", in Matt Matravers (ed.), *Punishment and Political Theory,* Oxford, Hart Publishing, 1999, pp. 48-79.

94 Robin Antony Duff, *Trials and Punishment,* Cambridge, Cambridge University Press, 1986, p. 233.

95 Matt Matravers, "What to Say?: The Communicative Element in Punishment and Moral Theory", in Matt Matravers (ed.): *Punishment and Political Theory, op. cit.,* p. 108.

96 Thomas Baldwin, "Punishment, Communication, and Resentment", in Matt Matravers (ed.), *Punishment and Political Theory, op. cit.,* pp. 124 ff.

be legitimate to punish someone for something which he does not agree to think of as wrong.

8 Punishment in Literature

The subject of punishment is a recurrent theme and one of the commonplaces of a great part of world literature. Literature has known how to put on record some of the transcendental themes of the philosophical debate, as these revolve around whether there is a right to punish, what are the forms and limits of punishment, and who has the right to impose punishment. Certain works of Aeschylus, Euripides, Aristophanes, Thucydides, Dante, Shakespeare, Molière, Swift, Montaigne, Tolstoy or Dostoyevsky are sterling proof of to what extent arguments regarding the subject abound in the world of letters of all times and places on the planet.[97] Here, we do not intend to analyze all these authors, that goes beyond the scope of our investigation. We shall limit ourselves to two classic works on the theme. They are: *Crime and Punishment* by Dostoyevsky and *A Clockwork Orange* by Anthony Burgess.

8.1 Crime and Punishment *by Fyodor Dostoyevsky*

The idea behind *Crime and Punishment* (1866) probably goes back to Dostoyevsky's days in prison. The work is partly a social novel in which money is a basic problem. In this regard, we find the thought of the young radicals, one of whom is the impoverished hero of the book, Raskolnikov. A nihilist in intellectual revolt against society, he waivers between good and evil. His destructive theory that humanitarian ends justify any means, even should these be evil, lead him to murder. In prison, his intellectual pride, which has driven him to breach the moral norms, allows him to realize that happiness cannot be attained through a rational planning of existence, rather, it must be sought through suffering. Other secondary characters, such as his wife Marmeladov, the prostitute Sonia, and Svidrigailov are also brilliantly portrayed. The work introduces a new dimension to the suspense of a murder mystery.

97 *Cf.* Sófocles, *Antígona,* in Colección Clásicos Inolvidables, Buenos Aires, El Ateneo, 2nd ed. 1950, María José Falcón y Tella, *La desobediencia civil*, Madrid, Marcial Pons, 2000, pp. 309-311; Translation into English of this second part by Peter Muckley, *A History of Civil Disobedience*, Genève, Diversités, 2004.

It mixes in social, philosophical and religious elements. The novel was an immediate success. Within the murky world of crime, there is a spiritual component which lights up Dostoyevsky's creation.[98]

In fact, the religious dimension does not come out as alien to punishment in Dostoyevsky. The idea of soul and mental suffering, by way of the guilty conscience, the process of expiation, tribulation or the torment in the soul occasioned by the offence, an offence which normal people consider a sin, are all present here. This moral suffering is exemplified through the literary character of Raskolnikov, who mentally tortures himself because of the need he feels of betraying himself as the author of his own crime.

Dostoyevsky characters are not of the same type as those of the great novels of Flaubert, Dumas or Balzac, the children of bourgeois society, humdrum, with their headaches, adulteries and petty domestic jealousies. Dostoyevsky creates his characters and places them at the limits of human normality, on the frontiers of the unstable. The majority are sinister and seem, indeed, to be possessed by the devil. However, these diabolic characters, thrown into the world, will they be regenerated? Only on one condition, answers Dostoyevsky, the condition of purification by means of suffering. Herein beat the conceptions of punishment as expiation, as a purge through which the subject experiences moral amendment. The unhappy Sonia says it to Raskolnikov, the murderer: "Get down on your knees in the middle of the square, shout out your crime in all directions so that all the world might hear it, hug the Holy Earth which you have stained with innocent blood and kiss it". It is the idea of humiliation, of recognition of sin, as a pre-condition for redemption from evil.

8. 2 A Clockwork Orange *by Anthony Burgess*

The anxiety which arises in the face of the so-called "treatment" carried out by rehabilitation penal policies has often found a literary expression rather than a criminological one. Embodied in novels, the situation of unease before the treatment of delinquents reaches greater audiences.

98 Fyodor Dostoyevsky (1821-1881), *Crime and Punishment.* Translation into English by Julius Katzer, Moscow, Raduga Publishers, 1985. Translation into Spanish, *Crimen y castigo*, Madrid, Ed. Fraile, 1981, p. 84. Harold Bloom (ed.), *Fyodor Dostoievsky's Crime and Punishment*, New York, Chelsea House Publisher's, 1988.

Probably one of the most widely read texts of literature – and the most seen in its film version – is *A Clockwork Orange* by Anthony Burgess.[99] Here, the central character changes from villain to victim on being subjected to treatment methods while in prison. When envisaging a terrible future – today a present – of gangs of thugs, youngsters disguised in various garb, using a threatening slang, rapists of women of all social conditions, Burgess raises the question to what extent it is moral to try to "cure" such behaviour. The only effective treatment would be – according to the author – a kind of therapy which would convert the recipient into a species of automaton, with no moral freedom of choice and no capacity for moral growth.[100] The crude behaviourism and the techniques such as those inflicted on Alex in *A Clockwork Orange* took place not only in fiction but equally in reality, where prisoners were used as guinea-pigs in experiments with psychotropic drugs, with substances like lithium or, in the most extreme cases, subjected to surgical operations to "cure" them of tendencies which induced them to commit crimes such as rape or pederasty.

In *A Clockwork Orange*, the hooligan attack and the impotence of its victims seem to exemplify a meeting between irremediable contraries and, when the leader of the rapist attackers falls into the hands of the police, the system begins to exercise not only structural and administrative violence upon him, but also therapeutic violence, incarnate in the behaviourist treatment of his criminal impulses. The reader has witnessed the brutal violence of the merciless aggressors and then contemplated the neutral State's "care program" and one might stare horror-struck when faced with first one, then the other, type of treatment.

9 Punishment in Theology

9.1 The Criminal as a Bad Person Who Needs Reforming

Many theorists see in retribution a detestable instinct, of Biblical origin, releasing society's old parricidal instinct: the Cain complex, which makes of the delinquent a species of scapegoat (*Sündenbock*) paying for its own and alien frustrations.[101]

99 Anthony Burgess, *A Clockwork Orange*, London, Heinemann, 1962.

100 Barbara Hudson, *Justice Through Punishment…, op. cit.*, pp. 19, 20 and 25.

101 Arthur Herbert Gray (1868-), "The Christian View of the Use of Punishment", in *Howard Journal*, 2, 1929, pp. 296 ff.

Escatology shows us this "eon", human time, as incomplete, but in a stage of culmination. It asks us to let the wheat and the tares grow, since, until the end of the world, there will be crimes and abuses of power, even though those who commit them have already lost the battle. The Biblical Original Sin has been wiped out, though its effects still live on in people and in social structures. These are the four escatological themes: Death, Judgment, Hell and Glory.[102]

9.2 The Christian Religion: Between Punishment and Pardon. The Biblical Teachings

Retributionist yearnings, to a certain degree, approximate revenge instincts, the returning of evil for evil. Many writers reject, as vile and petty, the abandoning of oneself to the blind, *vindicta* instincts. Some theologians arrive at the same conclusion (this is especially true among Protestants). For them, the throne of punitive justice is only claimed for God. They base this finding on many sacred texts which put the accent on justice being only in the hands of the Lord and not in those of men.

Such a belief is nothing new. Chapter 22 of Exodus places in the mouth of God the commandment "Thou shalt not kill", and Chapter 13 of St. Matthew tells of, and comments upon, the parable of the wheat and the chaff: "Men do not rip them up... That is a task for the Father along with his angels". There are many other Biblical quotations which could be used to back up the contention that punishment is the negation of Christianity, whose essence is, on the contrary, forgiveness. Thus: "Judge not that ye be not judged"; "Do not allow yourself to be overcome by evil, rather strive to overcome evil with good"; "Love thine enemies"; "Do good unto those that hate thee, pray for those who persecute and revile thee"; "Do not return evil for evil, nor curse for curse, rather indeed offer blessings"; "Do not take justice into thine own hands, beloved, give first place to the wrath (of God)"; "For it is written, Vengeance is mine, I shall do justice – saith the Lord; Rather, if thine enemy is thirsty, let him drink, if he hungers, let him eat"; "Whosoever doeth thus, heaps up burning coals upon his own head". Here is the idea that evil is not wiped out by another evil (*malum pasionis*), quite the opposite, evil is only conquered by the good (*bonum actionis*). Below, we shall examine some Biblical texts which serve as basis for the right to punish, as also

102 Antonio Beristain, *La pena-retribución y las actuales concepciones criminológicas, op. cit.*, pp. 130-132.

with the idea of forgiveness, and we shall distinguish between the teachings of the Old and the New Testaments.[103]

9.2.1 The Old Testament

Sacred Scripture, in various passages, admits *ius puniendi*, for instance, the above cited Chapter 22 of Exodus, where the precept of punishment by death is envisaged for the worshippers of idols, for those who kill a thief who robs by day, and the like. In general terms, present-day exegesis of Biblical texts, with rare exceptions, agrees with the conclusion that the Old Testament does not reprove *retributive* justice.[104]

9.2.2 The New Testament

As concerns the New Testament, exegetes debate much more over the theme of punishment. In fact, there do also exist New Testament texts which have punitive features. Recall, for instance, the classic quotation from Saint Paul to the Romans:

"For the Prince is a Minister of God for your good. But should ye work evil, tremble, because not in vain hath he unsheathed the sword, as the Minister of God, to exercise his justice, punishing he who worketh evil." (13. 4).

There are also Christ's words to Pilate: "Thou wouldst not have power had it not been given thee from on high".

Nevertheless, one of the characteristics of the New Testament, as opposed to the Old, is, precisely, that it is based on love and not fear, on a God become Man and friend, not on a God the Father who is quick to anger, on forgiveness and mercy rather than on vengeance and retribution.[105]

Indeed, the Evangelist demands forgiveness, though he admits the necessity for human penal justice:

---

103 J. Arthur Hoyles, *Punishment and the Bible*, London, Epworth Press, 1986. N. Lillie, "Towards a Biblical Doctrine of Punishment", in *Scottish Journal of Theology*, 21, 1968, pp. 449-461. Jeffrie G. Murphy, Jean Hampton, *Forgiveness and Mercy*, New York, Cambridge, 1989.

104 *Cf.* Richard Adamiak, *Justice and History in the Old Testament: the Evolution of Divine Retribution in the Historiographies of the Wilderness Generation*, Cleveland, J.T. Zubal, 1982.

105 Antonio Beristain, *La pena-retribución y las actuales concepciones criminológicas, op. cit.*, p. 127.

> If thy brother offend thee, see him and make him see, alone together, the two of ye. If he heedeth thee, thou hast won over thy brother. Should he heed thee not, call upon another or upon another two, so that the whole question be cleared up, supporting thyself with two or three witnesses. Should he not heed them, tell it to the community, and, if he heed not the community, consider him as a pagan or as a tax collector. (Matthew, 18. 15-17; Luke, 17. 3)

Along the same lines of forgiveness and mercy, the Scriptures say: "Do not repay evil with evil, nor insult with insult, but answer with blessings, for this are ye called upon"; "Should thine enemy be hungry, give him to eat, should he thirst, give him to drink, thus shalt thou bring out the colours to his cheeks"; "Do not be overcome by evil, overcome evil with the force of good" (Peter I, 3. 9; Romans, 12, 20ff). Forgiveness is thus set out as the salve between victims and delinquents. *Homo faber* works, but, should he abandon *homo pius*, he does not create.

How might one resolve this opposition between certain texts favourable to *ius puniendi* and others which recommend an endless mercy? According to Beristain: when the New Testament forbids retribution, it refers to individuals insofar as they are private persons, stripping away the attributes and the obligations of social authority. On the other hand, where social relations are treated of, punitive authority is permitted quite clearly.

The Biblical injunction to forgive does not exclude punitive sanction. Forgiveness destroys the punitive demand on guilt, but not the re-balancing demand of punishment. Forgiveness destroys the punitive exigency of third parties, but not the delinquent's self-requirement nor that of the common good. The State may and must recognize and meet the demands of punishment.[106]

What is unworthy and cruel is vengeance, a very different thing from social vindication or punishment. Greek mythology already symbolizes this in the dualism between *Nemesis* and *Themis*. The two lead in diametrically opposed directions. As we shall see, private revenge grows from the blind passion of the offended, while retribution is born of the personal, legal guilt of the delinquent. Private persons, in no way superior to the delinquent, exercise private revenge, but retribution is carried out by public authority, with a right delegated by God through the People. Whim, force, unlimited passion are the stuff of private re-

106 *Ibid.*, pp. 31-35.

venge, while proportional equality between crime and punishment limits retribution. Private revenge seeks the utmost harm for the offender as its supreme goal. In contrast, retribution attempts to secure reparation, and the recreation, of the legal order and social well-being.

In conclusion, taking into account modern exegetic orientations, and the text itself of Holy Scriptures, we might affirm that the objection of those who deny retributive justice, basing their arguments on Scriptural texts, lacks consistency. Reason forbids private revenge, but approves of public, social *vindicta*, of retribution. A private person may never impose punishment, not even the smallest, not even upon the greatest criminal, not even should he himself have been the victim of the crime. All right to punish is energetically refused the private man, though legitimate self-defence is recognized. Were it otherwise, the subject would be blinded by being the judge in his own cause.

Nevertheless, theologians, the classics, like the Spanish Theological School from the XVIIth century on, allow retribution in the hands of legitimate authority, which has received *ius puniendi* directly from God, and not from mere subjects – though by means of them. This theme is also seen when studying the rightness of the Death Penalty and of war, or when discussing: whether masters may whip their servants; teachers, their pupils; husbands, their wives, and so on... adding the comment – somewhat shocking today –"only and always when it is necessary".[107] This is the idea that:

- Authority "may" punish because God, Lord of All, has delegated power to it.
- Authority "must" punish because Society's conservation and the legal order demand punishment of crimes.

107 Cf. Francisco de Vitoria, *Relectio de potestate civili*.

Chapter III

Punishment in Law as a Reflection of Its Coercive Character

1 The Heteronomous Nature of Law as a "Presupposition" of Coercion

Human nature itself ensures that coexistence will not always be perfect and peaceable, it will be torn by conflicts whose solution is settled by normative codes which regulate the activity of everyone so that such activity might be compatible with that of all the rest.

One of the main, distinguishing marks of the law is that it is coercive. That is, its imposition is inexorable, it manifests *perseity*, as the Scholastics would say. If the legal norm is not fulfilled voluntarily, a penal sanction is imposed in its stead. This is as a "subsidiary" or compensatory supplement. Thus the delinquent is prevented from being at any advantage with respect to the other members of Society all of whom adhere to the legal code.

The coercive nature of the law is found in its relation to its *heteronomy*. As distinct from the ethical, which is autonomous, law is heteronymous. While the ethical norm is accepted freely by the subject, by each subject, for himself, so that finally he is the only judge along with his own conscience. In contrast, the law is imposed upon us from without, by a power alien to our own will, by a political power. Hence, no-one is judge in his own cause, one cannot be a legal party and a judge, the judge must be an impartial third party: "*nemo judex in causa propia*".

It follows from this also that, as to what concerns us here, it can be affirmed that *ignorance of the law is no excuse* and neither can the law's *contempt* serve as an excuse. This is opposed to what happens with moral norms. If we ignore them or do not accept them, they are not binding, at least not binding in the subjective sphere. Examples of how conduct not internally punished by ethical codes but which may, nevertheless, be punished by the law, whose sphere of influence takes in the entire population and whose origin is heteronomous, might include the following: the case of an anthropophague in a primitive tribe, for which eating human flesh is not a punishable offence, according to his ethical code; the case of the plane accident in the Andes when various passengers ate the flesh of their companions in order to survive, in a limit situation.

2 "Differences" between the Concepts of Coercion and Imperativeness

There is a term which is usually identified with coercion but which is, technically, not exactly equivalent. This is imperativeness (Sp. *Imperatividad*). While what is imperative refers to the plane of what is normatively foreseen, at the legislative level, regarding the sanction *in potencia*, coercion refers rather to the active carrying-out of the said sanction. It is the Aristotelian (hylomorphic) distinction between potency and act.

Punishment or sanction derives from the obligatory nature of the law and refers as much to the plane of coercion as to the plane of the imperative. The coercive is its carrying-out. The imperative is its normative prevision. On the imperative plane, sanction plays a part because it intimidates the population in general. This is its "general deterrence" role. On the coercive plane, the sanction acts with respect to the specific individual who has infringed against the penal norm and to whom it is applied as a punishment ("retribution"). In a third phase of the system, the Prison Administration authorities will try to resocialize, and reinsert the individual into mainstream life. This takes place in the period when punishment is executed ("special deterrence"). These three stages are clearly distinguished in the sanctioning *iter* (the proceedings).

3 The Coercive Nature of Law as "a Distinguishing Feature" between Law, Ethics and Customs

3.1 Coercion in Law

The legal is not the only normative order in human affairs. Other rules regulate coexistence in Society, apart from the law. These are such things as ethics, social usages, religion, and so on. Law is the only coercive system amongst all these kinds of regulation, the only one which is inexorably fulfilled, *for good or for evil*, voluntarily or enforcedly. It is precisely for this reason that punishment exists.[1] Given that there are

1 *Cf.* J. Guthier (dir.), *Le rôle sanctionnateur du droit pénal*, Fribourg, Suisse, Editions Universitaires, 1985.

individuals who are not willing to respect the norm first off, these are forced, in some way, to obey it by way of the norm's sanctionary aspect and they are not permitted to stray from the established order. We shall not yet go into the question of whether it is legitimate to impose the predominant system of values on others. Even though it be democratic, in most cases, it is a system imposed by the majority of the collective and so specific minorities and groups, not sufficiently heeded because of their lack of representation or economic power, might well feel themselves discriminated against.

3.2 The Weight of Guilt Upon the Conscience and Otherworldly Punishments in Morality

In ethics, there are no sanctions or, at least, they are not coercively enforced as they are in law. The only sanction, in case of non-fulfilment of a moral norm is of the nature of the *intangible* or *otherworldly* – the weight of conscience or punishment in a hypothetical future life. In Catholicism, this is represented by Hell and, in certain other religions, it takes the form of reincarnation as a lower order of being.

3.3 Social Group Exclusion in Customs

In social customs – the so-called rules of decorum or of manners, *moeurs, Sitte* – the only punishment stemming from their breach is social criticism. Where habits are concerned – that is, the usages one has such as rising or eating at specific hours of the day – or customs – that is, forms of behaviour of a specific circle or social group, for instance those which govern a lawyer's practice or the dress required by etiquette to attend certain events – it is *exclusion from the circle* that rules the norm in question. However, neither in the one case nor in the other, neither with habits nor with social customs, can their observance be coercively demanded.[2]

Should someone not greet a friend – a social usage – such behaviour might exclude him from that friend's friendship; should a recruit not salute a hierarchical superior, he might be forced to so salute or, refusing to do so, be taken to the cells. Should an individual not pay a

2 Eduardo A. Rabossi, *La justificación moral del castigo, op. cit,* pp. 81-83, referring to Alf Ross, in Chapter 3 of *On Guilt, Responsibility and Punishment, op. cit.*, pp. 37-38.

debt, in a card game amongst friends, perhaps none of the friends will henceforward play with him, and he may be excluded from the card-playing circle; if he who does not pay a debt is a tax-payer, the debt owing to the Inland Revenue, this may demand forced payment or, should the case arise, even confiscation of goods.

Punishments are different in the different cases. There is, for the legal norm, *forced fulfilment of that which is ordered or a substitute sanction*. In the case of the moral, we have *an intangible or next-worldly sanction*. Where social usage is concerned, *unpleasant comments or exclusion from the group* are to be found. Here, the first of these cases will occupy us. The other two, in the strict sense, are not sanctions, at least, not legal sanctions.

4 Coercive "Content"

4.1 The Law's "Obligatory" Efficacy as Primary Content

In what exactly does the coercion typical of the law consist? Normally, it is identified with the sanction. Still, this is not quite right. The aim of law is not to impose sanctions. The law has a sanctionary end but this is a subsidiary one. The *sanction* only comes into play *if and only if* the primary aim of law should fail.

The primary aim is *to make sure that what law orders is obeyed* (act) or *that deeds which it forbids are not done* (omission). The primary efficacy of law is conduct. The primary norms, for the majority of the legal profession, are norms of conduct. These consist in the *mandatory* (positive laws), the forbidden, *prohibitions* (negative), or the *permitted* (neutral behaviour).

4.2 The Law's "Punishment" Efficacy as Secondary and Subsidiary Content

Primary norms, however, are not always observed – norms of conduct aimed at the social collective. There are situations or individuals which breach the primary norm. This is when *secondary norms* arise. These are sanctionary, meant to be applied by judges and courts. Depending on the type of sanction, there are *perfect* norms which are accompanied by a return to the state preceding the infraction, for example, in the case of robbery, a giving-back of that which was stolen. There are *more than perfect* norms, where, apart from what happened in the case cited, there is also a sanction, a fine, for instance. If this were not so, one would be free to break the law and the delinquent would simply remain as he was before the robbery. *Less than perfect* norms also exist, where there is only a sanction and no restitution, and *imperfect* norms, when there is no sanction. This latter often happens in International Law, where States maintain their sovereignty without anyone being able to impose restrictions upon them, even though their leaders have broken the law, in despite of modern institutions such as the International Criminal Court – with all its limitations – trying to put an end to such situations.

5 Main "Types" of Punishment

5.1 Punishment and Deterrents

The traditional type of penal sanction is punishment. However, at the end of the XIXth century, the phenomenon of integrating deterrents into Criminal Law discipline was introduced. This end to the reign of punishment as the only consequence of a crime is a result of the inability of punishment to give an answer to a series of cases – essentially those of unchargeable but dangerous individuals.[3]

5.1.1 At the "Conceptual" Level, Dualist and Unitary Theories of the Relation Between Punishment and Deterrents. The Conceptual Difference and the Ever Greater Fusion-in-Practice of the Two Types of Punishment

The Classic School defends punishment, as against the Positivist School, which favours the deterrents. For people considered biologically and psychologically normal, free will is thought to obtain, responsibility, and a specific punishment is applied in terms of retribution. On the other hand, with people not considered so constituted, free will is denied and one talks of determinism, a deterrent, in the form of therapy, being considered more adequate than punishment. This dualist solution, which attempts to overcome the antinomy between retribution and preven-

3 Manuel Ayo Fernández, *Las penas, medidas de seguridad y consecuencias accesorias. Manual de determinación de las penas y de las demás consecuencias jurídico-penales del delito*, Pamplona, Aranzadi, 1997. José Antonio Choclán Montalvo, *Individualización judicial de la pena. Función de la culpabilidad y la prevención en la determinación de la sanción penal*, Madrid, Colex, 1997, p. 27.

tion, maintaining different roles for punishment and for deterrents, has its origin with Carlos Stoos, the author of the 1893 Swiss Penal Code.

The Spanish Code takes over this dual approach. Monist systems, with but one sanction, supported by certain members of the legal profession, are not usually adopted by Positive Law. Today, it is not usual to rely exclusively on punishment nor to do without it entirely and only apply deterrents – as Dorado advocates in his *Derecho Penal protector de los criminales*. That is, most professionals and most modern legal codes consider it right to apply both punishments and deterrents, each in its respective sphere of application.

Currently, there is also a coming-together of the two notions of punishment and deterrents, so distinct in their origins. Little by little, punishment is losing its exclusively retributive character to give place to preventive considerations. On the other hand, deterrents tend to be more limited in their aims and in their duration. The 1995 Spanish legal reform reflects this trend, narrowing the sphere in which deterrents are employed – as against the traditional system embodied in the 1970 Law of "Danger and Social Rehabilitation". That treated of post-crime deterrents, that is, measures applied to people whose dangerousness had been revealed in the commission of a previous crime.

The drawing together of punishment and deterrents causes the so-called crisis in the dual way system. The *rapprochement* between punishment and deterrents is seen at its clearest in Article 25.2° of the Spanish Constitution, where both types of measure are called upon to perform the same function: re-education and social reinsertion. However, punishment and deterrents do not only coincide in their special prevention roles, but rather, it is obvious that deterrents also fulfil a deterrent role. In this context, one might wonder what sense the distinction between the two still has, if both, in practice, are assigned the same ends of reinsertion and social re-adaption for the criminal. So, one talks of "a fraud in labelling". The proximity of punishment and deterrents, in truth, produces, at least at the theoretical-conceptual level, a degrading of the dualist system and the setting-up of a "*new monism*". Perhaps, then, the future will see us talking about "*penal sanction*" alone. However, for the moment, the Spanish system harbours the duality, punishment and deterrents – as the new Spanish Code has it.[4]

4 José Antonio Choclán Montalvo, *Individualización judicial de la pena...*, *op. cit.*, pp. 27-33.

5.2.2 Different Systems of "Carrying Out" Punishment and Deterrents

One usually speaks of three distinct systems of carrying out punishments and deterrents. These are defined according to the means used in applying them. They are: dualist systems; monist systems; and, vicarious or substitute systems.[5]

A *Dualist Systems*

Dualist systems, also known as the dual way, were introduced by Carlos Stoos when inserting deterrents into Penal Codes, as a way of fighting crime, alongside punishments. Dualism signifies the existence of two ways, via which the judge should impart justice. One is based on the guilt of the individual (punishment), and the other is founded on his danger to society (deterrents). The former is retributive, repressive and specific. It is *retributive* because it aims to pay back society for the harm caused it by the crime. It does this through punishment of the individual. It is *repressive* since it tries to intimidate the subject by repression, so that he does not transgress again; and, it is *specific* in that the length of punishment cannot go beyond that fixed by the law and by the judge.

This dualist system, or double way, is based on the fact that both means of combating crime – punishment and deterrents – should apply *accumulatively with preference given punishment.* It is clear that, when the individual has already served his sentence, but continues to be deprived of liberty because he is dangerous, then deterrents come into play.

B *Monist Systems*

Monist systems attempt to give a united response to the question of punishment or deterrents. They propose the use of *only one of these.* In no case does it consider using both, since it holds there is no great difference between the one and the other. Rather, it maintains, there are similarities since both presuppose a crime, have a legal character, are unpleasant and have the same goal, social defence.

C *The Vicarious System*

When two positions or ideas are in conflict, a third formula often arises which is *eclectic or mixed.* This is the case with the "vicarious system", so-called because it substitutes another, or stands in for it. This system

5 Juan Manuel Ramírez Delgado, *Penología. Estudio de las diversas penas y medidas de seguridad*, México, Porrúa, 1995, pp. 6-11.

sets out that we should *firstly use a deterrent* and that the time spent carrying out the deterrent should be *taken into consideration as regards the length of punishment*, if punishment is called for. If the authorities deem punishment unnecessary, once deterrents have been applied, punishment may be waived. Here, deterrents substitute for punishment. This system is based on the positivist ideas of Ferri.

5.2 Reparations

There are those who point out the possibility of a criminal's carrying on working in prison under the same economic conditions he would have if he were free, and of his paying part of his earnings to the victim. Still, this solution presents one immediate problem: the harm the crime causes has a social effect, even though it only affects the victim directly. Should private reparation satisfy a just demand of the victim, nevertheless, that overlooks the fact that the harm caused was public and that the response to the crime should also be public. It is said by some that penal sanction privatization must be avoided, that it takes us back to historical times past and gone, and that the public nature of punishment must be upheld. In spite of this, those like Beristain or Christie propose that criminal reparations should form a third species of penal sanction, together with punishments and deterrents, so as to compensate the victim, and hence re-establish public order and make for social defence. In this case, the accessory and partial nature of these reparations should be maintained, in regard to the primary sanction.

Chapter IV

Punishment in Criminal Law. Differences with Deterrents

1 Historical Analysis and Main Typology

1.1 Evolution of Punishment

1.1.1 From Punishment as Inflicting Pain to Punishment as Deprivation of Rights: Life – Capital Punishment; Freedom – Prison; and Property – Fines

For millennia, punishment of criminal acts was carried out through *private revenge*. Collective intervention was only used to placate the wrath of a god who was supposedly offended. An identification was made between crime and sin, an idea which informed penal physiognomy in a decisive way for years. In this evolution, the *talion* represented a timid attempt to overcome the absolute arbitrary nature with which punishment had erstwhile been applied. Nevertheless, what has been called "medieval punishment" continued until practically the second half of the XVIIIth century, when Criminal Law was humanized and secularized, breaking with its harshness and with its magical and sacred connections. It is then that punishment was conceived as a guarantee for collective order and the idea of hatred for, or revenge on, the criminal was overcome. The upholding of the guarantee became the responsibility of the State. Until then, the law essentially valued a prisoner's social position most, giving rise to brazen inequalities; punishments were very harsh and cruel and not always befitting the crime for which they were imposed. Punishment basically sought moral expiation and collective intimidation. Corporal punishments were extreme: mutilation, whipping, and so on. Capital punishment, accompanied by atrocious tortures was the punishment *par excellence*.[1]

---

1 Gerardo Landrove Díaz, *Las consecuencias jurídicas del delito, op. cit.*, pp. 15-17. C. Emsley, "The History of Crime and Crime Control Institutions", in Mike Maguire, Rod Morgan, Robert Reiner, *The Oxford Handbook of Criminology*, 3rd ed. Oxford, Oxford University Press, 2002. Christopher Hibbert (1924-), *The Roots of Evil; a Social History of Crime and Punishment*, 1rst ed. american, Boston, Little, Brown, 1963. Julius Makarewicz,

In other times, the passive subject of punishment greatly exceeded the living individual, responsible for and guilty of a crime. In ancient times, collective responsibility was ordained, animals and the dead were punished and inanimate objects were offered up to destruction, by way of punishment. As regards *collective punishment,* as we go back in time, we find it everywhere. Thus, in ancient China, all male relations of those guilty of high treason were decapitated: father, grandfathers, sons, grandsons, uncles and all their sons. Collective responsibility took many forms in ancient Israel. Jehovah punished all for the sins of one. Of Ivan the Terrible it is told that, in the course of his lunacy, he began to kill people "by families", instead of individually. A modern example of group punishment is that which took place at the death of Czar Nicholas II. Another example would be the holding responsible of all galley-slaves should one member escape. In Roman times, all the slaves under the master´s roof were killed if he were killed. In the Middle Ages, offspring were exterminated in cases involving high treason and rebellion. The deaths of Louis XVI and Marie Antoinette, of General Schleicher and his wife, of Mussolini and his lover are not far from this ancient practice.[2]

In some cases, apart from the psychological mechanisms which lead to the destroying of whatever surrounds the victim, in an attempt to restore public safety, the responsibility of the domestic community comes into play. This consisted of a closed group, all made to face the punishment to come: not only kinfolk but also slaves, servants and others. Even the animals belonging to the household were killed, along with the fruit trees in the garden. Here, we might speak of complete economic eradication.

Today, there is no killing of even the *dead.* Still, in the past, they thought in a different way. Sometimes, this was carried out to further punish the condemned, others, when the guilty one had died before having suffered, and only his lifeless remains were available, it was a means of venting ire and the unquenchable lust for revenge. In those times, the dead had the right to a decent burial, according to the norms and customs in force. In the other case, following ancient beliefs, the

La evolución de la pena, Madrid, Hijos de Reus ed. 1907. P. Rock (ed.), *The History of Criminology,* Aldershot, Dartmouth, 1994.

2 Hans von Hentig, *La pena, volumen I. Formas primitivas y conexiones histórico-culturales,* translation into Spanish by José María Rodríguez Devesa, Madrid, Espasa-Calpe, 1967.

dead could find no rest. Snatching eternal rest away from the dead was a form of torture and the equivalent of a punishment. Punishing the dead rests on the old idea that one could inflict harm and cause pain in the Great Beyond. The problem already preoccupied Plato. The profanation of a corpse is mentioned in the *Iliad*. It is immediately followed by underlining that this type of conduct provoked the wrath of the gods and is an ignominious crime. At basis, this is also the theme in *Antigone*. Two World Wars in the last century, and the collective hysteria they unleashed, built up new cases of the punishment of the dead. The urns of the leading Nazis, executed at Nuremberg, were destroyed and their contents stamped upon. Until 1947, there were the "punished" dead.

In Antiquity, it was not enough to execute the guilty and put an end to his life, as is shown clearly by a brief listing of the different procedures accompanying the death penalty, which added to the amount of cruelty and suffering. For instance, once beheaded by axe or by sword, the head was raised up on a spike or a post. According to a very ancient usage, the prisoner was always made to remain some time hanging from the noose, when we know that, for the dead to rest in peace, it is not enough that there should be a decent burial, keeping body and soul together, the body must also be intact and not mutilated. For those who died before execution, suicides, those who drowned, or were struck by lightning, the punishment was slowly weakened, being reduced to a dishonorable burial.

The *punishment in effigy* is a further instance of the idea we are here developing. When the criminal had escaped, dolls or drawings representing him as faithfully as possible were punished. Such effigies were of cloth, leather, grass or straw, and of life size. They were carried to the place of torture and were subjected to all the customary punishments: hanging, beheading, breaking on the wheel, even scarred with fire and whipped. Punishment in effigy played an important role in the trials of the Spanish Inquisition.

One writer, of a fine sensibility, has spoken of "souls of shadows, souls of mirrors, souls of portraits". In the shadow resides that part of personality which feeds desire, and she it is that is punished. The name too is one of those doubles of the physical person which accompanies him like a shadow or reflected image. In puberty initiation ceremonies, a new name is given the adolescent. The Romans, like all Mediterranean peoples, knew the charm of the portrait: "what is done to the portrait is suffered by the portrayed". This is a proof of the *magic* character of punishment in Antiquity, in an age when charms were the most potent means of defending one's very existence.

In prehistoric times, the *punishment of animals* took place too. The wild animal was something powerful, against whose power primitive man must affirm himself. While today we speak of hunting animals, there was a time when animals hunted man. From those primitive times, man has retained his fear of animals and his admiration for them. Animals were more rapid, stronger, and superior in a thousand ways. Without these ideas, we cannot understand the role played by animals in myth and in the history of religions. There lie the innumerable demons with animal forms. The pride of men was to have descended from stronger and more perfect creatures. The close relationship between man and animal stems from three types of fact: belief in the metamorphosis and "retro-metamorphosis" of men and animals; the idea that animals, like men, have a soul; and the holiness represented by animal life. The idea that man could transform himself into an animal is found throughout time and throughout countries. In India, it was the tiger-man, amongst us, the wolf-man. In South America, it is often the jaguar. A metamorphosis presupposes an identity of intertwining souls, to which corporal mutation is then added. Finally, even in Greek Mythology, there is a mixing of appetites and of concupiscence between man and animal. A French investigator has attempted to compile statistics on the "criminal" animals condemned. He treats of animals appearing before French courts, and other places, between 1120 and 1741. Amongst animals tried for murder, pigs take pride of place. Defenceless children were threatened by their voraciousness. The horned ox is also a demonic animal. A god in the form of a bull carried off the beautiful Europa, while another god in the guise of a wild boar killed the enchanting Adonis. In Sodomy, beast and man formed a group of criminals all equally guilty. Following Biblical precepts, animals too are doomed to death. As is well-known, sodomy itself was not a rare crime in the Middle Ages. Hanging an animal by the side of the condemned was a symbol of expiation.

Apart from the equating of an animal with the hated man, there are other observations which speak favourably of proceeding against animals as part of the campaign against the demons, primitively held to be like the vital spirit of the animal. The solemn execution of the animal may be seen in this light. It would have been much cheaper to simply kill the animal and have done with it. Instead of doing so, considerable expense and effort was gone to, to achieve a formal execution, including cremation in effigy.

Animals apart, in past times, punishment was even visited upon *lifeless things*. When speaking of the punishment of inanimate things, we are using a conscious simplification. Guilty things were not only destroyed by way of punishment, they were "expelled", that is, taken away across the frontier. This was the origin of the word "*exterminare*". The frontier prevented return. It is a magic fence which spirits may not cross, sometimes its character as a "great divide" was reinforced by the presence of a mountain or a river. In a similar fashion, inanimate things are punished by having their names taken away. Here again we can detect the relation with punishments imposed on the effigy, the shadow, clothing, and other "doubles" of the person involved.

On the other hand, when we speak of objects without life, we see how, the more we travel back in time amongst different cultures, the more we appreciate the difference between concepts of the past and concepts of today. In ancient times, there existed a widespread belief that every object, be it animate or inanimate, was imbued with a spirit. According to the earliest German conception, things with no life could commit the most outrageous crimes, if harm was caused by a thing's moving by itself, as in the cases of the oscillation or fall of a sword, a tree or a beam. As regards penal treatment of weapons, it is necessary to differentiate between objects which kill a man by their own specific weight, and the evil acts committed by men, with the help of a weapon or other instrument. In the first case, the weapon was thought of as brought to life and moved by an evil principle. Still today, in current law, amongst additional punishments we find the confiscation or ban on *instumenta sceleris*.

Another example of punishing lifeless things was found in the Privileges of Ratisbon of 1207. There, every house where a crime had been committed or an outlaw had been harboured was to be razed to the ground. The sites were to be left deserted and empty for all time. Punishment levied on historic buildings might seem to us somewhat primitive, but a civilized people like the Romans blocked up the access to the Curia where Caesar was assassinated, as if the place itself was guilty of what happened. In Shakespeare's Richard II, Bolingbroke complains that, amongst other injuries, enemies have destroyed his park and cut down the trees of his forest.

From whence springs the horror for the house of murder or the hatred against the four walls which have housed the evil-doer, sometimes only provisionally? What establishes the identity, not only of a man with his clothing, but also the house with he who lives in it? There exists the belief that the spirit of the dead fights to get back to his house. The essential factor justifying its destruction would be that the spirits of the dead, like living men, are anxious to have a home. To wipe out the house is then to drive out the spirits. When left out in the cold, they lose all hope. It is then that they seek the great wide world.

Like people, houses and cities have *a name*. Likewise, the name may be destroyed by way of punishment. Relations of regicides have to change their name. Conquered cities are not only razed, they also lose their old name. In 1945, the names of Eisenhower and Montgomery were given to streets in Prague, in October 1950, the signs were taken down again, by way of punishment. In Germany and Spain you can hardly find anyone with ease because of the constant street-name changes.

So far, we have spoken of the old *passive subjects* of punishment: collectives, the deceased, effigies, animals and lifeless things, besides living individuals. Below we discuss the *active subject* or the old possessor of the right to punish.

Nowadays, punitive power resides with the State or whoever it delegates. Before, there existed other bodies which could punish, were obliged to do so, and organized with this end in view. Firstly, we find what could be called the *automatism of punishment*. Like a rattle-snake trodden upon, punishment turns on the criminal, causing him great harm. An Eastern proverb has it that "you should have no truck with he who suffers from disgrace". This saying is not a reflection of mercilessness or wickedness, it rather rests on the old belief according to which every human failure contains a moral significance. Wherever a taboo or prohibition is broken, there will automatically arise an evil in the form of a punishment.[3] How simple, just and safe was that world. Police were not necessary, nor courts, nor executioners. The Forbidden punished by itself. Long life was above all a sign of perfection, a short existence, in a way, constituted a tacit reproach.

As regards children, the old and the weak, we speak of "showing them up", as regards adults, of *expulsion*. Whoever is thrown out of the group to which he belongs shows signs of not being good and not being open to improvement. Many expressions allow us to see how the sense of expulsion is identified with being bad. In English, the word *wretch* means "exiled", but it also has the sense of a bad person, a "throwaway" person. Expulsion from the group is considered an evil. In primitive societies, the collective is thought of as greater than the individuals which make up society. Giants, man-eaters and the Cyclops may live in solitude, but common mortals need to live in a group, since only united

3 Hans von Hentig, *La pena, op. cit.*, p. 111.

may they face the forces of nature and other human foes, wild beasts and ghosts. To the tribe or Germanic *Sippe* have been added other social formations. In India, it is the caste. There were Medieval cities from which, every year, all suspicious and disturbing elements were expelled. Proscribe, exile, excommunicate, these were the sanctions very much in use in ancient times. One might well revive the old Spanish verb "*bandir*" (bar from society), from whence we get the words "*banda*" (band) and "*bandido*" (outlaw).

Against attack by the forces of evil, apart from fire, water, and the mountain chain are protections. The exiled evil-doer upon an island is surrounded by a mechanic and magic ring of water. Beside fire and water, a delimiting function, finally a protective one, is attributed to mountains: "He who is beyond all mountains, he is safe and we are safe from him". Therefore, the pilgrim carries his load of sin beyond the dividing mountains. When people were condemned to go on a pilgrimage to the Holy Land, the sea was placed between the evil act he had carried out and the country where his guilt was laid down.

Besides the "automatism" of punishment and proscription, in primitive times, there was also the so-called "blood revenge". The duty to revenge was called up with every offence against one's life or one's physical integrity. Through vengeance, the clan or family group made up for any loss of strength. Collectives, which suffered and acted like individuals, were pitted against one another. For long periods of time, blood revenge was a sacred duty. Eventually it died out, turning first into a right then into a crime. Still, the duty to avenge came up against other, strong, social rules which are no less inviolable, like, for instance, the duty of hospitality.

Nor was *domestic discipline* foreign to primitive man as a means of sanction. Paternal power, normally vested in but one person, the strongest of the group, originally knew no bounds. According to the old Roman Legal Code, the woman could never abandon the power matrix of the male. This is the *patria potestas*. The disciplinary powers of the head of the family vary according to whether the wife, the daughter or the son is being treated of. This gave rise to different psychological conditions in each of the three cases. Disobedience formed the basis of intervention with regard to any of the kin. Amongst members of the family and the domestic animals, there was the slave, both in ancient and in colonial times.

Another series of power groups existed, true offshoots of paternal power. Amongst these we might cite Church discipline – which may even punish with excommunication – and the punishing prerogatives of the king, the guilds and the military. The earliest monastic punishments affected honour. Later, monastic prisons were established. The kings' domestic justice has remained up until today. In the Middle Ages, paternal, domestic discipline, and that of the guilds, had the same reach. Military justice doubtless still retains some traces of its birth in its close relation to family or tribal justice.

The sacred protection of society deserves a special mention. Here, *human sacrifices* played a part. Of all living creatures, man proved the most excellent victim. If sacrifice is a banquet, as far as our knowledge goes, human flesh hardly offended the gods, though human blood frequently did so. It is useful to classify human sacrifices according to their aim. Amongst the highest of all goods pursued was victory. An invisible enemy of the collective was the plague. In olden times, demons were the cause and the provokers of this and of other diseases. Hence they were not only treated by doctors, but also by witch-doctors. Plant and animal diseases also threatened the life of primitive man. In the Middle Ages, expiatory victims were also offered up as a remedy against them, proceeded by public prayers and charms. Similarly, a storm could be turned into good weather by means of human sacrifice. Rivers and waterfalls also received sacrifices of this type, as did volcanoes, so that they would remain quiet and not erupt. The sea and the ship belong mutually to one another. Even today, we make an offering of wine when launching a ship.

The victim offered the gods must be select and flawless. Hence, with human sacrifices, the highest quality must always be sought: beauty, youth, innocence, royal blood, first or only child, the qualities of a hero or of a saint. It was also important that the behaviour of the victim be irreproachable. Consider the case of Iphegenia, a beautiful virgin, sacrificed by Achilles.

In primitive times, punishment had a series of variants or additions. This is clearly seen with the Death Penalty, the punishment *par excellence* in ancient times. It was not enough to deprive the condemned of life, the greatest good, but the punishment must be decked out in especial harshness and cruelty. Such methods of capital punishment were used as the following: hanging – the gallows in all its different varieties – crucifixion, beheading by axe or sword, the guillotine was not then available, breaking on the wheel, suffocation by immersion, burning, burying alive, throwing off a cliff, quartering or stoning. Corporal punishment was also used. There was whipping or castration, humiliating punishments like the pillory or branding. Evolution in Criminal Law, as far as sanctions are concerned, consists precisely in the progressive substitution of capital punishment by privation of liberty and in the form of the death penalty, in extreme cases, as depriving of life but without going to the extremes of special additions or unnecessary suffering. *From punishment as affliction, we have passed onto punishment as privation of a good*: life (capital punishment); liberty (prison); or property (confiscation).[4]

We see an evolution in the history of thought insofar as crime and punishment are concerned.[5]

In the ancient world, in the East, as we have seen, responsibility was objective and collective. The East was the first stage of human development. What characterized Eastern thought is the suppression of the individual in the material substance of the community. Responsibility is collective, it comprises the family, with ancestors and descendants, and sometimes this is extended to include friends and acquaintances. Degrading and harsh punishments, principally corporal punishments, may be directed at any object, even against corpses. Society is despotic and theocratic. Criminal justice is administered by the divine, via emperors and kings, who represent it here on earth.

Ancient Greece might be pointed to as a second stage within the ancient world.[6] There, the divinity and fatality of crime and punishment stand out. From all this, the character of the Greek mythological hero seems to derive. He is a toy in the hands of outside forces, of destiny. He is deprived of all freedom and spontaneity, he is completely irresponsible as concerns his actions. In the Greek World, religion is of a fundamental nature; the human is made divine and the divine is humanized.

In Plato, punishment is in relation to his idea of evil and the determinism of knowledge. Plato proposes the complete immunization of society against a certain class of delinquent. He affirms that there are human natures which cannot be corrected and, hence, they must be separated from society or eliminated through capital punishment. Punishment is considered an act of justice and as the expiation of a crime,

4 Leon Shaskolsky Sheleff, *Ultimate Penalties: Capital Punishment, Life Imprisonment, Physical Torture*, Columbus, Ohio, 1987.

5 Fausto Costa, *Delitto e pena nella storia del pensiero umano*, Torino, Fratelli Bocca, 1928.

6 Tore Nilstun, *Aristotle on Freedom and Punishment*, Lund, Studenlitteratu, 19.

via which the delinquent learns, by pain, to know justice and truth.[7] In Greece also, the first utilitarian and contractualist doctrines are produced by the *stoics and by the epicurians.*

A third section in the ancient world must be given over to *Roman Criminal Law*, more especially to the work of Cicero. In the Latin world, as with primitive peoples, Criminal Law is based on private revenge. Only to a certain extent does it assume a public character. The city was constituted and, once the old family and regional justice was replaced by the jurisdiction of magistrates, crimes still continued to be divided into the public and the private. Vengeance and religious expiation for a long time continued to be the main goal of punishment. This can be assumed from the frequency with which capital punishment was used and from the atrocious methods of execution – *culleum, vivi combustio, bestis obiectio*, and so on.

A precursor in modern criminal science, of a positivist kind, is Seneca in his dialogues *De la ira* and *De la Clemencia*. Seneca was influenced more by Plato and Epicurus than by Zeno. Plato had defined punishment as a medicine for the soul. Like medicine, crime can produce suffering and therefore be apparently injurious. When dictated by reason, as it should be, however, like medicine, it produces the cure. What does the doctor do? In cases of light ailments, he tries to not radically alter the daily habits of the sick person and only prescribes the food, drink and the physical exercise which should be carried out. If the need arises, he will impose restrictions. Should these rules and restrictions not prove sufficient, he will forbid all food and impose abstinence upon the body. Finally, should all natural remedies fail, he will try blood-letting the patient to let the sickness out, without considering whether the treatment be a cruel one. In a similar fashion, the magistrate, insofar as this is possible, influences the spirit by his words, seeking the sweetest expressions to induce people to do right and to inspire justice, love, virtue, and the hatred of vice, within them. When this is not sufficient, he uses stronger language. Only in the last instance will he have recourse to punishment: beginning with the lightest punishments and continuing with more severe ones.

After the ancient world came the *medieval period* which saw the transition from Paganism to Christianity and the principle of redemp-

7 *Cf.* Plato, *Gorgias, Las Leyes* – Books IX and X- and the Book V of *La República*. *Cf.* also, Mary Margaret Mackenzie, *Plato on Punishment*, Berkeley, University of California Press, 1981.

tion. The basic right to punish was vested in God. The problem of crime and punishment became enormously complicated with Christian dogma as to the origin of evil, and discussions surrounding predestination and grace. Dogma included the dogma of original sin, for which man was thrown out of Paradise. Deriving from the theory of "Divine Delegation", punishment was conceived of as vengeance, but not private vengeance, but rather, public, and not earthly vengeance, based on hatred, but Christian revenge, divine, from Heaven, an expiation based on love – *zelo justitiae et amore Deo*. Only with Christianity did expiation assume a clear, spiritual experience, signification. What counts in punishment is the pain which redeems. Christianity, then, represents an evolution in the concept of the penal sanction, the highest valoration of the spiritual inner world.

Saint Augustine talks of Divine Retribution, Purgation, and Correction in his *City of God*.[8] According to his general idea, the world is divided into two parts, the Divine City and the Earthly City. The former is only populated by the chosen, and aims at knowledge, and at the affirmation of God. The latter is built by mortals and creates worldly happiness. Justice, in Saint Augustine, appears as Divine Retribution. God is essentially a Judge. He judges the transgression of Adam and continues to judge human actions from generation to generation. He will judge souls on the Day of Final Judgement. His Will is expressed in Holy Scripture and constitutes the Law. Before this, all uses and practices which do not conform to it must yield. To disobey the law is to fall into sin, against which God has instituted three types of punishment: punitive ones, purgation, and correction. The first of these are retribution for an eternal evil and were initially applied against original sin. Purgatory punishments are retribution for a transitory evil.

The doctrine of Free Will is one of the Patristic questions. Within Christian thought, we further find the opinions of *Saint Thomas Aquinas* concerning the right to punish. This is especially true of his *Summa Theologica*.[9] He develops the doctrine of Free Will as a condition for responsibility, if human actions were the product of necessity, we could not speak of justice.

8 Saint Augustine, *La Ciudad de Dios*, Book XX, Chapter I; Book X, Chapters 22-24; Book XV, Chapter VI; Book XXI, Chapter II.

9 Saint Thomas Aquinas, *Suma de Teología*, I, Part I-II, Madrid, Biblioteca de Autores Cristianos, 1989, Part I secundae, Quaest. 90-99; Part II secundae, Quaest. 9, 57, 60, 61 and 92.

After the Ancient and the Medieval worlds, we come to the third great stage, the Renaissance. Here, we find Humanism which placed Man and not God at the centre of things, setting off a reaction against the Scholastics. New ideas arose about the function of Criminal Law and responsibility with Thomas More's *Utopia* and Campanella's *City of the Sun*. Likewise, Hugo Grotius' *De jure belli ac pacis* deserves a mention. Grotius clearly establishes the relationship between crime and punishment, in connection with the question of merit. Punishment is just because it has crime as its cause. Grotius defines it thus: "*malum passionis quod infligitur ob malum actionis.*"[10] From this epoch also stems the contractualist theory of the origins of law, according to Hobbes in his *Leviathan*.[11]

A fourth stage was reached with the Enlightenment, with writers who tackle the subject of determinism and freedom, such as C. Tomasio or C. Wolf, or the autonomy of the subject and the identity of the person, like Leibniz. Seminal works appeared like Gian Battista Vico's *La scienza nova*, Montesquieu's *L'Esprit des lois* (which includes his principle of the division of powers), the Marquis of Beccaria's *Dei delitti e delle pene* (which consecrates the principle of penal legality).[12] Contractualism found its apogee in the thought of John Locke and of Jean-Jacques Rousseau – with the latter's idea of the General Will, the Empiricism of David Hume, the Utilitarianism of Jeremy Bentham, and the materialist ideas of de Holbach's *Sistème de la Nature*.

We could not consider examining the period of the XVIIIth century in its entirety without taking a close look at Italy. There, the Enlightenment showed itself in a series of thinkers of different, often opposed, tendencies. Just limiting ourselves to the strict sphere of our investigations, it is sufficient to record the doctrines of Antonio Genovesi, Gaetano Filangeri and Giandomenico Romagnosi, three names linked to three different penal principles: absolute justice, the pact or contract idea, and the concept of social defence.

10 Ugo Grotius, *De jure belli ac pacis*, Aalen, Scientia, 1993, Book II, Chapter XX, 1-9.

11 Thomas Hobbes, *Leviatán*, edition prepared by C. Moya and A. Escotado, Madrid, Editora Nacional, 2nd ed. 1983.

12 *Cf.* W.C. Pauley, "Beccaria and Punishment", in *International Journal of Ethics*, 35, 1924, pp. 404 ff. Coleman Phillipson (1878-), *Three Criminal Law Reformers: Beccaria, Bentham, Romilly*, Montclair, N.J., P. Smith, 1970.

However, all these theoretical currents take root more in the period after the XVIIIth century, with the second major evolutionary period of punishment.

1.1.2 From Capital Punishment to Prison. The Abolitionist Debate. Arguments For and Against Capital Punishment

The origin of Capital Punishment goes back to the dark night of Time. There are already cave paintings representing executions. In the evolution of the death penalty two steps can be distinctly discerned. One of these is the period before the *XVIIIth century*, when most, pre-enlightened minds were in favour of it: Socrates, Plato, Saint Thomas Aquinas, Erasmus, Luther, Goethe, Kant. In Ancient and Medieval times, capital punishment had a symbolic, magical, ritual, purificatory, irrational character as the re-establishment around the crime of the cosmic order. In this phase, another characteristic of the penalty is its gradually harshening nature, in the sense that its power came increasingly from added ceremonials. This can be clearly seen in Rome and amongst the Germanic nations. Canon Law represents a humanization and softening of Criminal Law, inspired by ideas of compassion and charity, as is reflected in such institutions as the Peace of God or religious asylum. Still, contrasted with these, we also find historical realities like the Inquisition, in the bosom of the Church.[13]

It is in the XVIIIth century – the Century of Lights, of the Illumination – when a new current of criticism began to flow against the death penalty. This gave rise to the *abolitionist movement*.[14] It is just after the age of utopias – Bacon's *New Atlantis* and Campanella's *City of the Sun*.

13 *Cf.* Daniel Sueiro, *La pena de muerte. Ceremonial. Historia. Procedimientos*, Barcelona, Alianza Editorial, 1974.

14 *Cf.* Cesare Beccaria, (1738-1794), *Dei delitti e delle pene: con una racolta di lettere e documenti relativi alla nascita dell'opera e alla sua fortuna nell'Europa del Settecento.* A cura di Franco Venturi, 1rst ed., Torino, G. Einaudi, 1978. There is translation into Spanish by J. A. de las Casas, Madrid, Alianza Ed., 1968; and translation, introduction and notes by Francisco Tomás y Valiente, in Madrid, Ed. Aguilar, 1969. Jeremy Bentham, *An Introduction to the Principles of Morals and Legislation*, 1rst ed. London, 1789; Oxford, Clarendon Press, 1823; ed. by H.L.A. Hart, J.H. Burns, London, 1970. See also, Herman Bianchi, René van Swaningen. With contributions of Elisabeth Barker (*et al.*), *Abolitionism, Towards a Non Repressive Approach to Crime: Proceedings of the Second International Conference on Prison Abolition*, Amsterdam, Free University Press, 1986. Michèle

As a consequence of the movement, there was a lessening of its application, together with a relative humanization and rationalization of the way it was carried out, later came the guillotine as a method of execution, and the suppression of torture. The death penalty ceased to be the basic punishment. This role was taken up by the punishment consisting in the deprivation of liberty.

Having completed this brief historical introduction, below, we concentrate more closely on the arguments and counterarguments, the "for" and "against", of capital punishment, around which the abolitionist debate turns.[15]

A primary argument is an *historical* one. Some people show themselves favourable to capital punishment precisely insisting upon its great antiquity and deep-rootedness at distinct stages and in different historical times. If it has always existed, this is for some good reason, its defenders seem to say. Still, every argument has its counter-argument, that is, the justice of an institution does not depend on its antiquity, we are not dealing with a quantitative problem, but a qualitative one and, moreover, the history of the death penalty is, on many of its pages, as dishonourable for Humanity as is that of the history of crimes. Until Galileo, Copernicus and Kepler, it was believed that the Sun circled the Earth, and not the other way about. Should we then continue to believe it? Further, at present, the death penalty is an anachronism, even though, as in the United States, there still exist Criminal Codes which allow it.

A second argument against it is the *rational* argument. This is the most important anti-death penalty argument. It runs: there exists no rational argument whatever in the death penalty's favour. Its existence is explained simply by the practical reason of social and political necessity, not by abstract, logical or *a prioristic* arguments.

A third factor to take into account, important to this work, since it is directly rooted in our subject (basis and aim of the criminal sanction), has to do with the possibly intimidatory (general deterrent) aspect, special deterrence, utilitarian, and retributive ends of capital punishment.[16]

Rodière, *L'abolition de la peine de mort*, Paris, Documentation Française, 1987. Thorsten Sellin, *Capital Punishment*, New York, 1967.

15 *Cf.* Bonnie Szumski, Lynn Hall, Susan Bursell (eds.), *The Death Penalty: Opposing Viewpoints*, St. Paul, Minn., Greenhaven Press, 1986.

16 *Cf.* Isaac Ehrlich, "The Deterrent Effect of Capital Punishment. A Question of Life and Death", in *Am. Ec. Rev.*, 65, 1975, pp. 397-417.

Though, at first sight, it might appear that the death penalty *intimidates* future delinquents a great deal, since it takes away the greatest good, life, this apparent argument in its favour is not borne out by statistical data. These show that the death penalty does not intimidate those to whom it is mainly addressed, the groups of criminals to whom it is usually applied: murderers and political prisoners. It does not intimidate murderers since 25% of them commit suicide (so it is useless to try to intimidate them with death), 50% are crimes of passion (whose protagonists act in a no-way-out situation, without stopping to reflect upon the punishment they will receive), and the rest are either psychopaths, incapable of feeling the psychological pressure of the punishment, or are professional killers who consider it a hazard of the trade, a professional risk. As regards political crimes, and especially cases of terrorism, it has been shown that the only thing the death penalty produces here is a glorifying effect, which raises them up in the eyes of some to the level of true martyrs who die for a better land.

What can be said of its *general deterrent* function? This is also questionable. It is enough to think of the last capital punishment in Spain on the 27th September, 1975, and its immediate aftermath of terrorist outbreaks.

The *utilitarian* basis too admits of some considerations. Is the death penalty useful for citizen security? It might appear so, though it should be said that such a reply presupposes equating a man with a dangerous animal – the born criminal, *l'uomo delinquente* Garofalo speaks of – as opposed to considering him open to betterment, along Western Christian lines. One thing is that the criminal has not been corrected yet, it is another entirely that he be incorrigible. The paradox is also produced of wanting to protect the life of men by killing some of them.

The *retributive, lex talionis,* expiatory argument – an eye for an eye, a tooth for a tooth – of Kant's Categorical Imperative is also not applicable to every type of crime. It does not apply in the cases of rebellion or of desecration of tombs, for example. Doing without such modern institutions as spontaneous repentance, amnesty or statutory limitations, leaves out of account that often the criminal is not free but, to a large extent, predetermined to commit crime by genetic factors, family and social pressures of different kinds, or is ignorant of the fact that evil is only ontologically reparable by good.

This ties in with the traditional Christian argument, so close to Western thought, that the *dignity* of man is a basic value, and that life is a sacred good, which it is not for the human being to dispose of, this privilege belonging solely to God. It insists that there is absolutely no paradox in concerning oneself with the life of *one* single man when daily the whole of Humanity is immersed in natural disasters, the massacres of war and starvation, given that, once again, it is not a quantitative problem but a qualitative one: even the life of but a single man deserves respect.

Finally, to the above should be added a series of *practical* arguments of differing types. Some are obviously irrational, such as that capital punishment is cheaper than imprisonment, or that the risk of escape from prison is too great or that it might be that prison-life may be a greater affliction than even losing one's life. On the other side, there are also arguments against capital punishment. There are the demoralizing effects which public executions produce on the citizenry at large, and its morbid attraction for some. Amongst these latter, we find the criminal-like and amoral figure of the *hangman* – the worst possible stigma, according to Unamuno – who ends up accustomed to killing and, what is worse, no longer feeling anything when he does kill.[17]

1.1.3 From Prison to Fines

A Arguments For and Against Prison. The Tendency to Shorten Prison Sentences

Deprivation of liberty accentuates the theory of the *difference between the goodies and the baddies.* Traditional dramatic productions tend to perpetuate the simplistic idea that there are good people on the one

17 Marino Barbero Santos, "Postulados político-criminales del sistema punitivo español vigente: presupuesto para su reforma", in *Nuevo Pensamiento,* 1975. *Pena de muerte: (el ocaso de un mito),* Buenos Aires, Ediciones Depalma, 1985. Amnesty International, *United States of America: The Death Penalty*, London, Amnesty International Publications, 1987. Hugo Adam Bedau, *Death is Different: Studies in the Morality, Law and Politics of Capital Punishment,* Boston, Northeastern University Press, 1987. Hugo Adam Bedau (ed.), *The Death Penalty in America; an Anthology*, Garden City, N.Y., Anchor Books, 1964. William L. Clay, *To Kill or not to Kill: Thoughts on Capital Punishment.* Edited by Michael and Mary Burgess, 1rst. ed., San Bernardino, California, Borgo Press, 1990. Tom Sorell, *Moral Theory and Capital Punishment,* Oxford, U.K. – New York, USA, B. Blackwell in association with the Open University, 1988. Karattoluvu Ganapati Subramanyan (1903-), *Can the State Kill its Citizen?* Introduction by S. Mohan Kumarangalam, Madras, Madras Law Journal Office, 1969.

side, bad, on the other. What is true is that a much more nuanced, and *complex*, approach to people and to situations than this simple dichotomy seems to reveal, is necessary. In reality, we are all good and bad at the same time, according to the moment. Contemporary art, literature and cinema struggle to show the complexity of reality rather than producing *discourses in black and white.*

Often people are condemned to prison, sometimes for a very long time, *in but a few minutes.* This is on the simple testimony of the police. Do all those men, young men, for the most part, often immigrants, guilty above all of not having social contacts, have the feeling that they have been properly judged? And, those others, amongst whom are included the non-guilty, innocent or not, spending long months in *preventive custody* before their trials even begin? Do they feel protected from all the dangers which our laws are made to preserve us from or do they not rather have the sensation that they have fallen into a trap? For instance, those drivers who, owing to a simple angry answer to a police officer have seen themselves carried before a correctional court for insulting an agent of public order. Such examples should suffice to show up the *often blind nature of the State machinery.*

Let us now try to imagine and to inwardly feel what it is like to be locked up in prison. Forget, for the moment, the purely abstract viewpoint from which we have been taught to think of prison – when putting to the fore order, public security, the general interest, the defence of social values, and the rest. It is no small thing to take away someone's freedom. Being locked up is an extremely painful evil, the not being able to come and go as one pleases, nor breathe the fresh air, nor meet with our acquaintances. We are dealing with a thing that makes no sense, that goes against the personality and against human sociability, the imposition of sterile suffering.

Moreover, there are few absolutes. *Cultural relativity* impregnates almost all sections of everyday life. Facts like homosexuality, drug-addiction, or bigamy are punishable in some countries but not in others. Behaviour such as blasphemy, witchcraft, or attempted suicide, which were punishable in the past, are no longer punishable. The relativity of the concept of what a crime is, *varying in space and in time,* results in the fact that the crime of yesterday is not one today, and the acceptable in one context may not be acceptable in some other. By the fact of having been born in such and such a place and not in another, in this or that epoch and not some other, one is deserving of imprisonment or not.[18]

There are a number of legally punishable acts which the system ignores or to which it turns a blind eye. This is the so-called "dark figure" of crime. This means that the penal system, far from taking action in all cases for which it has competence, leaves many cases unpunished, thus breaking with the principle and the values on which every legal code is based. These include the values of equality, security and justice which we find radically *falsified* if they are only applied to a limited number of situations, that is, *recorded* cases.

The need to always find a guilty party (the *necessary guilty one)*, to find someone against whom to set the legal machine running and who we can find guilty, by way of being a scapegoat, passes over the possible part played in his guilt by his environment, education, lack of economic opportunities and his family background. The cosmology of crime implies the existence of a fixed, an absolute point – a God at once Omnipotent and Omniscient. This idea is the idea of the Scholastics, and of a justice heir to the *Theology of the Final Judgment.*

Further, what is one to say of the *stigma*, which, in a large number of cases, the experience of trial and later imprisonment attaches to the condemned? This is without forgetting the later social rejection when the punishment has been fulfilled, all of which can, in the active subject of the crime, determine the perception of himself as a truly deviant character and lead him to live in accordance with that image, as if he were situated outside the law. Terms such as "delinquent", and the like, already imply a negative, emotive connotation, a *pejorative judgment.* The exclusion punishment provokes is clearly seen in the case of "junkies" who want to see the behaviour of those who sell drugs punished. They say: "It is not us, it is the dealers who should be prosecuted... " *To avoid rejection, they adhere to rejecting others.* In order to be able to live as they want with impunity, they place themselves on the side of the good and accept the idea of the existence of the bad side, to which others belong.

The penal system gives rise to effects totally at odds with those which a certain official discourse wishes to see reached in the amendment of the condemned. What is really obtained is that the system

18 *Cf.* Duncan Ivison, "Justifying Punishment in Intercultural Contexts: Whose Norms? Which Values?", in Matt Matravers (ed.), *Punishment and Political Theory, op. cit.,* pp. 88-108.

hardens the prisoner in his relations with the social order into which it is desired that he re-enter. This makes of the condemned *a new victim.* Given all the above, some abolitionist thinkers like Louk Hulsman wonder: Why could we not assimilate crime to the condition of a natural catastrophe, relegating it to *the sphere of the accidental,* from the point of view of suffered material losses? That is, instead of attributing certain catastrophic or gravely damaging events to specific persons, as is now done, they could be attributed to natural accidents. Might we not have recourse to the *civil* rules of indemnity, already applied in many spheres, rather than appealing to the ambiguous concept of guilt?

On the 14th May, 1981, Pope John Paul II was struck in the stomach by three revolver bullets. The following Sunday, his 61st birthday, he addressed the faithful who had congregated to pray in Saint Peter's Square, Rome, from the clinic where he was convalescing. He made a short speech in which he said: "I pray for the *brother* who has wounded me and whom I sincerely forgive". Neither the ordinary press nor the radio repeated these terms. One could read and hear: The Holy Father has forgiven his *adversary*; John Paul II has pardoned the *homicide*... The word "brother" was too surprising and uncomfortable to be reproduced in such circumstances. It was necessary to pigeonhole the event with the usual labels. It was an attempted assassination and one does not call an assassin "brother". It was, however, the word the Pope had intentionally chosen, avoiding defining himself as the victim of an aggressor, thus placing himself in *another universe* distinct from criminal justice.[19]

Sainz Cantero points out a series of factors leading to the failure of punishment by deprivation of liberty. Among them, we highlight the following: a) it neither *intimidates* the majority of criminals – precisely the habitual and most dangerous ones who have got used to suffering it – nor does it *correct*; b) there is the *abuse* of imprisonment, since its discovery as a punishment; c) we must recognize the fact that society *distrusts* those who come out of prison.[20]

To the above, we should add as arguments against imprisonment that it is "disturbing" and "stigmatizing" for the prisoner and his family

19 Louk Hulsman, J. Bernat de Celis, *Sistema penal y seguridad ciudadana: Hacia una alternativa*, Barcelona, Ariel, 1984, pp. 44-80.

20 José Antonio Sainz Cantero, "La sustitución de la pena de privación de libertad", in *Estudios Penales II. La reforma penitenciaria*, Santiago de Compostela, 1978, pp. 221 ff. D. Rothman, "Prisons: The Failure Model", in *The Nation*, 21 December 1974.

and too *costly* for society, in many ways, including the unbearable economic cost of prison management and the ungovernability of prisons.[21]

On the other side, prison subjects the individual to a terrible isolation and destroys his *sociability*.[22] It reduces the condemned to a state of immobility which is difficult to put up with for certain very active individuals. It deprives the criminal of any normal sexual activity, a deprivation extended to his wife, and which, within prisons, foments homosexual practices. It often generates bad memories of the prison or *jail psychosis*, whose effects and psychic sequels may last a lifetime. On the family level, it affects the prisoner and his closest relations by way of the loss of his company, often destroying conjugal unity. The prison ends up being *a school for delinquents*.[23]

However, not all elements are negative as regards imprisonment. Imprisonment is still necessary to neutralize dangerous individuals who threaten the community and the safety of citizens. Currently it is difficult to make the suppression of the prison system a reality, at least in the short run. We might say that it is an evil but a *lesser one*, which today fulfils a social function not covered by other institutions.[24]

Still, we might conclude by affirming that today the prison is in a state of crisis, in the same way as re-educational and social reinsertion methods are. In spite of all this, it does not seem possible nor opportune

21 *Cf.* André Normandeu, "Halte à la croissance des prisons!", in *Revue de Droit Penal et de Criminologie*, 1977. "Le mythe de la réhabilitation", in *Revue de Droit Penale et de Criminologie*, 1978.

22 Price-Lapedis, "Jail Inmates Also Are People Who Need People", in *Federal Probation*, September 1965.

23 José Antonio Sainz Cantero, "La sustitución de la pena de privación de libertad", *op. cit.*, p. 227. Nicolò Amato, *Diritto, delitto, carcere*, Milano, Giuffrè, 1987. *Nueva defensa social*, Buenos Aires, 1961. Marc Ancel, "Le problème de la peine de prison", in *Revue de Droit Penal et de Criminologie*, 1977. Emilio Dolcini, "La 'Rieducazione del condannato' tra mito e realità", in *Rivista Italiana di Diritto e Procedura Penale*, 1979.

24 James B. Jacobs, *New Perspectives on Prisons and Imprisonment*, Ithaca, NY, Cornell University Press, 1983. Norval Morris, *The Future of Imprisonment*, Chicago, University of Chicago Press, 1974. Of the same author see also, "Punishment, Desert and Rehabilitation", in Hyman Gross, Andrew von Hirsch (eds.), *Sentencing*, New York, Oxford University Press, 1981. *Madness and the Criminal Law*, Chicago, University of Chicago Press, 1983.

at the moment to completely do away with it.[25] Nevertheless, we can point up some of the *demands* which prison as punishment should meet in modern Criminal Law: its economical use, by way of *ultima ratio*, of *extrema ratio*; a taking into consideration that to be deprived of liberty should not mean that the condemned be shorn of all individual rights which a social and democratic State ruled by law recognizes. Likewise, capital punishment, where used, is normally no longer carried out with cruelty, since there is sufficient cruelty in depriving someone of their life, without piling on extras to this action, so too prison should be limited to the depriving of liberty, but never to the taking away of all rights.[26] Finally, the admirable modern tendency to shorten prison sentences should be pointed out, as also the prohibition on life imprisonment and the movement towards substituting other, less damaging punishments for imprisonment these days, fines, for instance.[27]

B Arguments For and Against Fines

Financial punishments, such as the seizure of property, are a modern institution. Within them, we find monetary punishments which consist in the payment of a sum of money. These punishments were not unknown to the Classical World. The word *poena* – from the Greek *poiné* – in its origin precisely indicated the fines listed by the Digest amongst the main, non-capital punishments. *Pre-modern*, monetary punishments above all had a private nature and were directed at reaching a pacific settlement of a conflict, as an alternative to vengeance. They were established between the guilty party and the offended party. They were a form of reparation, or the price paid for peace. This is as true for the *mulctae* of Roman Law, initially made up of cattle, then sums of money, as it is for the *guidrigildo* or the *fredo* which, in Germanic Law, substituted the exercise of *faida*, until it became perhaps the most widespread

25 Calvert R. Dodge, *A World Without Prisons : Alternatives to Incarceration throughout the World*, Lexington, Mass., Lexington Books, 1979.

26 Lorenzo Morillas Cueva, *Teoría de las consecuencias jurídicas del delito*, Madrid, Tecnos, 1991, pp. 48-51. *Cf.* also, Pinatel, “Le traitement des delinquants”, in *Revue de Science Criminelle et de Droit Pénal Comparé*, 1964. “La prison, peut-elle être transformée en institution de traitement?”, in *Annales Internationales de Criminologie*, 1969. Michelle Perrot (ed.), *L'impossible prison*, Paris, Seuil, 1980.

27 Borja Mapelli Caffarena, Juan Terradillos Basoco, *Las consecuencias jurídicas del delito, op. cit.*, p. 20.

of all penalties. Such punishments are also found in the *bonorum publicatio*, or confiscation of goods, of Roman Law. They continued to be used throughout Medieval and Canon Law. We have to wait for modern law codes before fines lose their reparations function.[28]

1.2 Deterrents. From the Classical to the Positivist School

Conceived in 1893 by the Swiss penologist Stoos, author of the draft bill of the Swiss Penal Code of the same year, they were meant as a complement to punishments, and as an effective means of social defence, in the fight against crime. "Deterrents" broke upon the scene of Criminal Law in a big way at the beginning of the XXth century. For this reason, deterrents are considered as having been born with *modern* Criminal Law. They constitute a method of fighting against crime and a legal consequence of crime. However, though the characteristics of these measures, and their very name, indicate that they are a modern creation, societies have fought against crime *since time immemorial* with a repressive and preventive apparatus which goes beyond the strictly criminal sphere. What is really modern about deterrents is their systematization at the end of the XIXth century. Still, even before this – though not yet called by the name "deterrents" – there were other measures included in many legal codes, among them the Spanish, such as police vigilance, the internment of the deranged, declared irresponsible, the isolation of beggars, or institutions which grew up for the education of minors.[29]

These could be thought of as those especial deterrents which are imposed upon people inclined to commit crime, *dangerousness* being a key concept here. It is also what distinguishes deterrents from punishments – according to the dual system. The latter are based upon the

28 Luigi Ferrajoli, *Derecho y razón. Teoría del garantismo penal, op. cit.*, p. 391.

29 Luis Jiménez de Asúa, "Las penas y las medidas de seguridad (Ponencia al tercer tema del VI Congreso Internacional de Derecho Penal)", in *El Criminalista*, 2nd series, t. II, Buenos Aires, Ed. V.P. de Zavalia, 1958. Of the same author see also *La ley y el delito*, Buenos Aires, Ed. Sudamericana, 6th ed., 1973. Gerardo Landrove Díaz, *Las consecuencias jurídicas del delito*, 5th ed. reviewed in colaboration with María Dolores Fernández Rodríguez, Madrid, Tecnos, 2002, p. 111. Gonzalo Rodríguez Mourullo, "Significado político y fundamento ético de la pena y de la medida de seguridad", in *Rev. Cen. Leg. Jur.*, Madrid, Reus, 1965.

guilt of the prisoner, the former, on the dangerous nature of the active subject of crime.

There are two types of deterrents: the ante- or pre-crime deterrents and the post-crime ones. The first are applied to people who, even though they have committed no crime, might do so. They exist to prevent their likelihood of doing so, a judgment of probability. The second are applied to people who have committed a crime. Both classes are enforced by legal authority, as distinct from measures carried out by the police, the government or the administration.[30]

2 A Different Concept of Law

In order to understand the basis and aims of punishment, one must begin from either a static or a dynamic angle.

From a static point of view, punishment would be the primary consequence of the crime, by way of retribution for it, the former being a necessary presupposition of the latter. In this sense, only so-called absolute theories may offer an explanation of punishment, giving it a basis: the crime committed.[31]

From the dynamic viewpoint, the penal sanction would have the same ends as the Criminal Law itself, that is, to avoid conduct forbidden by law. This aim is achieved by the general, legal threat and by the imposing and carrying out of specific sanctions, as much with a general deterrent effect as with a special deterrent effect, typical of relative theories.[32]

2.1 Punishment: Statism. Logical Aspects. Foundation. The Why. Justification. The Plane of "Ought-To-Be": "Why Should Punishment Exist?" Normativism

Retributionist theories, taking punishment as their starting point, fix more upon logical aspects. They elucidate the meaning of the word

30 Carlos García Valdés, *Teoría de la pena*, Madrid, Tecnos, 1985, p. 20.

31 P. Tremblay, "La stabilité de la peine: une perspective anti-évolutionniste", in *Revue Internationale de Criminologie et de Police Technique*, XXXIX, 1, 1986, pp. 31-49.

32 Manuel Ayo Fernández, *Las penas, medidas de seguridad y consecuencias accesorias. Manual de determinación de las penas y de las demás consecuencias jurídico-penales del delito*, Pamplona, Aranzadi, 1997, pp. 24-25.

"punishment" or the conditions for using sentences of the type "A punishes B". They deal with a static consideration of law, which seeks the "because", the justification for the right to punish and for the existence of punishment. These considerations they embody on the purely normative plane, the "ought-to-be": one punishes because there is a prior, illegal act.[33]

2.2 Deterrents: Dynamism. Teleological Aspects. The Goal. The "What-For". The Explanation. The Plane of "Being": "What Do Deterrents Exist for?" Naturalism

Utilitarianism – and, in general, the concept of deterrent, which it is usually partial to – offers, in turn, an ethical reply. It tries to morally justify punishment by appeal to its end. There is then no opposition between the two concepts since each offers a solution within a specific area: a logical conceptual aspect and an ethical end aspect. Both aspects are obviously different and must be separated with care. One thing is the clarification of meaning, or the conditions of use of punishment, and another, very different thing is the moral problem of the end of the act of punishing.

Deterrents take dynamic and teleological aspects into account.[34] They do not delve into the "because", but rather the "what-for", into the aims of punishment. Rather than going back in time to look for a prior crime which will logically justify the right to punish, what a deterrent does is to advance an explanation or, if you prefer, a justification, for punishment, albeit a teleological one. This explanation necessarily ties in with the facts, on the plane of being, for which the punishment is supposed to be useful. Rather than confronting a normative, legal phenomenon, moving on the plane of *Sollen*, we find ourselves facing a naturalist explanation, within the sphere of *Sein*, of facts, which punishment, especially in its guise of deterrent, tries to transform. This second outlook is governed by a causal explanation, through which a specific cause, the crime, will be followed, as a necessary effect, by the rehabilitation of the criminal and his reinsertion into society (the principle of causality). It behaves thus, rather than imputing to a supposed fact (of the form "if

33 Ignacio Muñagorri Laguía, *Sanción penal y política criminal…, op. cit.*, pp 43 ff.

34 *Cf.* on the topic, Francisco Felipe Olesa Muñiz, *Las medidas de seguridad*, Barcelona, Bosch, 1951.

crime A is committed") the corresponding legal consequence (punishment), by virtue of the *principle of imputation* – "if it is A, it ought to be B", which rules over the legal world.

3 Foundation or Justification

3.1 *The Questions: "Whether to Punish, Why, When and How to Punish, Forbid and Judge"*

Theorists usually distinguish between punishment's justification and its goal. When justification is spoken of, its necessity to maintain legal order, and its indispensability for community coexistence are alluded to. R. Maurach said that "a community that gives up its criminal law empire, gives up itself." Others talk of "social suicide." Nevertheless, abolitionist writers are not lacking who consider a society in which there are no punishments a possibility.[35]

However, though punishment might be necessary, it should be an *ultima ratio*, a final recourse when all other means of control and protection of society have failed. Criminal Law intervention can only take place when society is faced with unbearable legal infractions, punishment is a must when it is the only means of *sufficiently protecting* the social order. It is a recourse when we are faced with the need for a greater protection for society than that afforded by moral norms. Punishment thus takes the form of an evil, but it is a *necessary evil*. Principles of its subsidiary and effective nature are justificatory presuppositions of punishment.[36]

3.1.1 Is It Necessary to Punish?

As an inexorable, preliminary question, we must ask: Is it necessary to punish or not?[37] This question admits of two types of answer. There are

35 R. Maurach, *Tratado de Derecho Penal*, translation into Spanish and notes of Spanish law by J. Córdoba Roda, 1962, p. 63 – citation in Antonio Choclán Montalvo, *Individualización judicial de la pena*..., *op. cit.*, p. 51.

36 Gonzalo Rodríguez Mourullo, "Significado político y fundamento ético de la pena y de la medida de seguridad", in *Revista General de Legislación y Jurisprudencia*, 219, December 1965, pp. 28-29. José Antonio Choclán Montalvo, *Individualización judicial de la pena*..., *op. cit.*, p. 54.

37 R. Martin, "On the Logic of Justifying Legal Punishment", in *American Philosophical Quarterly*, 7, 1970, pp. 253-259. Toby, "Is Punishment Neces-

the negative or *abolitionist* answers, which do not recognize any justification for Criminal Law, and the *ius puniendi* of the State. Then there are positive answers to the problem, which might be placed under the head of *justificationist* answers. These recognize a need to punish. However, they plant ulterior problems as to the why, when and how of such punishment.[38]

A Negative Answer: The Abolitionist Systems

The abolitionist answer holds that punishment is not such a transparent and self-evident institution of crime control as some would have us believe. They say the role of punishment in modern society is not so obvious, but rather the consequence of an obscure effect of self-affirmation, on the part of existing institutions, more than anything logically derived from penal practices.[39] Though we are told the pattern of punishment is inevitable, to reaffirm the *status quo*, rather than maintain the existing institutional framework, we should – according to certain writers – put this framework in doubt and, as against considering how we might improve things like prisons, we should ask ourselves why they exist, and whether we could not do without them. Questions like those having to do with: who may punish; when they might punish; and how punishment should be carried out, today, only receive answers dictated by authority. They do not stem from logic or reason, and are based more on convention than on nature, and only thus are legal norms established. For Garland, we should not lose sight of the fact that all legal questions could be solved in another way, that, if the State's answers do not satisfy us, they can be replaced, that modern methods of punishment are neither obvious nor evident, but rather are in need of explanation. Punishments are usually explained by saying that all their flaws are remnants from the past or of a present which is about to disappear. Every criticism then is, in its attempt to find a way of reforming punishment, a hymn

sary?", in *Journal of Criminal Law*, September, 1964.

38 *Cf.* Thomas Mathiesen, *The Politics of Abolition. Essays in Political Action Theory*, Scandinavian Studies in Criminology, Oslo-London, Martin Robertson, 1974. "The Future of Control Systems – the Case of Norway", in David Garland, Peter Young (eds.), *The Power to Punish*, London, Heinemann, 1983.

39 Carlos García Valdés, *Teoría de la pena*, Madrid, Tecnos, 1985, p. 11.

to the future. However, what *abolitionists deny is precisely that punishment has any future.*[40]

The present is characterized by a change from optimism and faith in Criminal Law to a persistent pessimism and scepticism as to the logic and efficacy of modern penal institutions. This change of attitude began to emerge at the end of the 1960s. Contemporary methods, especially prison, present us with ideas which are increasingly more irrational, dysfunctional and counterproductive. The best known critique, and the best discussion, of the failings of punishment are to be found in the works of Michel Foucault.[41] Lawrence Stone, a critic of Foucault's, characterizes prisons of the last century as vestiges of the past, less necessary to maintain the social system than is the appendix for an individual's bodily system. Prisons survive simply and plainly because they have taken on a life of their own.[42]

During the greater part of the XXth century, the term "rehabilitation" was the key-word which sustained the ruling ideology of the penal system and institutional rhetoric.[43] Today, however, this term is no longer a talisman, the master key to the entire penal edifice. The idea of rehabilitation is in crisis and shows itself problematic, dangerous and, on occasions, impracticable. For something more than two decades, prison authorities have tried in vain to come up with a new philosophy, *a new rationale,* for punishment. Words so often used in the XIXth century, words and phrases like "incapacitation", "moral reform", "training", "correction", "rehabilitation", "prevention" have proved themselves insufficient and there are some today who talk of a new principle for punishment, that is, the presumption that crime and deviant conduct are social problems for which there might be a technical solution. How-

40 *Cf.*, from a critical point of view, Mendoza, "Hacia una posibilidad de un Derecho extra-penal", in *Libro Homenaje al Prof. Jiménez de Asúa,* Buenos Aires, 1964; and Karl Augustus Menninger (1893-), *The Crime of Punishment,* New York, Viking Press, 1968.

41 R. De Folter, "On the Methodological Foundation of the Abolitionist Approach to the Criminal Justice System. A Comparison of the Ideas of Hulsman, Mathiesen and Foucault", in *Contemporary Crises,* 10, 1986, pp. 39-62.

42 David Garland, *Punishment and Modern Society..., op. cit.,* pp. 3 ff.

43 J.L. de la Cuesta Arzamendi, *El trabajo penitenciario resocializador. Teoría y regulación positiva,* San Sebastián, 1982. F.T. Cullen, K.E. Gilbert, *Re-affirming Rehabilitation,* Cincinatti, 1982.

ever, when faced with the other slogan, "nothing works", and in order to find a solution once and for all, one should not set up remedies nor attempt "patchwork" (partial solutions) but one should go to the depths of the problem to thus prevent that "dark side" of the social order. Is there a right to punish? What are the limits of State power? These are not only scientific or academic questions. On the contrary, they are eminently practical ones. They go to the very roots of penal policy, to the sociology and history of punishment, rather than being simply policy ramifications. Half-way through the 1950s, the true basis, of what were considered axiomatic in Criminal Law, was called into question.[44]

Within the negative or abolitionist answers, those of the radical abolitionist Max Stirner; the holist, anarchist; and the post-Marxist abolitionist stand out. The philosophical presuppositions of such proposals are widely disparate. They go from the XVIIIth century myth of the "noble savage" and of an earlier, happy, primitive society ("the state of nature") to anarchist and Marxist-Leninist theories of the "New Man" and of a perfect, communist society of the future where there would be no room for either the State or social classes. The most radical abolitionist doctrines not only *do not* justify punishment, they do not even justify prohibitions, nor any type of penal or social coercion or restriction. This extreme stand is represented by the anarchist Max Stirner. For him, rules have no value. He showed himself in favour of rebellion against, and transgression of, all rules. Any such breach of rules should neither be prevented nor punished nor judged. This prohibition on judgment, although based on different postulates, reminds us of the Christian *nolite iudicare*, men should not judge their fellow men.

Less radical are the abolitionist theories which do not oppose all forms of social control, but only punishment and even Criminal Law itself. Here we are not dealing with amoral or egoistic theories like those of Stirner, but with moral and socially cohesive postulates, with reference to a higher order, which should regulate the society of the future. Along these lines, we find anarchist and libertarian writers like Godwin, Bakunin, Kropotkin, Molinari and Malatesta. These thinkers see in punishment an instrument of social control on the part of the dominant classes. In their place, they conceive of non-legal techniques of control, techniques that are of a moral or social kind. Some of these are: the "public *eye*"; the "*invisible force of moral education*"; therapeutic

44 David Garland, *Punishment and Modern Society..., op. cit.*, pp. 6-10.

solidarity; the social diffusion of vigilance and control; the *"pressure of public opinion"*.

This holist confusion between Law and Ethics, the post-revolutionary end of any social conflict, the self-correcting nature of the communist society and the future extinction of the State and, with it, Criminal Law is to be found in Marxism. We may think of Lenin and, above all, of Antonio Gramsci.

Finally, we should not forget the utopian moralism, and the regressive nostalgia for archaic and traditional models of community without law. Amongst present-day abolitionists, in the anarchist and *holist* tradition, we find the like of Louk Hulsman, Henri Bianchi and Nils Christie, who base their reformist projects on solidarity, on fraternity and on primitive methods of dividing up the national wealth.[45]

All these theories propose a model of *savage society*, lacking in all order and abandoned to the natural law of the strongest or, alternatively, the model of a *disciplinary society*, disciplined and totalized in which conflicts are controlled and resolved, or, even worse, prevented, by ethical-pedagogical methods of "order-internalization", or medical treatment, or social and even "political panoptism".[46] Both projects envisage a future utopia which stems from two opposing myths of the "state of nature". The one is a society without rules, the war of all against all – *bellum omnium contra omnes* – of the purest Hobbsean type. The other is of an idyllic, primitive society uncontaminated by inter-subjective conflicts, of which Rousseau spoke.[47]

B Positive Answer: Justificationary Systems

According to a useful distinction, put forward by XIXth century theorists of crime, theories of punishment, opposed to the abolitionist, which we have called justificationist, may be divided into two major categories: *absolute* or retributive; so-called *relative* theories or those of prevention.[48] We refer to both in detail later.

45 Louk Hulsman, J. Bernat de Celis, *Sistema penal y seguridad ciudadana: hacia una alternativa, op. cit.*, pp. 83 ff.

46 *Cf.* Pio Marconi, *La libertà selvaggia: Stato e punizione nel pensiero anarchico*, 1rst. ed, Venecia, Marsilio, 1979.

47 Luigi Ferrajoli, *Derecho y razón. Teoría del garantismo penal, op. cit.*, pp. 247-252.

48 John Braithwaite, Philip Pettit, *Not Just Deserts. A Republican Theory of Criminal Justice*, Oxford, Clarendon Press, 1990, p. 52.

3.1.2 Why Is It Necessary To Punish?

The question, "why punish?", may be understood in two different senses: 1. *Why does punishment exist,* that is, why do we punish?; 2. *Why should punishment exist,* that is, why must we punish? The methodological vice we detect in many of the answers to the question, why do we punish?, consists in a confusion of motivation with end; the "to be" (in fact or in law) with the "should-be" (axiological) of punishment, and, in some cases, *explanations* with *justifications,* or *vice versa.*[49]

A *Internal Legitimation* – "prohibitum quia peccatum", "ob malum passionis"

Absolute theories are retributionist. They consider punishment an end in itself, that is, as a "punishment", a "compensation", a "reaction", a "reparation" or "retribution" for the crime, justified by its intrinsic axiological value. Therefore, they do not consider it a means, still less a cost, but rather a meta-legal duty which is its own basis.

The characterization of absolute, or retributive, justifications are found in a well-known passage by Seneca, in the *quia peccatum.* As we can see, such justifications look to the past. Internal legitimation of punishment is *aprioristic,* in the sense that it is not conditioned by extra-punitive ends. Such theories are justified in the maxim that it is just to "repay evil with evil."[50]

Retributionist theories turn upon an internal legitimation. They would punish because there exists an evil, "*ob malum passionis*". This is the idea of legitimation: if something is illegitimate, unjust, by its very nature and essence, it must be forbidden. Something is either good or evil in itself, and so must be rewarded or forbidden. The world of the law does not count, only the internal sphere counts, the Moral.

B *External Legitimation* – "peccatum quia prohibitum", "ob malum actionis"

All utilitarian doctrines are relative. They justify and consider punishment only as a means to the realization of a utilitarian goal, that of the prevention of future crimes. Following the Seneca passage, in this case

49 Jescheck, *Tratado,* cited by José Antonio Choclán Montalvo, *Individualización judicial de la pena..., op. cit.,* p. 51. Igor Primoratz, *Justifying Legal Punishment,* Atlantic Highlands, N.J., Humanities Press International, 1989. Edmund L. Pincoffs, *The Rationale of Legal Punishment,* New York, Humanities Press, 1966.

50 Luigi Ferrajoli, *Derecho y razón. Teoría del garantismo penal, op. cit.,* pp. 253-254.

we punish *ut ne peccetur*, utilitarians look to the future. Justification for punishment is here conditioned by how adequate it is to the aim pursued, external to the unjust "in itself".

Prevention theories refer to an external legitimation: we punish because something is forbidden. This is the idea of validity: should something be prohibited, you must punish the infringement of this prohibition. Behaviour external to the subject is what matters, it is his acts which go against the law, "*ob malum actionis*". Should someone be bad but not commit an evil, external act, he is not open to punishment. However, contrariwise, if someone commits a bad act, sanctionable by law, forbidden by the law, then, even though he be a good person, he must be punished. The law is what matters.

1.1.3 How to Punish. Types of Crimes and Punishments

The question regarding how to punish refers to various themes at once, such as the quality of punishment and the judicial and legal measure of punishment, likewise, the methods of carrying them out. Only certain sorts of punishment fit each type of crime.

Punishments can be classified, in an essential manner, by appealing to *doctrinal* criteria or to *legal* postulates. The first classification concentrates on the "material object" on which the punishment falls; the second treats of its "gravity", as recorded in the Criminal Codes. Paying attention to doctrinal aspects, one may speak, first of all, of the Death Penalty, corporal punishment, deprivation of liberty, restrictions on freedom – banishment, confinement and exile – the taking away of rights, monetary punishments and moral punishments. Many punishments are collected under the head of loss of rights. Things such as losing one's nationality in the case of naturalized citizens, loss of ability to hold office, loss of the right to vote, suspension from public office, and so on. Monetary punishments include fines and cautions, while moral ones might be private or public upbraiding.[51]

When passing sentence, certain principles must be observed. These are things like: *in dubio pro reo*; the principle of necessity and the humaneness of punishments; the priniciple of the minimum necessary punishment; that of respect of persons; the principles of proportionality, equity and certitude of sentence; the legal pre-determination of the punishment. This final item requires that the evil of the punishments must exceed the good gained from the crime, thus indicating a mini-

51 Carlos García Valdés, *Teoría de la pena, op. cit.*, pp. 15 ff.

mum limit to them, on the other hand, it affirms that "anything in excess" is tyrannical, thus fixing an outer limit.

2.1.4 When Is It Necessary To Punish?

It is held that there exist retributive theories of punishment and utilitarian theories of deterrents when it comes to justifying the time for punishment. The former maintain this is when there is a crime. The latter hold it is when danger is present. In truth, as H.L.A. Hart has shown, the distinction between the two types rests on a mistake, and on a conceptual and terminological muddle. In fact, for this Oxford thinker, both theoretical directions, rather than being opposed, tackle distinct spheres and give answers to different questions. Retributive theories, in reality, treat of punishment "*distribution*", and look to the past. Utilitarian deterrent doctrines, on the contrary, deal with the question of the "*general goal*" of punishment, they cannot help but be future-oriented. This is the difference between the "*motive*" for applying punishment and the "*end*" it serves; the "why" and the "what for" of punishment, respectively.

A Retribution in Punishment

Punishment might be defined as "the privation or restriction of legal goods, imposed according to law by legal bodies on those guilty of a legal infraction".[52] Punishment must be characterized as:

- Personal
- Necessary and Sufficient
- Swift and Unavoidable
- Proportionate
- Individualized[53]

52 We find this definition in Cuello Calón, cited by Borja Mapelli Caffarena and Juan Terradillos Basoco, *Las consecuencias jurídicas del delito, op. cit.*, p. 29. *Cf.* also K.G. Armstrong, "The Retributivist Hits Back", in *Mind*, vol. 70, 1961, pp. 471-491; reimpr. in H.B. Acton (ed.), *The Philosophy of Punishment*, London, Macmillan, 1969. Andrew Ashworth, *Sentencing and Penal Policy*, London, Weidenfeld and Nicolson, 1983. M. Atkinson, "Justified and Deserved Punishments", in *Mind*, vol. 78, 1969, pp. 354-374.

53 Borja Mapelli Caffarena, Juan Terradillos Basoco, *Las consecuencias jurídicas del delito, op. cit.*, pp. 47-53.

B Danger in Deterrents. Post-crime Measures as Opposed to Pre-crime Measures

Punishments protective function is limited to just retribution for the breaking of the law by an individual who acts in a guilty way, that is, a citizen socially capable of doing so. The limitation applies as much materially as personally. However, the danger of certain criminals, as opposed to their criminal records, is not taken into account in such punishment. The deed committed thus only has recognition and symptom value as regards the criminals being a danger to society. Punishment must then be complemented by deterrents, based on the danger element, not on guilt. They should not depend upon the gravity of the deed, but on the character and threat represented by the author of the deed.

These deterrents – whose necessity is generally admitted today – might be pre-crime or post-crime. Certain sectors of the legal profession currently severely criticize pre-crime deterrents.

Pre-crime deterrents are those which are imposed on a person for the danger he represents, even before his committing any criminal act; they are *only* a function of the individual's perceived danger to society.

Post-crime ones are those imposed on a person for the same reason but only once he has committed a deed specified as a crime in Criminal Law.

Criminal Law holds to the principle that nobody should be declared a danger if his particular case has not been qualified by the law as such. The previous commission of a crime is demanded. This demand has a threefold guarantee function. It "reinforces the danger prognosis, it strengthens the existence of the principle of legality, and it reduces the function of the guarantee to tolerable limits." There is a tendency today to eradicate pre-crime deterrents. Pre-crime prevention can be effectively carried out via other channels, such as a more just legal regulation of the economic, family, work, political, educational or health systems. Pre-crime deterrents have always served totalitarian régimes. They have been amongst the favourite weapons for the most sordid machinations against human freedom and dignity.[54]

54 Gerardo Landrove Díaz, *Las consecuencias jurídicas del delito, op. cit.*, pp. 111-121.

3.2 The Justification Question in Punishment and in Deterrents

3.2.1 Punishment

A Free Will

There exists an intricate and secular debate over whether human action is the fruit of free will or, contrariwise, whether it represents but one more step in a causal connection of events not subject to choice. One or other of these options impinges upon the justification of punishment. Punishment and retributive theory rest upon the ideas of desert and justice, on the idea of human freedom. It is just and deserving that a man pay for his crimes if he is free when he commits them, and decides to do so making a misuse of this freedom. If there is freedom, there is responsibility and culpability. On the other hand, if one has not had the opportunity to choose, responsibility for any acts is not proportioned to that individual, he is not guilty of them. Such is the case with acts carried out under compulsion or *force majeur*. An illegal act is only punishable if it has been done based on a freely-willed decision. For retributive theories of punishment, the cause of crime lies in the freedom which the criminal abuses, and not in the human person himself. Hence, the punishment should act more on the crime itself than on the erring subject, as an act revealing the individual's free will.

B Guilt as a Value Judgment

To consider an individual morally responsible for an act is to make a judgment as to the moral value of that act, when the act consists in an offence, or when an attack on the rights of third parties, it may be a judgment in the form of moral reproach. When a moral reproach, in the form of a judgment, is pronounced, the personal responsibility of the agent is predicated for the commission of that specific action. The individual is guilty of the freely-realized act. He may only be legally excused because of circumstances which lessen his guilt, such as claiming it was an error, done in ignorance, under compulsion, and the like.

Guilt is at once the foundation and limit of punishment.[55] One may only punish the guilty person and may only punish him in proportion

55 Quintano Ripollés, "Culpabilidad y retribución como premisas de la justicia penal", in *Homenaje al profesor Luis Legaz y Lacambra. Estudios Jurídico-Sociales, Universidad de Santiago de Compostela,* 1950, pp. 1027 ff. *Cf.* also, by the same author, "La evolución del Derecho penal moderno ('contra corriente')", in *Anuario de Derecho Penal y Ciencias Penales,* 1957.

to his guilt and as far as that guilt may reach.[56] The function of the guilt principle as basis and "maximum" limit of punishment is beyond doubt. The polemical question arises as to whether there is room, and up to what point, to fix the penalty below the measure of guilt, paying attention to special prevention ends. Thus, the question arises as to what extent institutions like penal substitutes, overriding excuses, amnesty, reprieve, or the pardon of the person offended, conform to the guilt principle.[57]

The current concept of guilt has been the object of numerous *critical objections*. The truth is, the idea of guilt is frankly in a state of crisis, so much so that one can auger for it no other future than that of being superseded, in a more or less distant time. The debate between determinism and indeterminism here acquires capital importance. Insofar as we might deny free will, guilt will be thrown into doubt. Free will as an abstract quality of being human cannot be presupposed in the case of a specific man in a concrete social situation. In effect, there exists a lack of freedom. One would have to investigate to what extent the individual author of a crime enjoys the freedom to behave in a way different from the way he in fact did behave. That is, according to his abilities and personal circumstances, to the outer situation and to his internal state.

The *relative* nature of the idea of guilt, as regards value judgment and judgment of social character, also then presents itself. As Francisco Muñoz Conde says:

> Really, guilt in itself does not exist as an exclusive problem for the individual, rather, what exists is guilt with reference to others. Guilt is always a question of human coexistence... Coexistence presupposes communication between members of society, which reveals itself in what each expects in the behaviour of the rest, and vice versa, that is, a system of expectations is created. Punishment comes into play when expectations, the forms of conduct expected, are frustrated; hence, punishment also turns out to be a process of inter-relations presupposed by coexistence.[58]

56 José Antonio Choclán Montalvo, *Individualización judicial de la pena...*, *op. cit.*, p. 59.

57 *Ibid.*, p. 65.

58 Francisco Muñoz Conde, "El principio de culpabilidad", in *III Jornadas de Profesores de Derecho Penal*, Santiago de Compostela, 1975, p. 4. *Cf.* also Herbert Morris (1928-) (ed.), *Freedom and Responsibility*, Standford, Standford University Press, 1961. "Persons and Punishment", in *The Monist*,

For all the above, guilt has rather a *negative* function, that of determining if certain causes – mental illness or coercion – do not prevent us from holding the criminal personally responsible, in the light of sciences like Psychology and Psychoanalysis. Thus, it may be affirmed that, though free will exists in the abstract, it is impossible to show whether a specific person in a concrete situation has freely committed a determinate crime or not. The empirical existence of guilt, as a category, is a presupposition impossible to prove. Instead of trying to base punishment on guilt, it would have to be founded upon *necessity*, from a legal-social point of view, as a guarantee of the due proportionality between the gravity of the crime and that of the punishment. Punishment would thus be a sad necessity, useful to achieve societal coexistence and to avoid the committing of crimes, as far as this is possible.[59]

C Imputability and Moral Responsibility

The idea of punishment, at least according to the Spanish Classical School, corresponds to the metaphysical nature of the sanction, which stems from equally metaphysical presuppositions: an unreal idea of the human being (the criminal as a man with complete freedom), of his behaviour (crime as a manifestation of Free Will), and of the reality and function of Criminal Law (legal order as a demonstration of rational order, necessary to maintain in order to achieve absolute justice).[60] All are abstract approaches, and blind to reality. Man is responsible because he is free, says the theory, his acts may be imputed to him, and he is morally responsible for them.

52, 1968, pp. 475-501; reimpr. in *On Guilt and Innocence...*, *op. cit.*, pp. 39-58. "Guilt and Punishment", in *Personalist*, 52, 1971, pp. 305-321. *On Guilt and Innocence: Essays in Legal Philosophy and Moral Psychology*, Berkeley, University of California Press, 1976. "A Paternalistic Theory of Punishment", in *American Philosophical Quarterly*, 18, 4, 1981, pp. 263-271.

59 José Antonio Choclán Montalvo, *Individualización judicial de la pena...*, *op. cit.*, pp. 60-61.

60 Ignacio Muñagorri Laguia, *Sanción penal y política criminal...*, *op. cit.*, pp 58 ff.

D *Justice*

One of the characteristics of punishment is that it makes effective the idea of justice, broken by crime. However, what sort of justice are we here referring to?[61]

a Corrective and Equitable Justice: Reparations

A basic demand of justice is that the evil wreaked should be, as far as possible, repaired by the evil-doer. Aristotle spoke in this regard of corrective justice. The Greek philosopher thought of crime as an unjust act disturbing the "equilibrium" which ordinarily should exist amongst citizens. Punishment was to correct that injustice.

Crime is unjust insofar as there is an unequal relationship in which reciprocity is lacking between offender and offended. The offender causes damage without giving anything in exchange. The offended loses without receiving anything by way of compensation. Aristotle, then, urges that the balance broken be re-established. The situation is corrected when the advantage gained by the offender is annulled by the compensation received by the offended. Corrective justice tends to leave things as they were before the balance was broken by the crime. Equilibrium thus finds its level through punishment, at the mid-point between the loss by one party and the gain by the other. Punishment is at once conceived of as a "substraction": the criminal is deprived of the good thing he has ill acquired; and as "restitution": the victim is given back what had been taken from him. Here, there is no separation between Civil and Criminal Law. Corrective punishment is at once reparation to the victim and punishment for the criminal. Corrective justice justifies reparation, compensation, reparatory measures, such as indemnity, in short, the giving to each his own.

b Retributive Justice: Why Should the Offender Be Punished?

Today, the idea of retributive justice is in decline, in a century which puts utility before all else. Even the word "retributive" is in disuse in modern dictionaries. In France, it is found in neither Robert nor in Larousse, not even in Littré. One must go to old French dictionaries to find it. In English-speaking countries, the idea is retained, though it is significant that the term is avoided. "Just desert" is the preferred expres-

61 Maurice Cusson, *Pourquoi punir*? Paris, Dalloz, 1987, pp. 75-89. Wojciech Sadurski, "Distributive Justice and the Theory of Punishment", in *Oxford Journal of Legal Studies*, 5, 1, 1985, pp. 47ff.

sion. Still, retribution forms a natural part of punishment itself. Retributive justice has as its mission the regularization of reciprocal relations between two parties. It stipulates that there should be an "equivalence" between action and reaction.

Guilt plays an essential role. Though punishment inflicted upon an innocent party might prevent crime, most people are opposed to going about things thus, they consider it unjust, precisely because they do go along with this idea of retributive justice. It is only in the light of the idea of retribution that one may oppose the punishment of the innocent. One justifies striking back only and precisely because another has struck the first blow. This is the distinction between *attack* and *defence* which allows us to differentiate between crime and punishment. He who strikes and he who returns the blow are not put into the same category. Attacking first, the criminal loses all right not to be attacked, the which he had before, when he was innocent. Further, the punishment must fit the gravity of the crime. This is also a consequence of the principle of retribution. Proportionality is essentially explained in retributive terms. Should there be an intrinsic relation between crime and punishment, there must also be a relation between the importance of the one and of the other.

There exist four variants of retribution. They serve to give an answer to the question: Why do we punish?

1 Formal Retribution: For the Crime Committed

The first variant admits of little comment. One punishes for the crime committed. This is the idea of formal retribution. If you cease to punish, there ceases to be crime. Punishment is an essential element in the idea of crime.

2 Reciprocity: Because One Must Pay for One's Own Crimes

Retribution's second version assimilates crime to a debt and is based on the idea of reciprocity, the repaying of good by good, of evil by evil. This way of functioning is universal. It is found in children and amongst all known peoples. Reciprocity is the agreement between action and reaction, for the good as well as for the bad.

Amongst reciprocal relations, we might point to the following:

- *Swapping,* when one "good" is exchanged, or lent out, for another.
- *Mutual respect,* when one person refuses to harm another in exchange for a similar "abstention" on the part of that other.

- *Reparation*, through which one "harm" is compensated for by a "good".
- Finally, *retribution* where evil is repaid by evil.

3 Condemnation: Because It Is Deserved

The third "take" on retributive justice is the idea of suing, of reprobation, of reaffirmation of the norm, of a sentence. Here, punishment sets itself up in protest against evil, as a symbol of the indignation provoked by crime. A morally neutral reaction to crime would be inappropriate; it would not take into account the fact that crime is essentially a reprovable act.

4 Guarantee: To Give Honest People the Assurance that They Will Not Be the Only Ones Who Must Respect the Law

Retribution's fourth version might be called the "guarantee". In brief, the idea is as follows. The majority of citizens are voluntarily willing to subject themselves to the law. They would not do so, however, had they not the guarantee that the rest will do the same. Here, we punish not to reprimand the crime, but to honour the Social Contract. In the absence of punishment, criminals would enjoy a decisive advantage over non-criminals. Punishment annuls this advantage. Moreover, what is still more important, punishment offers virtuous citizens the guarantee that they will not be attacked with impunity.

E The Crime Considered Objectively, As an Infraction of the Legal Norm

The Spanish Classical School, in favour of punishments, placed punishment's responsibility in the commission of the act, insofar as this was a demonstration of the author's freedom. The responsibility thus placed, the School tried to objectify punishment by making it neutral. This is a Criminal Law based on the deed, not on the criminal.[62] What is important here is the objective aspect, crime in its objective guise. That is, crime is: "an action typified in law, illegal, guilty and punishable." The criminal's subjective circumstances have only a secondary relevance. Classical Criminal Law puts all its efforts into isolating the deed from the person and it does not recognize the basic idea of personality.

62 Ignacio Muñagorri Laguía, *Sanción penal y política criminal. Confrontación con la nueva defensa social, op. cit.*, pp. 88 and 139.

F Suffering as a Good, with Intrinsic Value in Itself

To affirm that the suffering which may afflict the criminal, as a consequence of punishment, is something having intrinsic value is an argument more reviled than defended. This is, nevertheless, what retributive theories of punishment believe in. They see, in the suffering which punishment occasions, a good in itself, rather than an evil at the service of a different good. We find here the difference between the "good in itself" and "the good as means." This idea was well-rooted in the very notion of revenge, where one evil makes up for another.

G Maximum Right to Punish Systems

As opposed to the arbitrary nature of absolutism, retribution offers at least a guarantee of, and a limitation on, the punitive power of the State. You can only punish when there exists a crime previously committed, and punishment must be proportional to the gravity of the said crime. This was a way of objectifying the application of punishment according to the idea of equality: "to the same crime, the same punishment". And, within the spirit of such laws, they should appear as the embodiment of the will of the citizens and as a guarantee that that will is being carried out.

In this sense, we might say that retributive systems are systems of "maximum Criminal Law", given that everything here must be "on the books" – *nulla poena sine lege.* However, it will not do to classify them thus, if we want to give some idea of their guarantee nature, which represents a brake on the abuses of the time before their introduction.

Ten axioms serve to show up this guarantee aspect:

1. *Nulla poena sine crimine*
2. *Nullum crimen sine lege*
3. *Nulla lex (poenalis) sine necesitate*
4. *Nulla necesitas sine iniuria*
5. *Nulla iniuria sine actione*
6. *Nulla actio sine culpa*
7. *Nulla culpa sine indicio*
8. *Nullum indicium sine accusatione*
9. *Nulla accusatio sine probatione*
10. *Nulla probatione sine defenione*

These principles and the legal, procedural guarantees expressed in them are respectively known as:

1. The principle of *retribution*, punishment must come after the crime
2. The principle of *legality*, in the loose or in the strict sense
3. The principle of *necessity* or of Criminal Law's economy
4. The principle of *harm*, or the offence of the act
5. The principle of *materiality*, or the exterior nature of the act
6. The principle of *guilt*, or personal responsibility
7. The principle of *jurisdiction*, again in a loose or in a strict sense
8. The principle of *accusation*, or the separation between the judge and the accusation
9. The principle of *the burden of proof*, or of verification
10. The principle of *contradiction*, of defence, or of refutation[63]

Neither is the idea of punishment and retribution too far from "merchantilist" thought, with the bourgeoisie as its originators. Even the terms "debt" and "pay" have historically been used synonyms for crime and punishment.

H The Fusion Law-Morality

The classic idea of punishment is proper to an epoch where crime is equated with sin, and the spheres of Law and Morality are mixed together, a world impregnated with religious concepts and metaphysical ideas of Criminal Law and of the right to punish. Little by little, this mentality was overcome, by virtue of the two swords principle: "Render unto Caesar what is Caesar's and to God what is God's."

I Crime as Sin

In primitive times, crime was considered an offence not only against the legal order, but also against the moral order. The criminal was considered an evil man who had to be corrected and amended, by way of an expiation for his guilt. The fact that there exist good men who are guilty of a crime and, the other way about, bad citizens who are innocent of crime was overlooked.

63 Luigi Ferrajoli, *Derecho y razón. Teoría del garantismo penal*, *op. cit.*, p. 93.

3.2.2 Deterrents

A Determinism and Social Necessity

According to determinist theory, individuals lack the freedom to act as they do and, so, do not deserve to be punished. At least, they should not be punished with a punishment as such, they should be subject to a deterrent.

An *extreme* version of determinism can be defended wherein the human being is *totally* controlled in his actions by factors foreign to his will and would not be free at all. Still, not all determinisms go to such lengths. There are *moderate* versions that hold that man is, to a certain extent and only to a certain extent, determined when he acts. This is a weak version of determinist theory which makes natural causality compatible with freedom. Human acts are caused, but among the causes are human freedom and human will. Freedom and causality are not mutually exclusive. What does indeed deny the possibility of freedom, and is opposed to it, is *compulsion*. Such, for instance, is the difference between the vulgar thief and the true kleptomaniac who, decide as he may, cannot stop stealing. Freedom would be the possibility of being different from how one is and, in the light of present desires, to carry out voluntary not instinctive acts.

Similarly, as opposed to *strong, extreme* or *absolute* indeterminism – which maintains the absence of causality altogether and is, hence, hard to defend – we find the *moderate, relative* or *weak* version of that doctrine, against a background of human freedom. In certain cases, it admits the possibility of actions conditioned by motives quite outside the will of the agent. In our view, only the eclectic, intermediate or moderate versions may be scientifically supported. They are the only determinisms that are defensible.

What exactly does it mean to say that an action is caused and not free? To say that something is the cause of an effect X implies, neither more nor less, than to say that it is a *sufficient* factor to produce such an effect. In this sense, we may say that, given the existence of a cause or series of causes, a certain effect must necessarily succeed. To affirm that all actions are caused – determinism in the strong sense – would be as much as to affirm that all choice, decision and human action are the necessary consequences of a preceding cause. Thus one says that some mental states are a consequence of mental causes, which, for the most radical theorists, would even be physical causes. This happens to such an extent that, if we change the cause or physical stimulus, we equally change the conduct. In this sense, psychiatric and neurological advances of recent years have shown that certain chemical or electric alterations may manipulate the emotions and prevent anger, fear or obsession, and produce well-being, relaxation, happiness or satisfaction. All this may be achieved by the use of medicinal drugs or neurological treatment. This presents a challenge to ordinary beliefs concerning responsibility and the ability to choose, especially if we should extrapolate from these experiments the message that all mental disorders derive from a preceding cause, most often a physical one. However, we may also reconcile freedom and determinism as not totally incompatible worlds. Despite there being an element of causality in our actions and choices, nevertheless, we still maintain a certain percentage of freedom in both. In weak versions, determinism and causality are compatible.

To understand this better, we must go back over the meaning of the word "freedom", and related terms. For those who hold the conciliatory thesis, *free means unconstrained, not necessary*. Still, a caused decision is not always a necessary decision. From the fact that the decision I took might obey a cause, we may not derive the fact that I did not desire to take that decision. Originally, a man was said to be free if he was not stopped from doing what he felt like doing by an outside force. The paradigmatic example of lack of freedom was time done in prison. Freedom thus meant the opposite of *compulsion*. An individual is free if his act is not compelled by a stronger force which gives him no option margin nor capacity for any choice whatever, a force that obliges him to act against his wishes. For instance, he is not free if he is locked up, or chained, or if someone threatens him with a pistol, so that he does something he does not want to do. Contrariwise, he is free if he decides what he wishes to do, without pressure from outside or inner forces, and if he so decides in accord with his nature and way of being. The statement that a decision is a free one implies something explicit and something implicit. The explicit is that he is not subject to compulsion. The implicit is that his decision was not a causally necessary consequence of anything.

There exists another argument, related to the above, that makes freedom and determinism compatible. According to this argument, the crucial thing, to know if an action is free, is to see if we could have behaved otherwise than we did, had we so desired. In this sense, there is absolutely no reason to assert that free actions are really possible if we are determinists. The same is true if we assimilate determinism to "*mechanicism*". That is to say, assimilate it to that type of determinism which leads to a rejection of freedom on the basis that deeds are physically caused, in an automatic or mechanical way, with no margin left for liberty. This, however, cannot be the case. Scientists may one day come to find physical and mechanical explanations for every physical question, but *not all questions are physical questions.* In the same way as the game of chess is governed by the rules of the game – which establish the possible moves of each piece –but each player, by daring, intelligence or stupidity, may carry out distinct moves, make different choices, so too human actions may remain free and be the responsibility of the acting subject, though they take place within certain causal limits. The same would be true if there were any rules for writing prose, rules of grammar, or of spelling. They would not prevent the individual writer from developing his own style.

The same is true of the distinction between *movement* and *action*: one is mechanical, the other is responsible and free. It is wrong, we say, to consider physical or psychological causes of bodily movement as also causes of actions. Thus, the physical, causal explanation of why the legs and arms move are useful, but human beings, insofar as they are beings endowed with intelligence and will, may move their limbs because "they want to." One thing is the causal explanation of why we raise a hand: because there is an impulse which stems from the brain and reaches that part of the body, thus moved by a stimulus. However, such a mechanical explanation for the hand's "movement" is not always sufficient to clarify the question of what was sought in the raising of the hand. Perhaps this might have been to make myself noticed, to put an end to a doubt and to formulate a question which intrigues me, to kill a fly, and so on. Nothing truly human automatically derives from movements that are physically or biologically caused. Intelligence, will and freedom do have a lot to do with the human. That is why we can suppress impulsive reactions like rage, shame or anger at, or forgiveness for, a person's evil act, especially if it be the case that it is someone who we cannot hold accountable for his actions. Our reaction is causally inexplicable. Causal explanation will not serve when we are dealing with the genuinely human and spiritual component that enters into action.

Here we also find the explanation for the possible existence of *"judgements and opinions."* If there were only absolute truth, black or white, one hundred percent true, it would make no sense that everyone may opine and give his own version of that truth; relative truth, my truth. If determinism in its strong variety were true, there would then be no possibility of forming judgments or of taking decisions. It is one thing for something to be true or false, this depends upon its agreement, or disagreement, with the facts. What now interests us, however, is not truth conditions. Rather, it is to highlight the fact that an individual can have a belief and formulate a judgment, independently of whether these approximate to truth. To admit the possibility, it is necessary to recognize some margin of freedom. This is a margin which allows us to distance ourselves from the axiomatic verification of the truth of such judgments.[64]

More objections could be made to determinism in its strong form. One of them rests on the idea that *all scientific knowledge is intrinsically "approximative."* Scientific theories always allow some small details to escape explanation. Therefore, there is always sufficient a field of action for indeterminism.

Deterministic theory makes it appear that the *"future"* may be as easily contemplated as the past, when, as we all know, the past and the future are of different natures. The past comes determined by that which has succeeded it. This is its proper definition: the past is like a rock of granite which cannot be changed. As against this, the future is quite other. It is open to the play of possibilities and to construction by human beings who act. The future is not found in any specific present moment, nor is it completely fixed. The future, unlike the past, remains open, the past is closed once and for all. We can act on the future.

Therefore, we should remind ourselves again that to know that determinism exists is one thing, but to pretend the universe is totally determined is something completely different. This last idea is not at all scientific. Were it otherwise, what field would then be open for human *creativity and freedom*? Perhaps we should not imagine that absolute indeterminism exists. There are clearly foreseeable events. Our universe is partly causal, partly probabilistic, and partly open: it is emergent. Radical determinism is criticized by Sociology, Philosophy and Psychology. Sociology criticizes it because it can never explain such important phenomena as *conflict, social change*, and perverse effects. To understand such realities recourse must be had to ideas of choice, decision, anticipation and freedom. The same is true of the psychological realm. There, no-one tries to deny the existence of compulsive behaviour, what is affirmed is that such behaviour is rare (considered pathological), generally linked to psychic defects. Most times, most people do not have the impression that they act compulsively, but rather, with a reasonable margin of freedom. Everyday life furnishes us with a great number of occasions where we have the possibility of choosing one answer from

64 Ted Honderich; *Punishment. The Supposed..., op. cit.*, pp. 113-158.

a whole range of answers. Only exceptionally are we carried away by extreme fury and lose control over our actions.

Individuals who commit crimes can be grouped under three general heads: those who are not responsible, those who are fully responsible, and those who are only partially responsible. We consider those decisions free which are taken by human beings who, with intelligence and free will, are able to distinguish between good and evil and who are not constrained to act against their will. However, that a decision be free does not imply that it escapes all outside influence. It simply means that this influence is not irresistible. A criminal's responsibility is diminished when his ability to resist temptation is diminished by a series of factors: immaturity, poverty, alcoholism, pressure of circumstances, amongst others. Juvenile crime is considered in a more indulgent way since it is more difficult for youth to control its impulses. For a poor man in dire need, it is more difficult to respect others' property than it would be for a rich man who has everything. It is more difficult to control one's emotions when one is drunk than it is for one who is sober.

It is difficult to resist certain temptations. Still, there exists the possibility of so doing. To recognize the freedom which criminals enjoy is to recognize their dignity as human beings. To deny a human being's ability to rationally choose is to deny his status as a person.[65]

B Dangerousness as a Probability Judgment

Determinism, even in its moderate version, affects the formulation of moral reproach, value judgments. Accepting that human action owes its cause to factors beyond the individual's control makes the only judgments possible utilitarian ones. This is true concerning the danger to society of the individual, as a question that worries the authorities who punish. When faced with the criminal's future, they must decide if it is probable that the criminal will go back to a life of crime. This is a probabilistic judgment.[66]

Starting from the fact that, in social life, *reactive attitudes* abound, such as gratitude, resentment, forgiveness, esteem, indignation, and the

65 Maurice Cusson, *Pourquoi punir?, op. cit.*, pp. 110-117.

66 Jean E. Floud, "Dangerousness and Criminal Justice", in *The British Journal of Criminology*, 22, 3, pp. 213-228. Jean E. Floud, Warren Young, *Dangerousness and Criminal Justice*, London, Heinemann, 1981.

like,[67] and concentrating for the moment on *resentment*, as society's most usual reaction to crime, we might hold that the human being has the capacity to modify, or even neutralize, that type of reaction when dealing with an abnormal or morally incapable delinquent, that is, an individual pre-determined to commit crime by factors beyond his will.

C *Responsibility or Social Necessity*

Social necessity is the idea which presides over the application of deterrents. Given that, to a large extent, the criminal is conditioned to commit crime, crime is seen as something necessary in all societies. It is then the State's task to respond to the social need it has to protect itself, in its turn, from such acts as break the law.

D *Utility. Utilitarianism* Ex Parte Populi, *as Opposed to Utiliarianism* Ex Parte Principis. *Security*

To seek for future utility, rather than retributive justice, is appropriate to the utilitarian attitude relative to punishment. Specifically, in these theories, we confront what is called *ex parte populi* utilitarianism. This is characteristic of contractualist and enlightenment Philosophy, and has as its starting point the welfare of, or the utility to, the governed and not to the governors. Utility to the governors is called *ex parte principis*. The laws, according to *ex parte populi*, are made for the citizens' utility.[68]

The idea of security is another for which deterrents are enacted. Deterrents are imposed to ensure that the crime will not be committed again in the future, and that people may go about where they will without fear of being attacked. Security is the absence of harm and the spiritual peace stemming therefrom. People enjoy security when they do not feel themselves exposed to crime. Security has to do with the scarcity of attacks on human life or goods. That is security's *objective* dimension. It also has to do with the feeling of peace and confidence which come from this. This is security's *subjective* dimension. Here, we need not indefinitely argue over the benefits of security. It is indispensable for there to arise any social fabric, without the which, no human

67 P. Strawson, "Freedom and Resentment", in *Proceedings of the British Academy*, XLVIII, 1962, pp. 1-25.

68 Ignacio Muñagorri Laguía, *Sanción penal y política criminal…, op. cit.*, pp. 48-53.

being can realize himself. Without some security, freedom and prosperity become inaccessible items.[69]

E The Subjective Aspect: The Offender. Crime in Its Social Aspect as a Breach of Social Order

Schools of thought defending punishment award primacy of consideration to objective aspects of crime. They consider a crime as an "illegal, guilty, typified and punishable act." Relative theories do not go about things in this way. They are in favour of deterrents and give priority to the other pole of punishment, that is, to subjective aspects. Here, the criminal is foremost, and they take into account that the same act, the same crime, is necessarily committed by many, widely different subjects, with different criminal personalities. To fit punishment to them is one of the characteristics of the measure to be adopted. Crime is nothing but a symptom that something is wrong in the individual, what he has done becomes of secondary importance. Further, crime is not considered so much in its objective aspect, that outlined above, as in its social repercussions or implications, as a breach or infraction of the social order. As opposed to Criminal Law "by the deed", here, we should rather speak of Criminal Law "by the author." This takes the author of the crime into consideration when analyzing Criminal Law. It is the fruit of such law, owing its existence mainly to criminological investigations.[70]

In any case, the act of which the crime consists should always be considered as limit-motive for penal intervention, as a security guarantee. Whatever the type of mental derangement, no matter how much it may reveal a dangerous personality in the author, this should never warrant punishment if the act itself cannot be included in the penal code. Should we once admit punishment not on the basis of the crime committed but, for example, on presumptions of future criminal activity, according as a person is more or less maladjusted, we should be allowing for all kinds of arbitrariness and abuses of power.[71]

Modern Criminal Law and Criminology struggle to unite the concepts of act and personality which had remained separate and unrelated in classical Criminal Law. The modern problem consists in establishing a balance between both elements: the act, on which the legality of pros-

69 Maurice Cusson, *Pourquoi punir?, op. cit.*, pp. 103-105.

70 Ignacio Muñagorri Laguía, *Sanción penal y política criminal..., op. cit.*, pp. 88-91, esp. p. 90.

71 *Ibid.*, pp. 91 and 92.

ecution depends, and the personality of the criminal, which serves as basis for individualized treatment.[72]

F *Suffering as a Means to the Good*

Utilitarian theories, taking off from prevention and deterrents, question the idea of retribution by way of one evil for another. They also question the suffering, which makes up the punishment, as a good thing in itself. Such suffering should, at the end of the day, be a means to a good end: reforming the criminal, social peace, intimidation to prevent future criminal acts, and so on.

Though we might justify the offender's or criminal's suffering, as those in favour of retributive justice try to do, on the basis of guilt, how might we justify someone's deliberate imposing of suffering on another? It may well be true that he is guilty, but who am I to set myself up as judge over another human being? In the extreme case, in the case of capital punishment, today, fortunately, in full retreat, how can we justify the clearly amoral figure of the hangman, a somebody who sets himself up as executor of death upon another human being? *To suffer is not the same as to inflict suffering*. The latter implies: establishing laws to say what is good or bad in a general way for all the component subpopulations of a State; someone to apply the laws thus established, but who himself is not free of prejudices of all kinds, of the possibility of error in judgment; and, someone to carry out sentences in institutions which often serve for everything except what they were initially designed for. All the above relates to the wider subject of the nature and justification of State coercion. Here, we leave it as simply noted.[73]

G *Minimum Right to Punish Systems*

Nineteenth-century liberalism gives way to relative theories and systems. These take account of the personal circumstances of the criminal, and not just legal guarantee and equality of treatment. Along these lines, we might qualify such movements as minimum systems of Criminal Law. That the principle of legality has suffered an evolution through time cannot be ignored, in light of the fact that, in its origins, in the Liberal State, it was embodied in laws and charters and Criminal Codes.

72 *Ibid.*, p. 139.

73 Gertrude Ezorsky, *The Ethics of Punishment*, Albany, State University of New York Press, 1972, pp. XXIV-XXV. J. Betegón, *La justificación del castigo, op. cit.*, p. 299-300.

Below, we consider this evolution. *Nulla poena sine lege*, meaning only that a crime must be foreseen by the law in an abstract manner, with maximum and minimum sentences attached, has been slowly losing its absolute character. Within sentence limits, the judge, especially in relative theories which favour deterrents, may exercise his power. Likewise, execution of punishment comes determined by social factors, and by the concrete reality of the individuals to whom it is applied. In this sense, we are dealing with minimum Criminal Law systems. These are systems that hold "all is permitted which is not expressly forbidden", rather than the reverse, which would read "all is forbidden which is not expressly allowed."

The principle of legality is no longer a simply formal principle. It has been transformed in accord with political and legal transformations. Retribution only fixes the framework. It only ensures that punishment must always come after the crime and must be proportional to the crime's gravity. Within such wide margins, this leaves sufficient space to accommodate a rich content of means aimed at, always present, preventive ends. When punishing, one spoke of expiation, of compensation. This was in line with the retributive *punishment*, of which Kant and Hegel spoke, that demanded that an evil be followed by a further evil. However, with the retributive *penal sanction*, punishment is considered a "bitter necessity." Sanction encompasses a wider, more modern sphere, for instance, it includes deterrents. Whoever imposes punishment here does not feel himself any longer "superior" to the criminal. We do not know what has caused the criminal to transgress nor do we know if, in some sense, society itself was not also responsible for the crimes committed within it. In a minimum Criminal Law case, there is a tendency to not impose unnecessary suffering. Suffering is only employed when one cannot prevent crime in any milder manner.

There was a time when it was held that "to each according to his rank." Thus, the noble who killed was decapitated while the plebian was quartered. Later came another idea which was "to each according to his property", that is, the rich found justice more indulgent than did the poor man. Subsequently, a better criterion was established, "to each according to his deserts." Today, we are approaching a time when the criterion will be "to each according to his necessities."[74] What must be avoided is that an excessive scientism should succeed an excessive "le-

74 Ignacio Muñagorri Laguía, *Sanción penal y política criminal...*, *op. cit.*, p. 74.

galism" in the penal sanction. It is as bad as the latter for it presupposes a lack of guarantees.

The principles enunciated are proper to the Rule of Law, where what is favoured is a "minimum Criminal Law." In contrast to this, we find the arbitrariness typical of absolutist or totalitarian states, with their "maximum Criminal Law codes." In the former instance, public power, especially in the criminal sphere, is rigidly limited and bound to law on the substantial and on the procedural planes. That is, public power is tied to relevant penal contents and to procedurally binding forms, respectively. Under maximum codes, public powers are *legibus soluti* or *totales*, that is to say, not disciplined by law and, hence, lacking in any limits or conditions.[75]

H The Fusion Law-Nature

We thus see that retributive theories, partisans of punishment, fused together Law and Ethics. Relative theories, defenders of the deterrent measure, keep both normative spheres governing human conduct separate, in order to bring about a new identification, that of Law with Nature. Law approximates to the natural sciences and professionals try to explain the phenomenon of criminality by appeal to physical and causal reasoning.

I Crime as Disease

Crime ceases to be considered a sin, as it was in earlier metaphysical and absolute conceptions. Now, it is considered an illness, with a biological and even genetic underlayer. The criminal is seen as someone ill who we try to cure. The idea of treatment takes the place of moral amendment, its predecessor.

4 Function and Aim

Debate over the function and goal of punishment has centred upon the two traditional theories of punishment: the retributionist and the utilitarian, or deterrent, theories. The former hold the suffering involved in punishment as something morally correct. It expiates the sin committed and compensates for the damage done. It is right because the criminal deserves it for being guilty of having committed the offence. Desert, a

75 Luigi Ferrajoli, *Derecho y razón. Teoría del garantismo penal, op. cit.*, p. 104.

concept with its eyes on the past, and of no future utility, is what justifies punishment. Within retributionism, there then exist different variants and conceptions but all share the common point of reference, the past – *punitur quia peccatum*. The latter (utilitarian) is a consequentialist sort of doctrine. It considers the only relevant aspects of an action are the good or the bad consequences the action produces. The deliberate suffering involved in punishment it considers only justified if it proves useful, that is, if through punishment, one can avoid or prevent future suffering – *punitur ut ne peccetur*.

Are these two theories irreconcilable? In their extreme versions they would be, for instance, should utilitarianism go so far as to justify punishing the innocent with the purpose of general prevention of future crime. Still, in their more modern, moderate, sense, retribution and utilitarian doctrines are reconcilable. In this way, we would have to avoid anchoring punishment in classic retributionism, in our time, generally overcome. We know that functioning in isolation, as the only punishment angle, such retributionism reverts to a cruel and primitive thesis, totally distanced from rationalism and the humanitarian values which Western culture has defended since the Enlightenment.[76]

4.1 Punishment and "Retribution"[77]

4.1.1 Varieties of Retribution

There are numerous variants on retribution, we group them here under four headings.[78] Each one gives a different answer to the retributionist question, "Why punish?" Below, we outline every one of these positions.

76 Jerónimo Betegón, *La justificación del castigo, op. cit.*, pp. 14-15.

77 K. Baier, "Is Punishment Retributive?", in *Analysis*, vol. 16, 1955, pp. 25-32; reimpr. in H.B. Acton, *The Philosophy of Punishment*, London, Macmillan, 1969, pp. 130-137. Eusebi, "La nuova retribuzione", in *Rivista Italiana*, 1983, pp. 914 ff. A.C. (Alfred Cyril) Ewing (1899-), *The Morality of Punishment with Some Suggestions for a General Theory of Ethics*, Preface by W.D. Ross, Montclair, N.J., Patterson Smith, 1970. "Punishment as a Moral Agency: An Attempt to Reconcile the Retributive and Utilitarian View", in *Mind*, 36, 1927, pp. 292-305. "Armstrong on the Retributive Theory", in *Mind*, 72, 1963, pp. 121-124. Gertrude Ezorsky, "Retributive Justice", in *Canadian Journal of Philosophy*, 1, 1972, pp. 365-368.

78 Jerónimo Betegón, *La justificación del castigo, op. cit*, pp. 70-71, note 129.

A There Exists an Intrinsic Good in Making the Guilty Suffer

The first type of answer is defended by what Ted Honderich calls "intrinsic retributionism." This consists in maintaining that we must punish because there is an intrinsic good in the suffering of guilty people.[79]

I confess I do not have the moral intuition to see where the intrinsic value lies in any situation where evil is balanced out by another evil. It is entirely unclear to me how anyone may reject vengeance but at the same time accept retributive punishment. Neither is it clear what is so valuable if we follow the line of the argument: we punish immoral acts or acts forbidden by law, totally independently of their moral *status*.[80]

B A Renewed Balance Is Struck between Benefits and Charges

The main retributionist line of argument, the second, regarding the why of punishment, invokes the idea of a balance between benefits and burdens.[81] Ashworth, regarding this, says that the general aim of punishment justification is "to restore the balance the offence disturbed. It is not just that the offender should be allowed to reap an advantage, and therefore law exists to subject him to a disadvantage to cancel (at least symbolically) what he has unjustly acquired."[82]

79 Ted Honderich, *Punishment: The Supposed Justifications*, Harmondsworth, Baltimore, Maryland, Penguin Books, 1969 (edition used by us). Ed. revised. Harmondsworth-Baltimore (etc.), Penguin, 1976. There is a previous edition: London, Hutchinson, 1969; and Harmondsworth, Penguin Books, 1984.

80 Carlos Santiago Nino, *Los límites de la responsabilidad penal. Una teoría liberal del delito*, Buenos Aires, Depalma, 1980, pp. 265 ff.

81 John Finnis, "Punishment and Pedagogy", in *Oxford Review*, 1967, 5, p. 83 and in "The Restoration of Retribution", in *Analysis*, 32, 4, 1972, p. 131.

82 Andrew Ashworth, *Sentencing and Penal Policy*, London, Weidenfeld and Nicolson, 1983, pp. 16-18. Wojciech Sadurski, *Giving Desert its Due, op. cit.*, pp. 225. Herbert Morris (1928-), *On Guilt and Innocence: Essays in Legal Philosophy and Moral Psychology*, Berkeley, University of California Press, 1976. (ed.), *Freedom and Responsibility*, Standford, Standford University Press, 1961. "Persons and Punishment", in *Monist*, 52, 1968, pp. 475-501; reimpr. in *On Guilt and Innocence..., op. cit.*, pp. 39-58. "Guilt and Punishment", in *Personalist*, 52, 1971, pp. 305-321. "A Paternalistic Theory of Punishment", in *American Philosophical Quarterly*, 18, 4, 1981. Also, Andrew von Hirsch, in *Doing Justice: The Choice of Punishment*, New York, Hill and Wang, 1976. Not in his *Past or Future of Crimes: Deservedness and Dangerousness in the Sentencing of Criminals*, New Brunswick, Rutgers Univer-

The first objection to this justification is that the fulfilment of the law is not always perceived of as a burden, and crime does not always imply an advantage. In many cases, the criminal's feelings of satisfaction are darkened by unpleasant emotions like fear, disgust or repentance. Rapists may be infected by syphilis or AIDS, the criminal may break his leg, conspiracy to murder or attempted murder may result in failure. The question then becomes: Must we punish crimes even though the evildoer derives no benefits or advantages from them?

Benefit-burden equilibrium theories do offer an answer to such a question. They say it is abstention and self-limitation which is the burden for which he obeys the laws, and freedom with no restrictions is the advantage the criminal reaps when breaking the law. His advantage then is the limitless exercise of his will. Still, is abstention always experienced as a burden by the obedient citizen who respects the law? Even where there is complete freedom, many people do not feel at all attracted to the idea of murder, and so, abstention implies no burden for them in the least.[83] Obedient citizens often do not feel constrained by the law, rather they feel perfectly free, and content to follow what they consider a just and rewarding course of action.[84]

In his 1981 work, *A Paternalistic Theory of Punishment*, Herbert Morris puts forward just such a theory. According to it, punishment, far from being a burden, is converted into a benefit since it helps the criminal understand that his offence constitutes an evil as much for himself as for others. The offender will be a better person after having experienced contrition through punishment. Morris' change of opinion since his stance held from 1968 to 1981 is perfect testimony to how difficult it is to clearly establish what makes for a burden and what makes for a benefit.

Sadurski, in his already cited 1985 work, considers that, after all, the burden involved in self-restriction and abstention is really no burden for,

---

sity Press, 1985. *Cf.* also by von Hirsch, *Censure and Sanctions*, 1993, and "Punishment, Penance and the State: A Reply to Duff", in Matt Matravers (ed.), *Punishment and Political Theory, op. cit.*, pp. 69-83. *Cf.* also from this point of view, George Sher, *Desert*, Princeton, NJ, Princeton University Press, 1987.

83 Margaret Falls, "Retribution, Reciprocity and Respect for Persons", in *Law and Philosophy*, 6, 1987, pp. 25-51.

84 *Cf.* Carlos Santiago Nino, *Los límites de la responsabilidad penal. Una teoría liberal del delito,* Buenos Aires, Astrea, 1980, pp. 263 ff.

at the end of the day, we continue to have options, and to have a choice is better than not having one. This is without taking into account the argument that, sometimes, it is better to have fewer options than to have a lot of them. In this sense, is it a burden on us that we cannot fly to Mars tomorrow? The point is that some benefits have a practical meaning for people, while others are lacking in importance. It turns out to be a weak basis for imprisoning someone that he has renounced burdens which were never perceived as such by him. Sher follows this line of argument in his 1987 book. He says that, though murder implies the breaking of a great moral restriction, the murderer has greater freedom than the ordinary citizen, that of being able to kill whom he pleases. Nevertheless, this is a freedom which the majority of people do not consider a benefit in any way. What, in this case, would be the re-equilibrium of benefits and burdens that the punishment should restore?

Further, in any society, there exists a great inequality of power and wealth, and the question of restoring the balance between benefits and burdens is indeed an arduous task. Here, when restoring benefits and burdens, how might we equilibrate the punishment of a poor person with that of a millionaire?[85]

On the other hand, before accepting this retributive argument justification, we should have to show that it is within the law's competence to wipe out feelings of self-gratification and, more, that their suppression would make the supposed frustration of the obedient citizen any the less burdensome.[86]

C *Punishment Annuls the Evil Caused, Restoring the* Status Quo *and Social Balance*

A third retributionist theory – closely related to the foregoing – invokes the Hegelian idea that the punishment wipes out the harm done, restoring the *status quo*.

It is evident that this theory suffers from the same defect as the one above. It takes for granted that a balance to be preserved exists between benefit and burden in society. The truth is far from this. What there really is is an initial situation where disequilibrium obtains.

85 John Braithwaite, Philip Pettit, *Not Just Deserts. A Republican Theory of Criminal Justice, op. cit.*, pp. 157-159.

86 Carlos Santiago Nino, *Los límites de la responsabilidad penal..., op. cit.*, p. 264.

D Punishment Presupposes Reprobation

More and more, the modern retributionist abandons ideas of social balance and annulment of advantages to cling to a fourth type of argument. According to this, sanction and punishment are justified because they imply reprobation and denouncement. Lord Denning was an outstanding defender of this viewpoint.[87] Some defend the moral ignomy by a series of consequentialist considerations:

- It strengthens the inhibitions *vis-à-vis* crime in society.
- The denunciation contributes to societal identity. Society sees itself as a self-respecting community.[88]
- The lack of moral outrage would lessen the importance of those laws which have been broken.

Still, quite a number of retributionists, especially von Hirsch in 1986 and Nozick in 1981, hold that upbraiding criminal conduct is not a good in itself unless good consequences flow therefrom.[89]

A strong, retributionist tradition exists which holds that formal punishment is not the way to maximize moral stigma possibilities. The stigma is something which arises amongst the community. Hence, it is silly to assume that carrying legal conflicts beyond the community and submitting them to the courts might be a good way to feed such social stigma. For instance, Christie speaks of a sort of stealing of the conflict from the victims of crime by the State. Insofar as we formalize and rationalize criminal justice, the community sees itself deprived of the pedagogical possibilities of clearing up the matter.[90]

In other works, it is argued that the way to exploit the power of reprobation would be to displace its sphere of action and change repressive social control into moral social control.[91] Take Nozick. He justifies

87 Lord Denning, *Report of the Royal Comisión on Capital Punishment*, London, HMSO, 1984.

88 Andrew Oldenquist, "The Case for Revenge", in *The Public Interest*, 82, 1986, pp. 72-80, esp. p. 75. And, of the same author, "An Explanation to Retribution", in *Journal of Philosophy*, 9, 1988, pp. 464-478.

89 Robert Nozick, *Philosophical Explanations*, Oxford, Clarendon Press, 1981, pp. 363-97.

90 Nils Christie, "Conflicts as Property", in *The British Journal of Criminology*, 17,1, pp. 1-15.

91 John Braithwaite, "Restorative Justice", in M. Tonry (ed.), *The Handbook of Crime and Punishment*, New York, Oxford University Press, 1998.

punishment in that it "reconnects" the criminal with the right values from which his crime had disconnected him. He is unclear as to what "reconnection" exactly means, except in that it does not imply remorse, repentance or any other sort of correct value interiorization. Rather, we punish offenders because we wish these values to have "a meaningful effect on his life", in the sense that he should understand, though not necessarily accept, such values.[92]

4.1.2 The Ideas of Repression, Expiation, Revenge, *malum passionis. Lex Talionis,* Repaying One Ill with Another. Differences between Retribution and Revenge

Absolutist or retributive doctrines are based upon the maxim that it is just to repay evil with evil. It is said that *the desire for vengeance is to the law what sexual desire is to marriage*. Even today, the idea of vengeance often hovers over courts of justice. Even if it be true that today its most brutal form has been overcome, yet vengeance and Criminal Law are not ideas completely alien to each other.[93] This is a principle which is of ancient origins, and is founded upon the blood-revenge common to all primitive legal systems.[94] It was already present in the shape of a divine precept in the Hebrew Tradition. It was transmitted, even despite of the evangelical precept of forgiveness, to the Christian and Catholic Tradition by a whole gamut of churchmen, from Saint Paul through Augustine and Aquinas to Pope Pius XIIth.

The concept turns upon three basic, religious-style ideas: *vengeance – ex parte agentis*; *expiation – ex parte patientis*; and, *restoration of balance* between punishment and crime.[95] These ideas, typical of reactionary penal thought are based on the survival of ancient beliefs which confuse the Law with Ethics. They see a necessary nexus between the following: guilt and punishment; punishment and restoring of the

92 Robert Nozick, *Philosophical Explanations, op. cit.*, p. 375. John Braithwaite, Philip Pettit, *Not Just Desserts..., op. cit.*, pp. 160-166.

93 Susan Jacoby, *Wild Justice: The Evolution of Revenge*, London, Collins, 1985. Leonard Orland, "From Vengeance to Vengeance: Sentencing Reform and the Demise of Rehabilitation", in *Hofstra Law Review*, 7, 1978, pp. 29-56. R. Verdier (ed.), *La vengeance*, vol. I, Paris, Cujas, 1980. E.A. Westermarck, "The Essence of Revenge", in *Mind*, 7, 1898, pp. 289-310.

94 Maurice Cusson, *Pourquoi punir?*, Paris, Dalloz, 1987, pp. 29 ff.

95 Luigi Ferrajoli, *Derecho y razón. Teoría del garantismo penal, op. cit.*, p. 254.

violated natural order; the *lex talionis* and the purification of the criminal by punishment. These are all concepts of a magic kind and, to a large extent, irrational. Reactionary penal thought entered a crisis with the advent of the Enlightenment. They were taken up again by Kant and Hegel ready for the XIXth century.

Still, in fact, these doctrines continue to be unable to overcome the obvious objection, formulated by Plato, that is, *what has once been done cannot then be undone*. It is their irreparable nature which sets off criminal from civil penalties. Only in the latter is there room for repairing the damage done.[96]

The only acceptable moral reason for retribution, as regards punishing a person, lies in the fact that he has committed an offence, understanding by that that the moral guilt of the offending agent is a sufficient and necessary condition for a justified punishment, always so long as the intensity of the punishment be *equal* to that of the offence. One would have to add that this is so while the punishment is compatible with the dignity and moral autonomy of the agent, the offender, who by his behaviour has brought upon himself the selfsame punitive action.

The greater part of conduct considered deserving of repression by retributionists is that which is based on moral demands embodied in religious-style rules of the kind laid out in Medieval Canonical Law. Within this context, it is no surprise that punishment should have a strong, expiationary component of a religious hue – *punitur quia peccatum est*. This concept, combining punishment and the repression of sinful behaviour, attracted the criticism of writers like Grotius or Pufendorf, who revealed the overriding necessity to elaborate a lay Criminal Law to be administered by State authorities. This would set aside from being specified as punishable all simple thoughts and intentions, and would limit itself to only conduct, including outward conduct within the reach of the law. This would be conduct that did not fulfil the rules of the sovereign and which sinned against society and its members.

The retributive idea in its pure form, in Kant for instance, has been the object of severe criticism. Curiously enough, this often came from some of Kant's earliest intellectual followers like Karl Grolman or Arthur Schopenhauer. Schopenhauer formulated a stinging criticism of Kant, thus: all retribution for a present evil which inflicts a pain which cannot be made up for by future consequences is pure vengeance. Recently, this type of criticism has been revived by writers like Claus Roxin or

96 *Ibid.*, pp. 254-255.

Giorgio del Vecchio. Del Vecchio estimates that the evil brought about by the crime can never be overcome by another evil, even if employed by the good. Within English-speaking countries, similar arguments are found in the classic works of Hobbes, Bentham, Judge Holmes or, more recently, J. Hospers.[97]

Contractualist theories, for example in John Locke's version, talk of a state of nature, before the constitution of civil society, where great instability existed, since everyone took justice into his own hands by way of private vengeance. That is why the social pact arose. It was to yield up a part of natural liberty in order to gain more legal security. Thence appeared the figures of the State and the Judge, as impartial third parties – *nemo judex in causa propia*. This imposes sanctions through legal proceedings, in such a way, at least in theory, that they are objective, coldly and rationally calculated so that the reach of the State apparatus' reply should meet the breaches of the legal system suffered. It does not deal with forgiving the offender, but rather with institutionalizing the sanction. Should we have to set up a moral scale, at the very bottom would come *vengeance*, which puts a man on a par with his enemies, and, at the highest point, would come forgiveness, which makes him superior to them. At some intermediate point we should find the *institutionalized penal sanction*, which, though in some cases it inflicts a *controlled pain*, it does not, like revenge, consider that *the more harm that is caused*, the more satisfaction is obtained, the lust for vengeance satiated.

The idea of a correspondence between the extent of the offence and that of the retributive answer is precisely one of the greatest practical difficulties in any punishment theory. This is because the exact equality or equivalence of such an answer, so sought after in theory, is in practice totally unworkable. Most often the talionic idea – *an eye for an eye, a tooth for a tooth* – of equal treatment is totally unrealizable. The only offence open to a completely equivalent response would be homicide. The rest of them – rape, blackmail, counterfeiting, grave desecration, and the like – are never repaid in the same coin. If they are paid back in units of different measurement, however, how can the one be compared with the other? How many oranges equal a certain number of apples?

97 Hobbes *Leviatán*, Madrid, Editora Nacional, 1979. Translation into Spanish by A. Escohotado, p. 248. J. Betegón, *La justificación del castigo, op. cit.*, pp. 115-120.

What equivalence is there between an old and a young eye, or between a myopic and a hypermetropic one?

Further, there are cases where equality does not imply uniform treatment, but rather *proportional* treatment. We must remember that equality implies not only treating equals equally, but also treating inequalities unequally in proportion to their inequalities. Here again, we come up against the difficulty of when we should treat unequally, and in what measure we should fix the inequality.

From all the above, we might conclude by affirming that the *lex talionis* should be rejected in its literal sense – an eye for an eye. Even in its wider and somewhat improper sense, as equivalence of treatment, it is difficult to really quantify. Taken to the extreme, we might appreciate that offences are something which *should* always turn out to be graver than the punishments, minimizing the suffering and hurtful consequences these have upon the criminal. The only solution for the retributionist is to be guided by intuition, with all the drawbacks this implies for *objectivity and impartiality.*

Greater still are the problems should we try to measure not the gravity of the offence but the agent's level of intentionality. In such a case, we would abandon forever the objective world and enter into the subjective dimension of guilt, where such factors as the delinquent's imputability level come into play. A psychologically balanced subject is not the same as a psychopath incapable of feeling the psychological pressure of punishment and, to a large extent, predetermined in his actions. Therefore, we must affirm that retribution, measurement and *lex talionis*, while they do represent an advance over and above vengeance, are much closer to some idealized world than to any real one.

Under real social conditions, retributive punishment is clearly immoral, given that the criminal is rarely a free and autonomous agent, rather he is a mere object of his own passions, and genetic, familial, and socio-economic conditioning. These might include: psychological instability; affective and cultural deprivation in infancy; social ostracism and a subjective situation of need. To these, some would add also the corruption of the System. Marx speaks of the Capitalist System as seriously conditioning the individual in the real world, alienating him from his own freedom and converting him into an anti-social being, a future, active criminal. He talks of the system's promotion of selfish sentiments; its lust for wealth; the social inequalities it generates, its unbridled competitiveness, its creation of artificial needs in the consumer society.[98]

Finally, as another distinctive note separating vengeance from retributive punishment, it should be pointed out that, against the State's sanctioning apparatus' reply to crime which is *necessary* – and which always comes into play whenever there is a crime, and always to the same extent as it does with similar crimes – the reply stemming from revenge motives may not follow any previous pattern set in the treatment of other, similar offences to which it might have fallen victim. Institutionalized, retributive punishment is not a "private" act. Vengeance is. It is not a matter between offender and offended. There the offended party can choose to answer or not. Legal punishment is a "public" act. There is a judge or a tribunal. Above their individual wills is the will and the rule of law. The judge serves this law impartially. He is even subject to it in the carrying out of his task.

We should also distinguish between expiation and vengeance. Vengeance means making the criminal pay. Expiation means that the criminal himself pays. Revenge theory deals with all crime as if it were of the same type of physical violence: you have hurt someone, you will be hurt. Expiation behaves as if all crimes were business transactions: you took something from someone, you must pay an equivalent value back.[99]

4.1.3 The Backward Glance – *punitur quia peccatum est.* The *Vergeltungstrafe*

Punishment is justified in the crime. It should, then, look backwards. This is not, however, at least usually, only to find its *raison d'être* ("there is no punishment without a crime"), but to remind itself that what is important is to look obsessively backwards. This is retributive punishment: the *Vergeltungstrafe*. Opposed to this is the punishment with an end in view: the *Zweckstrafe*. It is more important to punish because there is a crime – *quia peccatum est* – than in order that there should be no repetition of crime – *ut ne peccetur*.

98 Jerónimo Betegón, *La justificación del castigo, op. cit.*, pp. 121-141.

99 Enrique Eduardo Mari, *La problemática del castigo. El discurso de Jeremy Bentham y Michel Foucault*, Buenos Aires, Hachette, 1983, p. 102. Heiko H. Lesch, *La función de la pena*, Cuadernos "Luis Jiménez de Asúa", Madrid, Dykinson, 1999, pp. 7-9.

4.1.4 The Reconciliation of Retribution with Modern Liberal Theories, as a Guarantee of Proportionality and as Legality Principle over and against the Arbitrary Nature of Absolutism, and as but one Function of the Punishment which to a Certain Extent Is Always Necessary

Continental thought, like English-speaking pragmatism, has seen a resurgence of retributive theories, though not of the Continental, Kantian, Hegelian sort, of a moral and metaphysical bent, but rather in their classic guise, as heirs to Liberal, Political Philosophy. This has made the guarantee its banner in the penal world. That is, as a just proportioning between crime and punishment. The guarantee is thus based on the prohibition against punishing beyond the gravity of the crime. This should not be done even for preventive reasons, since it goes against human dignity to use man as a means. Limitation criteria quite foreign to the retribution idea born with Kant and Hegel are offered up. The limitation on punishment is foreknown in order to assure the criminal the minimum suffering and society, the necessary dissuasion. The approach is more the idea of proportion than that of retribution. We find Wertheimer here, following Hart, or John Rawls. In this way, abuses like National Socialist authoritarianism, and the penal terror it imposed, are avoided. Their so-called criminal law was dressed up by the Kiel School to service the political aims of the Third Reich.[100]

4.2 Deterrents and "Prevention"

4.2.1 The Idea of Security

Obviously, as already mentioned, the deterrent measure is mainly concerned with security. We have seen how punishment was oriented towards compensatory and retributive justice. If we take this existing legal *binomy* between security and justice into account, deterrence gives pride of place to the former, while punishment lauds the latter.

4.2.2 The Forward-Looking Glance, so that the Criminal Should Not Transgress Again – *punitur ut ne peccetur.* The *Zweckstrafe*

Relative theory postulates are radically opposed to absolute theories, defenders of punishment. They, for their part, are in favour of deterrent measures, with their basis in Enlightenment humanitarian and utilitarian doctrines. During the Enlightenment, the sense of punishment no

100 Borja Mapelli Caffarena, Juan Terradillos Basoco, *Las consecuencias jurídicas del delito, op. cit.*, pp. 36-37.

longer resided in the idea of guilt and the carrying out of justice, but rather in the protection of Society and the idea of security, that is, the avoiding of future, punishable acts – *poena relata ad effectum*. The preventive aim of punishment was placed foremost amongst its functions. The goal of this policy was not to punish the criminal because he had acted badly – *quia peccatum est* – but to deter others, or he himself, from committing future crimes – *ut ne peccetur*. This is end-geared punishment (*Zweckstrafe*), as against retributive punishment (*Vergeltungstrafe*).[101]

5 Main Jurisprudential Theories

5.1 Punishment and "Absolute Theories". Punishment as an End in Itself[102]

5.1.1 "Divine" Retribution

For the divine retribution thesis, there exists a divine order of things which cannot be infringed. Should the order be disturbed, man sets himself against God and violates His Law. This occasions a punishment to expiate the evil done. Here we have the overriding idea to be found in Traditional Catholic Writers, from Thomas Aquinas to Stahl, Jarcke, J. Bekker and Walter. This type of theory is reproached for its basically metaphysical nature. It is only understandable by an act of faith.

5.1.2 "Moral" Retribution. Immanuel Kant: Punishment as a Moral Necessity and as a Categorical Imperative

In Kant, the subject of punishment justification is mainly discussed in "Metaphysical Principles of the Theory of Law", more especially in the second part, with reference to Public Law, and in the section headed "*Von Strafe und Begnadigungsrecht*" (On the Right to Punish and on Pardon).[103]

101 José Antonio Choclán Montalvo, *Individualización judicial de la pena…, op. cit.*, p. 68.

102 J. Cottingham, "Varieties of Retribution", in *Philosophical Quarterly*, 29, 1979, pp. 238-246.

103 Kant, *Die Metaphysik der Sitten*, ed. by W. Weischedel, Suhrkamp Taschenbuch Verlag, Band VIII, Frankfurt am Main, 1982. We use the 10th ed. Frankfurt, 1993, vol. VIII, pp. 255 ff. Heiko H. Lesch, *La función de la pena, op. cit.*, pp. 8-11. Jerónimo Betegón, *La justificación del castigo, op.*

Firstly, Kant defines the right to punish as "the right the sovereign has to painfully afflict the subject as a consequence of his transgressing the law". Two characteristics of punishment as retribution emerge from this definition. They are: the existence of a prior crime – *seiner Verbrechens* – and therefore of guilt; the existence of pain – *Schmerz* – or suffering as a consequence of punishment. Hence, here, punishment cannot be considered from a utilitarian perspective as the search for a good, even should this be for society as a whole. Utilitarian reasons are absent from the definition. Criminal Justice is conceived of as an absolute necessity, in a categorical imperative way.[104]

In Kant, penal law is a categorical imperative. Kant went so far as to affirm that, right up to the last murderer who was in prison should be executed, otherwise the whole of society ran the risk of converting itself into an accomplice in the violation of justice, even in the extreme case of a dissolution of civil society by consent of its members, or if a community inhabiting a desert island decided to abandon it and disperse themselves.

In the well-known Kantian contribution, punishment is just retribution, deprived of any aim whatever – *poena absoluta ab effectu*. It represents the cause of an evil act as compensation for a guiltily carried out, breaking of the law – *malum passionis propter malum actionis*. That is the punishment's content is *lex talionis*, "if you have killed, you must die." The function of punishment is the carrying out of justice. For Kant, Criminal Law unconditionally binds, it is a categorical imperative. It may only be applied when caused by a crime, and only because a law has been broken. Holding the presupposition that man is morally free, the injury inflicted by a penal law is the injury imposed by the legal obligation to not infringe upon the outward freedom of others. One punishes not as goal-directed retribution, but because someone has committed a crime. It is not so that the criminal will not commit a crime in the future, since that would be prevention. According to Kant, prevention treats the person as a means to an end, and not as an end in

cit., pp. 17-60. Tom Sorell, "Punishment in a Kantian Framework", in Matt Matravers (ed.), *Punishment and Political Theory, op. cit.*, pp. 10-28.

104 *Cf.* also Mario A. Cattaneo, *Dignità umana e pena nella filosofia di Kant*, Milano, Giuffrè, 1981, pp. 320-328.

himself. Possible effects which punishment might produce on the criminal or on society in the future turn out to be irrelevant.[105]

Another characteristic of imposing punishment, in Kant, is, insofar as the measure to be applied is concerned, the idea of equality in its *lex talionis* guise.[106] Thus, Kant holds the death penalty is ideal for homicide, as against abolitionist doctrines like those of Beccaria and the Enlightenment punishment reformists.[107] Kant only allows of two exceptions to his rule regarding the absolute necessity to punish the homicide with death. These are the two cases in which honour is at stake. That is, for crimes of infanticide and when death is caused by a duel. The German thinker also speaks of the right to grace (*ius aggratiandi*) as a right reserved to the sovereign, a right he should administer with care, given that, badly used, it might give rise to even greater injustices. The sovereign should exercise his grace where the injuries are directed at his own person, never in cases of crimes produced amongst the subjects. That would represent the very greatest injury to the victim injured.

Betegón affirms that Kantian penal philosophy revolves around two central ideas: the respect for human dignity and the principle of equality. This last is an *a priori* rule when fixing upon the *quantum* of a just punishment.[108]

Human dignity is encapsulated in the second formulation of the categorical imperative: "Act in such a way that you might use Humanity, as much in your own person as in that of any other, always as an end, at the same time, and never simply as a means." Few writers have escaped the temptation to critically point out the tremendous contrast between the postulates of autonomy and human dignity *and* some of the punishments Kant proposes. These are very cruel, in consonance with the *lex talionis*. For instance, castration for pederasty and rape. It is, however, true that the German philosopher himself recognized that he was setting forth an ideal system which, in some cases, might prove imperfect in a phenomenal world. Still, insofar as what he expressly advocates,

105 José Antonio Choclán Montalvo, *Individualización judicial de la pena...*, *op. cit.*, pp. 56-57.

106 *Cf.* Heiko H. Lesch, *La función de la pena, op. cit,* p. 11.

107 *Cf.* S. Byrd, "Kant's Theory of Punishment: Deterrence in its Threat, Retribution in its Execution", in *Law and Philosophy*, vol. 1, 1989, pp. 151-200.

108 *Cf.* Mario A. Cattaneo, *Dignità umana e pena nella filosofia di Kant*, Milano, Giuffrè, 1981.

Kant is in favour of root suppression of torture and of physical abuse, the which too often accompany the carrying out of punishments.

In Kant's Penal Philosophy, the absolute equality, *lex talionis* principle tends to suppress that inequality created by the crime. When cancelling this out through an equal and opposite action, perfect retribution is achieved. Once the suffering is over, the criminal returns to the situation of equality which obtained before he broke the Law of Universal Freedom. He also regains the respect of the community and so recovers his civil standing.

For Kant, "law is the limitation on the liberty of each as a condition for the liberty of all, insofar as this is possible with a general law", "to the law is joined the faculty of exercising coercion on he who violates it." Coercion comes to be identified with freedom, given that coercion is necessary to conserve freedom in the world of real coexistence. In Kant's words, "if a certain use of liberty is the very obstacle to that liberty according to general laws, then the coercion opposing the crime coincides with liberty. Or, what is the same, coercion is an impediment to an obstacle in the way of liberty. Or, what is the same, coercion accords with law", "(coercion) shows itself as an act contrary to the liberty realized in order to reject the act itself, contrary to the other, and, from thence, because two negatives make an affirmative, it shows itself as an act that restores liberty." In Kant, coercion is *the negation of the negation* of law, and it re-establishes the legal order. This coercion is not left in private hands – as distinct from personal revenge – but is institutionalized in the legal authority of the State. The State is titular owner of the *ius puniendi*.

This is at least a first reading of Kant. Jerónimo Betegón offers a second reading, of the "Pre-Critique" studies known as "Moral Lessons."[109] In one of these, under the title "Award and Punishment", Kant distinguishes between intimidatory or preventive punishment and retributive punishment. Another penal text, which might be brought in to give a reading of Kant not merely in the key of retribution, is a letter of the German philosopher to an old disciple, the doctor and philosopher

109 The original German title is "Eine Vorlesung Kants über Ethik", Berlin, 1924. There is translation into English, "Lectures on Ethics" by L. Infield, London, Methuen and Co. Ltd. 1rst. ed. 1939, reimp. 1979; and translation into Spanish, "Lecciones de Ética", by R. Rodríguez Aramayo and C. Roldán Panadero, with introduction and notes by R. Rodríguez Aramayo, Barcelona, ed. Crítica, 1988.

Johann Benjamin Erhard. Here Kant counterpoints the moral punishment with the human. The former is identified with theological punishment, administered by divine authority. The latter is of a legal nature. Only the first is absolutely retributive, alien to any consideration of the criminal's guilt. The second, in contrast, admits of empirical and prudential considerations and is administered by human beings.

An argument, likewise counter to the existence in Kant of only a retributive basis to imposing punishments, may be extracted from a work which is not strictly penal. This is the "Introduction to the Theory of Law", more particularly, those passages dedicated to the right of necessity. As one of the cases, together with equity, which illustrate the right, there is what Kant calls "Mistaken Right" (*Zweideutigen Recht*). This consists in the "taking away of someone's life who has not threatened me always and only when my own life is in danger." An example might be a shipwrecked man who, in danger of death, throws overboard his partner in misery, to keep himself afloat and so to be able to save his own life. The curious thing is the justification Kant gives for such conduct. He does not consider it *exempt* from punishment (*inculpabile*), but rather as being unsusceptible to punishment (*inimputabile*). Kant treats it as an example of the non-imputable, not as a case of pardon or the right to grace.

Here we connect with the subject of the guilt principle in Kant's penal philosophy. Punishment is seen as the legal effect of moral guilt (*demeritum*). The evildoer must be judged as worthy of punishment (*strafbar*) or punishable, since he has deserved it by his conduct, always, however, supposing the crime manifests the requisite intentionality. For it to do so, it must satisfy a double demand. One is *imputation*, there must exist a sincere intention to carry out the punishable act. The other is that there must be *imputability*, this demands a balanced mental state when the crime is committed.[110]

110 *Cf.* Jeffrie G. Murphy, *Kant: The Philosophy of Right*, London, MacMillan, 1970. Wolfgang Naucke, "Le droit penal retributif selon Kant", in *Retribution et Justice Penale, Travaux et Recherches de l'Université de Droit, d'Economie et des Sciences Sociales de Paris*, Paris, P.U.F., 1983. Gioele Solari (1872-1952), "Kant e la dottrina penale della retribuzione", in *Rivista di Filosofia*, 20, 1929, pp. 25-58.

5.1.3 "Legal" Retribution. Georg Wilhelm Friedrich Hegel: Punishment as a Logical Necessity of the Dialectic Method. The Synthesis between a Thesis (the Law) and Its Antithesis (the Crime), the Negation of the Negation of the Law

Hegel's theory regarding punishment's basis only takes up but a small part of his vast work. It appears especially well-collected in his Legal Philosophy and shares a great many of the presuppositions of Kantian theory.[111] It is also a retributive theory, based on the equality relation which should mediate in the reparation of the crime.[112] Nevertheless, the Hegelian thesis is distinct from the Kantians' in regard to punishment, as they envisage an express denial of the need for an empirical equivalence between crimes and their punishments.

The unjust or illicit (*Unrecht*) reflects the antithesis between law-in-itself, which is the thesis, and the individual will. Within the illicit, what most interests us is crime. This is the most grave type of the illicit. The criminal act, or crime, "helps to polarize the natural individual will and the General Will, as embodied in State institutions."[113] The concept

111 G.W.F. Hegel, *Grundlinien der Philosophie des Rechts* (Berlin, 1821), Frankfurt am Main, Suhrkamp Verlag, 1978. There is translation into Spanish by A. Mendoza de Montero, in Juan Pablos Editor, Méjico, 1980. Also in México, UNAM, 1975. Buenos Aires, Ediciones Claridad, 1937; and translation into English by T.M. Knox, Oxford, Oxford University Press, 1962. Cf. also Jerónimo Betegón, *La justificación del castigo, op. cit.*, pp. 60-94. Samuel Walters Dyde, "Hegel's Conception of Crime and Punishment", in *Philosophical Review*, 7, 1898, pp. 62-71. Luciano Eusebi (a cura di), *La funzione della pena: il commiato da Kant e da Hegel*, Milano, Giuffrè, 1989. Ossip Kurt Flechtheim (1909-), "Hegel and the Problem of Punishment", in *Journal of the History of Ideas*, 8, 1947, pp. 293-308.

112 *Cf.* Ulrich Klug, "Para una crítica de la filosofía penal de Kant y Hegel", in *Problemas actuales de las Ciencias penales y de la Filosofía del Derecho. Homenaje al profesor L. Jiménez de Asúa*, Buenos Aires, Ed. Pannedille, 1970. *Cf.* also of the same author, *Skeptische Rechtsphilosophie und humanes Strafrecht*, Berlin-New York, Springer, 1981. Peter G. Stillman, "Hegel's Idea of Punishment", in *Journal of the History of Philosophy*, 14, 1976, pp. 169-182. F.J. Stawell, "Hegel's Theory of Punishment", in *International Journal of Ethics*, 7, 1896-1897, pp. 95-96.

113 L. Hinchman: "Hegel's Theory of Crime and Punishment", in The Review of Politics, 44, 1982, p. 541. Rolf-Artur Baermann (1948-), *Sittlichkeit und Verbrechen bei Hegel*, Frankfurt am Main, Lang, 1980. D.E. Cooper, "Hegel's Theory of Punishment", in Z.A. Pelczynski (ed.), *Hegel's Political Phi-*

of crime is the same as the act which comes from a free being, but which is an attack upon all free beings. The overcoming (*Aufheben*) of crime (*des Verbrechens*) is the re-establishment, the restitution, of law. This is achieved by punishment, the synthesis of the said dialectic process.[114] Punishment thus comes to constitute the annulment of the crime. It is the negation of the negation of Law, the harm suffered for the harm done, in the way of question and reply. Taking this proposition to its logical conclusion, punishment should inevitably follow crime, by its very nature and, so, in consequence, State intervention would not be needed to impose it from outside.

Going yet further, should we interpret Hegel's work literally, punishment should be included in the *right of the guilty*, a species of moral therapy, which would educate the criminal, giving to suffering a curative and expiatory effect, through which the criminal achieves repentance. The delinquent would here have a right to moral correction.[115] Yet, it seems strange to talk of a right that cannot be avoided, when one of the characteristics of subjective rights is that they are freely exercised. Moreover, we are here dealing with a right which in principle no-one wants to exercise. On the other side, as J.E. McTaggart points out, it appears improbable that the citizen of a modern State would come to admit a kind of moral magistracy on the part of the State organization, in a similar sense to the way a son respects his parents or the believer, his God. One should not confuse the Legal and Ethical spheres.

Another thing is that Hegelian punishment would be a *necessary condition for the existence of rights*. This is the idea that only when we punish certain forms of conduct do we admit the prior existence of rights which must now be re-established. This is to be found in relation to the distinction between *performative utterances* – of an operative

---

losophy: Problems and Perspectives, Cambridge, Cambridge University Press, 1971, pp. 151-167.

114 Heiko H. Lesch, *La función de la pena, op. cit.*, pp. 16 ff.

115 *Cf.* J.E. McTaggart, "Hegel's Theory of Punishment", in *International Journal of Ethics*, 6, 1896, pp. 479-502. There is a reviewed version in the work of the same author, *Studies in Hegelian Cosmology*, Cambridge, Cambridge University Press, 1918, chapter 5. Recently included in the compilation by Gertrude Ezorsky, *Philosophical Perspectives on Punishment*, Albany, State University of New York, 1972, pp. 40-55. There is a reply to this article by F.J. Stawell, "Hegel's Theory of Punishment", in *International Journal of Ethics*, vol. VII, 1896-1897, pp. 95 ff.

nature, that signify the carrying out of something – and *constatative utterances* – of a merely descriptive type, which limit themselves to expressing a "true" or "false" judgment about something. *Promises* would be utterances of the first type. These induce us to fulfil what we promise. *Orders* are another example. These lead to the carrying out of what is mandated, also *subjective rights*, which should grant the owner the possibility of their real putting into practice. In other words, certain states of things, to exist, require certain prior procedures. One of these proceedings is punishment, necessary for the existence of rights.[116]

In Hegel, the right to punish stems from respect for personal dignity and is a natural, inalienable and absolute right whose negation implies the negation of all rights and moral obligations. Here, we are dealing with a *mandatory right*, a right independent of any benefit whatever which its exercise may grant us. J.G. Murphy, when speaking of a right to be punished, does not use the term in a literal sense. It is rather an allusion to the fact that, via punishment, one receives one's just deserts, *what one has brought upon oneself* through choices freely made.[117]

5.1.4 Francis Herbert Bradley's Retributionism

F.H. Bradley was a XIXth century English philosopher whose inclusion here serves to complete our analysis of Kantian, Hegelian, pure retributionism. It is interesting to observe how he reveals his originality as a defender – almost alone on the Anglo-Saxon scene with the exception of perhaps the Idealists Bernard Bosanquet and T.H. Green[118] – of the retributive theory of punishment. Predominantly, this world had been for decades under the sway of ethical utilitarianism, empiricism and pragmatism.

Bradley's treatment of punishment offers support for the retributionist's stand if we concentrate our attention only on the first chapter of *Ethical Studies* (1876), his main work. There we find a strong criticism levelled at utilitarianism. These pages have led the likes of H. Rashdall, J.D. Mabbott or S.I. Benn to not hesitate in including Bradley amongst the unequivocally retributionist band of writers. Nevertheless,

116 Jerónimo Betegón, *La justificación del castigo, op. cit.*, pp. 80-81.

117 J.G. Murphy, "Moral Death: A Kantian Essay on Psychopathy", cited in Jerónimo Betegón, *La justificación del castigo, op. cit.*, p. 90, note 168.

118 B. Bonsanquet, *The Philosophical Theory of State* (1899), and *Some Suggestions on Ethics* (1918). T.H. Green, *Lectures on the Principles of Political Obligation*, 1885.

as J. Betegón remarks, it is difficult to deny that between this work and his "Some Remarks on Punishment" article there exists a theoretical abyss.[119]

In the article, Bradley evolves from retributionism to a defence of *social Darwinism* to justify punishment, alluding to natural selection within an antagonic existence, where the most inept, and incapable of social adaptation will be progressively eliminated. Bradley comes to this conclusion after the analysis of two possible types of retributionism. Thus, he distinguishes between *a normal growth* of the theory and *a diseased growth*. By a diseased growth of retributionism, Bradley means that understanding of the phenomenon of punishment which sees criminal conduct – totally or partially – as the action of a *morally diseased being*. A person lacking in the volitional capacity and who, therefore, can hardly be considered a moral agent. By this move, the idea of justice is relegated to a secondary position. *Justice is dethroned* and only, what Bradley nominates, the *principle of social surgery* can give an account of the nature and function of punishment. The surgery is conceived of as a means or, better, a remedial operation appropriate to the evil which society has suffered. Such terms remind us of medieval allusion to the death penalty as a remedy against disease when it amputates from the social body the infected member to sanitize the rest. Punishment is thus given the form of a *medicinal remedy that both benefits the criminal and protects society*.[120]

5.1.5 Contractualist Retributionism

According to retributionist doctrine, in primitive periods, man lived in a state which today we would call "natural", a state where each individual is guided by his own instincts and whims, obeying his personal satisfactions, not hesitating to hurt others in order to attain his desires. Life in

119 F.H. Bradley, "Some Remarks on Punishment", in *International Journal of Ethics*, IV, April 1984, pp. 269-284; also published in F.H. Bradley, *Collected Essays*, Oxford, Oxford University Press, 1969, pp. 149-164. Jerónimo Betegón, *La justificación del castigo, op. cit.*, pp. 94-113. *Cf.* also, D.J. Crossley, "Bradley's Utilitarian Theory of Punishment", in *Ethics*, 86, 1975, pp. 200-213. P. Johnson, "Bradley and the Nature of Punishment", in Anthony Manser, Guy Stock (eds.), *The Philosophy of F.H. Bradley*, Oxford, Clarendon Press, 1984, pp. 101 ff.

120 *Cf.* also, H. Rashdall, "Mr. Bradley on Punishment", in *International Journal of Ethics*, 4, 1984, pp. 241-243.

society was then a perpetual *bellum privata*. One of the main drawbacks to the state of nature was that there the strongest and most daring always prevailed, even if by tyranny and injustice, over the weakest and most cowardly. To avoid this unbearable situation human beings made a pact to set up authority and a *civil society*, yielding part of their original freedom in exchange for greater legal security. From this one may deduce that a prime object and essential end of punishment is the safety and tranquility of individuals and the re-establishment or reparation of the damage caused (by crime) to the commonwealth and to private persons. The pact, or social contract, is in the nature of a hypothetical or theoretical, rather than an historical, reality. In the State succeeding the pact, authority would have the right to punish, though only within certain limits, like that of the ban on an abusive exercise of the *ius puniendi*.[121]

Even in the state of nature, a *right to legitimate self-defence* when life was threatened would have existed. This was always considered an innate and inalienable right, given that it is subordinate to the instinct of self-preservation. However, it is not considered that the State's right to punish stemmed from the yielding up of this natural right. The latter is exercised *after* the offence, the attack, the crime, while the right to self-defence is exercised, and ends, with the counter-act against a physical injustice, and may not survive the immediate danger without losing its legitimacy. In effect, we recognize that, should the counter-act of defence go beyond its just limits, and is excessive, it comes to resemble vengeance more than right. The right to punish, then, cannot have its basis in such a natural right.

Further, the capacity to punish presupposes the right to command and cannot correspond to any one individual alone. Any other individual must be considered *equal* in the pact. Applying punishment perforce implies some *authority* encharged with doing so. Without this, the idea of punishment disappears, to give place to the idea of vengeance, once again. The state of nature is precisely characterized by the absolute equality existing between all men. It would therefore be absurd to talk of a cessation of a right which could never have existed, as is the case with the *ius puniendi*.

Finally, there are those who hold to a third contractualist formula. They maintain that individuals became aware that they lacked an author-

121 Manuel de Lardizabal, *Discurso sobre las penas*. Introduction by Antón Oneca. Madrid, *Revista Estudios Penitenciarios*, 174, July-September 1966. Madrid, 1967, pp. 78 and 79.

ity with coercive power over them, in order for them to live peacefully. In view of this, all signatories to the pact conceded to the collective the faculty of punishing them, of sanctioning them, should they carry out any acts contrary to the common good. However, again the problem arises that *then* man could not have transferred more than he ever had (the right to punish). Consequently, for instance, society would have no right, of an inalienable sort, whatever to take away any good from any man, more especially his very life. Over such goods, the individual himself, under the new notion of a punishing law, would have no right at all.[122]

According to this version of retribution, the contractualist, there would exist a tacit pact within civil society, within the State, geared to a just distribution of burdens and benefits amongst all members of the collective. In such a way, every legal system comes to have two faces. *For the majority* of its addressees, disposed to abide by it, it would appear as a compromise to *compensate them* for their abstaining from disobedience, by way of the punishment of the disobedient. On the other side, *for the minority* of potential transgressors of the agreed upon pact, the legal system would appear as a single whole comprised of *orders backed up by threats*. This contractualist-type argument grants some reasons for being faithful to what has been pacted.[123] There is a *prima facie* obligation to fulfil promises, and a tacit State compromise to redistribute goods, after their initial distribution, would see itself altered by any crime that might be committed.

5.1.6 Other Retributionist Theories

The retributionist concept of punishment had been openly theorized by others, even before Kant and Hegel. It had been expressed by Campanella, Selden, Leibniz and Genovesi. After Kant and Hegel, it was to

122 *Cf.* Juan Malvenda Campos, *La pena.* Memoria de Prueba para optar al grado de Licenciado en la Facultad de Ciencias Jurídicas y Sociales. Imp. Austral. Recoleta. 1935, pp. 62-65, esp. p. 64.

123 *Cf.* John Finnis, "The Restoration of Retribution", in *Analysis*, 32, 4, 1972, pp. 131-135. A.V. Hirsch, *Doing Justice: The Choice of Punishment*, New York, Hill and Wang, 1976, pp. 46-49. J.G. Murphy, "Marxism and Retribution", in *Philosophy and Public Affairs*, 2, 3, Spring 1973, pp. 217-243. H. Morris, "Persons and Punishment", in *The Monist*, 52, 4, October 1968, reimpr. in *On Guilt and Innocence. Essays in Legal Philosophy and Moral Psychology.* Berkeley. University of California, 1976, pp. 39-58. W.D. Ross, *The Right and the Good*, Oxford, Clarendon Press, 1965, p. 60. Jerónimo Betegón, *La justificación del castigo, op. cit.*, p. 84.

receive even more force by a considerable number of philosophers and jurists. Among them, we might single out: in Italy, Pellegrino Rossi, Antonio Rosmini, Terenzio Mamiani, Enrico Pessina, Tancredi Canonico, Giuseppe Maggiore, Giuseppe Bettiol and, recently, by Vittorio Mathieu. In Germany, we find Ludwig Heinrich Jacob, Julius Friedrich Abegg, Albert Friedrich Berner, Hans Welzel, Karl Binding and, in the first editions, the Treaty of Maurach. In England, there was the Victorian judge, James Fitzjames Stephen, and, in more recent times, adding to the anti-correctionalist tendency developed years ago in the United States under the name the "Justice Model", we find the liberal orientations of Morris, Hawkins and Fogel.[124] There are too the moralists of the "deserved-punishment" school like Singer and Dershowitz, and alarmists, like van Haag and von Hirsch.[125] In Spanish Penal Science, retributionist thought is represented by Cuello Calón, amongst others. Today, it is almost impossible to find retributionism in the strong sense defended by anyone. The idea of retribution pure, with no other end in view, is not defended, even though a retributive essence to punishment is indeed recognized.[126]

5.2 Deterrent and "Relative Theories". Deterrents as a Means to an End

The utilitarian and deterrent justification, of so-called relative theories, has its remote forebears in Plato, Aristotle and Epicurus. It develops as a legal and political doctrine with the Iusnaturalism and Contractualism of the XVIIth century, when the foundations of the Rule of Law

124 D. Fogel, *We are the Living Proof: The Justice Model of Corrections*, Cincinnati, Anderson Pub., 1975. Gordon Hawkins, "Punishment and Deterrence: The Educative, Moralizing, and Habituative Effects", in *Theories of Punishment*, Bloomington, London, Indiana University Press, 1971. D. Greenberg, "Reflections on the Justice Model Debate", in *Contemporary Crises*, vol. 7, 1983, pp. 313-327.

125 *Cf.* S.A. Lazaridis, « La rétribution dans la philosophie pénale anglo-saxonne d'aujourd'hui », in *Archives de Philosophie du Droit*, 28, 1983, pp. 91-108. Luigi Ferrajoli, *Derecho y razón. Teoría del garantismo penal, op. cit.*, pp. 255-256. José Antón Oneca, *La prevención general y la prevención especial en la teoría de la pena*, Salamanca, 1944. Johs Andenaes (1912-), *Punishment and Deterrence.* Preface by Norval Morris, Ann Arbor, University of Michigan Press, 1974.

126 José Antonio Choclán Montalvo, *Individualización judicial de la pena…, op. cit.*, pp- 57-59.

and modern Criminal Law were laid down by thinkers like Hobbes, for whom it was unnecessary to worry about any past evil, since we should rather bother ourselves with future good. After Hobbes come others like Locke, Pufendorf, Thomasius, Montesquieu, Voltaire, Beccaria, Blackstone, Filangieri, Pagano, Hume, Bentham and von Humboldt, whose names are linked to a conjunction of called-for, guarantee principles, such as that of natural law.[127]

5.2.1 General Deterrence Theories

A *The Goal of the Greatest Security for the Greatest Number of Non-Offenders: To Punish Less*

Amongst deterrence theories, we might distinguish between two variants. One seeks the greatest possible utility available to protect the majority of the people, which is made up of non-criminals. The other adjusts the end of punishment to the minimum necessary suffering which must be inflicted upon that minority formed by the criminal class. The first is called general deterrence and the second goes by the name of special deterrence.

"The Greatest Happiness of the Greatest Number" is the utilitarian political formula first proclaimed by Beccaria and later repeated by Bentham. An earlier inkling of the second version is found in Montesquieu's maxim "all punishment not deriving from necessity is tyranny."[128]

Taking the two variants together, we should have four groups of relative or utilitarian doctrines:

- Negative General Deterrence or *intimidation*. This assigns punishment the role of dissuading people through example and threat of punishment.
- Positive General Deterrence or *integration*. This gives punishment the positive task of reinforcing loyalty to the constituted order amongst associates.[129]

---

127 *Cf.* Manuel Ayo Fernández, *Las penas, medidas de seguridad y consecuencias accesorias..., op. cit.*, pp. 25-27.

128 Luigi Ferrajoli, *Derecho y razón. Teoría del garantismo penal, op. cit.*, pp. 261-263.

129 T. Hoernle, Andrew von Hirsch, "Positive Generalpraevention und Tadel", in *Goldtdammer's Archiv für Strafrecht*, 142, 1995.

- Negative Special Deterrence or *incapacitation*. Here, punishment has the negative function of eliminating or neutralizing the criminal, one way or another.
- Positive Special Deterrence or *correction*. This awards punishment the place of positively correcting the condemned.

B Main Jurisprudential Theories

a "Negative" General Deterrence, General Intimidation. Do Punishments Really Deter? Main Modalities

Negative general deterrence theories have the virtue of being the only theories which do not confuse the Legal and the Moral or the Natural, since they pretend to an axiological neutral proposition. In this, they directly connect with the Enlightenment tradition, which theorized with the greatest possible force the separation between Ethics and Law.

Within the doctrines we may make out two subgroups: 1) Theories of intimidation exercised by the generality of citizens, through the threat of the punishment contained in the law; 2) Those of intimidation also directed by all the citizens, but through example.

Before going on to analyze each of these outlooks separately, we might here plant the question, do punishments truly intimidate?[130]

It is difficult to deny, with any certainty, that punishment may intimidate, at least a specific sort of potential criminal. When the police go on strike, or when they are immobilized for one reason or another, criminality increases in a significant way. This is what we might expect. Would anyone suggest motorists would continue to respect parking regulations if there were no fines?

Our question is entirely other. Perhaps, the earlier affirmation is only valid for the majority of citizens, who, anyhow, are willing to obey the laws, but this may not necessarily be applicable to criminals. It may be that criminals are too impulsive, unpredictable and irrational to be frightened off by a distant and uncertain sanction. This too is true, to a certain extent. Were the world perfectly rational, threat of punishment and of penalization would be enough to dissuade everyone from committing evil deeds and crime. We live, however, in an imperfect, and none too rational world. Many people let themselves be carried away by the impulses of the moment and do not listen coldly to reason. This is why the effectiveness of punishment is limited. There will always be

130 Thorsten Sellin (1896-), "L'effet intimidant de la peine (Etude de Sociologie Criminelle) ", in *Rev. Sc. Cr.*, 1960, pp. 579 ff.

individuals capable of satisfying their desires no matter what the cost, never mind what the price they may have to pay.

At first sight, it might appear that some "punishment" or "exemplary sentence" should dissuade men from the commission of crime. Nevertheless, it is not so. It is not true that only the most severe punishments may intimidate. As they are only passed in extreme cases, potential criminals tell themselves, quite rightly, that such a thing will never happen to them. The greater the system's *regularity* in functioning when imposing punishment, the greater will its dissuasive effect be. That is why it is essential that the criminal should know that he will be tracked down and punished, that he should consider punishment as a kind of corollary to crime, necessarily bound up with it. Beccaria already held that "certainty of punishment has a greater value than does its severity." So, for instance, people feel more intimidated by a 10% probability of receiving a year's sentence than they do when there is a 5% probability of a two year stretch in prison. It is a greater terror to believe they are definitely going to be imprisoned, even if only for a day. Length of punishment has only a secondary importance. For the rest, from what is known of prison experience, what is hardest are the first few days and months, much more so than succeeding days and months. All the foregoing is not applicable to monetary sanctions, where people are much more sensitive to their severity – and their amount – than their probabilities. For example, we feel more intimidated by a 2,000 Euro fine, with a 5% probability of imposition, than we do by a 1,000 Euro fine whose probability of being effected is 10%.

Here, it is worth pointing out that *punishment frequency tends to diminish as severity increases*. Montesquieu already signalled as much. The law's atrocity is an impediment to its being carried out. Whenever punishment is beyond all bounds, impunity is preferable. Therefore, one should either punish often or punish severely. You cannot do both at once. At least, this is true for democratic countries. Laws considered too severe are rarely applied. The inverse is also true. Frequency of punishment will be increased when severity is lessened.

We might conclude, with Maurice Cusson, that the dosage of deterrent or intimidatory effect corresponds to a series of maxims:[131]

– The hierarchy of punishment. Severity of punishment should be graded as a function of the gravity of the crime.

131 Maurice Cusson, *Pourquoi punir?, op. cit.*, pp. 117 ff.

- Penal deficit. Punishment should cause the guilty party a greater amount of damage than the advantage he obtained from the crime.
- Length of imprisonment. Increase in length of prison sentence does not appear to produce any correlative increase in intimidatory effect.
- Fines. The higher the quantity involved in the fine, the greater will be its dissuasive effect.
- Deterrents. These have no notable intimidatory effect, especially upon recidivists.

1 Intimidation by "Threat"

The first aspect the negative, general deterrent goal may adopt is that of intimidation through the threat the Criminal Law contains. This is the view of the aim of punishment of authors like Anselm Feuerbach, Giandomenico Romagnosi, Francesco Maria Pagano and Arthur Schopenhauer. It is then substantially taken up by Carmignani, Francesco Carrara, and innumerable later jurists.

At first sight, it might seem trivial to assert that Criminal Law serves to threaten. In truth, any legal norm, not only criminal ones, is comprised of sanctionary efficacy, together with obligatory efficacy. The former is the imposition of a substitute sanction in case of nonfulfilment. Obligatory efficacy is the carrying out of what is ordered, or the omission of what is forbidden. To say that threat is involved is as obvious as saying that prescriptions are there to persuade. This is the practical function of all legal norms: to guide behaviour by establishing agreeable effects for behaving thus and disagreeable ones for failing to do so. Similarly, penal sanctions have incentive effects for prescribed, or permitted, acts, and disincentive effects for forbidden acts. We can even affirm that punishment is nothing but the disincentive effect imposed by Criminal Law to guarantee its own efficacy and to dissuade people from its breach. As a secondary norm, following the classic distinction, the penal norm always has as goal the securing of a primary norm or a norm of behaviour.

It might be objected, against intimidation by threat, that a similar end justifies punishment, as a way of guaranteeing penal prohibition efficacy, but it does not justify the prohibitions themselves. Still, it may be argued, in negative general deterrent through threat's favour, that it serves as a rational basis for Criminal Law's three guarantee principles, precisely because of its formal character. We here recall that these three principles are as follows:

– The Penal Legality Principle. This states that, if Criminal Law's purpose is to prevent crime, this must be achieved through the exact fixing of crimes "on the books" insofar as penal threat goes, given that only foreseen acts may be prevented and people dissuaded from doing them. Non-foreseen acts are not covered, no matter how injurious they might be.
– The Materiality of Crimes Principle. It is only possible to prevent the outward behaviour of individuals, not inner states of mind or subjective situations, such as dangerousness, malignity, infidelity, immorality or psychic-physical abnormality.
– The Personal Responsibility and Culpability Principle. Acts to be prevented by penal threat are only those that are conscious and voluntary. They do not include those that are not guilty because they are not intentional or those that are due to chance, *force majeur*, or, even, acts by third parties. It also completely excludes the punishing of the innocent.

Further, general deterrence, in its negative form, as threat to the collective, is aimed at the general population and not at every individual criminal in particular. Thus, equal or personalized treatment – having rehabilitatory ends in view, or individual or social therapy as a goal – is avoided. Avoiding these pitfalls, it avoids the danger of treating the criminal as a guinea-pig.

What is outlined above offers guarantees against *Criminal Justice terrorism*. Such terrorism is one of the drawbacks attendant upon negative general deterrence by example. Not all are advantages, however. Another type of danger looms. This is the danger of *Criminal Legislative terrorism*. Since the penal threat serves as a counter-stimulus, countermotive, or psychological coercion, it might be, erroneously, believed that it would be more effective the stricter the punishments it threatens are. This might lead to the imposing of draconian punishments, and even to a truly tragic extreme: the Death Penalty for all crimes. We should then never forget another, no less important end, than that of crime prevention, which must be served. This is *the prevention of excessive and uncontrollable punishments*. The potential damage of crimes prevented by punishment must never make us forget the damage punishment for the prevention of crimes may cause.[132]

2 Dissuasion by "Example". The Exemplary Punishment

Deterrent by example is present in the works of Grotius, Hobbes, Locke, Pufendorf, Thomasius, Beccaria, Bentham, Filangieri and, in general, the XVIIth and XVIIIth century Iusnatualists. The idea of punishment's exemplary role is subject to the Kantian objection, according to which no person should be used as a means to ends that are foreign to him. It makes no difference how praiseworthy they might be. From this viewpoint, the exemplary function idea as a justification for Criminal Law is expressly immoral. It legitimates punishments guided by the utmost severity. Above all, it allows punishments stripped of every certainty and guarantee. Some of these might be: *exemplary punishment*, or the *punishment of the innocent*, irrespective of who the real guilty party is. Such is the practice we find, for instance, in the case of the carrying out of reprisals.

Even without arriving at these extremes, deterrence by example may result in discretional and unequal punishments, depending solely on the amount of social alarm or political convenience that is floating around. Because of these social fashions, the condemned may be used as a scapegoat, under the Machiavellian principle that *the end justifies the means*. Reducing legal reason to political reason, or to "Reason of State", inevitably leads to *penal terrorism*.[133]

b "Positive" General Deterrence, Generic, Stabilizing or Integrating, Tending to Achieve Cohesion and Social Solidarity

Against the traditional idea of general deterrence, as the intimidation of potential criminals, there is a deterrence of positive affirmation of Criminal Law. It reinforces "the social conscience of the norm", by way of punishment, as Hassemer says. It "confirms the reign of the norm", echoes Jakobs, or it ratifies "an attitude of respect for law", in Armin Kaufman's words. Finally, it represents "an affirmation of basic legal convictions", as Mir Puig synthesizes.[134] Baratta says that we are deal-

132 Luigi Ferrajoli, *Derecho y razón. Teoría del garantismo penal, op. cit.*, pp. 277-281.

133 *Ibid.*, pp. 276 and 277.

134 *Cf.* Lorenzo Morillas Cuevas, *Teoría de las consecuencias jurídicas del delito, op. cit.*, pp. 25-28.

ing here with the re-establishment of confidence, and the reparation (or prevention) of the negative effects which the breaking of the law produces for the stability of the system, and for social integration.[135]

General positive deterrence theories are not exactly new. Precedents may be traced to James F. Stephen and Lord Devlin's *expressive* or *denunciatory* theories, or, above all, to Gabriel Tarde's late XIXth century *realist* theory. He speaks of the utilitarian basis of punishment stemming from the values socially attributed to the irrational factors of indignation and of hate provoked by crime and satisfied by punishment.[136] On the sociological plane, Günter Jakobs' theory really does not add much to Émile Durkheim's deviation theory. For Durkheim, punishment was a factor in social stabilization which acted on honest people, reaffirming collective sentiments and their solidarity as against social deviants. Perhaps, the difference is that Durkheim only meant to *explain* how punishment worked, Jakobs tries to *justify* it or axiologically legitimate it.

For Mig Puig, we must make a distinction between two positive tendencies in general deterrence theory:[137]

The Tendency to Broaden ius puniendi*: Hans Welzel and Günter Jakobs*

The most immediate of the first tendency may be found in Hans Welzel. For him, Criminal Law assures the positive nature of the ethical-social acts already in place. These are such things, for example, as respect for others' lives, for health, for liberty, for property, and the rest. Having such a role, *ius puniendi* sets out to punish any attempt at the destruction, or endangering, of the ethical-social conscience and the law-abiding attitude of citizens.

Günter Jakobs, in turn, considers the function to be the maintenance of the norm as a "role model" for all social relations. Jakobs takes

135 Alessandro Baratta, "Integración-prevención: Una 'nueva' fundamentación de la pena dentro de la teoría sistémica", in *Cuadernos de Política Criminal*, 1984, p. 535. Freud, *Totem y Tabu*, Frankfurt, 1981, p 40 ff. *Cf.* also, José Antonio Choclán Montalvo, *Individualización judicial de la pena…, op. cit.*, pp. 77 ff.

136 *Cf.* Gabriel Tarde (1843-1904), *Penal Philosophy*, translation into English by Rapelje Howell, with preface of the editor Edward Lindsey and introduction by Robert H. Gault, Montclair, N.J., Patterson Smith, 1968, c. 1912.

137 Santiago Mir Puig, "Función fundamentadora y función limitadora de la prevención general positiva", in *Poder y control*, 1986, pp. 51 ff.

his cue from Luhman's idea of law as an instrument of social stabilization, action-guiding, and reinforcing the institutionalization of expectations. Thus, punishment is seen as a cohesive factor in the social-political system through its capacity to restore collective confidence – once broken by crime – and through the law's stability and its ability to renovate citizen loyalty to institutions.

Welzel's vision, no less than Jakobs', in Mir Puig's estimate, tends to promote Criminal Law intervention by way of the positive, general deterrent. Doing away with *ius puniendi* limits will lead to legitimation and development of a crime policy lacking in democratic legitimation. Further, it will result in Criminal Law interference in matters of individual conscience, and this is clearly inadmissible.[138]

The Tendency to Limit ius puniendi*: Winfried Hassemer, Hans Zipf, and Claus Roxin*

Against this first tendency, Mir Puig sets forth the option of a different sector of legal opinion which, while sharing the basic ideas of positive, general deterrence, develops a limiting interpretation of general intervention.

Winfried Hassemer considers Criminal Law as affirming and insuring basic laws. This norm insurance may come about by the making of criminal, or aggravating, already existing penalties, but also by the decriminalization and the attenuation of punishment, by the simple conviction that such measures are ideal for improving social coexistence. Hans Zipf and Claus Roxin see things along similar lines.[139]

---

138 *Cf.* Hans Welzel (1904-), *Das deutsche Strafrecht: eine systematische Darstellung*, Berlin, de Gruyter, 1969; and, of the same author, *Abhanlungen zum Strafrecht und zur Rechtsphilosophie*, Berlin-New York, de Gruyter, 1975.

139 Winfried Hassemer, "Fines de la pena en el Derecho penal de orientación científico-social", in *Derecho Penal y Ciencias sociales*, Bellaterra, 1982. Hans Zipf, "Alteraciones dogmáticas en los fines de la pena de la prevención especial y de la prevención general", in *Estudios Jurídicos sobre la reforma penal*, Córdoba, 1987. Claus Roxin, *Iniciación al Derecho Penal del hoy*, translation, introduction and notes by Muñoz Conde and Luzón Peña, Sevilla, 1981. "Sinn und Grenzen staatlicher Strafe", in *Juristische Schulung. Zeitschrift für Studium und Ausbildung*, pp. 377-387; there is Spanish translation, "Sentido y límites de la pena estatal", by Luzón Peña, in *Problemas básicos del Derecho Penal*, Sevilla, Universidad de Sevilla, 1981. "Schuld, Prävention und Verantworlichkeit im Strafrecht", in *Fest.*

C *Main Representatives of These Theories*

a The "Psychological" Theory of Johann Paul Anselm Feuerbach

Below, we paraphrase and cite Feuerbach. For him, the State should serve as the medium through which it becomes psychologically impossible for the citizen to do harm; through which, the citizen is programmed to not break the law, to decide never to do so...[140] The only means open to the State to do this is by influencing feelings with feelings, and overcoming certain inclinations with contrary inclinations, the motive behind some acts with another, opposed motive. How all this is done is set out below. Man craves pleasure, avoids pain because, above all, he would shun unpleasantness, the which goes against his nature. Therefore, he would also cede something of happiness if this allows him to obtain more happiness somewhere else, he bears some small infelicity, should this help him escape some greater pain. Breaking the law is avoided if each citizen knows for sure that any infraction leads to a greater evil than would follow from his not having satisfied the urge which might lead him to break the law. How then is this conviction to be awoken in the citizen? Many theorists hold that the State has to cause evil (punishment) to dissuade people from other evils (crime). The possibility of punishment, once represented, deters people from crime. This is the belief of all who see the end of punishment as dissuading people from committing other crimes. This presupposes that the simple representation of punishment imposed upon some criminals will be, in effect, sufficient psychological motive for third parties to not commit similar crimes to the ones punished. Is a psychological motive at the same time a legal one? How can the right to impose an evil upon a man exist simply because the pain caused may be turned to advantage by the State? It would mean treating a man as a thing, for the criminal too is a man.[141]

Bockelmann, 1978, pp. 279 ff. There is translation into Spanish, "Culpabilidad, prevención y responsabilidad en Derecho Penal", in *Culpabilidad y prevención en Derecho Penal*, Madrid, 1981. Santiago Mir Puig, "Función...", *cit.*, p. 57.

140 Johann Paul Anselm Feuerbach, *Anti-Hobbes*, Huyesen, 1797; *Ist Sicherung vor dem Verbrecher Zweck der Strafe und ist Strafrecht Präventionsrecht?*, in V. Almendingen, Feuerbach, Grolmann (eds.), Bibliothek für die peinliche Rechtswissenschaft und Gesetzkunde, I.2, Herborn and Hadamar 1798, pp. 1 ff.

141 Feuerbach, *Anti-Hobbes, op. cit.*, pp. 40 ff., 43, 44 ff.

From this, it follows that evil's tie to crime has to be threatened by a law. The law is general and necessary. It applies to all, it threatens with punishment everything which is stipulated as punishable, and it sets up any punishment precisely because there now exists a law which is a necessary legal consequence of this particular crime. Whoever commits this certain action must suffer the punishment, nobody committing it should escape punishment. Crime and punishment are mutually conditioned. You cannot desire the one without the other. No-one may decide to act contrary to a law and not expect to suffer in turn some evil. The end of law, and the threat contained in it, is therefore the intimidatory effect of punishment which is intermingled with crime.[142]

The general deterrent that Feuerbach speaks of is then, at first sight, prevention stemming from punishment's threatening nature. So, his theory is rather a psychological one. It turns upon punishment threat by Criminal Law, more than being in itself a theory of punishment. Feuerbach seems to have taken his ideas from Fichte. By way of punishment, we should enable the citizen to obtain a counterweight to his criminal impulses. These must be overcome in such a way that arbitrariness becomes psychologically determined according to law. Feuerbach further binds together the basis and the end of punishment to State Security. He holds that to punish – with the single aim of causing harm to a person, to the detriment of his moral dignity – is, in reality, a right only God has. On the other hand, nobody at all has the right to cause damage with no motive whatever in view. He says: "Hence, he who imposes punishment degrades himself to the same level as he who is deserving of punishment". Feuerbach concludes that the objective of punishment can therefore be no other than dissuading others from committing crimes, from creating new crimes. It is necessary to seek to convince the individual that crime necessarily calls forth punishment, that a greater evil will follow any discontent he might feel at not satisfying his impulses towards breaking the law, to overcome his criminal impulses. He must then come to know that the threat of punishment envisaged by the law will be implacably put into practice. Law contains a threat; the exercise of law makes that threat a reality.[143]

142 *Ibid.*, p. 49.

143 Heiko H. Lesch, *La función de la pena, op. cit.*, pp. 23-28, esp. p. 25.

b Jeremy Bentham: The *Panopticon* as a Global Institution

The *Panopticon* or *Inspection House* that Jeremy Bentham designed in 1791 is considered by Michel Foucault as the true summary of knowledge-power principles.[144] It has the shape of a circular building, with individual cells all around the perimeter. The windows and lighting are such that the inmates can be clearly seen from the central control tower, though this remains opaque to those inmates. It is, thus, an architectonic form designed to individualize bodies and to make those bodies the constant subjects of the knowledge and the power of the authorities in the central tower. This constant inmate visibility and vulnerability induces self-control in them. Therefore, punishment becomes less and less necessary and is replaced by gradual obedience to the mandates of power. It gives way to a smooth yet effective domination structure, independent of the people making up that structure. Bentham, like the official in Kafka's Penal Colony, might say, with regard to his penal device: "Up to this point have I intervened, from here on the machine works alone."[145]

Similarly we might point up the parallel between Bentham's Panopticon and Erving Goffman's *Total Institution*. We might well wonder if the archetectonics, the Panoptic system, its principles, are not indeed the same as those behind the influential *Asylums* by Goffman. He speaks of *total institutions* which he defines as "places of residence and of work, where a large number of people in the same situation, for an appreciable period of time, share a daily routine, formally administered, while they are closed up therein." Goffman admits that prisons are a notable example of total institutions, though so too are other establishments whose

144 *Cf.* Jacques-Alain Miller, "La machine panoptique de Jeremy Bentham", in *Ornicar. Bulletin Périodique du Champ Freudien*, Paris, 3, May 1975. María Jesús Miranda, "Bentham en España", in *El Panóptico*, Madrid, Ediciones de La Piqueta, 1979. Walter Mutsumi Navakwe (1940-), *Punishment and Prevention of Crime in Jeremy Bentham's Thought*, 1983, Microform. Clifford D. Shearing – Philip Stenning, "From the Panopticum to Disney World: The Development of Discipline", in Anthony Doob, Edward L. Greenspan (eds.), *Perspectives in Criminal Law: Essays in Honour of John Ll.J. Edwards*, Aurora, Canada Law Book, 1984.

145 Franz Kafka, *En la colonia penitenciaria*, Barcelona, Emece Editores S.A., 1976. Enrique Eduardo Mari, *La problemática del castigo…, op. cit.*, esp. pp. 135 ff.

members have not broken the law. In this sense, he makes the psychiatric hospital his paradigmatic instance of the total institution.[146]

c Émile Durkheim: Punishment as a Form of Revenge Affirming Social Solidarity

According to Durkheim, punishment was *originally* the social reaction of a passionate nature which society – collectively or as a social body – exercised upon those responsible for a criminal act. Against the opinion of many modern theorists who see a rationally calculated social reaction in punishment, Durkheim highlights its passionate nature.

For him, only *later* does the law rationalize passion. When legal forms appear, passion is weakened, or, if we allow the expression, it is rationalized. This does not mean that passion disappears. Passion is of the essence of the reaction to crime. What happens is that advanced society Criminal Law tends to try to appear dispassionate. As a passionate reaction, punishment is a display of vengeance, both in primitive and in advanced societies. The difference resides in the rational canalization of vengeance.

The passion underlying punishment is not idle, but rather, is very useful, from the social point of view. The basic idea is that the criminal should come to feel shame at the crime he has committed. Should the punishment achieve this effect, his function has been fulfilled, since *shame* implies an internal transformation of the person guilty of crime.

For Durkheim, punishment's uses are multiple. They begin with the *expiation* involved in paying for what one has done. This is the prime function of punishment as passion: *he who does the misdeed must pay*. Through this, the victim or his nearest relations are satisfied. Together with this goal, another, perhaps more important, is to be found. This is the achievement of *social cohesion*, making for social defence, the which was attacked by the crime going against "decent people." Social defence is not better achieved by punishing more. *Trivialization* of punishment must be avoided, along with any disproportion between sanction imposed and damage caused.

Durkheim avers that Criminal Law has undergone evolution with the switch from a *repressive* system to a *restitutive* legal system. The former is characteristic of primitive, religiously-based societies. The

146 Erving Goffman, *Asylums*, Harmondsworth, Penguin Books, 1968. *Internados*, Buenos Aires, Amorrortu, 2nd ed. 1970. Enrique Eduardo Marí, *La problemática del castigo…, op. cit.*, pp. 191 ff.

latter is the hallmark of rationalist, lay societies. Added to the general evolution of law – from repressive to restitutive – Durkheim underlines two laws governing Criminal Law's evolution. The law of quantitative variation and the law of qualitative variation.

According to the first law, "intensity of punishment is greater the less advanced the type of society and the more absolute is central power." Punishment is more severe in societies not too advanced and in absolutist States.

Qualitative variation may be expressed thus: "punishments depriving people of liberty, and nothing else, for periods of time which vary according to the gravity of the crime, increasingly tend to become the standard type of repression." Punishments evolve from the corporal, of greater or less severity (the death penalty, mutilations) to the imposition of deprivation of liberty, as the main type of penal sanction amongst the repressive systems of civilized countries.[147]

5.2.2 Theories of "Special deterrence"

A The Idea of the Minimum Amount of Suffering for the Minority of Deviant Subjects: To Punish Better

Within deterrent aims, special deterrence takes as its target the specific, individual criminal. This is against the general deterrent that has the whole of society as its addressee. Special deterrence, then, acquires its utmost meaning when punishment is carried out. Here, the ideal is not the honourable and wholly humanitarian one of *punishing less*, it is rather to discipline and employ technology to *punish better*. To reach this goal, it sets out a disjunctive program: correction, for the reformable criminal, or elimination, for the incorrigible. Respectively, these twin prongs are known as positive special deterrence and negative special deterrence.

Special deterrence, along the double edges given, has its origin, according to some, like Foucault, with the opening of the Modern Age, during the Enlightenment. Nevertheless, others, like Luigi Ferrajoli, hold that Foucault's opinion stems from an error in perspective, and

147 Émile Durkheim, "Deux lois de l'évolution pénale", in *L'Année Sociologique*, 4, 1899-1900, pp. 65-95. Gregorio Robles, *Crimen y castigo (Ensayo sobre Durkheim)*, op. cit., pp. 88-124. Leon Shaskolsky Sheleff, "From Restitutive Law to Repressive Law: Durkheim's The Division of Labor in Society Revisited", in *Archives Européenes de Sociologie (European Journal of Sociology)*, 16, 1975, pp. 16-45.

that truly corrective theory and legislation did not grow up until the second half of the XIXth century. For them, it arose "parallel with the diffusion of organicist theories of the body social, healthy or sick, which required the clinical eye and the therapeutic experiments of those in power" to be tended correctly.[148] Enlightenment theories, in contradistinction, according to Ferrajoli, show themselves partisans of general rather than special deterrents.

B *Main Jurisprudential Theories*

a "Negative" Special Deterrence, Tending to Eliminate or Neutralize the Incorrigible Offender

Cusson refers to neutralization, basically by means of prison.[149] He says that neutralization should not be carried out except where it may be comfortably predicted that the miscreant will carry out new crimes when once set free. American criminologists have been interested for years in neutralization, but only under certain conditions. These are: when the neutralized criminal cannot be easily replaced within the group he consorts with; when prison is not able to exercise its "criminogenic" effect on him, and when he will fall back into his life of crime on leaving prison.

Neutralization also has its "costs." These are both monetary – it costs to keep him behind bars – and in terms of suffering – for both the criminal and those around him. Historically, neutralization has been a common practice. In all ages, there has been a desire to neutralize unruly and unpredictable individuals. They have been banished, mutilated, killed... Even today, the wish to put dangerous people at a safe distance is felt throughout all stages of the legal process: the police, the courts, and so on.

The question is: how to identify the future, recidivist risk that calls for neutralization in prison? Every individual is a world. There are no two criminals who are the same. American criminologists speak of "selective incapacitation" here. The problem turns upon the ability to predict, since prediction, for man, certainly has its limits. In this regard, two sets of conundrums arise: "false positive" ones and "false negative" ones. The former consists in predicting that an individual will commit crime again when, in truth, he will not. The latter is the contrary case

148 Luigi Ferrajoli, *Derecho y razón. Teoría del garantismo penal, op. cit.*, p. 264.

149 Maurice Cusson, *Pourquoi punir?, op. cit.*, pp. 117-150.

where it is held he will not break the law, when, in fact, he does. Given this panorama, the majority of criminologists are more preoccupied by imprisonment which could have been avoided than by crimes which might have been prevented. Problems of prediction error appear more chronic where violent crimes are concerned, not only because of their greater gravity, but also because they are more difficult to predict. Violent crimes are rare and, the rarer a phenomenon, the more unpredictable it is.

Criminal behaviour is neither totally predictable, nor absolutely unforeseeable. In the current "state of the art", "prediction tables" prove more useful than clinical experience, usually of some psychiatric kind. Prediction tables are devices which place various criminal group characteristics in relation to each other. Conclusions reached through these establish a set of general variables related to recidivism. They are:

- *Past delinquence.* Whenever a greater number of crimes have been committed by any criminal in the past, the greater will be the risk of future criminal acts. The past is indicative of the future. The more deeply-rooted a habit, the more difficult will it be to eradicate it.
- *Crime precocity.* The younger the criminal when he commits his first crime, the greater will be his tendency to break the law again.
- *Age.* The younger a delinquent, the greater his bent towards the commission of new crimes. With age, passions dim.
- *Instability in the work situation.* The more often a criminal has changed his job, the greater will be his tendency to future crime. People with a steady and interesting job have more to lose if caught "red handed".
- *Stimulants.* The more drugs or alcohol which a criminal consumes, the greater his likelihood of falling into the life of crime again. Excessive consumption of alcohol and drugs both destroys self-control and requires money to keep consumption up.

b "Positive" Special Deterrence, Tending towards the Re-Education of the Occasional Offender

There are individuals who do not fit the category of incorrigible criminals. In fact, they are the majority. With regard to them, positive special deterrence should be employed. Through this, re-education and social reinsertion of the correctable criminal is attempted. This measure is advisable for the greater part of common crimes, the majority of the perpetrators of which are often poorly socialized people. The re-education program is useful for them.

C *Main Representatives of these Theories*

In its present form, the ruling deterrence (as the end of punishment) methods stem from the Enlightenment, though later they yielded to XIXth century retribution theories. They re-emerged strongly in the last third of the same century. Three main currents may be discerned, each having a specific geographical location. They were: Correctionalism in Spain, the modern course heralded in Germany by von Liszt, and Positivism in Italy. What stands out in von Liszt is his tripartite division of punishments – the intimidatory, the correctional, and the inoculating. These he linked with three criminal categories – occasional, state, and incorrigible. Positivism in Italy tried to substitute deterrence for punishments. Finally, Spanish correctionalism, especially Dorado Montero's, attempted a Criminal Law that would protect the best interests of the criminal.

a Spain and Religious "Moralist" Theories: "Correction" or Moral Improvement of the Offender. Crime as Moral Pathology. There Are No Incorrigible Offenders, Only Offenders Not Yet Corrected. The *Poena Medicinalis* – the Medicine of the Soul. Pedagogic and Beneficient Conception

Moralist doctrines of corrigible criminal amendment, of course, are of ancient origin.[150] They are fruit of the spiritual idea of Man, inspired by Free Will, they develop this concept. They were already formulated by Plato and, later, taken up by Saint Thomas Aquinas. Prime amongst such doctrines is the *poena medicinalis*, following which, the State may not only punish the criminal, it may also force him to become good. This idea of punishment as pedagogy, not completely ignored by Roman Law, informs Canonical Medieval Law. It is also found in Thomas More, who on the threshold of the Modern Era, spoke for the first time of the deprivation of personal liberty as a punishment geared to re-education. The late Enlightenment Giambattista Vico, taking crime as the fruit of ignorance, differentiated between types of punishment to impose according to the prisoners capacity to show "shame" and to suffer pangs of conscience for their faults. While also assigning amendment as the aim of punishment, thinkers like Hobbes, Grotius, Pufendorf, Thomasius and Bentham, nevertheless are not typical of this tradition which is more closely linked to the Judeo-Christian, the Platonic, and the Medi-

150 *Cf.* Philip Bean, *Punishment: A Philosophical and Criminological Inquiry*, Oxford, M. Robertson, 1981, p. 47. Barbara Hudson, *Justice Through Punishment. A Critique of the 'Justice' Model of Corrections*, op. cit., p. 3.

eval ethos than to that of the Enlightenment. Punishment as a medicine for the soul is found in Thomas Aquinas and even before. Its roots are found in the Biblical idea of suffering as a means to expiate sin, and to reconcile Man with God. The same is true of the penitential and liberating force of confession, of repentance, of remorse, in the truest Jewish, Catholic, or indeed simply religious, tradition.

Such ideas see in punishment, more than an evil for which one must suffer, a medicine which may cure the soul, something beneficial for the criminal, with a teaching role. They regain vitality in the XIXth century, inspired by two modern versions of the theme. These are: the Catholic, held by Karl David August Röder, Vincenzo Garelli, Francesco Filomusi Guelfi, Vincenzo Lanza, and Francesco Carnelutti; and the Idealist, represented in Italy by Ugo Spirito, taking them up from Eduard Henke. All these ideas are salvaged from the drawback – outlined by Kant and often implicit in punishment – of treating a man as a means rather than an end. However, they do often suffer from the fact that they often bring trailing in their wake lugubrious ideas of a retributive hue regarding punishment. According to retributive theories, cure is only attained through pain – *non fit redemptio sine effusione sanguinis.*[151]

1 The *Besserugstheorie*. Karl Christian Friedrich Krause and Karl David August Röder

Correctionalist theory, as noted, arises in full bloom in the first half of the XIXth century in Germany at the hands of Karl August Röder, in his *Comentatio an poena malum esse debeat.* This, in turn, is inspired by Krausist philosophical presuppositions. Here, punishment is seen as:

> The rational and necessary means of aiding the unjustly predetermined Will of a member of the State to control himself, because, and insofar as, the disharmony which springs from his disorder wounds the entire organism of the State.[152]

151 *Cf.* Luigi Ferrajoli, *Derecho y razón. Teoría del garantismo penal, op. cit.*, pp. 265-266.

152 K.D.A. Röder, *Las doctrinas fundamentales reinantes sobre el delito y la pena*, translation into Spanish by F. Giner, Madrid, 1876, pp. 212 ff. Karl Christian Friedrich Krause (1781-1832), *Grundlage des Naturrechts oder philosophischer Grundiss des Ideals des Rechts*, Freiburg, Haufe, 2003.

For Röder, Criminal Law only rests completely satisfied when the outer damage caused by the disordered will, and the inner damage to the criminal himself, should have been totally repaired, in the one case, and extirpated, in the other. The criminal is viewed as a being incapable of making good use of his outer liberty. Therefore, he must be educated and morally reformed in order for him to regain that capability. So, the amendment correctionalism advocates does not limit itself to the mere external legality of acts, it would reach a legal and a moral reform by exercising a beneficial influence on the soul, the thought, the feelings, and the will of the condemned.[153]

2 The Spanish Correctionalist School. Francisco Giner de Los Ríos, Luis Silvela, Concepción Arenal and Pedro Dorado Montero

Correctionalist Theory had great repercussions in Spain. Giner de Los Ríos, Concepción Arenal, Luis Silvela and, fundamentally, Pedro Dorado Montero all take up special detterent ideas, though they do not see correction as the be-all-and-end-all of punishment.[154] The transforming thesis of the last cited author is notorious, with its idea of Criminal Law as law protecting the criminal.[155]

Dorado Montero said that the radical transformation which was to come in ideas of punishment, and, from them, in social life at large, would consist in totally abandoning punishing criminals and in never ever using punishment on them. This should be replaced by tutor-like deterrents.[156] For him, punishment is a means to social existence, but not a permanent one. It is only used in the current circumstances of

---

153 José Antonio Choclán Montalvo, *Individualización judicial de la pena...*, *op. cit.*, pp. 72-73.

154 Francisco Giner de los Ríos (1839-1915), *Estudios jurídicos y políticos*, Madrid, J. Casano, 1921. Francisco Giner de los Ríos, Alfredo Calderón, *Resumen de Filosofía del Derecho*, Madrid, V. Suárez, 1898. Luis Silvela, *El Derecho Penal en principios y en la legislación vigente en España*, Madrid, R. Fé, 1903. Concepción Arenal de García Carrasco (1820-1893), *Estudios penitenciarios...*, Madrid, V. Suárez, 1895. *Obras Completas de Concepción Arenal*, Madrid, V. Suárez, 1895-1929. Agustín Fernández Albor, "Los fines de la pena en Concepción Arenal y en las modernas orientaciones penitenciarias", in *R. E. P.*, 180-181, 1968, pp. 11-62.

155 Pedro Dorado Montero, *El Derecho protector de los criminales*, Madrid, 1915.

156 Pedro Dorado Montero, *Bases para un nuevo Derecho Penal*, Buenos Aires, Depalma, 1973, p. 8.

life. Once punishment can by replaced by more economic, milder, intelligent and efficient ways of dealing with the problem of crime, it will disappear, scorned as useless and irrational.

In a certain way, his thought may be considered utopian, that of a free thinker imagining a future by transforming the present.[157] This, however, should not lead us to disqualify it, for who can truly discern with exactitude what is realizable and what is not? Social reality is in constant change and evolution. Utopia, no matter how far off it may appear, presupposes the ability to see possibilities, to bring to light the apparently impossible, separating it from the possible, uniting dreams with reality, finally throwing light upon the validity of constructions considered by some definitive, knowing that man is the only maker of his own history.[158]

b Germany and "Finalist" Theories. Franz von Liszt in His Marburgh Program: Crime as Social Pathology. The Individualization of the Punishment: Ends Differ With Different Type of Offender

The majority theory points out that deterrent to future crimes, acting upon the criminal so that he will never repeat his crime, is achieved via a three-dimensional path. It should *correct* the correctable, what is known these days as "resocialization", and considered the most specific, and what special deterrent attempts to make the most constructive aspect of its task. Still, this is not the only role it has. It also *intimidates*, by the sentence, all who remain who may be intimidated. It *makes innocuous* and inoffensive those who are neither correctable nor open to intimidation. It does this by imprisonment and loss of liberty. Such possibilities are adjusted to the different types of criminal in the following manner:[159] for *occasional* criminals, not in need of correction, punish-

157 José Antón Oneca, *La utopía penal de Dorado Montero*, Salamanca, Universidad de Salamanca, 1950.

158 Ignacio Muñagorri Laguía, *Sanción penal y política criminal…, op. cit.*, pp. 109 and 111-113.

159 Franz von Liszt, "Die deterministischen Gegner der Zweckstrafe" (1893), in *Strafrechtliche Aufsätze und Vorträge*, 2, 1905, pp. 25 ff. "Der Zweckgedanke im Strafrecht", in *Strafrechtliche Aufsätze und Vorträge*, Berlin, 1905; 1970 (reimpresion). Wolfgang Naucke, "Die Kriminalpolitik des Marburger Programms 1882", in *ZStW*, 94, 1982, pp. 525 ff. Schöch, "Das Marburger Programm aus der Sicht der modernen Kriminologie", in *ZStW*, 94, 1982, pp. 864 ff. T. Würtenberger, "La doctrine de Franz von Liszt de la culpabi-

ment will be an intimidatory threat; for *habitual, incorrigible criminals,* punishment brings with it "innocuous-rendering" imprisonment for an indeterminate time, "penal servitude" (*Strafknechtschaft*); for *corrigible* law-breakers, punishment represents correction and resocialization. The typology already had its origin with Karl Grolman, at the end of the XVIIIth century, and was further developed by von Liszt in his famous 1882 Marburgh Program.[160]

The new emphasis displaced the deed done from the centre of Criminal Law. It surreptitiously came united with a fight against the short prison sentence which was ineffective as an educational measure, though good for the prisoner. Nevertheless, von Liszt never fought against the long prison sentence. For him, severe and continuous punishment must prove an aid for any criminal thought likely to commit crime again.[161]

Goal-oriented theory is less conditioned by philosophical presuppositons than are spiritual doctrines of amendment. It reflects the existing class-structure of society, without bothering to seek any axiological, naturalistic, or teleological justification for punishment. An obvious proof of classism is von Liszt's way of identifying "irrecoverable" types. He refers to them as the "proletariat", as "beggars, and tramps, individuals of both sexes, dedicated to prostitution and alcohol, crooks and lowlifes physically and morally degenerate." Von Liszt sees the "chiefs of staff" of this group as being formed by habitual criminals. The goal theory of punishment, or von Liszt's ends doctrine has exercised as great, or even greater, influence on European punishment theory than the other special deterrent speculations we have looked at. It forms the theoretical and programmatic basis for the International Criminal Law Union set up in 1889 by von Liszt himself, together with Adolphe Prins and Gerard van Hamel. The Union developed the principle of personalized and differentiated punishment up to its utmost consequences.[162]

---

lité et de la responsabilité pénale", in *Travaux du Colloque de Philosophie Penale (12-21 January 1959)*, Paris, Dalloz, 1961. Heiko H. Lesch, *La función de la pena, op. cit.*, pp. 31 ff.

160 Luigi Ferrajoli, *Derecho y razón. Teoría del garantismo penal, op. cit.*, p. 263.

161 *Cf.* José Antonio Choclán Montalvo, *Individualización judicial de la pena..., op. cit.*, pp. 69-71.

162 Luigi Ferrajoli, *Derecho y razón. Teoría del garantismo penal, op. cit.*, pp. 268-270.

1 "Individual Intimidation", For the Occasional Offender

Punishment efficacy must be measured, not only, nor even principally, by its influence on criminals – these, after all, are the people on whom punishment's threat has been wasted – but rather by its power over the great multitude of souls, hovering between vice and virtue, who determine their conduct by conscience. Here, we should point out that the majority of crimes are not committed by habitual or career criminals, but by occasional law-breakers. The point is to see how far the threat of possible punishment, the essence of Criminal Law, and punishment itself act as inhibiting effects when it comes to the commission of crimes. Do they really serve as elements of social control?[163] From this perspective, we might assert that the intimidation effect affects occasional law-breakers more than habitual criminals. It also works better with regard to acts of less importance – ignoring parking rules, say – than to grave infractions. Murder or sexual crimes, which ignite a burning social reaction, are, in spite of this, less susceptible to being put a stop to through general intimidation. The reason, or one of them, is that Criminal Law is the only social institution which reproves minor infractions, while the serious stuff is also open to reproach by other orders governing human conduct like Religion or Ethics.[164]

2 "Resocialization", Reinsertion and Re-Education, for the *Zustandverbrecher*. Differences between the Concepts of Reinsertion and Re-Education. The Problem of White Collar Delinquents

The question of resocialization raises another, that of the efficacy of punishment in the face of certain types of crime like, for instance, white collar crime. When referring to this, robbery, larceny and other of the classic crimes against property do not enter into our field of study. However, many white collar crimes do. Economic delinquency is, technically speaking, a species of white collar crime. Some authors even equate the two. *White collar crimes* are crimes committed by respectable people, high society individuals, in the exercise of their profession. They take the form of fraud, malpractice, monopolies, and the like rather than crimes of violence.[165] If the delinquents are "decent", "respectable", "well-

163 Ignacio Muñagorri Laguía, *Sanción penal y política criminal…, op. cit.*, p. 123.

164 *Ibid.*, p. 124.

165 Sutherland, *White Collar Crime*, 2nd ed., New York, 1961, pp. 9 ff. Richard A. Posner, "Optimal Sentences for White-Collar criminals", in *American*

regarded" and "economically stable", it would seem that, in principle, it would not be necessary to resocialize or re-educate them, unlike common criminals, who are often raised in marginalized environments, with a faulty upbringing within the lower-middle or working class. The paradox even arises where there is a kind of "Wild West morality", with its frequent individualist perversion that sometimes comes to consider these white collar crooks heroes. "Robbing the taxman is not like robbery at all" may be heard in the mouth of the man in the street.

Punishment in the face of economic crime therefore presents a debatable, ethical problem. Some actions, on the books as white collar crimes, do not meet with a strong enough general disapprobation: this occurs with tax fraud. In other cases, a civil or administrative sanction is considered as being more appropriate than punishment.[166]

While still little empirical investigation has been done into the necessity and efficiency of white collar crime sanctions, it appears that they are beneficial in the realm of general crime deterrence, and, though less so, in some aspects of special deterrent.[167] Criminal theorists deny the possibility of re-educating these law-breakers, mainly because they already have a high level of socialization.[168] They are well-educated people, "of respectability and high social status" (Sutherland), "well-to-do individuals" (Posner), "honourable gentlemen" of the best society.

However, should we consider that the relevant socialization, in terms of punishment, is not to know and practice table-manners to the point of perfection, how to greet people or how to dress, but rather the ability to live in society without grossly breaching its laws, we must then conclude that white collar criminals will have to alter their frames of mind, their *Gesinnung*. A person who has broken the law and is, hence, a criminal may well be formally adapted to society. On the other hand, a person totally outcast from society may very well break no law, commit no crime. In the first instance, *re-education* is called for. In the second, what is needed is *reinsertion*. The particular "re-personalization" of white collar criminals must be achieved by routes different from those

Criminal Law Review, 17, 1980, p. 409.

166 In Great Britain and Australia there have been critics to criminal penalty regarding the *antitrust* laws.

167 Antonio Beristain, *La pena-retribución y las actuales concepciones criminológicas, op. cit.*, p. 150.

168 Miguel Bajo Fernández, *Derecho Penal económico aplicado a la actividad empresarial*, Madrid, Civitas, 1978, pp. 81 ff.

followed in the case of common criminals. This could perhaps be by the shock and the "stigmatization" of a prison term, through the "blow" of a privation of a professional right or of personal freedom.

Not a few criminologists exist who reject prison for white collar criminals. A "professional" white collar criminal will behave very well in jail, but, once on the streets again, or in his office, with his cheque-book, then the old saying proves true "the Devil is a Gentleman." If, on the other hand, he is but an occasional or situational white collar criminal, then his falling back into crime will depend precisely on the occasion or situation, for as the old saw says: "the Devil makes work for idle hands." Nevertheless, prison is costly, especially for dealing with "educated" prisoners, whose psychic configuration, like that of their families, is especially prone to the serious prejudices which prison provokes in its inhabitants.

Fines, perhaps, would be better suited to white collar criminals. Why take away their freedom? Let them return what they have taken, and pay a substantially large fine. Thus we aid in diminishing social and economic inequalities. Or, if they are sent to prison, the length of time should be short, exemplary, but be accompanied by financial sanctions. In any case, the excesses suggested by the 1950-1960 utopian advocates of resocialization should be avoided, especially those of the North American school. This came to push for exaggerated prison sentences which would retain the criminal for much longer periods than the law stipulated for his crime, with the supposed justification that this would give time sufficient for re-education. It is essential to never forget that the punishment must never outdo the limit of guilt, no matter what the pretext might be in terms of "benefit" to the condemned.

However, while fines should probably be more often applied against white collar criminals than prison is, since they are less inhuman, more effective, and more fitting to their crimes, still, the risk is run that white collar criminals will benefit more, comparatively, by such measures than the common criminal. More fines should also be levied upon them, and fewer prison sentences. Another danger with "gentlemen" thieves is that they may hide their handsome stash either within the country or abroad, in order to thus annul the effects of fines. This might be solved by new legislation limiting banking secrecy. Insofar as concerns the drawback involved in the just "recompense" for fraud, where the fine imposed is of too small a sum, given the quantity of monies whisked away, obviously fines should be raised. Contemporary experts still debate a further problem, regarding the impossibility of imposing certain punishments on corporate bodies. This is solved, in part, by acting mediately against the representatives, managers, or personnel responsible for these entities, since they are the true agents of the crime.[169]

3 "Rendering Harmless" – Via Life in Prison or the Death Penalty – for Habitual, Recidivist Criminals. The Problem of the Incorrigible or Born Criminal: Does Such Exist? Cesare Lombroso's Thesis

Cesare Lombroso's specific contribution to criminology is his close observations of the criminal, the practical motivation behind his most important publication, *L'uomo delinquente*.[170] Following a study method similar to that employed when studying (other) "natural" objects, Lombroso believed he had "discovered" a type of abnormal human being, the "born criminal". He defined his specimens in predominantly somatic and physiological terms. By analogy with savages and "coloured" races, he explained their anomalies by "laws" of atavism and degeneration. This gave rise to a new pseudo-Science, Criminal Anthropology.[171]

Positivism, in its most grandiose version, that of Auguste Comte, attempts the investigation into all forms of human life and behaviour. It holds that social and psychological phenomena obeyed the same type of causal laws that were applicable to the natural world. This idea was taken up by theorists of crime, by politicians, and by Prison Administrations, in their attempt to lessen the crime rate. If human behaviour obeys causal laws, then, in principle, the causes of crime could be uncovered and eradicated. The most celebrated positivist criminological theories, for a time, were those of "atavism", as spoken of by Lombroso. Lombroso affirmed that certain people were predetermined to commit crimes since they were less evolved than other people. This was "evident" from cranial irregularities. By examining convicts, it would be possible to deduce which of them had such irregularities, in brief, which of them were "born criminals". These would be incorrigible wretches who must be imprisoned for long periods of time to prevent them causing harm to their fellows. They should be distinguished from people who were criminals because of "circumstances or by accident", and who indeed

169 Antonio Beristain, *La pena-retribución y las actuales concepciones criminológicas, op. cit.*, pp. 135-176.

170 Cesare Lombroso, *L'uomo delinquente in rapporto all'antropologia, alla giurisprudenzia ed alla psichiatria,* Torino, Bocca, 1878.

171 Fausto Costa, *Delitto e pena nella storia del pensiero umano, op. cit.*, pp. 198-202.

could be reformed. Though today the idea of finding cranial deformations might appear ridiculous, biological positivism has had a long and continuing history. Even now, we have certain difficulties in giving up the biological labels of the "natural criminal", we might, for instance, consider the fashionable XYY chromosome theory of the late 1960s.[172]

c Italy and "Naturalist" Theories of "Positivist" Punishment: Crime as a Natural Pathology. Substitution of Punishment by Deterrents

More radically, Italian positivist criminology did not only bind punishment to the dangerousness of the criminal, and assign to the binding thus formed an essential place for special deterrence, but it even, and in consequence, attempted a wholesale substitution of punishment by deterrents. This implied a renouncing of punishment's influence. Positivism denied that punishment had any effect.

Therapeutic theories of punishment, especially worked out by the Positive School of Enrico Ferri, Raffaele Garofalo, Eugenio Florian and Filippo Grispigni, also had an impact upon the English-speaking world. In particular, they affected Barbara Wooton and, even if based on different premises, the theories of the old Soviet Union. There are traces of such theories in the work of Lenin, of Evgenii Pashukanis and Petr I. Stucka.[173] Application of deterrents should serve a double function. They should "cure" the condemned and they should also segregate or neutralize him. The first is necessary because he is really a sick man, the second, because he also represents a threat to society.[174]

For such theories, the criminal is an anthropologically inferior being, more or less deviant or degenerate and, hence, any punishment must have a therapeutic and orthopedic function. The criminal is no longer a being endowed with Free Will, his behaviour is subject to a strong determinism. In this, he is equivalent to an animal whose conduct is at the mercy of the laws of natural necessity. Three main ideas are here intermixed: Lombroso's, Darwin's and Spencer's. They are: the "born" or "natural" criminal; species selection ("survival of the fittest"); and, society as a "social organism". The theories we shall examine hold that the State should exercise a scientific control more than a moral

172 Barbara Hudson, *Justice Through Punishment...*, *op. cit.*, pp. 7-15.

173 Barbara Wootton (1897-), *Crime and the Criminal Law: Reflections of a Magistrate and Social Scientist*, 2nd ed, London, Stevens, 1981.

174 *Cf.* Jose Antonio Choclán Montalvo, *Individualización judicial de la pena...*, *op. cit.*, p. 73-74.

inspection. Through medical practices of a therapeutic or surgical sort – hygenic-preventive measures, therapeutic-repressive measures, surgical-eliminative measures, according to type of criminal: be he occasional, passionate, habitual, demented or born – the State will handle crime.[175]

d France and the New Social Defence: Marc Ancel and His Differences with the Postulates of Filippo Gramatica

Modern School international relations led to the founding of the International Criminalist Association by Franz von Liszt, Adolphe Prins and Gerard van Hamel. From 1924 on, this was altered to the International Association of Criminal Law. On the basis of that, the Genovese Professor Filippo Gramatica created The International Society for Social Defence.[176]

Italy and France kept up the special deterrent orientation with this so-called "Social Defence".[177] In its birthplace, Germany, von Liszt's special deterrent ideas were the stars of a season, and then they were rapidly eclipsed by retributionism. In Italy and France, they dragged on. First, the more extreme version of Filippo Gramatica arose. He set out the motto, "not a punishment for every crime, but a measure for every person." He suggested substituting "antisocial behaviour" for crime, "danger" for guilt, and "deterrent" in place of punishment.[178]

This radical concept, out of Gramatica, implied an elimination of Criminal Law, for what would be left of it if crime, guilt and punishment disappeared? These would now be replaced by Social Defence, based on antisocial behaviour and its cure, the deterrent. The whole represents a serious threat to personal rights when faced with State intervention.[179]

---

175 Luigi Ferrajoli, *Derecho y razón. Teoría del garantismo penal, op. cit.*, pp. 266-267. José Antonio Choclán Montalvo, *Individualización judicial de la pena..., op. cit.*, pp. 73-75. E. Ferri, *Principios de Derecho criminal.* Translation into Spanish by J.A. Rodríguez Muñoz, Madrid, 1933, pp. 247-249. *Sociologia criminale,* II, Torino, 1930, p. 77.

176 Societé Internationale de Défense Sociale, «Programme Minimum de la Société Internationale de Défense Sociale », in *Cahiers de Défense Sociale,* 1973, pp. 23 ff.

177 *Cf.* Juan Malvenda Campos, *La pena, op. cit.*, pp. 69-70.

178 Filippo Gramatica, *Principi di difesa sociale*, Padova, Cedam, 1961.

179 José Antonio Choclán Montalvo, *Individualización judicial de la pena..., op. cit.*, pp.74-75.

This led to the eclectic, Parisian-directed movement of Marc Ancel. He maintained the Defence primacy of special deterrence, *but* still recognized the principles of man's responsibility and of his guilt.[180]

Deriving from Ancel's variety of postures perhaps, the New Social Defence defines or refers to itself as a "movement", refusing to make a School of itself, or to make penal practice conform to any unitary directives.[181]

e The U.S.A. New Penology

For the rest, purely pragmatic-style correctionalism experienced extraordinary good fortune at the end of the XIXth century, in the United States. This was quite independently of Continental European Culture. In 1870, the Cincinnati Congress announced the insensitivity of "determinate punishment". It thus opened the stage for the New Penology, based on the *non-fixed sentence*, on the putting forward of alternatives to imprisonment and, in the space thus cleared, introducing exemplary punishments. The judge could choose to impose stiff sentences or to waive sentence altogether.[182]

5.3 "Eclectic, Mixed" Theories

There have always been eclectic, intermediate or mixed theories of various kinds. Sometimes we find "additive" theories, limiting themselves to putting different punishment ends and functions in the "same pot" for everyone to take what he needs. This does not seem the ideal way of going about things since, without rhyme or reason, we are limited to juxtaposing punishment goals which often take off from presuppositions which are mutually incompatible. In Germany, such a mishmash is found in the Constitutional Tribunal. It is not consistent to affirm that the incompatible is really compatible, the result of the equation only disorganizes punishment's goals. These ends often collide, far from solving contradictions, a new source of confusion is introduced.

So-called "union" theories now arise, dialectic theories which try to unite positive aspects of different punishment theories in a higher

180 Antonio Beristain, *La pena-retribución y las actuales concepciones criminológicas, op. cit.*, pp. 60 ff.

181 Ignacio Muñagorri Laguía, *Sanción penal y política criminal..., op. cit.*, p. 211.

182 Luigi Ferrajoli, *Derecho y razón. Teoría del garantismo penal, op. cit.*, p. 269.

idea, eliminating the weaknesses of each, through a "complement and limitation" dialectic system.[183] Perhaps this is the case with the theory we examine below.

5.3.1 Guiding Idea: The Reconciliation of Punishment with Deterrents

Against absolute theories of retribution, and relative deterrent theories, be they general or special, we find so-called intermediate, eclectic, mixed, or "union" theories. These reconcile punishment and deterrence, together with all sanction aims, according to where they are applied. This tendency now appears uppermost in both current law, among experts, and in jurisprudence.

5.3.2 Main Jurisprudential Theories

A compromise solution was developed in Germany by Merkel, in his "Margin of Freedom Theory" (*Spielraumtheorie*). Here guilt serves as the limit beyond which deterrent ends may not go.

Mir Puig, investigating the German doctrine, sees two major branches, which we look at below. One is of conservative hue, and close to retributionist approaches. The other, of progressive colouration, approximates deterrent ideas. What is clear is that, today, there exist multiple tendencies within the eclectic, hard to classify, theories and they have an endless number of nuances to which all are susceptible.[184]

A The Conservative Thesis, Close to Retributionist Ideas

a The 1962 German Ministerial Project

The conservative thesis sees in retribution the foundation stone of punishment. Here, deterrent has but a mere complementary role. Retribution is prime. Such a position may be identified with the above Project.

b Hans Welzel, Reinhart Maurach and Hans-Heinrich Jescheck

Though not trying to restore the *lex talionis*, in this section, we include writers who could be labelled traditional. In Spain, for instance, the tradition is developed by, amongst others, Rodríguez Devesa, Rodríguez Mourullo, Casabó Ruiz, Sáinz Cantero, Landrove Díaz, Cuello Calón

---

183 Heiko H. Lesch, *La función de la pena, op. cit.*, pp. 41-42.

184 Lorenzo Morillas Cueva, *Teoría de las consecuencias jurídicas del delito, op. cit.*, pp. 31-34.

and Barbero Santos. In Germany, the advocates are Hans Welzel, Reinhart Maurach and Hans-Heinrich Jescheck.[185]

B The Progressive Thesis, Close to Preventive Ideas

a The Alternative German Project

The Nazi's manipulation of Liszt's ideas, and the later rise in fortune of retributionist movements as a reaction to that use, resulted not only in the eclipsing of Liszt himself, but also Germany's abandonment of special deterrent postulates in general. From the 1960s on, in Germany, a sector of criminal science began what has come to be called the "back to Liszt" movement. With this, the special deterrent returned and reached its apogee with the Lisztian-inspired Alternative Project. Still, it remains to be pointed out that this renaissance of special deterrent premises did not mean, for many of the authors involved in the Project, an adhesion to any exclusive idea of punishment as regards special deterrence. What it did mean was that such deterrence would be accepted during the executive phase of punishment.[186]

The German Alternative Project, devised by German professors, indicates a way for them to overcome the defects of the situation they then found themselves in. Bauman describes his intentions regarding sentencing in something like the following terms: Treatment is not imposed, it is offered. This is because treatment without the collaboration of the treated is a complete failure. The place where treatment takes place should be organized in such a way that a basic value is given to the decisions of the person detained, reacting against any bureaucratization of the centre, through prior conversations between the said detainee and members of the institution, after the manner of colleagues, as a team (never more than fifteen detainees at once), aided by psychologists, pedagogues, social workers, sociologists, and a legal professional. The inmate and the team may appeal to the directors of the centre. This procedure will produce more discussion than it will decisions. Still, within the centre, it will uphold the principle of liberty. In this sense, the detainee may decide, for instance, what to do with his spare time. The

185 *Cf.* Reinhart Maurach, *Deutsches Strafrecht: ein Lehrbuch*, Karlsruhe, C.F. Müller, 1954. Hans-Heinrich Jescheck, "Die Krise der Kriminalpolitik", in *Zeitschrift für die gesamte Strafrechtswissenschaft*, 1979. "Linee direttive del movimiento internazionale di riforma penale", in *L'Indice Penale*, 1979.

186 Lorenzo Morillas Cueva, *Teoría de las consecuencias jurídicas del delito*, *op. cit.*, pp. 28-30.

week will be 30 hours long, divided into 5 days. A minimum of 10 hours per week will be given over to therapy. Once half the sentence has been completed, there will be the possibility of deciding whether probation is in order. In any case, this must be decided once 15 years of sentence has been completed. In short, a very different institution to the classic is envisaged. There, it is hierarchy, authority and, come to the pinch, recourse to violence, to keep the institution going, which are the central concerns.[187]

b Eberhard Schmidhauser and Claus Roxin

While, as with any classification, it is open to debate, perhaps, here we might include, within this more progressive and deterrent orientation the Spanish authors: Antón Oneca, Cerezo Mir, Luzón Peña, Muñoz Conde, and Mir Puig. In Germany, the following deserve special mention: the contributions of Eberhard Schmidhauser and Claus Roxin. According to the last named, a series of stages or phases should be distinguished in the *iter penal*, a distinct function and aim of punishment corresponds to each phase. At the moment of legal threat, on the part of the legislator, general deterrent obtains. When applying or carrying out justice, sentencing by the judge, retribution is foremost. When executing punishment, the Prison Administration's task, then, special deterrent and tutelage of the condemned comes into play.[188]

1 General Deterrence in the "Legal Threat" by the "Legislator"

It must never be forgotten that punishment comes stipulated in law as an answer to crime. Even though punishment achieves its greatest reality in practice at the moment of its execution, the enormous importance of punishment as something normative must be underlined. Punishment's embodiment in the penal norm is a moment in its existence quite as real as the moment of its execution. Its norm presence is not purely static, but, in a way, impinges upon social functioning.[189]

---

187 Ignacio Muñagorri Laguía, *Sanción penal y política criminal…*, *op. cit.*, pp. 162-164.

188 José Antonio Choclán Montalvo, *Individualización judicial de la pena…*, *op. cit.*, pp. 85 and 87.

189 Ignacio Muñagorri Laguía, *Sanción penal y política criminal…*, *op. cit.*, pp. 124-126.

2 Retribution at the "Adjudication" of Justice by the Judge

There is a second stage to the application of punishment, in the *iter*. This is adjudication by the judge. This is when justice is carried out. Until now, this was just a simple general thing foreseen in the Criminal Law. It is here that retribution plays its central role. To any crime committed, a certain legal consequence, with a proportional criterion attached, is attributed. This is applied by the judge. Thus, retribution does have its place in the criminal law process. It is not to be understood in the primitive sense of expiation. It is, rather, a guarantee of legality.

3 Special Deterrence in the "Execution" of Punishment by the "Prison Administration"

Together with legal *pre-determination* (on the codes) and judicial *determination* (by the judge) of punishment, there is the third phase of the *iter* which is known as *post-determination*. This is the measure of punishment in its execution stage. Is it right to modify the length of punishment once within the place of punishment's execution? Is it lawful for the Prison Administration, or even the judge, to reduce or increase the sentence as a consequence of treatment's results? An answer in the affirmative would be possible if we postulate that the end of punishment is to re-educate the prisoner and to ensure his correction. Still, this goes against Criminal Law as a guarantee system, based upon the ten axioms we outlined earlier. Nevertheless, this is indeed the American New Penology's solution to our riddles. It advocates the *non-fixed sentence*. The point is, for instance, whether we should cut down the prison sentence if the prisoner repents, becomes a "new" person and no longer needs to be incarcerated. If the rule – rather than the exception – is that people change (amongst them criminals) with the passing of time, is it not more logical to reduce prison sentences, which anyway are destined to later be reduced at the executive stage? This would avoid the structural defect of excessively long prison sentences. What good does it do to make provision for very severe sentences in law if later they will be waived at the Administrative level where they are carried out, systematically and discretionarily waived there? Why would one promote punishment harshness when passing sentence and then indulgence in prisons? That is, between the *malum quod antea denunciatum* and the actual *impositum*. The coincidence of the two is a hallmark of legality principles, of certainty and penal equality.

The explanation of this apparent schizophrenia lies in the double end pursued by punishment. It wishes to be exemplary at the time of sentencing, but compromising when carrying sentences out. The first goal is met by the court's assigning harsh punishments. The second has to do with the good conduct which prison discipline imposes upon the prisoner. This latter is open to negotiation if the condemned shows signs of repentance, the which is necessary should he desire to benefit from reduction in sentence. This confers totalizing and strongly potent powers upon the prison institution. It becomes an immense and uncontrollable power. The organs responsible for the supervision of the conduct vital for living in prison thus are converted into a species of despotic referee, with limitless power. The prisoner turns into a mere thing, in the hands of other men, wounded in dignity, even if those controlling his destiny were the very wisest of men. Also, the condemned is deprived of all certainty of expectations, of any immunity from the arbitration of another human being.

6 The Clash or Struggle between Schools of Punishment

A group of writers, especially Italians, see two Schools of Criminal Law with two different general conceptions of the law, and different views as to its basis and goal, particularly. The Classic School is a partisan of punishment and of absolute theories. The Positive School is in favour of deterrents, and of relative theories. The reason we treat them separately here, though we have dealt with them briefly earlier, has no other purpose than to give some account, in a succinct way, of who the main representatives are.

6.1 The Classical School of Absolute Theories, in Favour of Punishment.Carrara

The Classical School is a consequence of the impassioned work of Beccaria. Through it, he gave birth to the "scientific" penal system, in full harmony with human rights' claims, thus re-establishing the dignity of the human being. In the process, he counteracted the excesses of primitive justice, dominant since Antiquity, and still living on into the Middle Ages. In Italy, within the Classic School of Criminal Law, we find Pellegrino Rossi's system, with its absolute basis of penal justice. We see Carmignani's thought on the subject, Antonio Rosmini's ideas, the polemic debate between Mamiani and Mancini, or the later development of the School with Carrara.

Carrara, chief exponent of this school, revealed the following as some of that School's prime postulates: The reason for, and the limits on, the State's right to punish; the guarantees claim to due process for the individual; and the opposition to the then barbaric punishments with which the criminal was punished. The Italian School's doctrines had an influence well beyond the Alps, in France and Germany.[190]

6. 2 *The Positivist School of Relative Theories, in Favour of Deterrents. Enrico Ferri*

The origins of the Positive School go back to Carlo Cattaneo and penal reform. Some of its main exponents are: Roberto Ardigò and Giovanni Bovio, with his critique of penal reason; Cesare Lombroso, and his study of the criminal; Enrico Ferri, on Criminal Sociology; or, Raffaele Garofalo, with his "natural crime" ideas and his biological concept of punishment.[191] Cesare Lombroso founded Criminal Anthropology. Enrico Ferri, integrating the data of Anthropology with those of Psychology and Statistics, identified the "Science" of Criminal Law as a branch of Sociology.[192] Raffaele Garofalo, one of the School's greatest writers, and an adherent of Lombroso's, also followed this line of investigation.[193]

190 *Cf.* Fausto Costa, *Delitto e pena nella storia del pensiero umano, op. cit.*, pp. 153-181. Juan Manuel Ramírez Delgado, *Penología. Estudio de las diversas penas y medidas de seguridad, op. cit.*, pp. 34-35.

191 *Cf.* Fausto Costa, *Delitto e pena nella storia del pensiero umano, op. cit.*, pp. 181-227.

192 Enrico Ferri (1856-1929), *Criminal Sociology*, translation into English by Joseph I. Nelly and John Lisle; ed. by William W. Smithers; introduction by Charles A. Ellwood and Quincy A. Myers. Pietro Nuvolone, "Le sanzioni criminali nel pensiero di Enrico Ferri e nel momento storico attuale" in *Revue Penale Suisse*, 1956, pp. 345 ff. And of the same author, "Il rispetto della persona umana nell'esecuzione della pena", in *Justitia,* 1956. "El problema de la reeducación del condenado", in *Revista Mexicana de Derecho Penal*, 1966.

193 Raffaele Garofalo, *Criminologia. Studio sul delitto e sulla teoria della repressione*. P. I, Chap. I, I. Ed. II, Torino, Bocca, 1891.

7 Different Conceptions of the State: From the Police State to the Welfare State. From a Culture of Subjects to One of Citizens

Within the family circle, we believe, the parents should prove friends, not merely guardians. We might say the same of the State, in light of historical experience.[194] In history, we witness the passing from a Police State, primarily, it seems, interested more in the pure pleasure of punishing and exacting retribution than anything else, to a State which cares for the criminal and tries, insofar as possible, to help him break from the vicious circle in which heretofore he has found himself. From a culture of subjects the way opens up to a culture of citizens, where there are not only duties – at basis, the duty to obey those in power – but also rights, conceded under the aegis of law.[195]

Once the "Police State" has been transformed into the "Welfare State", the citizen goes from being an enemy to the laws – an enemy who must be corrected so that he breaks the law no more – to being an individual in a difficult situation and who, in many cases, and precisely as a citizen, has a certain right to social re-incorporation, should he err.[196] Such a right comes from the contemporary State's obligation to assure citizens social participation in public benefits, and, among those citizens, the criminal.[197]

---

194 *Cf.* Fernando Falcón y Tella, *Tridimensionalismo y Derecho*, Madrid, Servicio de Publicaciones, Facultad de Derecho, Universidad Complutense de Madrid, 2004, pp. 35-55. Review by Juan Antonio Martínez Muñoz, in *Foro. Revista de Ciencias Jurídicas y Sociales. Nueva Época*, Facultad de Derecho, Universidad Complutense de Madrid, 0, 2004, pp. 317-320. *Cf.* Also, Fernando Falcón y Tella, "La familia, el Estado, la Iglesia: Pasado y nuevos horizontes", in *Anuario de Derechos Humanos, Nueva Época*, Madrid, Instituto de Derechos Humanos, Facultad de Derecho, Universidad Complutense de Madrid, vol. 5, 2004, pp. 189-215, esp. pp. 196 ff. José Antonio Choclán Montalvo, *Individualización judicial de la pena..., op. cit.*, p. 88.

195 *Cf.* Antonio Beristain, *La pena-retribución y las actuales concepciones criminológicas, op. cit.*, pp. 100-101.

196 V.A.C. Gatrell (1941-), "Crime, Authority and the Policeman-State, 1750-1950", in Francis Michael Longstrech Thompson (ed.), *The Cambridge Social History of Britain, 1750-1950*, 3 vols. Cambridge.

197 Ignacio Muñagorri Laguía, *Sanción penal y política criminal..., op. cit.*, pp. 136 and 137.

7.1 The Absolutist Theocratic State: Negative General Deterrence. Penal Terror

From before Ancient Rome's fall right up until the end of the XVIIIth century, the State apparatus adopted is the Absolute State. The main form of government is Absolute Monarchy in which there exists a king, monarch, or sovereign with absolute powers. He holds a supreme position, hence is he called Your Highness or Your Majesty. The title explains his position above the commonalty of mere mortals. This sovereign received his power direct from above – the theocratic theory of power. In the Middle Ages, he comes to be styled "King, by the Grace of God", monarch *legibus solutus.*

The State thus conceived was a power imposing Draconian punishments, based upon an axiomatic application of penal laws, *more geometrico.* Punishment was *the* principle sanction and the predominant goal of said punishment here was retribution. Negative, general deterrence played an important part together with punishment. This was the intimidation of the community so that it would abstain from committing any new criminal offences. In the service of this great goal, a whole system of gruesome punishments was installed. Anything went to achieve the final goal of putting an end to crime and of achieving obedience to the law. It was, in brief, penal terror. Any penal guarantee had to await the coming of the Enlightenment and the Rule of Law to establish itself in its different forms.

7.2 The Rule of Law

By the "rule of law" is understood that State construction where power, brute force, is subject to law. Law and power are in continue historical, dialectic combat. The rule of law adopts different historical guises: from the XIXth century Liberal State, passing through the Social State, to arrive at the Social Democratic State, by way of synthesis. All these are rule of law.

Each of the States mentioned, and examined in these sections, has presupposed some particular foundation as to Criminal Law and, in consequence, determinate ways of conceiving the function of punishment. This confirms the validity of the assertion: the foundation and end of State punishment depends on the function ultimately attributed to the State itself.[198]

7.2.1 The 19th-Century Liberal *Rechtsstaat*

A Thesis. Liberty. Formal Focus: To Remove Obstacles

After the fall of *Ancièn Régime* absolute monarchies, and after the French Revolution, there arose, as a theoretical construct and a political reality, the Rule of Law. In its first phase, this revealed itself as the Liberal *Rechtsstaat*.[199] As the name itself indicates, the ruling idea governing this is the liberty of all at all levels: economic, political, and constitutional. Matched, respectively, by: liberal economics and the Physiocratic School, Liberal Parties, and written Constitutions. The idea here is to seek for the maximum liberty possible only curtailed by respect for the liberty of all others. From this it follows that the axis around which all turns is the individual, the State duly limiting itself to "formally" guaranteeing respect for the rules of the game which will permit the exercise of the liberty of all. The State becomes a neutral, abstaining State.

B Preponderant Goals: Retribution, and General Positive Prevention

In the reign of Liberal Criminal Law, punishment was attributed both a prevention of crime function and a retribution for crimes committed function. Thus, there existed a discrepancy at the level of theory between two different currents of liberal thought: the preventionist, of utilitarian provenance, and the retributive, bound to absolutist ideas of punishment, basically Kant's and Hegel's.

7.2.2 The Social *Rechtsstaat*

A Antithesis. Equality. Material Content: Promote Basic Effectivity Conditions

The interwar period – that between the two World Wars which marked the XXth century – saw Totalitarianism become a major player. There appeared on the scene Italian Fascism, German National Socialism, and Soviet Communism. Having overcome this stage, after the Second World

198 Thomas Hill Green (1836-1882), "The State's Right to Punish", in *Journal of the American Institute of Criminal Law and Criminology*, 1, 1910-1911, pp. 19-43.

199 Jeffrie G. Murphy, "Retribution and the State's Interest in Punishment", in J.R. Pennock, J.W. Chapman (eds.), *Criminal Justice, Nomos XXVII*, New York University Press, 1985, pp. 156-164. "Retribution, Moral Education and the Liberal State", in *Criminal Justice Ethics*, 4, 1985, pp. 3-10.

War, there arose with Lord Beveridge the Social Welfare State. Now the State apparatus did not exclusively seek out liberty, via formal guarantees, but also delved into, and pursued, equality and a solid material content to such principles. It was not enough to solely remove obstacles nor to grandly proclaim formal equality before the law. It was also necessary to promote the conditions to make such liberty and equality an effective reality, in a proportional way, rather than in any uniform one, in order to compensate for real, inevitable, natural inequalities like the different share of talents, of luck, or those of social ones such as wealth. To gain this end, the State must intervene. It must be a "tutor" State.

B Preponderant Goal: Special Prevention

If Liberal Criminal Law allowed attribution to punishment both a deterrent and a retributive function (according as it served the empirical or the ideal man), Social State Criminal Law could do nothing else but confer a deterrent function on punishment. This deterrent aimed at fighting crime, combating delinquency as a real phenomenon of social existence, and aimed to effectively stop, on the plane of facts, a criminality which was on the increase throughout the XIXth century. This is the phase of special deterrence, proper to the Positive School, which favours deterrence over punishment.

7.2.3 The Social and Democratic *Rechtsstaat*

A Synthesis of the Above

Article 1°, 1 of the 1978 Spanish Constitution uses the expression "Social and Democratic *Rechtsstaat*" to define the model of State adopted by the Spanish *Magna Carta*. It is a State model which would unite the Liberal and the Social States, going beyond both. Doubtless, the Liberal State adopts the idea of the rule of law, that is, the demand for formal guarantees, certain limits to protect society from the State. If the principle governing the Liberal State was the limiting of State action, the Social State blossomed later as an active motor in social life, occupying itself, together with formal demands, with effectiveness of what was consecrated by those formal guarantees. We move thus from the impartial referee-State to the guardian-State. The former prides itself on its non-interference, typical of liberalism. The latter is the Welfare State, an interventionist State. Historically, the Liberal and the Social State find themselves in dialectic relation of thesis and antithesis. The Social Democratic State is the synthesis stemming from this dialectical process.

B Aims: Positive General Deterrence, Special Prevention within Certain Limits, and Retribution as a Guarantee

The interventionist principle which obtains in the Social State, might lead, as it has in some countries, to a Criminal Law more occupied in its own efficacy than with serving all citizens. Punishment is, at times, a weapon which the State wields against society. It then might produce efficacy, but also something not quite so laudable, penal terror. This is the danger into which might fall any Criminal Law aimed predominantly at efficacy. To avoid this risk, as with every dangerous weapon, punishment must submit to instructions for use and application, that is, within certain limits.

In a Social and Democratic State, in its Criminal Law, general deterrent should adopt two guises. They are: the intimidatory deterrent, also known as negative general deterrent, and the integratory general deterrent, also called positive general deterrent. General intimidatory deterrent should be limited. It must also set itself up as socially integrating, and then, general deterrence will necessarily appear as a stabilizing, correct form of intimidation and not as penal terror, more befitting an Absolute State of the *Anciѐn Régime.*

Democratic Criminal Law must always develop under strict subjection to the limits proper to the principle of legality, both in its formal as in its material mode. It should not only serve the majority, but also respect and take care of minorities. The dignity of the criminal must be respected, avoiding torture and the Death Penalty, offering the condemned possibilities for resocialization and social reinsertion, as laid down by Article 25 of the Spanish Constitution. No imposition of any one specific system of values may be pursued. Obstacles to social reinsertion, like criminal records, must be cleared away.[200]

8 Factual Plane. Critical Examination of Deviations in the Theories Considered in Light of the Facts

8. 1 On Absolute Theories

Critics of retributionism question its very presuppositions since it admits *free will* and this is an empirically undemonstrable and a meta-

200 *Cf.* Santiago Mir Puig, *Función de la pena y teoría del delito en el Estado social y democrático de Derecho,* 2nd. ed. revised, Barcelona, Bosch, 1982, pp. 19-43.

physical idea. It makes no sense to see retribution through punishing behaviour which no person can control and which carries him away deterministically.

Others place other retributionist postulates in doubt. Klug is a case in point. He questions the "categorical imperative" of Kant and Hegelian dialectic when they justify punishment. For Klug these are but *empty formulae* which contribute nothing, mere linguistic paraphrases: "'the negation of the negation' is but some linguistic structure, it is neither objective nor is it concrete." However, in a purely abstract order, any act, and therefore crime, implies "authorization for counter-change, or what is the same, makes this legally possible... this does not also, at the same time, make it normatively *necessary*."[201]

On the other side, it makes no sense at all to *add to the evil of the crime, the evil of the punishment*. Evil is only resolved by good, not by some counter-weight evil. Moreover, since *lex talionis*, no-one has yet found a formula to validly quantify the amount of retribution required.

Critics of retributionism not only question its presuppositions, they also throw doubt upon its pretended effect of being *legal security*, providing proportionality.[202]

8. 2 On General Deterrence Theories: The Offender as "Scapegoat"

Against general deterrent theories, many criticisms have been brandished. The deepest of these point out how they mean the instrumentalization of man, and the undermining of his dignity, when conceiving him as but a simple means to attain a useful end, as a scapegoat. The question then arises whether it is right to inflict an evil upon someone so that others will never commit evil. Is it right to punish one man not in consideration of he himself, but having a regard for others, even should the intimidation prove effective?

Pure, general deterrent could lead to a policy of State penal terror. Taken to extremes, we should face draconian punishments, with no consideration of guilt to act as a brake.

201 Ulrich Klug, "Para una crítica de la filosofía penal de Kant y Hegel", in *Problemas actuales de las Ciencias penales y de la Filosofía del Derecho. Homenaje al profesor L. Jiménez de Asúa*, Buenos Aires, Ed. Pannedille, 1970.

202 Borja Mapelli Caffarena, Juan Terradillos Basoco, *Las consecuencias jurídicas del delito, op. cit.*, pp. 37-38.

Another argument raised against general deterrent is that there exist many groups of both crimes and criminals upon which it has never been possible to test the general deterrent effect of the punishment. The average person, in normal circumstances, – he who least needs it – indeed lets himself be intimidated, but this is not true of other population groups, the authentic, potential criminals, like *professional*, paid criminals. They see punishment as a risk or a hazard of the trade. Then there are occasional and impulsive criminals, for instance, the individual who commits crime in the throes of passion, in the heat of a row, without stopping to think what the legal consequences of his action will be, nor what the gravity of the sentence that will be imposed on him might be. Something similar happens with those we consider psychopaths, incapable of feeling the psychological pressure of punishment, a punishment which may even exercise upon the perverse individual a *vis atractiva*. Think, for example, of Jack the Ripper or of serial killers. Much the same sort of thing might be said of other grave crimes. The criticism remains. Still, the ineffectiveness of punishment on certain criminals is answered on the basis that punishment's efficacy is shown precisely when dealing with citizens who do not commit crimes, for, without general deterrents, they might commit them.

According to current statistics, the true effect of Criminal Law's general deterrent, to be taken into account, does not depend so much on the gravity or severity of the punishment threatened by the law as it does on other factors, especially on how often the threat is made good in practical life, the knowledge that it will always be inexorably imposed whenever there is a crime committed. *A light punishment certain to be applied intimidates more than a potentially stiff sentence whose application is doubtful.* Social effects and consequences are also decisive factors for many – loss of employment, loss of reputation. Such things often increase efficacy in preventing greater crimes more than does the imposing of the punishment itself.

General deterrent is also criticized because it makes no provision for resocialization, re-education, and reinsertion of the condemned. It is too busy concerning itself with the effect of the punishment on the community to bother with the individual criminal.[203]

General deterrent theories are not, then, all advantage. The "positive" general deterrent, especially, aimed at producing social group soli-

203 Lorenzo Morillas Cueva, *Teoría de las consecuencias jurídicas del delito, op. cit.*, pp. 24-25.

darity and cohesion, has its drawbacks and dysfunctions. The price paid for solidarity through punishment is sometimes very high. With punishments, the group centres more on the law and considers it good without stopping to question what social interests it serves. What is worse, the criminal becomes a scapegoat and prevents people asking why crimes are committed and what the social conditions are that foster them. This can lead to *intolerance* which is always a potentially destructive sentiment and, taken to the limit, gives rise to that type of *fanaticism* where the individual believes that those who are not like him, and not like the majority, must be destroyed. The Salem Witch Hunts are a case in point. There we find a Puritanism and a self-righteousness that mixed together true elements of catharsis with collective hysteria, a fiery mix that is a permanent source of intolerance and divisiveness. *Social solidarity is positive, but not at the price of collective blindness, which so often accompanies mass phenomena*, because, then, what was functional from one standpoint becomes dysfunctional from another.[204]

8. 3 On Special Deterrence Theories: The Offender as "Guinea-Pig"

Special deterrence offers great advantages since it acts on the individual criminal, making possible, or attempting to make possible, that in future he will lead a life that is law-abiding. This is the idea of resocialization around which special deterrence revolves. This represents a humanization of punishment, aimed at a specific person and trying to reform him.

Not all are advantages, however, with the special deterrent movement. Against it, one might argue that it does not allow for any *delimitation* of the right to punish, since, if dangerousness is the decisive criterion when passing sentence, what may occur is that that might be great whereas the crime committed was minor. In such cases, the principle of guilt and that of dangerousness counsel entirely different measures of harshness. Something similar is true in the cases where resocialization is not possible, here, life in prison would be suggested by special deterrence. If the punishment imposed on the criminal must last until he is resocialized, the limits laid down by *ius puniendi* would often see themselves completely transgressed because the dangerousness risk would have it so. This would be a total breach of the principle of legality's fixing of margins, and of the principle of guilt, for punishment. *A sensu*

204 *Cf.* David Garland, *Punishment and Modern Society…*, *op. cit.*, pp. 76-81.

contrario, when grave crimes are committed, but the criminal does not have a high degree of dangerousness and is adapted "correctly", rigorously observing special deterrence, dangerousness and reinsertion as criteria, we should find ourselves with the paradox of not having to punish with a long sentence, despite the fact that the crime was very serious indeed, simply because we are dealing with criminals with a high grade of good adaptability.

Further, should dangerousness be the decisive factor, in cases where this obtains, in spite of the fact that no crime whatsoever had been committed, we could impose pre-crime measures, and this implies an absolute violation of the principle of legality too. It punishes for crimes not yet realized. Carried to its ultimate consequences, special deterrence theory seems to ask: "If a crime might be avoided and anticipated, why wait until it has been committed?" The answer should be that otherwise we act against the principle presumption of innocence and legal security. It would impinge upon respect for the individual liberties guaranteed every human being by the Constitution.

These doctrines, taking the State as teacher, tutor or therapist, and crime as pathology (it seems irrelevant to them whether this be moral, natural or social), are the most anti-guarantee and anti-liberal of theories. They justify models of Criminal Law tending to the limitless. The criminal's moral and inner freedom is badly perturbed, it makes little difference if by the priest or by the psychiatrist, while, at the same time, his body, his outside or physical freedom, is confined to prison. If treatment is not shared by the criminal, this, in turn, is an added affliction to his imprisonment.[205] Perhaps that is why treatment doctrines have their apogee in totalitarian regimes of the inter-war years.

Resocialization is an idea which is currently in crisis.[206] Alone, it cannot justify Criminal Law. Today, there is a debate over whether to abandon treatment and resocialization ideology. Many reproach the approach with being cowardly and ineffective, with regard to criminals

205 *Ibid.*, pp. 74-75.

206 *Cf.* Antonio García-Pablos de Molina, "La supuesta función resocializadora del Derecho Penal: utopía, mito y eufemismo", in *Anuario de Derecho Penal y Ciencias Penales*, 32, September-December 1979, pp. 645-700. And his *Estudios Penales*, Barcelona, Bosch, 1984. Francisco Muñoz Conde, "La resocialización del delincuente, análisis y crítica de un mito", in *Cuadernos de Política Criminal*, 1979; also in *La reforma del Derecho Penal*, Barcelona, Bellaterra, 1980.

that may put Society in danger. Others go further and assert that it really wants to regenerate souls and not only bodies in order to ensure the domination of men by the power of the system. What legitimates the majority's imposing its vision of things upon the minority of the population which deviates from such a vision? On what basis do we legitimate an attempt to influence the education and the fates of other adult human beings against their own wills? Why cannot people live in their own fashion at the edges of society? This is the general tenor of the objectors to the resocialization and treatment idea.

Going still farther, there are those who affirm *it is society which should be resocialized, eliminating the injustices found there, injustices which lead to infractions of norms.* Psychoanalytical theories consider punishment of criminals to be nothing more than a mode by which society turns them into scapegoats, into sacrificial victims, upon which the population can discharge its antisocial impulses and which makes up for people's not having committed the crime themselves.

In any case, the debate over the question whether we should resocialize for moral or for legal reasons remains open. Is it sufficient that the individual's outer behaviour does not contravene the laws, or is it essential to amend the inner sphere as well? Only Religion or Ethics may delve into such regions, and then only in a guiding fashion, never as externally coercive measures. To force moral reform upon anyone is incompatible with that most basic of all civilized values: respect for the human person. It certainly, irremediably, contradicts the principle of liberty and autonomy of conscience. The individual is sovereign over his own mind, over himself. Were it otherwise, then apparent philanthropy degenerates into iniquitous despotism.

Other correctionalist ideologies – Italian Positivist and the Marburgh Program differentiation, apart from the value of liberty – further contradict the principle of *equality*, when putting forth an idea of the criminal as an abnormal and inferior being. Taken to extremes, they result in inhuman doctrines like those of "breeding" or "eugenic elimination", based on the idea that the State should lend Nature a hand, and thus, together with natural selection, an artificial type of punishment selection, of some Orwellian sort. The theories in question strike not only at the values of liberty and equality, but also at the *dignity* of the person being treated and at one of the basic principles of the Democratic State, *tolerance* and equal respect for differences. They therefore violate the first right of every man which is the liberty to be himself, and to go on being the way he is.[207]

The attempt to inculcate moral values into the criminal is incompatible with a pluralist society. If we enforce religious codes and ethical beliefs we simply propagate the dominant system of values, which are not necessarily the best. It is a means of manipulation through power. We should not forget that Western societies, where we live, are, in the great majority of cases, bourgeois societies, where penal laws represent the interests and values of the ruling classes. The democratic idea of majority rule must be made compatible with respect for minorities. As Henry David Thoreau said, in his day, against a North American system which began an unjust war, "a majority of one who has more right on his side is already a majority one." Perhaps this is not the case in the majority of criminal acts, but, in a certain way, we should command sufficient flexibility to be able to put ourselves in the criminal's shoes, even if only hypothetically, in order to consider if we ourselves – having lived his infancy, had his lack of economic, family and educational opportunities – would not have reacted like him, pitting ourselves against the system. Sometimes legality can be unjust. Not all laws are just. There are legitimate occasions where the sufferer should object to an unjust law, or, if it comes to the crunch, even disobey it.

Over and against these extreme solutions, there are intermediate and conciliatory stands. For example, one writer proposes offering the criminal not moral suggestions and concrete values, in particular, but rather a "plurality of possible ways", the kind of plurality which can be found in any heterogeneous society. The offender could thus choose for himself. Along similar lines, others suggest social, emancipatory therapy, this would attempt to educate the criminal but without any indoctrination. Some object that such alternatives simply leave the offender to his own devices, that they are too liberal. They consider the delinquent to be like a child who needs to be guided in his steps towards resocialization because otherwise he would lose his way.

Another attack on special deterrence centres on the fact that it treats exclusively the subjective side, the inmate, leaving aside the crime altogether. Thus, it introduces a great deal of *legal insecurity* when not applying equal punishment to equal crimes, only concentrating on separate individuals. Possible *uncertainty* and *arbitrariness*, when at the

207 Luigi Ferrajoli, *Derecho y razón. Teoría del garantismo penal, op. cit.*, pp. 270-273.

mercy of psychologists, educators and psychiatrists may lead the prisoner to be treated like a guinea-pig upon whom new treatments are tested. Moreover, a treatment where the treated does not wish to be cured is nonsense, and a violation of the freedom of the individual who is now condemned to be helped.

Special deterrence, on the plane of reality, could open up penal practices and punishment models which might be limitlessly oppressive, paternalist, persuasive, forcing unwanted acculturation on the prisoner and violently manipulating his personality. Only think of what occurred in an authoritarian culture like that of the Nazis. Remember too the experience of Soviet penal, insane asylums and the re-education schools of China. These are the degenerate and abusive forms that special deterrent doctrine might take.

On the practical plane, as opposed to our theoretical investigations, it has been argued that resocialization cannot always be achieved, that it is utopian. Special deterrence then appears to us as ineffective to change reality and to attain its sought-for goals. Is it not unrealistic to imagine anyone will be resocialized in prison, which, rather than helping to this end, is often a school for delinquents and a place where he who tries to become "resocialized" is frequently attacked by his own companions? Further, even should the prisoner wish to co-operate and be cured, and even if prison conditions were in fact ideal, still certain means and personnel would be required which the penitentiary establishments simply lack. We are not, of course, talking about prisons having few television, games, and the like, as if such things were the main aids in resocialization. In prisons, there is too much bureaucratization and there are too few resocialization resources. The panorama offered by the jail of today is a desolate one, as regards resocialization, and much else. Prison is a "criminogenic" place. It incites to crime. Repression and education are incompatible postulates, in the same way as are deprivation of liberty and liberty itself. And liberty is the very presupposition and the ideal greenhouse for true education.

The resocialization idea should be re-worked to make it viable, for it is not a bad idea. Morillas Cueva puts it thus: "We must not fall into the schematism trap which demands a clean decision between resocialization, 'yes or no?', or between punishment or treatment. Co-existence is possible. The idea of resocialization should neither be extinguished nor mystified, it must only be relativized and hence adjust itself to social necessities". That is, it must become compatible with other, less oppressive instances of social control. It must employ social-political-style global means which would promise a juster and more egalitarian society.[208] For the moment, the only thing we may expect from the prison is that it become as little repressive as possible and, therefore, as little desocializing and anti-educational as possible.

8.4 On Mixed Theories

Critiques of mixed theories are born of the inanity of the mixed theory project, which tries to make retribution and deterrent compatible. Given that absolute theories and relative ones inhabit entirely different worlds – the former ideal, the latter, practical – their incompatible nature is directly obvious.

- Absolute theories stem from the demand for Justice, from the idea of punishment, within the theoretical-conceptual framework, and so, they are removed from the imperfections of the real world. Transforming their speculations into reality does not concern them.
- Relative theories come from the demand that punishment has to do with the human inclination to attack others – general deterrence – or from the need to counteract the deformation the individual undergoes as reflected in his crime – special deterrence. They always take reality into account, and its imperfections - that is, the question whether or not punishment really solves legal, criminal cases. This, for absolute theories, is an absurd question.[209]

208 Lorenzo Morillas Cueva, *Teoría de las consecuencias jurídicas del delito, op. cit.*, pp. 30-31 and 38-42, esp. p. 42. Borja Mapelli Caffarena, Juan Terradillos Basoco, *Las consecuencias jurídicas del delito, op. cit.*, pp. 40-42. F. Allen, *The Decline of the Rehabilitative Ideal,* New Haven, 1981. J. Andenaes, "The Morality of Deterrence", *University of Chicago Law Review*, vol. 37, 1970, pp. 649-664, reimpr. in G. Hawkins, F. Zimring (eds.), *The Pursuit of Criminal Justice,* Chicago, The University of Chicago Press, 1984. M. Anquetil (*et al.*), *La peine, quel avenir?: approche pluridisciplinaire de la peine judiciaire. Actes du Colloque des Centre Thomas More des 23-24 mai 1981,* Paris, Editions du Cerf, 1983.

209 Borja Mapelli Caffarena, Juan Terradillos Basoco, *Las consecuencias jurídicas del delito, op. cit.*, p. 43.

9 Normative Plane: The Aims of Punishment in the Spanish Legal System

9.1 The 1978 Spanish Constitution

Article 25. 2 of the Spanish Constitution reads:

> Deprivation of liberty punishments and deterrence are aimed at re-education and social reinsertion and may not consist in hard labour. He who is condemned to prison and serving his sentence enjoys all the basic rights set out in this Chapter, with the exception of those which are expressly limited because of the sentence passed, because of the sense of the punishment and prison law. In all cases, the inmate will have the right to remunerated work and to corresponding Social Security benefits. He shall also have access to culture and to the integral development of his personality.[210]

This constitutional intent cannot be interpreted as an irreflexive special-deterrent absolutism. The article cited does not annul the principle of guilt, nor special-deterrent ends, it only induces us to recognize special-deterrent aims in the carrying-out of sentences when these are socially possible.[211]
Other constitutional articles, conditioning the nature of State Criminal Law would be:[212]

- Regarding personal dignity, inherent rights, and free development of personality; Article 10.
- On punishment proportionality; Article 15.
- That punishments may not be inhuman nor degrading, and the prohibition of the Death Penalty; Article 15.
- Criminal Punishment not to be either moralizing or used to impose any determinate ideology; Article 16.
- Punishments limited to only he who is guilty, through his own actions; Article 17. 1.

210 *Cf.* Lorenzo Morillas Cueva: *Teoría de las consecuencias jurídicas del delito, op. cit.*, p. 43.

211 *Cf.* José Antonio Choclán Montalvo, *Individualización judicial de la pena…, op. cit.*, pp. 88 ff.

212 José Antonio Choclán Montalvo, *Individualización judicial de la pena…, op. cit.*, p. 89.

The constitutional proclamation in Article 25.2, on re-education and social reinsertion of the condemned, when putting people in prison and when applying deterrents, have been the subject of much debate. The ideas of re-education and social reinsertion have been subjected to severe criticism, because of their possible moralizing content, their tie to treatment ideology (therapeutic intervention in personality) or their tendency to refer only to the outcast criminal, and not to the socially integrated. In despite of all, we cannot ignore what is positive in these ideas, finally taken up by the profession, for they allow us to avoid a purely segregationist concept of the prison, they humanize punishment, and they allow institutions – prison substitutes or institutions mitigating the harshness of sentences – to orient themselves towards special deterrence. Such is the case with prison benefits.[213]

Constitutional limits upon deterrent ends must inevitably take off from public order and the Constitution's basic, organizing principles. Hence, first, we must look at Article 1. This sets forth the higher values of the Legal Code: "Freedom, Justice, Equality and Political Pluralism". Article 10 later establishes that "the basis of public order and social peace" rests on "the dignity of the person, inviolable rights which are inherent, the free development of personality, respect for the law, and for the rights of others". These constitutional principles imply, as a result, proportionality as a general deterrent limit, for otherwise penal terror could lead to the imposing of disproportionate punishments that would harm human dignity, to the extent that the prisoner would become instrumentalized, whereas man should always be an end in himself, not a means to an end, no matter how laudable that end might be. On the other hand, re-education and reinsertion may not be geared to achieving any change in the prisoner's personality. It is limited, no more and no less, to obtaining from him future conduct which will be respectful of the law and of the rights of others.[214]

213 Mercedes García Arán, *Fundamentos y aplicación de penas y medidas de seguridad en el Código Penal de 1995*, Pamplona, Aranzadi, 1997, Chapter II, pp. 31 ff.

214 Mercedes García Arán, *Fundamento y aplicación de penas y medidas de seguridad en el Código Penal de 1995*, *op. cit.*, pp. 35-38.

9.2 The 1995 Criminal Code

The promulgation of the 1995 Code, together with the derogation of the old Dangerousness and Social Rehabilitation Law (containing pre-crime deterrent possibilities), brought with it a considerable modification in deterrents.[215] From then on, the only cases where deterrent could be applied are those where "having committed a crime" (a post-crime measure), the author should find himself in a non-imputable situation, because of exculpating circumstances: like mental aberration or psychic alteration, of one sort or another, of a greater or lesser intensity, complete intoxication and alteration in perception which gravely conditioned his perception of reality. As an absolute precondition of deterrent application, then, the person must have committed some act on the books as a crime, when his dangerousness found outer expression, and where there is some high probability that he will commit future crimes – a *judgment of dangerousness.* This judgment goes along with a check on the relation between dangerousness and probable future crime – *dangerousness diagnosis.* The person must have been declared, at a judicial hearing, caught in one of the so-styled "dangerous states" which correspond to exculpation for mental or psychic alteration, intoxication or alteration of perception. The concurrence of the cited exculpations with the crime is a necessary, though not a sufficient, condition. A "dangerous diagnosis" is also required, as a something added. It is not enough that it be registered that the individual has committed a crime, and that his condition is covered by one of the above cases – either completely or partially – that admits exculpation, it is further obligatory to formally establish "criminal dangerousness" as a "criminal prognosis" of future crime. Moreover, deterrents may not be more burdensome nor of longer duration than is the sentence abstractly applicable to the actual crime committed. Neither must it exceed the limit needed to prevent the criminal's future dangerousness (cf. Article 6.2 Criminal Code).

According to Spanish Criminal Code Articles 96 and 105, a catalogue of deterrents applicable is as follows:

Depriving of Liberty Deterrents:

1. Internment in a Psychiatric Centre.
2. The same in a De-Habituation Centre.
3. The same in a Special Education Centre.

215 *Cf.* Gracia Martín (coord.), *Las consecuencias jurídicas del delito en el nuevo Código Penal español,* Valencia, 1996.

Non-Deprivation of Liberty:
1. Prohibition on residing or staying in specific places.
2. Loss of right to drive motor vehicles.
3. Loss of licence or permit for firearms.
4. Professional Debarment.
5. Deportation of non-legal resident foreigners.
6. Other measures listed in Article 105 of the Code, that is:
   - Obligation to reside in certain place.
   - Placement in Family Care.
   - Subject to some formative-style program, educational, cultural, professional, sex educational, and the like.

Despite all this, internment in some establishment continues to be the deterrent *par excellence* throughout European penal codes when treating those who have committed crimes but who cannot be held responsible.

The 1995 Spanish Criminal Code keeps the application of the so-called "vicarious system". This applies depriving of liberty punishment and deterrent together. It is used in cases where the agent is semi-not responsible and declared guilty of a crime. Though here there is diminished responsibility, the resultant punishment takes into account incomplete exoneration, but still is attended by the need to apply a deterrent which should accord with this semi-not responsible situation.[216]

9.3 Constitutional Court Case Law

The expressions "ends" and "functions" of punishment refer to not altogether equivalent phenomena. Each should be used on a distinct reasoning plane. The former indicates what the penal norm should finally and essentially "pursue". The latter is "how" to do this or how this should be done. The first is summed up as: punishment pursues as its end the avoiding of certain forms of human behaviour for the protection of certain legal goods. The second may be put thus: penal functions are general and special deterrent, in their positive and negative versions.

The Spanish Constitutional Tribunal itself is aware of these diverse planes and the terminological ambiguity when it points out:

216 Mercedes García Arán, *Fundamentos y aplicación de penas y medidas de seguridad en el Código Penal de 1995*, *op. cit.*, pp. 127-154.

> In effect, as distinct from what happens regarding those organs responsible for interpreting and applying laws, the legislator, when establishing punishments, obviously lacks a precise table to guide him in univocally relating means and ends. It is not only necessary to pay attention to the essential and direct aim of protecting what corresponds to the norm. He has other legitimate ends which he might pursue via punishment, and the legislator must also attend the diverse forms in which punishment operates, and these might be labelled its functions or its immediate ends (SCT 55/1996, f.j. 6).

On penal functions, a great part of constitutional case law has been taken up by interpreting the express constitutional declaration: "depriving of liberty punishments and deterrents will be geared to re-education and social reinsertion" (Article 25. 2). The lack of any other mention of punishment functions has presented the Tribunal with the question of whether such functions are the only functions constitutionally admitted punishment. This would imply that, for instance, punishment may only be admissible – or, at least, prison – for those individuals who require resocialization, and only so long as they needed it. Should this, perhaps, be the preponderant function, or is it, in any case, but *one* of the functions of punishment?

Another question thrown upon the Constitutional Court tapis, related to the foregoing, derives from the placement of Article 25. 2. The Article comes among articles dealing with fundamental rights open to constitutional protection, and, so, the question which presents itself is: does there exist a basic right to re-education and social reinsertion? If the answer is "yes", what would be the content of such a right?[217]

The Tribunal soon takes up these questions, and does so choosing a cautious reading, while, from the guarantee for the accused and the condemned point of view, it offers a restrictive reading of the precept in question. Synthetically, its interpretation is the following: Article 25. 2 "does not express a unique function for punishment, neither does it contain a pronouncement as to *the* functions of punishment. It does not contain a subjective right, but only a binding mandate directed to the penitentiary legislator and the Prison Administration as to how they should fashion the execution of a certain type of punishment, the taking-away of liberty. Nevertheless, this mandate does not imply that

217 *Cf.* M.R. Gardner, "The Right to be Punished. A Suggested Constitutional Theory", in *Rutgers Law Review*, 33, 1981, pp. 838-864.

every aspect of prison life must be ruled only or primarily by the resocialization mandate."[218]

10 The Axiological Plane: Punishment and Rights. Is there a Right to Punish?

It is held that the State has a *prima facie* obligation to protect the rights of those individuals which it governs, rights which may see themselves threatened by criminal acts. It is a *prima facie* obligation, too, to try, insofar as possible, to prevent these infractions before they take place. Still, certain principles exist which regulate how far this protection must be carried out. All individuals, including criminals, begin by being titular owners of rights such as those to life, liberty, property, amongst others. These rights are as much rights against the State as they are against other individuals. By virtue of these rights, the citizen also has a series of obligations towards others. He has, first of all, the obligation to respect their rights and to not disturb them. Should he fulfil that obligation, his own rights will remain intact. If, however, he does not fulfil this first obligation, he loses his own rights and the State may act against him. It may take away his liberty (prison), his property (confiscation) or, even, in specific cases, his life (Capital Punishment).[219]

All this notwithstanding, *we are under no obligation* to punish the law-breaker because he *deserves* it. Rather, it is a case of *having the right* to punish him because *some individuals* deserve it.[220]

Further, the only end that allows Humanity to interfere with the freedom of other men is self-defence. The only reason why he who may exercise power, in a just fashion, over other members of a civilized community, against their will, may do so is to prevent harm coming to oth-

218 Gonzalo Rodríguez Mourullo, *Delito y pena en la jurisprudencia constitucional*, Madrid, Civitas, 2002, pp. 104-115, esp. p. 106. José Antonio Choclán Montalvo, *Individualización judicial de la pena..., op. cit.*, p. 91. Mercedes García Arán*: Fundamentos y aplicación de penas y medidas de seguridad en el Código Penal de 1995, op. cit.*, pp. 32-33.

219 Wolfgang Naucke, "Generalprävention und Grundrechte der Person", in W. Hassemer, K. Lüdersen, W. Naucke, *Hauptprobleme der General-prävention*, Frankfurt am Main, 1979; there is a translation into Italian, "Prevenzione generale e diritti fondamentali della persona", in *Teoria e prassi della prevenzione generale dei reati*, Bologna, 1980.

220 Ted Honderich, *Punishment. The Supposed..., op. cit.*, pp. 158-169.

ers. The criminal's "own good", be it physical or moral, is not sufficient excuse for intervening. You cannot make him act in a determinate way simply because it may make him happier, or a better person, nor even because he might then be more prudent, wiser, or even more just.

Punishment immediately plants a question as concerns rights.[221] This problem might be formulated as follows: Punishment, by its nature, deprives someone of a right: life or liberty or property. How then can defenders of rights defend punishment? Is it at all possible to reconcile punishment, a violation of rights, with rights? Could there exist a moral right to sanction? Would this not, in fact, be the recognition of a right to violate rights? What of affirming, with Hegel, that the criminal has a right to the punishment which will allow him to reinsert himself in society? Might we recognise an individual right to restrict one's own rights?

On the other side, "what sort of right would the right to punish, and to be punished, be"? Would it vary, as a function of time, place, occasion contingencies, from one country to another and from one historical epoch to another, depending on the circumstances which surround the infraction? Does the delinquent *not* have rights, or does he have *some* rights, but not others, or is it that he possesses all rights, but they are in "suspension"? Has the criminal given up his rights, has he renounced them, have they been taken away by someone else, or are both these last things true?

Perhaps, the perpetrator of a crime agrees to his own punishment, giving the sovereign power the authorization to punish him (Hobbes). This would be as if, to not be victims of murder, we assented to die should we, in turn, ourselves become murderers (Rousseau). Thus we accept to subject ourselves to authority, be it that of the State or of some other body, and abide by its decisions. More, should we agree with some principle, later we can never oppose its application, no matter how negative the consequences of it might be turn out for us.[222]

221 *Cf.* Milton Gordinger, *Punishment and Human Rights*, Cambridge, Mass., Schenkman Pub. Co.; Morristown, N.J., distributed by General Learning Press, 1974. Graven, "La limitation du droit de punir de l'État par les droits de l'homme", in *Revue de Droit Penal et de Criminologie*, 1955.

222 Dudley Knowles, "Punishment and Rights", in Matt Matravers, *Punishment and Political Theory*, Oxford and Portland, Oregon, Hart Publishing, 1999, pp. 28-41. David A. Hoekema, *Rights and Wrongs: Coercion, Punishment and the State*, London-Cranbury, N.J., Selingsgrove Susquehanna Univer-

What would still exist in all cases is the right of the innocent to not be punished.

sity Press, 1986. "The Right to Punish and the Right to Be Punished", in H. Gene Blocker, Elisabeth H. Smith (eds.), *John Rawls Theory of Social Justice: An Introduction*, Athens, Ohio University Press, 1980, pp. 239-269.

Chapter V

Punishment in Other Spheres Distinct from Criminal Law

1 Administrative Sanctions

1.1 Administrative Law

The following principles should rule in cases of Public Administrative sanctioning:[1]

- *Legality and typified sanctions.* Public Adminstrative punishing power may only be exercised when such punishment has been expressly stipulated by some norm having the status of law.
- *Non-Retroactivity.* Sanctions cannot be back-dated. An exception is made here when an earlier sanction would prove more favourable to the breaker of the norm.
- *Guilt.* The demand for the guilt element in sanctioning crime is, with no doubt whatever, admitted in Criminal Law, but there are more doubts in the case of Administrative Law, in Spain, at least, since the Constitution is silent on the subject. Theorists have had to deduce the guilt demand from declarations in the Constitution made concerning the dignity of the person. Jurisprudence and the majority of legalists demand the concurrence of imputability and of dolo, or negligence, also in cases of administrative infraction. The two most important corollaries of the guilt principle are: the exclusion of objective responsibility and the non-qualification of the different administrative infractions attending only on the result.
- *Proportionality.* That an infraction of an administrative nature should carry with it much greater penal consequences to those belonging to the crime itself has long been a worry for legal professions. They have often pointed out that such consequences should not exceed the higher limit established for the faults.

---

1 Borja Mapelli Caffarena, Juan Terradillos Basoco, *Las consecuencias jurídicas del delito, op. cit.*, pp. 22-28.

- *Non bis in idem*. Application of this principle has three important effects:
  a) Administrative sanctioning must cede before action by the courts, and may not intervene until the courts have issued their findings.
  b) If the courts find there is a crime or a fault, administrative sanction is thereby ruled out.
  c) In the opposite case, the Administration must respect the declaration of the facts which arose during the trial, when acting *a posteriori*. This is because the State cannot admit any double evaluation, or discrepancy, concerning the same set of proofs.

Administrative sanction might be defined as: "any evil inflicted by the Administration upon an employee as a consequence of illegal conduct, established by administrative process and having a purely repressive end in view."[2] These requisites are almost always fulfilled in the case of *fines*. Apart from fines, the most frequent sanction, administrative punishment habitually consists of the *loss of rights* which is recognized, and regimented, in administrative ordenances themselves – loss of driving licence, closing of establishments, loss of civil servant career, temporary or permanent professional inhabilitation, and the like. Civil service and corporate sanctions are normally called *disciplinary sanctions*.

Administrative sanctions have a punitive character. They are one more manifestation of the penal power of the State.[3]

1.2 Tax Law

In Tax Law, there exist penal infractions – so-called tax evasion – which are open to penal sanctions, but there likewise exist administrative sanctions. Tax infractions are characterized in law because they are sanctionable even when they are simple *negligence*. This does not prevent people from committing tax infractions where greater guilt is attached to these same lesser faults – they may, for instance, include reckless carelessness or even malice.

2 Suay Rincón, *Sanciones administrativas*, Bolonia, 1989.

3 J.R. Parada Vázquez, "El poder sancionador de la Administración y la crisis del sistema judicial penal", in *RAP*, 67, 1972; "Evolución y constitucionalización de las infracciones administrativas", in *PJ*, 2, 1982.

The objective element in tax infractions is made up of *acts or omissions*. Tax infractions do not admit so-called imperfect forms of execution. The object of the act or omission is tributary duty: tributary credit, other money loans (like retentions or fractional payments), the duty to fill out tax returns, accountant dues, and so on.

Those subject to punishment, "infractors", are physical or legal persons who carry out the acts or omissions specified at law as tax infractions.

Tributary sanctions make up the *remedy* envisaged by the Legal Code for infraction of tax duties, which are essentially analogous to punishments applicable to criminal acts. This is as much because of the structure of the norms that go to make them up as it is of their goal and form of application. The nature of these sanctions is overwhelmingly *repressive*.

Different classes of tax sanction exist: 1) Monetary sanctions, generally fines. 2) Loss of rights sanctions, with an accessory character; they always accompany fines. Sanctions are gradable. They depend on the amount of good or bad faith shown by the tax dodger, on the repeated commission of the infraction and the amount of resistance put up, negative resistance to, or obstruction of, the Inland Revenue investigation. Such grading is of general application to all tax infractions. Specific circumstances of the infraction are also graded according to such things as the economic status of the offender, the amount of economic damage caused to the Tax Office, the spontaneous fulfilment of obligations and formal duties, their delay, and so forth.[4]

1.3 Labor Law

In the Spanish Legal Code, Public Administration intervention in labour relations is of long standing. Today, it takes many forms. Among its functions, inspection and control of fulfilment of labour laws, by those responsible for these, are to be noted. Applying sanctions to non-compliers is part of this task. Inspection is the responsibility of the *Inspec-*

4 Fernando Pérez Royo, *Los delitos y las infracciones en materia tributaria*, Madrid, IEF, 1986. Ramón Falcón y Tella, *Análisis crítico de jurisprudencia en materia de prescripción de las infracciones y sanciones tributarias*, Madrid, IEF, 1990. Miguel Ángel Martínez Lago, "Infracciones y sanciones tributarias (Derecho Financiero y Tributario)", in *Enciclopedia Jurídica Básica*, vol. III, Madrid, Civitas, 1995, pp. 3582-3586.

ción de Trabajo. A basic idea here is the "breaking of the social order." This can be subdivided thus: work infractions; social security concerns; employment and unemployment benefit control; and, also, emigrant and immigrant control, migrant movements and foreign workers. This means that the idea of social order infraction now greatly overflows the strict framework of labour relations. This is true as much in the sphere of what as of who it oversees. Today, it extends to social security relations, to co-operative work, and to working population movements. Infractions fall under three headings, according to their importance or gravity: light, grave, very grave. Parallel to infraction grading, we find the law dividing sanctions into light, grave and very grave.[5]

1.4 City Bylaws

Typical urban sanctions are fines. The quantity falls between minimum and maximum limits. Exact amounts here are fixed according to the general principle that urban infraction may never mean any economic benefit for the rule-breaker.[6]

2 International Sanctions

Nowadays, in Public International Law, there are two distinct procedures to assure norm efficacy. On the one hand, we find *individual* actions directly adopted by States harmed by international crime. These measures, called *auto-tutorage*, are proper to *decentralized* societies (of the past). On the other hand, there are *collective* measures, institutionally adopted. In contemporary international law, the term sanction is reserved for the second type of measure, applied because of a decision

5 Manuel Alonso Olea "Sobre la doble garantía material y formal para la imposición de sanciones administrativas a empresarios en materia laboral", in *Revista Española de Derecho del Trabajo*, 39, 1989. R. Escudero Rodríguez, "El nuevo marco legal de la potestad sancionadora de la Administración en el orden social", in *RL*, 11, 1988. Fermín Rodríguez-Sañudo, "Sanciones administrativas (Derecho del Trabajo y Seguridad Social)", in *Enciclopedia Jurídica Básica*, vol. IV, Madrid, Civitas, 1995, pp. 6060-6063.

6 *Cf.* Luciano Parejo Alfonso, "Infracciones y sanciones urbanísticas", in Enciclopedia Jurídica Básica, vol. III, Madrid, Civitas, 1995, pp. 3585-3589.

made by an international organization. This is indicative of the growth in international *solidarity*.[7]

International organizations with the ability to impose this type of sanction are those which have competence for the maintenance of peace and international security, that is, the *United Nations* and its *regional branches*.

Within the United Nations, main competencies fall to the *Security Council*, in cases of threats to the peace, breaking of the peace, or acts of aggression. This body may make recommendations or decide on the measures to adopt. Nevertheless, before making up recommendations or taking decisions, it may adopt provisional measures, such as a cease-fire order, retreat of forces to positions held on a certain date, and the like. These measures, prior to sanctions, seek to achieve the immediate and the minimum establishment of a state of peace.

Sanctions the Security Council may impose take two forms. First, there are sanctions which do not imply the use of force, they are of a political or an economic kind. They may take in the total or partial interruption of economic relations, and of communications: rail, sea, air, postal, telegraphic, and the rest. They may involve a breaking-off of diplomatic relations. Measures of these types have been applied by the Council in various cases, in the realm of international practice. We could cite the case of South Africa, as a consequence of its *apartheid* policy. Here, an arms embargo was imposed. The case of Rhodesia might also be mentioned, where steps were taken against the established rascist regime. On another plane, there was the armed invasion of Kuwait by Iraq. There is a long "and so on".

Secondly, the Council likewise may adopt sanctions which imply the use of force – by air, sea, or land. Here, we encounter such actions as demonstrations of force, armed blockades, and the rest.

The insoluble discrepancies between the old two superpowers – the USA and the USSR, in the Cold War epoch, and with their right to veto Council actions – led to a situation where the United Nations became inoperative for a long time.[8]

7 J. Lynch, "Crime in International Perspective", in James Q. Wilson, Joan Petersilia (eds.), *Crime*, San Francisco, CA, Institute of Contemporary Studies, 1995, pp. 11-39.

8 V. Gowlland-Debbas, *Collective Responses to Illegal Acts in International Law*, Dordrecht, 1990. J. Combacau, *Le pouvoir de sanctions de l'ONU (Étude théorique de la coercition militaire)*, Paris, 1974. María Paz Andrés

The United Nations General Assembly also has its competencies, though they are secondary, in the fields of sanction imposition and the making of recommendations.

A series of points on the subject of international sanctions arises which it might prove fruitful to examine. First of all, they are exclusively used with regard to violations of international norms of an imperative nature. These are things like acts of aggression, colonial domination by the use of force or serious breaches of human rights; this confirms the extant difference between international offences and international crimes. They are judged according to their consequences. In the case of the second, sanctions may be imposed. The first give rise to the simple obligation to repair the damage done.

Finally, the subject of sanction efficacy or obligatory force might be touched on here. From the strictly legal viewpoint, it remains for us to distinguish between when a recommendation might have been adopted, and when, a sanction. The first, as the name shows, is not obligatory. The second is.

One of the other greatest recent achievements, in the international sphere, is the growing determination to hold some of the worst violators of human rights personally responsible for their crimes. The arrest of Pinochet, the International Crime Tribunal for Rwanda, and the trial of ex-Prime Minister Jean Kambada for the crime of genocide, the criminal prosecution of Slobodan Milosevic, or the creation of the International Criminal Tribunal, are outstanding achievements and the clearest demonstration that no-one should be above the law, or beyond the reach of international justice.

It only took four years for a sufficient number of States to ratify the Statute of Rome of the International Criminal Tribunal, when even its most optimistic advocates thought it would take decades. Its becoming a reality in 2002 represented a major historical landmark. Still, the struggle must continue to make it a strong institution. The only power, the USA, and some other powers, have not backed up the Tribunal, have even employed active means to weaken it, perhaps fearing a decrease in their own sovereignty, and becoming scared at the possibility that their

Sáenz de Santa María, "Sanciones internacionales (Derecho Internacional Público)", en *Enciclopedia Jurídica Básica*, t. IV, Madrid, Civitas, 1995, pp. 6063-6065.

own leaders or members of the armed forces might come under an international jurisdiction.[9]

3 Civil Responsibility. Penal Clauses of Some Contracts

The legal consequence of penal infraction, an offence, or a fault, is the imposition of punishment upon the person responsible. For every crime or offence there grows up a legal action to punish the guilty party, but civil actions might also sprout to call for restitution for the thing done, reparation for the damage caused, and indemnity for the injuries sustained, by the punishable deed. On the other hand, a series of cases exists where a deed, described by the law as a crime or offence, gives rise to civil, not criminal, responsibility. On this subject, Article 1902 of the Spanish Civil Code says: "He who causes harm by act or omission to another, where there is guilt or negligence, is obliged to repair the damage caused". Civil responsibility takes in: 1. Restitution. 2. Reparation of damage caused. 3. Indemnity for injuries.

In the demand for civil responsibility springing from crime, two possibilities are open: sueing for a civil action independently of the criminal, in some other trial, or taking the civil and the criminal in one trial together. The latter is the course pursued in Spain. Thus, Article 1902 says: "Civil obligations stemming from crimes or offences are governed by the Criminal Code." However, this treating of both aspects together does not cause confusion. As legal professionals point out, the private nature of civil responsibility is shown as much in its renouncability, as in its "ultra-personal" character. It allows for situations unthinkable in Criminal Law. The Private Law aspect of civil responsibility reveals itself in that it is transmissible to heirs of the person responsible and, equally, to heirs of the injured party. This is in complete contrast to Criminal Law and the public nature of punishment.

9 Paul Gordon Lauren, "Nuevos retos para los derechos humanos. El futuro a la luz del pasado", in *Anuario de Derechos Humanos, Nueva Época*, t. V, Instituto de Derechos Humanos, UCM, 2004, pp. 369-386, esp. pp. 372-375. Lecture delivered in the II Jornadas Internacionales "Nuevos retos de los derechos humanos", organized by the Instituto de Derechos Humanos of the Facultad de Derecho of the Universidad Complutense of Madrid, in November 2003. Translation into Spanish from the English original, "New Challenges for Human Rights: The Future in Light of the Past", by Fernando Falcón y Tella.

In Civil Law, we also find so-called contractual responsibility. This is a remedy the creditor may count on when a debtor does not pay. Its keynote is that it requires that the failure to pay back the debt has caused the creditor harm and that the debtor should then be subjectively chargeable.

Punishment is also to be found, outside Criminal Law, in certain penal clauses attached to specific contracts.[10]

10 J.M. Reyes Monterreal, *Acción y responsabilidad civil derivada de delitos y faltas,* Madrid, 1958. Enrique Ruíz Vadillo, "Responsabilidad civil (art. 20 del Código Penal)", in *Comentarios a la Legislación Penal*, V, I, Madrid, Edersa, 1985. F. Soto Nieto, *La responsabilidad civil derivada del ilícito culposo*, Madrid, 1982. José María Luzón Cuesta, "Responsabilidad civil por delito (Derecho Penal)", in *Enciclopedia Jurídica Básica,* t. IV, Madrid, Civitas, 1995, pp. 5916-5922. Fernando Pantaleón Prieto, "Responsabilidad contractual (Derecho Civil)", in *Enciclopedia Jurídica Básica*, t. IV, *op. cit.*, pp. 5922-5927.

Chapter VI

Conclusions

1 Dialectic and Reconciliation of Ends

As with many fields of study, a suitable answer to what should be the foundations and ends of punishment does not admit of one single, unique answer. There is no simple objective that might be valid for "the right to punish". Retribution – not in its metaphysical and archaic sense, but rather as a presupposition and limit of *ius puniendi* – should be combined with general and special prevention objectives. Even something so laudable, at first sight, as the goal of resocialization must be subject to certain limitations if we do not wish to fall into therapeutic abuses.

Once again, the key word is the noun *dialectic*. Indeed, rather than looking in one single direction, the field of vision must be widened in order to see that we are facing a complex problem which demands equally complex solutions. Further, the answers and the conciliatory solutions of various schools should not limit themselves to pigeonholing their projects. They must use them as poles in continuous struggle and interchange. That is, in a dialectical fashion. From the opposition to contraries comes forth synthesis which, in turn, will not be static and definitive, given once and for all, but open to revision and always willing to incorporate new perspectives and new emphases. Hence, in this book, we have analyzed the subject of punishment in various disciplines and branches of knowledge, not limiting ourselves to the legal nor, with the legal, to Criminal Law.

2 Resocialization of Society and Not Desocialization of the Offender

Criminological, secular evolution reveals that the perfection of Criminal Law does not consist in the *abolition* and *negation* of punishment, as might at first appear. Rather, it consists in its *sublimation*, *elevation*, and *betterment*. This is the same as occurs in the field of psychology. Traumas are not avoided, they are resolved. The best way to resolve them is not by denying their existence but by overcoming them once clear note has been taken of their existence. There will always be criminals, there will always be punishment for them. The level to which penology may aspire does not depend on the quantitative volume of its application. That is determined by outside factors, such as criminality. The important thing is the qualitative aspect of punishment. Punishment should be clear-cut and final. Its ends should be adapted to the higher ideal of Justice. One must aim at a greater *personalization* of punishment that would insist upon special prevention.[1]

3 The Value of Conflict

It is important to *not* presuppose that all conflicts must necessarily, always, be resolved. The search for a once-and-for-all solution is an ethnocentric Puritan idea. A majority of people fervently adhere to this idea that all conflicts can be resolved. A step forward, albeit it a small one, would be to speak of *conflict management.* Conflicts may be resolved, but one may also learn to live with them. A higher step still would be where one could talk of *being concerned about conflict. Active participation in conflict* might perhaps be a more suitable phrase, since this places the accent more than on results on the simple act. "Winning is not the important thing, the important thing is to take part."

As Durkheim would say, "Criminality is, to a certain extent, an integral part of a good society." If we consider it is society which generates conflict, we might ask: What good does it then do to speak of resocializing the delinquent so that he will adapt to a society which is not ideal, but is rather conflictive within itself? To talk of resocializing the delinquent would only make sense where the society wishing to convert the malefactor was a just one, with a just social order and a just legal system. Where this is not the case, what purpose would resocialization serve? Should we not first begin by resocializing society? Why should one socialize a young man if, when he comes out of prison, he must return to a broken home, in the city slums, with no job, and surrounded by friends and cohorts who are criminals? We suggest, as distinct from

1 Antonio Beristain, *La pena-retribución y las actuales concepciones criminológicas, op. cit.*, p. 99. Raymond Saleilles (1855-1912), *L'individualisation de la peine*, Paris, F. Alcan, 1898, 3rd ed. 1927, introduction by Gabriel Tarde; *The individualization of Punishment,* translatión into English by Rachel Szold Jastrow, introduction by Roscoe Pound, Boston, Little Brown, 1911.

the resocialization of the delinquent, the *resocialization of society*, making it less unjust, less socially unequal, and with structures which would more and more make people not turn to crime. In any case, viewed in its negative aspect, we must *prevent the desocialization of the criminal by society itself*.

Success in treatment would not depend, either exclusively or mainly, on the success of applying prison sentences or the other punishments, but rather, to a great extent, on the model of society we produce, that is to say, on an extrapenitentiary factor. Though behaviour in prison might be exemplary, it is an assisted behaviour. Still, what happens when prison assistance disappears, and the individual once again enters the outside world and his movements are no longer limited to the enclosed space of the prison? In this regard, it has been well said that "*It is very difficult to educate people for freedom under conditions which do not admit of freedom*."[2]

4 Visions, Dreams and Utopias

This book is based on the belief that ideas change the world. Not ideas alone, however. Ideas may help change the world when the right conditions prevail.

All the extraordinary advances in the history of humanity began with visions, dreams and utopias. Nothing can be done without the will and the ability to imagine, to go beyond the experience of the pre-established order and to dream, and to consider not only what is, but also what *could be*. Visions alter the mental schemata of humanity. They throw the practices of millennia into doubt and allow progress. It was historical visions which allowed Galileo to discover that the Earth moved around the Sun, and not the opposite, which allowed Columbus to discover America and see that our planet was not a flat disc but a sphere. Visions showed men that kings and emperors should not be considered representatives of divinity, that social division into estates or casts should not be viewed as something natural. Visions proclaimed the equality of all human beings and contemplated slavery and *apartheid* with moral outrage. They enforced the equality of women's rights with those of men, at least formally. Visions condemned torture and genocide as repugnant practices.

2 José Antonio Choclán Montalvo, *Individualización judicial de la pena…*, *op. cit.*, pp. 95-99.

Such visions bring out the best that is in us. They are sources of inspiration that make us dream while awake. They are the vehicles of hope for the future which lift our spirit even in the times of greatest calamity. No great achievement has been attained without a visionary mind first dreaming of it, raising it above what for millennia had been considered the *correct* and true way, and challenging the established order.

Visions alone, however, cannot convert themselves into reality. For this to happen, people are needed – men and women dedicated to action – political leaders, poets, philosophers, with the ability to inspire in others a belief in change, people capable of going beyond their own desires and of doing something altruistic for the rest of mankind, of confronting powerful, hidden interests and of presenting a fierce opposition which, at times at the risk of their lives, they will stand by, putting up with frustrations and fears, but never surrendering to downheartedness.[3]

5 The Reparation of Damage. Towards a Conciliatory System

In day-to-day life, when we do harm to somebody, we attempt to compensate them for the injury we have caused them. Why does the State, in the developed countries, not do the same? Or, at least, why do we not extend the ability of the aggressor to compensate the victim and diminish the role of the State and of Criminal Law, making these instruments of last recourse, a final possibility when a peaceful solution to the dispute has failed? In all systems where a strong State is not in evidence, compensation for victims seems the most commonly followed path.[4]Ordinary people, the entire population, should convert themselves into *participants* and not be mere *spectators*. They should be *producers of solutions, not consumers of them*. We should seek settlements

3 *Cf.* Aung San Suu Kyi, *Freedom from Fear*, New York, Penguin, 1995 ed., p. 183. Paul Gordon Lauren, "Nuevos retos de los derechos humanos. El futuro a la luz del pasado", *op. cit.*, p. 381. Nicolás López Calera, *¿Es posible un mundo justo? Estudios de Filosofía jurídica y política*, Granada, Universidad de Granada, 2003; and Nicolás López Calera (ed.), *La palabra contra el terrorismo*, Granada, 2004.

4 Nils Christie, Los límites del dolor, op. cit., pp. 128 ff.

rather than give orders, compensate instead of taking reprisals, do good rather than cause evil.[5]

Two basic questions arise concerning the limits upon the right to punish:

- The first occurs when the victim desires revenge. If the victim insists on vengeance, would it be right to let him inflict pain on the criminal, if he be willing to do so? The reply would seem to be "no". Vengeance is not ethical. Ontologically, evil is not resolved by applying an opposite evil, it is only resolved by applying good to it.
- The second has to do with a contrary situation. If the victim forgives, a new question arises: Should we always let the victim show generosity, extend a pardon? What would we say about a serious crime? Can the community demand that the delinquent pay for his offence even though the victim has forgiven him? The answer appears again to be given by ethics. Pardon affects the personal sphere, but the breach of the external social order demands punishment. However, why is this? Moreover, what if there is no risk of recidivism?

It is precisely to control the diverse cruel measures of different individuals that the "balance" arose, the common system of measurement which the State imposes. However, in the same way as the generality of law may often demand the aid of equity, of justice in concrete cases, in order to avoid *summum ius, summa iniuria*, it is often the case that the punishment is tailored to the individual. If no two people are equal, there can be no two equal punishments. The weighting between Justice with a capital, abstract and universal, and justice in any specific case should be applied case by case with acumen, and, at the same time, with controls. At all costs, that the criminal become a *scapegoat* or *fallguy*, or equally *a guinea pig*, must be avoided. Therefore, once again, there must be someone or something *that guards the guardians*, puts brakes and limits, checks and balances, upon the punitive power of the State.

6 The Is-Ought Question

If someone orders us to do something quite obviously unacceptable – for instance, to throw ourselves from a window – our reply would

5 Cf. Mark S. Umbreit (1949-), *Crime and Reconciliation: Creative Options for Victims and Offenders*, Nashville, Abingdon Press, 1985.

surely be to disobey, no matter how strong the ties to authority might be, or the respect due the one ordering, or the power that person might have over our will. We should simply say something like: "I am sorry, I cannot throw myself out. Should I do so, I would probably die and I do not want to die".

Answers like the above, in different contexts, are daily presented by thousands of human beings, without questioning the technical decorum or formal accuracy of them. In truth, it is not exactly right to say that "we cannot" throw ourselves from the window, at least if we are not physically impeded from doing so, by paralysis or because we are tied up. On the plane of fact, of being, of facts, nothing prevents us from doing so. Indeed, we should rather say something like: "I am sorry, but no matter how much I appreciate you, I must not obey you in this case because it is not morally correct to take a life and, if I leap into the void, that is what I shall be doing." Notice here the change of nuance. We have moved from the plane of "can" to the plane of "ought-to" do. It is a fact that not everything we can do we should do and, contrariwise, not everything we have to do, we can do. Here, we are not moving upon the "factual" plane, that of facts, of reality, rather we are on that of the ought-to-be, of values, in agreement with certain ethical codes of Morality, Religion or Natural Law.

Why set this example? What we wish to highlight here is how often the two planes are confused: the plane of being and the plane of the ought-to-be; facts and values. Or, we might say, an "explanation", a causal description of deeds and their effects, is confused with its "justification." The latter being a value judgement, conforming with the idea of justice. Similarly, we often confuse what cannot be with that which it would be better if it did not occur.

In the debate on punishment – and imprisonment, as the most important type of punishment in the legal world – we should never mix dreams with reality, utopias with facts, neither must we, however, ever forget, in an attempt to be overly hard-headed, that dreams serve to change reality. In this regard, it is important to balance realism with idealism so that they level at just that point where virtue is found, well below sterile dreaming, but also well above a paralyzing realism. We must dream but without losing sight of reality. Often, in the discourse on punishment, when mistaking the plane of being with that of the ought-to-be, such discourse sins by being excessively crude or excessively unrealistic and, what is worse, by being unaware that it is falling into this confusion of planes.

7 Flexibility as a Virtue

On the subject of punishment, there always arises, as the clinching argument which ends all further discussion, the *dictum* to the effect that punishment is unavoidable in every society, for no society wishes to abolish it, as it is a means of keeping order and avoiding the chaos and social anarchy which would ensue if everyone did whatever they wanted to do, with no fear of reprisals. Still, is this true? Allow us to offer some considerations which might, at the very least, place in doubt the absolute veracity of such an assertion when taken as an untouchable and absolute dogma.

It is the eternal dilemma: What is the best defence? Should we raise high walls of commands and prohibitions, with the corresponding punishments for those who fail to stay within them? We must not forget that a wall can always be knocked down, scaled or mocked by a tunnel carved beneath it. The same goes for penal sanctions and prison walls, should the guilty person feel too much pressure on him. The safety of society resides more in socially adapted men than in high prison walls. Is it not perhaps more effective to form *free* individuals, capable of answering for their actions, to foment a greater confidence in the fact that the social order will be respected because it is just, rather than making it respected for fear of the punishment to be visited on those who do not obey its laws?

We know we might be labelled idealists, dreamers, who propose unreachable utopias. However, let us begin the argument again, on another level, that of personal relations within the family setting. In the long run, what is more effective, setting up a prison system – allow us the metaphor – with fixed hours for going out and coming home, enforce a dress code, and a thousand and one other rules concerning every question, to be imposed on the children by the parents? The former, fed up, and sometimes rightly so, will systematically disobey them, when they can, and will cover up what they do. Or, might it not be better to build a system of trust and freedom, of responsible personality formation, where the parents lay down a few basic rules of the game – the fundamentals – but leave the rest open to the children so that, in the continuous play of trial and error, they will strengthen their wills and learn to be responsible and free? With the passage of time, given the first scenario, the children will have grown up hyper-protected or, contrariwise, they will be totally rebellious. In the second scenario, we shall have created responsible beings, well capable of taking their own decisions. Something similar happens with the State and its punishments.

Allow us another image: Which resists a hurricane wind better, the trunk of a hundred-year-old oak or a rush on the banks of a lake? Rigidity or flexibility? The tree trunk appears the stouter, but it also offers a greater resistance to the wind force that, when the case arises, will be able to smash it in pieces or uproot it at a blow. As against this, the rush will bend, offering less resistance and will survive with its greater flexible structure the onslaughts of contrary forces. The same occurs with a rigid, totalitarian society or with a liberal and democratic system, respectively, with a purely vindicative goal behind punishment or with a relative and individualized theory of penal treatment.

Let certain critics not say that then everyone would do whatever they felt like and that anarchy would make social life impossible. If it is true that, sometimes, *there is no greater injustice than disorder* and that *force makes the law when the law loses its force*, why should it be that a punitive system which limits itself to punishing the least must therefore be less effective in the fight against criminality?

Let us think of society and imagine it as a great *pressure cooker*, one of those we use to cook in. Let us ask ourselves for a moment what happens within such a cooker should we close the safety valve. This would prevent the pressure from escaping and the pot would explode causing a gigantic mess. Something similar happens with dissidence, not only the civilized sort but also, at a lower level, that which goes against the entire system. To a certain extent, the expression of dissent must be permitted. The clear banking on freedom will prove misguided in certain cases and crime will break out. Nevertheless, on the brighter side, freedom allows the pressure to escape and society, as a whole, as if it were one big pressure cooker, will not explode.

This is the same mechanism employed in *vaccines* to prevent infection by certain diseases. Vaccines work by injecting a small quantity of the virus which produces the disease in the healthy organism. It is administered in a dose not sufficient to make the individual fall ill, but still in a dose great enough for the organism to produce antibodies which serve as defence mechanisms against the disease. In this fashion, the body will be better prepared in future to confront the evil. Similarly, society must allow a certain degree of tolerance towards controlled dissent. This should not be brutally suppressed, but properly channelled.

BIBLIOGRAPHY

ABEL, Charles F., MARSH, Frank H., *Punishment and Restitution: A Restitutionary Approach to Crime and the Criminal,* Westport, Conn., Greenwood Press, 1984.

ABRAHAMSEN, David (1903-), *The Psychology of Crime,* New York, Columbia University Press, 1960.

ACTON, H.B. (Harry Burrows) (1908-) (ed.), *The Philosophy of Punishment,* London, Macmillan, 1969.

ADAMIAK, Richard, *Justice and History in the Old Testament: the Evolution of Divine Retribution in the Historiographies of the Wilderness Generation,* Cleveland, J.T. Zubal, 1982.

ADAMSON, C., "Punishment After Slavery: Southern State Penal Systems, 1865-1890", in *Social Problems,* 30, 1983, pp. 555-569.

"Toward a Marxian Penology: Captive Criminal Populations as Economic Threats and Resources", in *Social Problems,* 31, 1984, pp. 435-458.

ADLER, Jacob (1913-), *The Urgings of Conscience: A Theory of Punishment,* Philadelphia, Temple University, 1992; edition of 1985 by Jacob ADLER.

AGARWAL, Rajendra Saran, KUMAR, Sarvesh (eds.), *Crimes and Punishment in New Perspective,* Delhi, Mittal, 1986.

AGULHON, Maurice, "Présentation", in *L'impossible prison,* Paris, Editions du Seuil, 1980.

ALARCÓN BRAVO, Jesús, "Tratamiento del joven delincuente", in *Delincuencia Juvenil. Estudio de su problemática en España,* Ministerio de la Gobernación, Madrid, 1972, pp. 215 ff.

ALEXANDER, Franz (1891-), STAUB, Hugo, *The Criminal, the Judge and the Public: A Psychological Analysis,* New York, Macmillan, 1931; translation into English by Gregory ZILBOORG, Glencoe, Ill., Free Press, 1956; New York, Collier Books, 1962.

ÁLVAREZ GONZÁLEZ, Norberto, *La tendencia a sufrir el castigo: una contribución a la teoría de la culpa,* Alcalá, Universidad de Alcalá de Henares, Servicio de Publicaciones, 1996.

ALLEN, Francis A., The *Decline of the Rehabilitative Idea: Penal Policy and Social Purposes,* New Haven, Yale University Press, 1981.

ALONSO OLEA, Manuel, "Sobre la doble garantía material y formal para la imposición de sanciones administrativas a empresarios en materia laboral", in *Revista Española de Derecho del Trabajo,* 39, 1989.

AMATO, Nicolò, *Diritto, delitto, carcere*, Milano, Giuffrè, 1987.

AMNESTY INTERNATIONAL, *United States of America: The Death Penalty*, London, Amnesty International Publications, 1987.

ANCEL, Marc, "Des mesures qui seraient indiquées au lieu et place de la peine, pour tenir compte des nécessités d'une defense social humaine", in *Rev. Pent. Et de Dr. Pen.*, 1951.

"Les doctrines nouvelles de la défense sociale", in *Revue de Droit Penal et de Criminologie*, 1951-1952, pp. 47 ff.

"Droit pénal et défense sociale", in *Rv. Sc. Crim.*, 1953, pp. 144 ff.

"Penas y medidas de seguridad en Derecho positivo comparado", in *ADPCP*, t. IX, fasc. III, 1956, pp. 443 ff.

"Peine et réeducation dans l'evolution du droit pénal", in *Etudes et documentation*, Ministère de la Justice, Direction de l'Adm. Penit., Paris, 1959.

"Responsabilité et défense sociale", in *Rev. Sc. Crim.*, 1959, pp. 179 ff.

"Défense sociale et prophylaxie criminelle", in *Hommage à Georges Heuyer*, Paris, Presses Universitaires de France, 1961.

"Défendre la défense sociale?", in *Rev. Sc. Crim.*, 1964, pp. 188 ff.

"Droit pénal classique et défense sociale", in *Revue Penal Suisse*, 1965, pp. 1 ff.

"De la vengeance expiatoire au traitement des delinquants", in *L'évolution du Droit Criminel Contemporain (Etudes Lebret)*, Paris, 1968.

"La noción de tratamiento en las legislaciones penales vigentes", in *Tratamiento penitenciario, Revista de Estudios Penitenciarios*, 1968.

"Le problème de la peine de prison", in *Revue de Droit Penal et de Criminologie*, 1977.

La défense sociale, Paris, Presses Universitaires de France, 1985.

ANDENAES, Johs (1912-), "Almenprevensjion-illusjion eller realitet?", in *Nordisk tidsskrift for kriminalvidenskab*, 33, 1950, pp. 103-133.

General Prevention. Illusion or Reality? Theories of Punishment, Bloomington-London, Indiana, University Press, edited by Stanley E. GRUPP, 1971.

Punishment and Deterrence, preface by Norval MORRIS, Ann Arbor, The University of Michigan Press, 1974.

"The Choice of Sanction. A Scandinavian Perspective", in TONRY, M. –ZIMRING, F. (eds.), *Reform and Punishment*, Chicago, The University of Chicago Press, 1983.

"The Morality of Deterrence", in *University of Chicago Law Review*, vol. 37, 1970, pp. 649-664, re-ed. in HAWKINS, G. – ZIMRING, F. (eds.), *The Pursuit of Criminal Justice*, Chicago, The University of Chicago Press, 1984.

ANDERSON, Digby (ed.), *This Will Hurt: The Restoration of Virtue and Civic Order*, London, Social Affairs Unit, 1995.

ANDRÉS SAENZ DE SANTA MARÍA, María Paz, "Sanciones internacionales (Derecho Internacional Público)", in *Enciclopedia Jurídica Básica*, t. IV, Madrid, Civitas, 1995, pp. 6063-6065.

ANQUETIL, Michel (*et al.*), *La peine, quel avenir?: approche pluridisciplinaire de la peine judiciaire. Actes du Colloque du Centre Thomas More des 23-24 mai 1981*, Paris, Editions du Cerf, 1983.

ANTÓN ONECA, José, *La prevención general y la prevención especial en la teoría de la pena*, Salamanca, 1944.

La utopía penal de Dorado Montero. Introduction by Francisco MALDONADO, Salamanca, Universidad de Salamanca, 1950.

"Los fines de la pena según los penalistas de la Ilustración", in *R. E. P.*, 1964, pp. 415 ff.

AQUINAS, Saint Thomas, *Suma de Teología*, Madrid, Biblioteca de Autores Cristianos, 1989.

ARAGAO, Antonio Moniz Sodre de, *As tres solas penais: clássica, antropologica e critica: studo comparativo*, 8th ed., Rio de Janeiro, Feitas Bastos, 1977.

ARDAL, P., "Does Anyone Ever Deserve to Suffer?", in *Queens Quarterly*, 91-92, 1984, pp. 241-257.

ARENAL DE GARCÍA CARRASCO, Concepción (1820-1893*), Estudios Penitenciarios...*, Madrid, V. Suárez, 1895.

Obras completas de Concepción Arenal, Madrid, V. Suárez, 1895-1929.

ARISTOTLE, *Ética a Nicómaco*, introduction and notes by Miguel CANDEL, translation into Spanish by Francisco P. SAMARANCH, Madrid, Santillana, 1997.

ARMSTRONG, K.G., "The Retributivist Hits Back", in *Mind*, vol. 70, 1961, pp. 471-491; re-ed. in H.B. ACTON (ed.), *The Philosophy of Punishment*, London, Macmillan, 1969.

ASHWORTH, Andrew, *Sentencing and Penal Policy*, London, Weidenfeld and Nicolson, 1983.

"Criminal Justice, Rights and Sentencing", Paper to the *Australian Institute of Criminology Sentencing Conference*, Canberra, 1986.

ASSOCIATION INTERNATIONALE DE DROIT PENAL, *VI Congrés International de Droit Penal*, Milano, Giuffrè, 1957.

ATKINSON, M., "Justified and Deserved Punishments", in *Mind*, vol. 78, 1969, pp. 354-374.

AUBERT, Vilhelm, *Om straffens sosiale funksjoner*, Oslo, 1954.

"Legal Justice and Mental Health", in *Psychiatry*, 21, 1958, pp. 101-113.

AUBERT, Vilhelm, MATHIESEN, Thomas, "Forbrytelse og sykdom", in *Tidsskrift for samfunnsforskning*, 3, 1962, pp. 169-193.

AUDIT COMMISSION, *Helping With Inquiries: Tackling Crime Effectively*, London, HMSO, 1993.

AUSTIN, John L., "Alegato en pro de las excusas", in *El lenguaje común. Ensayos de Filosofía Analítica* (comp. V.E. CHAPPEL), Madrid, Tecnos, 1971.

AVVANZINO, Pierre, HEUGHEBAERT, Serge, *La sanction et le soin*, Lausanne, Réalités Sociales, 1987.

AXELROD, Saul, APSCHE, Jack (eds.), *The Effects of Punishment on Human Behaviour*, New York, Academic Press, 1983.

AYERS, Edward L. (1953-), *Vengeance and Justice: Crime and Punishment in the Nineteenth Century American South*, New York, Oxford University Press, 1984.

AYO FERNÁNDEZ, Manuel, *Las penas, medidas de seguridad y consecuencias accesorias. Manual de determinación de las penas y de las demás consecuencias jurídico-penales del delito*, Pamplona, Aranzadi, 1997.

BACIGALUPO, Enrique, *Delito y punibilidad*, 1st ed., Madrid, Civitas, 1983.

BAERMANN, Rolf-Artur (1948-), *Sittlichkeit und Verbrechen bei Hegel*, Frankfurt am Main, Lang, 1980.

BAIER, K., "Is Punishment Retributive?", in *Analysis*, vol. 16, 1955, pp. 25-32; re-ed. in H.B. ACTON, *The Philosophy of Punishment*, London, Macmillan, 1969, pp. 130-137.

BAIRD, Robert M., ROSENBAUM, Stuart E. (eds.), *Philosophy of Punishment*, Buffalo, N.Y., Prometeus Books, 1988.

BAJO FERNÁNDEZ, Miguel, *Derecho penal económico aplicado a la actividad empresarial*, Madrid, Civitas, 1978.

BALDWIN, Thomas, "Punishment, Communication, and Resentment", in MATRAVERS, Matt (ed.), *Punishment and Political Theory*, op. cit., pp. 124-133.

BANKOWSKI, Zenon, MUNGHAM, Geoff, *Essays in Law and Society*, London-Boston, Routledge & Kegan Paul, 1980.

BARATTA, Alessandro, "Criminologia liberale e ideología della difesa sociale", in *La Questione Criminale*, 1975.

"Sistema penale e marginazione sociale", in *La Questione Criminale*, 1976.

"Criminologia critica e politica criminale alternativa", in *Revue Internationale de Droit Penal*, 1978.

"Integración-prevención: una 'nueva' fundamentación de la pena dentro de la teoría sistémica", in *Cuadernos de Política Criminal*, 1984.

BARBERO SANTOS, Marino, "La pena de muerte. Problema actual", in *Anales de la Universidad de Murcia*, 1964; and in *Estudios de Criminología y Derecho Penal*, Universidad de Valladolid, 1972.

"Consideraciones sobre el estado peligroso y las medidas de seguridad, con particular referencia a los Derechos italiano y alemán", in *Estudios de Criminología y Derecho Penal*, Universidad de Valladolid, 1972.

"Postulados político-criminales del sistema punitivo español vigente: presupuesto para su reforma", in *Nuevo Pensamiento*, 1975; and in *Sistema*, 10, July 1975.

Pena de muerte: (el ocaso de un mito), Buenos Aires, Ediciones Depalma, 1985.

BARIL, Micheline, *L'envers du crime*, Montreal, Centre International de Criminologie Comparée, Les Cahiers de Recherches Criminologiques, Université de Montreal, 1984.

BARNER, H.E., *The Story of Punishment*, Boston, The Standford Co., 1930.

BAUDRILLARD, Jean, *Oublier Foucault*, Paris, Ed. Galilée, 1977.

BAUMAN, Z., "The Social Uses of Law and Order", in D. GARLAND, J.R. SPARKS (eds.), *Criminology and Social Theory*, Oxford, Oxford University Press, 2000.

BAUMANN, Jürgen, "Schuld und Sühne als Grundproblem heutiger Strafrechtspflege?", in BAUMANN, Jürgen (hrsg.), *Misslingt die Strafrechtsreform?*, Neuwied, Luchterhand, 1969, pp. 8 ff.

BAYER, R., "Crime, Punishment and the Decline of Liberal Optimism", in *Crime and Delinquency*, April 1981, pp. 169-190.

BEACH, George K., *Tolstoy's Question, by What Right Do Some Persons Punish Other Persons?*, s.i., s.n., 1980.

BEAN, Philip, *Rehabilitation and Deviance*, London, Routledge & Kegan Paul, 1976.

Punishment: A Philosophical and Criminological Inquiry, Oxford, M. Robertson, 1981.

BEAUMONT, Gustav de (1802-1866), TOCQUEVILLE, Alexis de (1805-1859), *Système pénitentiaire aux Etats-Unis et de son application en France*, Paris, Charles Gosselin, 3rd ed, 1845; *On the Penitentiary System in the United States*, Philadelphia, 1833 ; Carbondale, 1964.

BECCARIA, Cesare, Marquis of (1738-1794), *Dei delitti e delle pene: con una raccolta di lettere e documenti relativi alla nascita dell'opera e alla sua fortuna nell'Europa del Settecento.* A cura di Franco VENTURI, 1st ed. in NUE nuova serie, Torino, G. Einaudi, 1978. Translation into Spanish, *De los delitos y la penas*, by J. A. DE LAS CASAS, Madrid, Alianza Ed., 1968; and translation, introduction and notes by Francisco TOMÁS Y VALIENTE, Madrid, Ed. Aguilar, 1969. Translation into English, *Of Crimes and Punishments*, by H. PAOLUCCI, New York, Bobbs Merrill, 1963.

BECKER, Gary S., "Crime and Punishment: An Economic Approach", in BECKER, LANDES (eds.), *Essays in the Economics of Crime and Punishment*, New York-London, Columbia University Press, 1974.

BEDAU, Hugo Adam, "Concessions to Retribution in Punishment", in J.B. CEDERBLOM, W.L. BLIZEK (eds.), *Justice and Punishment*, Cambridge- Massachusetts, Ballinger Publishing Co. 1976.

"Retribution and the Theory of Punishment", in *Journal of Philosophy*, 75, pp. 601-620.

Death is Different: Studies in the Morality, Law and Politics of Capital Punishment, Boston, Northeastern University Press, 1987.

BEDAU, Hugo Adam (ed.), "Capital Punishment in the United States", in *The Howard Journal*, 19, 1960.

The Death Penalty in America; An Anthology, Garden City, N.Y., Anchor Books, 1964.

BELEZA DOS SANTOS, J., "O fin da prevençao especial nas prisoes criminais. Valor e limites", in *Boletim do Ministerio da Justiça*, 73, 1958.

BENDA, Ernst (*et al.*), *Hat Strafe Sinn?: aus juristischer, psychologischer, ethischer und pastorales Sicht nehmen Stellung.* Hrsg. by Balthasar GAREIS and Eugen WIESNET, Freiburg im Breisgau, Herder, 1974.

BENN, Stanley I., "An Approach to the Problems of Punishment", in *Philosophy*, 1958.

"Punishment", in EDWARDS, P. (ed.), *The Encyclopedia of Philosophy*, New York, Macmillan and the Free Press, 1967, vol. VII, pp. 29-36.

BENNETT, T.H., *Tackling Fear of Crime: A Review of Policy Options*, Cambridge, Institute of Criminology, 1989.

BENTHAM, Jeremy, *Tratados de Legislación penal y civil*, t. I, pp. 66-95, and t. IV, pp. 311-314, Villalpando, Madrid, 1821.

"El Panóptico", "Memoria", in Francisco FERRER Y VALLS (ed.), *Principios de Legislación y de Codificación*, Madrid, Imprenta de D. Tomás Jordán, 1834. Madrid, Ediciones La Piqueta, 1979.

An Introduction to the Principles of Morals and Legislation, 1st ed. London, 1789; Oxford, Clarendon Press, 1823; ed. by H.L.A. HART, J.H. BURNS, London, The Athlone Press, 1970.

The Rationale of Punishment, London, Robert Howard, 1830.

BERGALLI, Roberto, *¿Readaptación social por medio de la ejecución penal? Notas a propósito de la Ley penitenciaria nacional argentina y del Proyecto de reforma de la Parte General del Código penal* (1974), Madrid, Instituto de Criminología, Universidad de Madrid, 1976.

La recaída en el delito: modos de reaccionar contra ella, Barcelona, Sertesa, 1980.

BERISTAIN, Antonio, *La pena-retribución y las actuales concepciones criminológicas*, Presentation by Elías NEUMAN and Eugenio Raúl ZAFFARONI, Buenos Aires, Depalma, Criminología Contemporánea, 1982.

BERLIN, Isaiah, Sir, *Two Concepts of Liberty*, Oxford, Oxford University Press, 1958.

BEST, Joel, *Random Violence: How We Talk About New Crimes and New Victims*, Berkeley, California, University of California Press, 1999.

BETEGÓN, Jerónimo, *La justificación del castigo*, Madrid, Centro de Estudios Constitucionales, 1992.

"Nota a la reedición del 'Discurso sobre las penas' de Lardizabal", in *Anuario de Derechos Humanos, Universidad Complutense de Madrid*, 3, 1985, pp. 669-682.

BETTIOL, Giuseppe, "Stato di diritto e misure di sicurezza", *Congreso de Diritto Penale*, Bressanone, 1961, Padova, Cedam, 1962.

"Il mito della rieducazione", in *Rivista di Diritto e Procedura Penale*, 1963.

BEYLEVELD, Deryck, *The Effectiveness of General Deterrence Against Crime: an Annotated Bibliography or Evaluative Research*, Cambridge, Institute of Criminology, 1978.

A Bibliography on General Deterrence Research, Westmead, Saxon House, 1980.

BIANCHI, Herman, WANINGEN, René van. With contributions by Elisabeth BARKER (*et al.*), *Abolitionism, Towards a Non Repressive Approach to Crime: Proceedings of the Second International Conference on Prison Abolition*, Amsterdam, Free University Press, 1986.

BLACK, D., "Crime as Social Control", in *American Sociological Review*, 48, 1983, pp. 34-45.

BLANSHARD, Brand, "Retribution Revisited", in E.H. MADDEN, R. HANDY, M. FARBER (eds.), *Philosophical Perspectives on Punishment*, Springfield , Ill., Charles C. Thomas, 1968.

BLONDIEAU (*et al.*), *Rétribution et justice pénale*, preface by Michel VILLEY, Paris, P.U.F., 1983.

BLOOM, Harold (ed.), *Fyodor Dostoievsky's Crime and Punishment*, New York, Chelsea House Publisher's, 1988.

BLUMSTEIN, Alfred, COHEN, Jacqueline, NAGIN, Daniel (eds.), *Deterrence and Incapacitation: Estimating the Effects of Criminal Sanctions on Crime Rates*, Washington, DC, National Academy of Sciences, 1978.

BLUMSTEIN, Alfred, COHEN, Jacqueline, MARTIN, S.E., TONRY, M.H. (eds.), *Research on Sentencing: the Search for Reform*, Washington, National Academy Press, 1983.

BOIX REIG, Javier, "Significación jurídico-penal del artículo 25.2 de la Constitución", in *Escritos Penales*, Valencia, 1979.

BOOK, A.S., "Shame on You: An Análisis of Modern Shame Punishment as an Alternative to Incarceration", in *William and Mary Law Review*, 40, 1999, pp. 653-686.

BÖRJESON, Bengt (1932-), *Om pafoljders verkningar*, Uppsala, 1966

BOTTOMLEY, A. Keith, "The Failure of Penal Treatment – Where Do We Go From Here?", in John BALDWIN, A. Keith BOTTOMLEY (eds.), *Criminal Justice*, London, Martin Robertson, 1978.

Crime and Penal Politics: The Criminologist's Dilemma, Hull, Hull University Press, 1989.

BOTTOMS, Anthony E., "Reflections on the Renaissance of Dangerousness", in *Howard Journal*, 16, 1977, pp. 70-97.

"Neglected Features of Contemporary Penal Systems", in David GARLAND, Peter YOUNG (eds.), *The Power to Punish*, Aldershot, Gower, 1983.

"The Philosophy and Politics of Punishment and Sentencing", in C. CLARK, R. MORGAN (eds.), *The Politics of Sentencing Reform*, Oxford, Clarendon Press, 1995.

BOTTOMS, A., PRESTON, R.H. (eds.), *The Coming Penal Crisis: A Criminological and Theological Exploration*, Edinburgh, Scottish Academic Press, 1980.

BOULAN, Fernand, "Les droits de la victime: un choix de politique criminelle", in BOULAN, Fernand (*et al.*), *Problèmes actuels de science criminelle*, Aix en Provence, Presses Universitaires d'AixMarseille, 1985.

BOUTELLIER, Hans J., *Crime and Morality – The Significance of Criminal Justice in Postmodern Culture*, Dordrecht, Netherlands, Kluwer Academic Publishers, 2000.

BOUZAT, Pierre, "Le controle de l'execution des mesures de défense sociale", in *L'individualisation des mesures prises à l'egard du delinquant*, Paris, Cujas, 1954.

BOX, Steven , *Power, Crime and Mystification*, London, Tavistock, 1983.

Recession, Crime and Punishment, London, 1987.

BRADLEY, Francis Herbert (1846-1924), "Some Remarks on Punishment", in *International Journal of Ethics*, vol. IV, April 1894, pp. 269-284. Also published in F.H. BRADLEY, *Collected Essays*, Oxford, Oxford University Press, 1969, pp. 1949-1964.

BRAITHWAITE, John, "Challenging of Criminal Law and Just Deserts: Punishing White-Collar Criminals", in *Journal of Criminal Law and Criminology*, 73, 1982, pp. 723-763.

Crime, Shame and Reintegration, Cambridge, Cambridge University Press, 1989.

"Restorative Justice", in Michael H. TONRY (ed.), *The Handbook of Crime and Punishment*, New York, Oxford University Press, 1998.

BRAITHWAITE, John, PETTIT, Philip, *Not Just Deserts. A Republican Theory of Criminal Justice*, Oxford, Clarendon Press, 1990.

BRIGHT, Jon, *Turning the Tide: Crime, Community and Prevention*, London, Demos, 1997.

BROWNLEE, Ian, *Community Punishment: A Critical Introduction*, London, Longman, 1998.

BUCHANAN, James M., *The Limits of Liberty. Between Anarchy and Leviatan*, Chicago, The University of Chicago Press, 1975.

BUENO ARÚS, F., "A propósito de la reinserción social del delincuente (artículo 25.2 de la Constitución española)", in *Cuadernos de Política Criminal*, 1985.

BURGESS, Anthony, *A Clockwork Orange*, London, Heinemann, 1962.

BURGH, Richard W., "Do the Guilty Deserve Punishment?", in *The Journal of Philosophy*, 79, 4, 1982, pp. 193-210.

BUSTOS RAMÍREZ, Juan (1935-), *Manual de Derecho Penal español. Parte general*, Barcelona, Ariel, 1984, pp. 20-41.

BYRD, S., "Kant's Theory of Punishment: Deterrence in its Threat, Retribution in its Execution", in *Law and Philosophy*, vol. 1, 1989, pp. 151-200.

CALLIESS, Rolf-Peter, *Theorie der Strafe im demokratischen und sozialen Rechtstaat: ein Beitr. z. Strafrechtsdogmatischen Grundlagendiskussion*, Frankfurt am Main, Fischer-Taschenbuch Verlag, 1974.

CAMUS, Albert, KOESTLER, Arthur, *La pena de muerte*, Buenos Aires, Emecé, 1st ed. 1972.

CAPELLA, Juan Ramón, *Sobre la extinción del Derecho y la supresión de los juristas*, Barcelona, Fontanella, 1970.

CARACCIOLI, Iro, *I problemi generali delle misure di sicurezza*, Milano, Giuffrè, 1970.

CARCASIO, Pasquale, GUICCIARDI, Luigi Maria, *Le pene e le misure di sicurezza: manuale pratico secondo il vigente codice penale*, Milano, Giuffrè, 1966.

CARLSON, Rick J. With the collaboration of David K. De WOLF and Priscilla De WOLF, *The Dilemas of Corrections*, Lexington, Mass., Lexington Books, 1976.

CARRARA, Francesco, "Emenda del reo assunta como unico fondamento e fine della pena", in *Opusculi di Diritto Criminale*, vol. I, 4 ed, Tipografia Ciachetti, 1885, pp. 191 ff.

CARROLL, J.S., "A Psychological Approach to Deterrence: The Evaluation of Crime Opportunity", in *Journal of Personality and Social Psychology*, 36, 12, 1978, pp. 1512-1520.

CASCAJO CASTRO, J.L., "Los fines de la pena en el orden constitucional", in *La Ley*, 4028, 3rd May 1996.

CASTRO PÉREZ, "Consideraciones sobre la pena", in *Anuario de Derecho Penal y Ciencias Penales*, 1967.

CATTANEO, Mario A.: *La filosofia della pena nei secoli XVII e XVIII*, Ferrara, De Salvia Ed., 1974.

Il problema filosofico della pena, Ferrara, Editrice Universitaria, 1978.

"Fondamenti filosofici della sanzione penale", in *Problemi della sanzione. Società e diritto in Marx, Actas del XXI Congresso di Filosofia Giuridica e Politica*, Roma, Bulzoni, 1978, pp. 41-100.

Dignità umana e pena nella filosofia di Kant, Milano, Giuffrè, 1981.

"Pena, I. Filosofia del Diritto", in *Enciclopedia del Diritto*, vol. XXXII, 1982, pp. 701-712.

"Hobbes Theory of Punishment", in K.C. BROWN, *Hobbes Studies*, Oxford, Blackwell, 1965, pp. 287 ff.

CAVADINO, M., DIGNAN, J., *The Penal System: An Introduction*, London, Sage, 1992.

CAVALLA, Francesco, *La pena come problema: il superamento della concezione razionalistica della difesa sociale*, Padova, CEDAM, 1979.

CEDERBLOM, J.B., BLIZEK, William L. (eds.), *Justice and Punishment*, Cambridge, Mass., Ballinger Pub. Co., 1977.

CENTRO DE INVESTIGACIONES CRIMINOLÓGICAS, *Estigmatización y conducta desviada. Recopilación de Rosa del Olmo*, Venezuela, Universidad de Zulia, Facultad de Derecho.

CLARKE, D., "Marxism, Justice and the Justice Model", in *Contemporary Crises*, 2, 1978, pp. 27-62.

CLARKE, Ronald V., "Situational Crime Prevention: Its Theoretical Basis and Practical Scope", in M. TONRY, N. MORRIS (eds.), *Crime and Justice: An Annual Review of Research*, vol. 4, 1983, pp. 225-226.

CLARKE, Ronald V., CORNISH, Derek B. (eds.), *The Reasoning Criminal: Rational Choice Perspectives on Offending*, New York, Springer Verlag, 1986.

CLAY, William L., *To Kill or not to Kill: Thoughts on Capital Punishment*. Michael and Mary BURGESS, 1st ed., San Bernardino, California, Borgo Press, 1990.

CLEMMER, "Observation on Imprisonment as a Source of Criminality", in *Journal of Criminal Law*, 1950.

COBO DEL ROSAL, BOIX REIG, "Derechos fundamentales del condenado. Reeducación y reinserción", in *Comentarios a la Legislación Penal*, I, Madrid, 1982.

COCOZZA, Joseph J., STEADMAN, H.J., "Prediction in Psychiatry: An Example of Misplaced Confidence in Experts", in *Social Problems*, 25, pp. 265-276.

COFFEE, J.C., TONRY, M., "Hard Choices: Critical Trade-offs in the Implementation of Sentencing Reform through Guidelines", in TONRY, Michael, ZIMRING, F. (eds.), *Reform and Punishment*, Chicago, University of Chicago Press, 1983.

COHEN, J., "Incapacitation as a Strategy for Crime Control: Possibilities and Pitfalls", in TONRY, Michael, MORRIS, Norval (eds.), *Crime and Justice*, 5, Chicago, University of Chicago Press, 1983, pp. 1-84.

COHEN, M.L., GROTH, A.N., "The Clinical Prediction of Dangerousness", in *Crime and Delinquency*, 34, 1978, pp. 28-39.

COHEN, Stanley, "The Punitive City: Notes on the Dispersal of Social Control", in *Contemporary Crises*, 3, 1979, pp. 339-363.

"Social Control Talk: Telling Stories About Correctional Change", in David GARLAND, Peter YOUNG (eds.), *The Power to Punish: Contemporary Penalty and Social Analysis*, London, Heinemann, 1983.

Visions of Social Control: Crime, Punishment and Classification, Cambridge, Polity Press. Oxford-New York in association with B. Blackwell, 1985.

COMBACAU, J., *Le pouvoir de sanctions de l'ONU (Étude théorique de la coertion militaire)*, Paris, 1974.

CONKLIN, W., *The Impact of Crime*, New York, MacMillan, 1975.

COOPER, D.E., "Hegel's Theory of Punishment", in Z.A. PELCZYNSKI (ed.), *Hegel's Political Philosophy: Problems and Perspectives*, Cambridge, Cambridge University Press, 1971, pp. 151-167.

COOK, P.J., "Research in Criminal Deterrence: Laying the Groundwork for the Second Decade", in MORRIS, Norval, TONRY, Michael (eds.), *Crime and Justice – An Annual Review of Research*, Chicago, University of Chicago Press, 1980.

COPELLO, Mario Alberto, *La sanción y el premio en el Derecho*, Buenos Aires, Losada, 1945.

CÓRDOBA RODA, Juan, *Culpabilidad y pena*, Barcelona, Bosch, 1977.

"Las penas y sus fines en la Constitución", in *La reforma del Derecho Penal*, Barcelona, Bellaterra, 1980.

COSTA, Fausto, *Delito e pena nella storia del pensiero umano*, Torino, Fratelli Bocca, Biblioteca de Scienze Moderne, 1928. Translation into Spanish, *El delito y la pena en la historia de la filosofía*, México, 1953.

COTTINGHAM, J, "Varieties of Retribution", in *Philosophical Quarterly*, 29, 1979, pp. 238-246.

COURTOIS, G., "La vengeance chez Aristote et Seneque à la lumière de l'anthropologie juridique", in *Archives de Philosophie du Droit*, 28, 1983, pp. 29-66.

CRAWFORD, A., *Crime Prevention & Community Safety : Politics, Policies & Practices*, London, Longman, 1998.

CRESSEY, D.R., "Hypotheses in the Sociology of Punishment", in *Sociology and Social Research*, 39, 1955, pp. 394-400.

CROATIA, MINISTARSTVO PRAVOSUDA, *Della responsabilità penale e delle pene (a cura del Ministero della Giustizia della Repubblica Popolare di Croazia)*, Zagrabia, s.n., 1950.

CROSSLEY, D.J., "Bradley's Utilitarian Theory of Punishment", in *Ethics*, 86, 1975, pp. 200-213.

CUELLO CALÓN, Eugenio, *Moderna penología*, T. I., Barcelona, Bosch, 1958.

CUESTA ARZAMENDI, José Luis de la, *El trabajo penitenciario resocializador. Teoría y regulación positiva*, San Sebastián, 1982.

CULLEN, Francis T., GILBERT, Karen E., *Reaffirming Rehabilitation*, Cincinatti, Ohio, Anderson Publishing Co., 1982.

CULLEN, Francis T., LINK, B.G., TRAVIS, L.F., WONZIAK, J.F., "Consensus on Crime Seriousness: Empirical Reality or Methodological Artifact?", in *Criminology,* 23, 1985, pp. 99-118.

CUSSON, Maurice, *Délinquants pourquoi?,* Paris, Armand Colin, Montreal, Hurtbuise HMH, 1981.

Le contrôle social du crime. Preface by Alain PEYREFITTE, 1st ed., Paris, P.U.F., 1983.

Pourquoi punir?, Paris, Dalloz, Collection Criminologie et Droits de l'Homme, 1987.

CUTLER, Antony, NYE, David, *Justice and Predictability,* London, MacMillan, 1983.

CHAMBLISS, William J., "Functional and Conflict Theories of Crime: The Heritage of Émile Durkheim and Karl Marx", in CHAMBLISS, William J., MANKOFF, Milton (eds.), *Whose Law? What Order?,* New York, 1976.

CHAMBLISS, William J., SEIDMAN, Robert B., *Law, Order and Power,* 2nd ed, Reading, Mass., Addison-Wesley Pub. Co., 1982.

CHOCLÁN MONTALVO, José Antonio, *Individualización judicial de la pena: Función de la culpabilidad y la prevención en la determinación de la sanción penal,* preface by Siro GARCÍA, Madrid, COLEX, 1997.

CHRISTIE, Nils (1928-), "Reaksjonenes virkninger", in *Nordisk tidsskrift for kriminalvidenskab,* 49, 1960, pp. 129-144.

"Forskining om individual-prevensjon kontra almenprevensjon", in *Lov og Rett,* X, 1971, pp. 49-60.

"Conflicts as Property", in *The British Journal of Criminology,* 17, 1, pp. 1-15.

Limits to Pain, Oxford, Martin Robertson, 1982. Translation into Spanish by Mariluz CASO, *Los límites del dolor,* México, Fondo de Cultura Económica, 1984.

D'AGOSTINO, Francesco (1946-), *La sanzione nell'esperienza giuridica,* Torino, Giappichelli, 1989.

DAHL, N.O., " 'Ought' and blameworthiness", in *Journal of Philosophy,* 1967.

DAHRENDORF, Ralf, *Law and Order,* London, Stevens, 1985.

DALGARD, Odd Steffen, *Abnorme lovovertredere. Diagnose og prognose,* Oslo, 1966.

DAVIS, L.H., "They Deserve to Suffer", in *Analysis,* 32, 1972, pp. 136-140.

DAVIS, Michael, "How to Make the Punishment Fit the Crime", in *Ethics,* 93, 1983, pp. 726-752.

DE CAVARLAY, Bruno Aubusson (*et al.*), *Le Pénal en première ligne ou en dernier ressort,* Paris, CESPID, 1984.

DE FOLTER, R, "On the Methodological Foundation of the Abolitionist Approach to the Criminal Justice System. A Comparison of the Ideas of Hulsman, Mathiesen and Foucault", in *Contemporary Crises,* 10, 1986, pp. 39-62.

DEIGH, John, "On the Right to Be Punished: Some Doubts", in *Ethics,* 94, 1984, pp. 191-211.

DELMAS-MARTY, Mireille, *Modèles et mouvements de politique criminelle,* Paris, Economica, 1983.

DE MATTIA, Angelo, "Merito e ricompensa", in *Rivista Internazionale di Filosofia del Diritto*, vol. XVII, VI, pp. 608-624.

DEMOS, R., "Some Reflections on Threats and Punishments", in *Review of Metaphysics*, 11, 1957, pp. 224-236.

DENNING, Lord, in *Report of the Royal Commission on Capital Punishment*, London, HMSO, 1984, s. 53.

DERSHOWITZ, Alan Morton, *Fair and Certain Punishment*, New York, McGraw Hill, 1979.

DINITZ, Simon, CONRAD, John P., "Thinking About Dangerous Offenders", in *Criminal Justice Abstracts*, 10, 1978, pp. 99-130.

DODGE, Calvert R., A *World Without Prisons:Alternatives to Incarceration throughout the World*, Lexington, Mass., Lexington Books, 1979.

DOLCINI, Emilio, "La 'Rieducazione del condannato' tra mito e realità", in *Rivista Italiana di Diritto e Procedura Penale*, 1979.

DOLINKO, D. "Some Thoughts about Retributivism", in *Ethics*, 101, 1991, pp. 537-559.

DONZIGER, Steven R. (ed.), *The Real War on Crime*, New York, Harper Perennial, 1996.

DORADO MONTERO, Pedro, *El Derecho protector de los criminales*, vol. I and II, Madrid, 1916.

Bases para un nuevo Derecho Penal, preface by M. RIVACOBA, Buenos Aires, Depalma, 1973.

DOSTOYEVSKY, Fyodor (1821-1881), *Los hermanos Karamazov*, Barcelona, Bruguera, 9th ed., 1974.

Crime and Punishment, translation into English by Julius KATZER, Moscow, Raduga Publishers, 1985. Translation into Spanish, *Crimen y castigo*, Madrid, Ed. Fraile, 1981.

DOYLE, J.F., "Justice and Legal Punishment", in *Philosophy*, 42, 1967, pp. 53-67; re-ed. in H.B. ACTON, *The Philosophy of Punishment, op. cit.*, pp. 159-171.

DRAGONETTI, Jacinto, *Tratado de las virtudes y de los premios*, Villamil, Madrid, 1836.

DRAPKIN, Israel (1905-), *Crime and Punishment in the Ancient World*, Lexington, Mass., Lexington Books, 1989.

DUBOW, Fred, McCABE, Edward, KAPLAN, Gail, *Reactions to Crime: A Critical Review of the Literature*, Washington, DC, National Institute of Law Enforcement, US Department of Justice, 1979.

DUFF, Robin Antony, *Trials and Punishments*, Cambridge-New York, Cambridge University Press, 1986.

Intention, Agency and Criminal Liability, 1990.

"Alternatives to Punishment – or Alternative Punishments", in W. Cragg (ed.), *Retributivism and its Critics*, Franz Steiner, 1992, pp. 43-68.

"Penal Communications: Recent Work in the Philosophy of Punishment", in *Crime and Justice, An Annual Review of Research*, 20, 1995.

Criminal Attempts, New York, Clarendon Press, 1996.

"Punishment, Communication, and Community", in MATRAVERS, Matt (ed.), *Punishment and Political Theory, op. cit.*, pp. 48-69.

"Response to von Hirsch", in MATRAVERS, Matt (ed.): *Punishment and Political Theory, op. cit.*, pp. 83-88.

DUMM, Thomas L., *Democracy and Punishment: Disciplinary Origins of the United States*, Madison, Wis., University of Wisconsin Press, 1987.

DUPRAT, Catherine, "Punir et guérir. En 1819, la prison des philanthropes", in *L'impossible prison*, Paris, Du Seuil, 1980.

DURHAM, Alexis M., "Crime Seriousness and Punitive Severity: An Assessment of Social Attitudes", in *Justice Quarterly*, 5, 1988, pp. 131-154.

DURKHEIM, Émile, *De la division du travail social*, Paris, Alcan, 1893; Paris, Presses Universitaires de France, 5th ed., 1998.

Les règles de la méthode sociologique, Paris, Alcan, 1895 ; Paris, Presses Universitaires de France, 10th ed., 1999.

"Deux lois de l'évolution pénale", in *L'Année Sociologique*, 4, 1902, pp. 65-95 ; also in *Emile Durkheim on Institutional Analysis*, ed., translation and introduction by Mark TRAUGOTT, Chicago, The University of Chicago Press, 1978, pp. 153-180 : "Two Laws of Penal Evolution"; re-ed. as chapter 4, "The Evolution of Punishment", in Steven LUKES, Andrew SCULL (eds.), *Durkheim and the Law*, Oxford, 1983.

Les formes elementaires de la vie religieuse (Le système totémique en Australie), Paris, Alcan, 1912 ; Paris, Librairie Générale Française, 1991, introduction by Michel MAFFESOLI.

L'éducation morale, Paris, Alcan, 1924; translation into English, *Moral Education*, New York, 1973; translation into Spanish by M.L. NAVARRO, Buenos Aires, 1947.

DWORKIN, G., BLUMENFELD, D, "Punishment for Intentions", in *Mind*, 1966.

DWORKIN, Ronald M., "Lord Devlin and the Enforcement of Morals", in *Yale Law Journal*, 75, pp. 986 ff.

Taking Rights Seriously, Cambridge –Massachusetts-, Harvard University Press, 6th ed. 1978. London, Duckworth & Co. Ltd, 3rd ed., 1981; translation into Spanish by Marta GUASTAVINO, Barcelona, Planeta-Agostini, 1992.

"What is Equality? Part 1", in *Philosophy and Public Affairs*, 10, 1981, pp. 185-246.

DYDE, Samuel Walters, "Hegel's Conception of Crime and Punishment", in *Philosophical Review*, 7, 1898, pp. 62-71.

EHRLICH, Isaac, "The Deterrent Effect of Capital Punishment. A Question of Life and Death", in *Am. Ec. Rev.*, 65, 1975, pp. 397-417.

ELIAS, Norbert, *The Civilizing Process. i. The History of Maners*, Oxford, 1978; *ii. State Formation and Civilization*, Oxford, 1982.

EMSLEY, C., "The History of Crime and Crime Control Institutions", in Mike MAGUIRE, Rod MORGAN, Robert REINER, *The Oxford Handbook of Criminology*, 3rd ed. Oxford, Oxford University Press, 2002.

ERIKSON, T. Fai, "Notas sobre sociología de la desviación", in *Estigmatización y conducta desviada,* comp. by R. del OLMO, Centro de Investigaciones Criminológicas, Venezuela, Universidad de Zulia, Maracaibo.

ESCUDERO RODRÍGUEZ, R., "El nuevo marco legal de la potestad sancionadora de la Administración en el orden social", in *RL,* 11, 1988.

ESER, A., "Resozialisierung in der Krise?", in *Festschrift für K. Peters,* 1974.

ETTINGER, Clayton James (1881-), *The Problem of Crime,* New York, R. Long & R.R. Smith, 1932.

EUSEBI, "La nuova retribuzione", in *Rivista Italiana,* 1983, pp. 914 ff.

EUSEBI, Luciano (a cura di), *La funzione della pena: il commiato da Kant e da Hegel,* Milano, Giuffrè, 1989.

EWING, A.C. (Alfred Cyril) (1899-), *The Morality of Punishment with Some Suggestions for a General Theory of Ethics,* Preface by W.D. ROSS, Montclair, N.J., Patterson Smith, 1970.

"Punishment as a Moral Agency: An Attempt to Reconcile the Retributive and Utilitarian View", in *Mind,* 36, 1927, pp. 292-305.

"Armstrong on the Retributive Theory", in *Mind,* 72, 1963, pp. 121-124.

EZORSKY, Gertrude, "Retributive Justice", in *Canadian Journal of Philosophy,* 1, 1972, pp. 365-368.

"The Ethics of Punishment", in EZORSKY, G. (ed.), *Philosophical Perspectives on Punishment,* Albany, State University of New York Press, 1972.

(ed.), *Philosophical Perspectives on Punishment,* Albany, NY, State University of New York Press, 1972.

FALCÓN Y TELLA, Fernando, *Tridimensionalismo y Derecho,* Madrid, Servicio de Publicaciones, Facultad de Derecho, Universidad Complutense de Madrid, 2004. Review by Juan Antonio MARTÍNEZ MUÑOZ, in *Foro. Revista de Ciencias Jurídicas y Sociales. Nueva Época,* Facultad de Derecho, Universidad Complutense de Madrid, 0, 2004, pp. 317-320.

"La familia, el Estado, la Iglesia: Pasado y nuevos horizontes", in *Anuario de Derechos Humanos, Nueva Época,* 5, 2004, Madrid, Instituto de Derechos Humanos, Facultad de Derecho, Universidad Complutense de Madrid, pp. 189-215.

FALCÓN Y TELLA, María José, *La desobediencia civil,* preface by Fernando GARRIDO Falla, Madrid, Marcial Pons, 2000. Review by: Guido SARACENI, in *Rivista Internazionale di Filosofia del Diritto,* 3, July-September, 2001, pp. 424-426; Paula LÓPEZ ZAMORA, in *Revista de Estudios Políticos,* 111, pp. 312-315; Beatriz CASTRO TOLEDO, in *Revista de la Facultad de Derecho de la Universidad Complutense de Madrid,* 1999-2000, pp. 243-266; Oscar María PRIETO GARCÍA, in *Anuario de Derechos Humanos del Instituto de Derechos Humanos de la Facultad de Derecho. UCM,* 2001, pp. 1026-1035; Juan Antonio MARTÍNEZ MUÑOZ, in *Veintiuno. Revista de Pensamiento y Cultura,* 53, Spring 2002, pp. 146-148; Pedro RIVAS, in *Anales de la Cátedra Francisco Suárez,* 34, 2000, pp. 447-450. Translation into English by Peter MUCKLEY, first part, *Civil Disobedience,* preface by Martti KOSKENNIEMI, Leiden-Boston, Martinus Nijhoff, 2004; and second part, *A History of Civil Disobedience,* Genève, Editions Diversités, 2004.

Lecciones de Teoría del Derecho, Madrid, Servicio de Publicaciones de la Facultad de Derecho, Universidad Complutense de Madrid, 1st ed. 2001, 2nd ed. 2003.

"Fundamento y finalidad de la sanción penal desde el punto de vista iusfilosófico", in *Libro Homenaje a Antón Oneca,* Preface by José ITURMENDI MORALES, (forthcoming).

FALCÓN Y TELLA, Ramón, *Análisis crítico de jurisprudencia en materia de prescripción de las infracciones y sanciones tributarias,* Madrid, IEF, 1990.

FALLER, Lincoln B., *Turned to Account: The Forms and Functions of Criminal Biography in Late Seventeenth and Early Eighteenth Century England,* New York, Cambridge University Press, 1987.

FALLS, Margaret, "Retribution, Reciprocity and Respect for Persons", in *Law and Philosophy,* 6, 1987, pp. 25-51.

FEELEY, Malcolm M., *The Process is the Punishment,* New York, Russell Sage, 1979.

FEELEY, M., SIMON, J., "The New Penology: Notes on the Emerging Strategy of Corrections and its Implications", in *Criminology,* 30, 4, 1992, pp. 449-474.

FEINBERG, Joel (1926-2004), "On Justifying Legal Punishment", in *Nomos III, Responsibility,* ed. by C.J. FRIEDRICH, New York, Liberal Arts Press, 1960, pp. 152-167.

"Problematic Responsibility in Law and Morals", in *Philosophical Review,* 1962.

"The Expressive Function of Punishment", in *The Monist,* 1965.

Doing and Deserving, Princeton, NJ, Princeton University Press, 1970.

Social Philosophy, Englewood Cliffs, Prentice Hall, 1973.

Harm to Others, Oxford, Oxford University Press, 1986.

FERNÁNDEZ ALBOR, Agustín, "Los fines de la pena en Concepción Arenal y en las modernas orientaciones penitenciarias", in *R. E. P.,* 180-181, 1968, pp. 11-62.

FERNÁNDEZ LIRIA, Carlos, *Sin vigilancia y sin castigo: una discusión con Michel Foucault,* Madrid, Libertarias/Prodhufi, 1992.

FERRAJOLI, Luigi, *Derecho y razón. Teoría del garantismo penal.* Preface by Norberto BOBBIO, translation into Spanish by Perfecto Andrés IBÁÑEZ, Alfonso RUIZ MIGUEL, Juan Carlos BAYÓN MOHINO, Juan TERRADILLOS BASOCO and Rocío CANTARERO BANDRÉS, Madrid, Trotta, 1st ed. 1995, 2nd ed. 1997, 3rd ed. 1998.

FERRI, Enrico (1856-1929), *Sociologia Criminale,* II, Torino, 1930; *Criminal Sociology,* translation into English by Joseph I. NELLY and John LISLE; ed. by William W. SMITHERS; introduction by Charles A. ELLWOOD and Quincy A. MYERS.

Principios de Derecho Criminal, translation into Spanish by J.A. RODRÍGUEZ MUÑOZ, Madrid, 1933.

FEUERBACH, Johann Paul Anselm (1775-1833), *Anti-Hobbes,* Huyesen, 1797.

"Ist Sicherung vor dem Verbrecher Zweck der Strafe und ist Strafrecht Präventionsrecht", in ALMENDINGEN, FEUERBACH, GROLMANN (eds.), Bibliothek für die peinliche Rechtswissenschaft und Gesetzkunde, I. 2, Herborn y Hadamar, 1798.

FINE, B., KINSEY, R., LEA, J., PICCIOTTO, S., YOUNG, J. (eds.), *Capitalism and the Rule of Law: From Deviance Theory to Marxism,* London, 1979.

FINNIS, John, "Punishment and Pedagogy", in *Oxford Review*, 5, 1967.

"Meaning and Ambiguity in Punishment (and Penology)", in *Osgooge Hall Law Journal,* 10, 1972, pp. 264 ff.

"The Restoration of Retribution", in *Analysis,* 32, 4, 1972, pp. 131-135.

Natural Law, Natural Rights, London, Oxford University Press, 1980.

FITZGERALD, Patrick John, *Criminal Law and Punishment,* Oxford, Clarendon Press, 1962.

FLECHTHEIM, Ossip Kurt (1909-), "Hegel and the Problem of Punishment", in *Journal of the History of Ideas,* 8, 1947, pp. 293-308.

FLEW, Antony Garrad Newton (1923-), "The Justification of Punishment", in *Philosophy,* 29, 1954, pp. 291-307. Re-ed. in H.B. ACTON, *The Philosophy of Punishment, op. cit.,* pp. 83-104.

FLOUD, Jean E., "Dangerousness and Criminal Justice", in *The British Journal of Criminology,* vol. 22, 3, pp. 213-228.

FLOUD, Jean E., YOUNG, Warren, *Dangerousness and Criminal Justice,* London, Heinemann, 1981.

FOGEL, D., *"We are the Living Proof": The Justice Model of Corrections,* Cincinnati, Anderson Pub., 1975.

FORER, Lois (1914-), *Criminals and Victims: A Trial Judge Reflects on Crime and Punishment,* New York, Norton, 1980.

FOUCAULT, Michel, *Surveiller et punir : naissance de la prison,* Paris, Gallimard, 1975 . Translation into English by Alan *Sheridan, Discipline and Punish : The Birth of the Prison,* New York, Vintage Books, 1979. Translation into Spanish, *Vigilar y castigar,* México, Siglo XXI, 1966.

"La poussière et le nuage" in *L'impossible prison,* Paris, Du Seuil, 1980.

FREUD, Sigmund (1856-1939), *Civilization and Its Discontents,* London, 1930; New York, 1962.

"Criminality from a Sense of Guilt", in "Some Character-Types Met with in Psycho-Analytical Work", in *id., Collected Papers,* IV, ed. by J. *Riviere,* New York, 1959; in *Imago,* 4, 1915-1916.

Totem y tabu, Frankfurt, 1981.

FREUND, Julien, *Sociologie du conflit,* Paris, Presses Universitaires de France, 1983.

FRIEDMAN, Lawrence Meir (1930-), *Crime and Punishment in American History,* New York, Basic Books, 1993.

FROMM, Erich, *On Disobedience and Other Essays,* London, Routledge & Kegan Paul, 1984.

GAES, Gerald (1947-), "Correctional Treatment", in M. TONRY (ed.), *The Handbook of Crime and Punishment,* New York, Oxford University Press, 1998.

GAHRINGER, Robert Ervin, "Punishment and Responsibility", in *Journal of Philosophy,* 66, 1969, pp. 291-306.

"Punishment as Language", in *Ethics,* 76, 1960, pp. 46-48.

GALEA, Daniel Ferdinandus, *De personalitate poenae in doctrina D. Covarruviae*, Romae, Institutum Utriusque Iuris Pontificiae Universitatis Lateranensis, 1971.

GALLIGAN, Denis James, "The Return to Retribution in Penal Theory", in *Crime, Proof And Punishment: Essays in Memory of Sir Rupert Cross*, London, Butterworths, 1981.

GARABEDIAN, "Social Roles in a Correctional Community", in *Journal of Criminal Law*, September, 1964.

GARCÍA ARÁN, Mercedes, *Fundamentos y aplicación de penas y medidas de seguridad en el Código Penal de 1995*, Pamplona, Aranzadi, 1997.

GARCÍA BASALO, J. Carlos, *Algunas tendencias actuales de la Ciencia penitenciaria*, Buenos Aires, Abeledo-Perrot, 1970.

GARCÍA GARCÍA, J., "El cumplimiento de las penas privativas de libertad: repercusiones de la parte general del Proyecto de Código Penal de 1992", in *Cuadernos de Política Criminal*, 53, 1994.

GARCÍA MAYNEZ, Eduardo, "El mito de Prometeo y Epimeteo y las finalidades del castigo", in *Dianoia. Anuario de Filosofía*, México, UNAM, 1979.

GARCÍA-PABLOS, Antonio, "La supuesta función resocializadora del Derecho Penal: utopía, mito y eufemismo", in *Anuario de Derecho Penal y Ciencias Penales*, 32, September-December 1979, pp. 645-700.

"Hacia una revisión de los postulados de la Criminología tradicional", in *La Ley*, 16 March 1983.

Estudios Penales, Barcelona, Bosch, 1984.

Problemas actuales de la Criminología, Madrid, Edersa, 1984.

"La resocialización de la víctima: víctima, sistema legal y política criminal", en *Criminología y Derecho Penal al servicio de la persona (Libro homenaje al profesor Antonio Beristain)*, San Sebastián, 1989, pp. 193-198.

Manual de Criminología. Introducción y teorías de la criminalidad, Madrid, Espasa-Calpe, 1998.

Tratado de Criminología, Valencia, Tirant Lo Blanch, 1999; 3rd ed. 2003.

Criminología. I, Salamanca, Ciencias de la Seguridad (CISE), 2004.

Introducción al Derecho Penal, Madrid, Editorial Universitaria Ramón Areces, 2005.

GARCÍA RIVAS, *El poder punitivo en el Estado democrático*, Cuenca, 1996.

GARCÍA VALDÉS, Carlos, *La nueva Penología*, Madrid, Publicaciones del Instituto de Criminología, Universidad Complutense de Madrid, 1977.

Teoría de la pena, Madrid, Tecnos, 1985.

GARDNER, M.R., "The Right to be Punished. A Suggested Constitutional Theory", in *Rutgers Law Review*, 33, 1981, pp. 838-864.

GARLAND, David, "Durkheim's Theory of Punishment: A Critique", in *id.* and Peter YOUNG (eds.), *The Power to Punish*, London, 1983.

Punishment and Welfare: A History of Penal Strategies, Aldershot, Gower, 1985.

"The Criminal and his Science", in *British Journal of Criminology*, 25, 2, 1985, pp. 109-135.

"The Punitive Mentality: Its Socio-Historical Development and Decline", in *Contemporary Crises*, 10, 1986, pp. 305-320.

"British Criminology Before 1935", in *British Journal of Criminology*, 28, 1988, pp. 131-147.

Punishment and Modern Society. A Study in Social Theory, Chicago, The University of Chicago Press, 1990.

"Criminological Knowledge and its Relation to Power: Foucault's Genealogy and Criminology Today", in *British Journal of Criminology*, 32, 4, 1992, pp. 403-422.

"Penal Modernism and Postmodernism", in T. BLOMBERG, S. COHEN (eds.), *Punishment and Social Control*, New York, Aldine de Gruyter, 1995.

"The Limits of the Sovereign State: Strategies of Crime Control in Contemporary Society", in *British Journal of Criminology*, 36, 4, 1996, pp. 445-471.

"Governmentality and the Problem of Crime: Foucault, Criminology, Sociology", in *Theoretical Criminology*, 1, 2, 1997, pp. 173-214.

The Culture of Control. Crime and Social Order in Contemporary Society, Chicago, The University of Chicago Press, 2001.

GARLAND, David, YOUNG, Peter, *The Power to Punish: Contemporary Penalty and Social Analysis*, London, Heinemann Educational Books, Atlantic Highlands, N.J., Humanities Press, 1983.

GAROFALO, J., "The Fear of Crime: Causes and Consequences", in *The Journal of Criminal Law & Criminology*, 72, 2, 1981, pp. 839-857.

GAROFALO, Raffaele, *Criminologia. Studio sul delitto e sulla teoria della repressione*, Torino, Bocca, 1891.

GATRELL, V.A.C. (1941-), "Crime, Authority and the Policeman-State, 1750-1950", in THOMPSON, Francis Michael Longstrech (ed.), *The Cambridge Social History of Britain, 1750-1950*, 3 vols. Cambridge.

GAUBATZ, Kathlyn Taylor, *Crime in the Public Mind*, Ann Arbor, MI, University of Michigan Press, 1995.

GAYLIN, Willard, ROTHMAN, David J., "Introduction", in Andrew von HIRSCH, *Doing Justice: The Choice of Punishments*, New York, Hill and Wang, 1976.

GELIN, Marcel, *La peine justifiée*, Trévoux, Imprimerie J. Jeannin, 1922.

GENDERS, Elaine, PLAYER, Elaine, *Grendon : A Study of Therapeutic Prison*, Oxford, Oxford University Press, 1995.

GENDIN, S., "The Meaning of Punishment", in *Philosophy and Phenomenological Research*, 28, 1967, pp. 235-240.

"A Plausible Theory of Retribution", in *Journal of Value Inquiry*, V, 1970, pp. 1-16.

"Insanity and Criminal Responsibility", in *American Philosophical Quarterly*, 1973.

GENDREAU, P., ROSS, R., "Reivivication of Rehabilitation: Evidence from the 1980s", in *Justice Quarterly*, 4, 3, 1987, pp. 349-407.

GEPHART, Werner, "Die non-rationalen Elemente der strafrechtlichen Rationalisierung. Die Lehre Émile Durkheims", in BRIDE, Brun-Otto, HOFFMANN-RIEM, Woflgang (eds.), *Rechtsproduktion und Rechtsbewusstsein*, Baden-Baden, Nomosgesellschaft, 1988, pp. 177-194.

GERBER, Rudolph J., McANANY, Patrick D. (eds.), *Contemporary Punishment: Views, Explanations ad Justifications,* Preface by Norval MORRIS, South Bend, University of Notre Dame Press, 1972.

GERMAIN, C., "La sanction", in *Travaux du Colloque de Philosophie Penale (12-21 January 1959),* Paris, Dalloz, 1961.

GIALLOMBARDO, "Interviewing in the Prison Community", in *Journal of Criminal Law,* 1966.

GIBBENS, "Les problemes posés par le traitement psychiatrique des delinquants", in *Revue de Science Criminelle,* 1958.

GIDDENS, Anthony, *Durkheim,* Hassocks, Sussex, 1978. London, Fontana, 1986.

The Constitution of Society: Outline in the Theory of Structuration, Berkeley, University of California Press, 1984.

The Nation-State and Violence, vol. II of *A Contemporary Critique of Historical Materialism,* Berkeley, University of California Press, 1985.

GILLING, Daniel., *Crime Prevention: Theory, Policy and Politics,* London, UCL Press, 1997.

GIMBERNAT, Enrique, "¿Tiene un futuro la dogmática jurídico-penal?", in *Estudios de Derecho Penal,* Madrid, 1967.

"El sistema del Derecho Penal en la actualidad", in *Anuario de Ciencia Jurídica,* I, 1971, pp. 278 ff.

GINER DE LOS RÍOS, Francisco (1839-1915), *Estudios jurídicos y políticos,* Madrid, J. Casano. 1921.

GINER DE LOS RÍOS, Francisco, CALDERÓN, Alfredo, *Resumen de Filosofía del Derecho,* Madrid, V. Suárez, 1898.

GLOVER, M.R., "Mr. Mabbott on Punishment", in *Mind,* 48, 1939, pp. 498-501.

GLUECK, Sheldon, *Crime and Correction: Selected Papers,* Cambridge, Mass., Addison-Wesley Press, 1952.

GOFFMAN, Ervin, *Assylums,* Harmondsworth, Penguin Books, 1968. *Internados,* Buenos Aires, Amorrortu, 2nd ed., 1970.

GOLDMAN, A.H., "The Paradox of Punishment", in *Philosophy and Public Affairs,* 9, 1979, pp. 42-58.

"Toward a New Theory of Punishment", in *Law and Philosophy,* 1, 1982, pp. 57-76.

GOODE, E, "Round Up the Usual Suspects: Crime, Deviance, and the Limits of Constructionism", in *The American Sociologist,* 25, 1994, pp. 90-104.

GORDINGER, Milton, *Punishment and Human Rights,* Cambridge, Mass., Schenkman Pub. Co.; Morristown, N.J., General Learning Press, 1974.

GOTTFREDSON, M., HIRSCHI, T., *A General Theory of Crime,* Standford, Standford University Press, 1990.

GOWLLAND-DEBBAS, V., *Collective Responses to Illegal Acts in International Law,* Dordrecht, 1990.

GRACIA MARTÍN (coord.), *Las consecuencias jurídicas del delito en el nuevo Código Penal español,* Valencia, 1996.

GRAMATICA, Filippo, *Principi di difesa sociale,* Padova, Cedam, 1961.

GRAVEN, "La limitation du droit de punir de l'État par les droits de l'homme", in *Revue de Droit Penal et de Criminologie*, 1955.

GRAY, Arthur Herbert (1868-), "The Christian View of the Use of Punishment", in *Howard Journal*, 2, 1929, pp. 296 ff.

GREEN, Thomas Hill (1836-1882), "The State's Right to Punish", in *Journal of the American Institute of Criminal Law and Criminology*, 1, 1910-1911, pp. 19-43.

GREENBERG, D., "Reflections on the Justice Model Debate", in *Contemporary Crises*, vol. 7, 1983, pp. 313-327.

GROSS, Hyman, *A Theory of Criminal Justice*, New York, Oxford University Press, 1979.

GROVES, Byron W., NEWMAN, Graeme, *Punishment and Privilege*, Albany, N.Y., Harrow and Heston, 1986.

GROTIUS, Hugo (1583-1645), *De jure belli ac pacis libri tres*, Aalen, Scientia, 1993.

GULOTTA, Guglielmo, *Psicoanalisi e responsabilità penale*, Milano, Giuffrè, 1972.

GUNN, J., MADEN, A., SWINTON, M., *Mentally Disordered Prisoners*, London, Institute of Psychiatry, 1991.

GURVITCH, Georges (1894-1965), "Social Control", in *id.* and Wilbert E. MOORE (eds.), *Twentieth Century Sociology*, New York, 1945.

GUTHIER, J. (dir.), *Le rôle sanctionnateur du droit pénal*, Fribourg, Suisse, Editions Universitaires, 1985.

HAAG, Ernest van den, *Punishing Criminals*, New York, Basic Book, 1975.

HAFERKAMP, Hans, *Kriminalität ist normal – Zur gesellschaftlichen Produktion abweichenden Handelns*, Stuttgart, Ferdinand Enke Verlag, 1972.

"Zur Notwendigkeit handlungstheoretischer Analysen der Kriminalität und der Kriminalisierung", in ARBEITSKREIS JUNGER KRIMINOLOGEN (Hrsg.), *Kritische Kriminologie*, 1974.

HAFFE, Bernhard, "Hat emanzipierende Sozialtherapie noch eine Chance?", in *Seminar: Abweichendes Verhalten. III.* Ed. by LÜDERSEN and SACK, *Die Gesellschaft Reaktion auf Kriminalität*, Frankfurt am Main, 1977.

HAGAN, John, *Deterrence Reconsidered: Methodological Innovations*, Beverly Hills, Sage Publications, 1982.

HAMILTON, V.L., RYTINA, S., "Social Consensus on Norms of Justice: Should the Punishment Fit the Crime?", in *American Journal of Sociology*, 85, 1980, pp. 1117-1144.

HAMPTON, Jean, "The Moral Education Theory of Punishment", in *Philosophy and Public Affairs*, 13, 3, 1984, pp. 208-238.

"Correcting Harms versus Righting Wrongs: the Goal of Retribution", in *UCLA Law Review*, 39, 1992, pp. 201-244.

HARDING, Christopher (1951-) – IRELAND, Richard W., *Punishment: Rethoric, Rule and Practice*, London-New York, Routledge, 1989.

HARE, R.M. (Richard Mervin), *Freedom and Reason*, New York, Oxford University Press, 1965; re-ed. 1980.

HART, H.L.A. (Herbert Lionel Adolphus), "Prolegomenon to the Principles of Punishment", in *Proceedings of the Aristotelian Society*, 1959-1960. Re-ed. P.

LASLETT – W.G. RUCINAM (eds.), *Philosophy, Politics and Society*, 2 serie, Oxford, Blackwell, 1962, pp. 158-162. Also in H.L.A. HART, *Punishment and Responsibility, op. cit.* And in *Theories of Punishment*, Bloomington, London, Indiana University Press, 1971. Translation into Spanish by Jerónimo BETEGÓN, "Introducción a los principios de la pena", in Jerónimo BETEGÓN, Juan Ramón de PÁRAMO ARGÜELLES, *Derecho y Moral. Ensayos Analíticos*, Barcelona, Ariel, 1990.

"Punishment and the Elimination of Responsibility", London, 1962. Also in H.L.A. HART, *Punishment and Responsibility, op. cit.*

The Morality of Criminal Law, Jerusalem, Hebrew University Magnes Press, 1964.

Punishment and Responsibility: Essays in the Philosophy of Law, Oxford, Clarendon Press, 1968; New York, Oxford University Press, 1982.

HART, H.M., "The Aims of the Criminal Law", in *Law and Contemporary Problems*, 23, 1958, pp. 585-593..

"Criminal Punishment as Public Condemnation", in R.S. GERBER, P.D. McANANY (eds.), *Contemporary Punishment, op. cit.*, pp. 12 y ss.

HASSEMER, Winfried, "Fines de la pena en el Derecho penal de orientación científico-social", in *Derecho penal y ciencias sociales*, Bellaterra, 1982.

HAWKINS, Gordon, "Punishment and Deterrence: The Educative, Moralizing, and Habituative Effects", in *Theories of Punishment*, Bloomington, London, Indiana University Press, 1971.

HAY, Douglas, "Property, Authority and the Criminal Law", in *id. et al., Albions Fatal Tree: Crime and Society in Eighteen Century England*, Harmondsworth, 1975.

HEGEL, Georg Wilhelm Friedrich (1770-1831), *Grundlinien der Philosophie des Rechts*, Berlin, 1821 ; Frankfurt am Main, Suhrkamp Verlag, 1978. Translation by A. MENDOZA DE MONTERO, in Mexico, Juna Pablos ed., 1980. Also in México, UNAM, 1975. Translation into English by T.M. KNOX, Oxford, Oxford University Press, 1962.

HENTIG, Hans von, *La pena, Volumen 1, Formas primitivas y conexiones histórico-culturales*, translation into Spanish by José María RODRÍGUEZ DEVESA, Madrid, Espasa-Calpe, 1967.

HERMANS, H.L.C., *Het verbeurde recht: het verbeuren van recht als gevolg van strafbare feiten of van niet strafbare, door de wet als onrechtmatig beschouwde gedragingen*, Arnhem, Gouda Quint, 1986.

HIBBERT, Christopher (1924-), *The Roots of Evil; a Social History of Crime and Punishment*, 1st ed., Boston, Little, Brown, 1963.

HILL, Frederic, *Crime, its Amount, Causes, and Remedies*, New York, Garland Pub., 1984.

HINCHMAN, L., "Hegel's Theory of Crime and Punishment", in *Review of Politics*, 44, 1982, pp. 523-545.

HIRSCHMAN, Alfred O., *The Rethoric of Reaction: Perversity, Futility, Jeopardy*, Cambridge – Massachusetts – Harvard University Press, 1991.

HIRST, P., "The Concept of Punishment", in Robin Antony DUFF, David GARLAND (eds.), *A Reader on Punishment*, Oxford, Oxford University Press, 1994.

HOBBES, Thomas, *Leviathan*, London, J.M. Dent, *Leviatan*, 1st ed. 1651; Madrid, Editora Nacional, 1979, translation into Spanish by A. ESCOTADO.

HODGES, D.C., "Punishment", in *Philosophy and Phenomenological Research*, 18, 1957, pp. 209-218.

HOEKEMA, David A., *Rights and Wrongs: Coercion, Punishment and the State*, London-Cranbury, N.J., Selingsgrove Susquehanna University Press, 1986.

"The Right to Punish and the Right to Be Punished", in H. Gene BLOCKER – Elisabeth H. SMITH (eds.), *John Rawls Theory of Social Justice: An Introduction*, Athens, Ohio University Press, 1980, pp. 239-269.

HOERNLE, T., VON HIRSCH, Andrew, "Positive Generalpraevention und Tadel", in *Goldtdammer's Archiv für Strafrecht*, 142, 1995.

HOFSTATTER, Peter Robert (1913-), "Pena y reprochabilidad desde el punto de vista social-psicológico", in *Sexualidad y crimen*, translation into Spanish by Enrique GIMBERNAT, Madrid, Reus, 1969.

HOLBACH, F., *Justice Laudative*, Bruxelles-Paris, Larcier, Pedone, 1904.

HONDERICH, Ted, *Punishment: The Supposed Justifications*, Harmondsworth, Baltimore, Maryland, Penguin Books, 1969. Harmondsworth-Baltimore, Penguin, 1976. London, Hutchinson, 1979; Harmondsworth, Penguin Books, 1984; Cambridge, Polity, 1989.

HOUGH, James Morden, "The Impact of Victimization: Finding from the British Crime Survey", Paper prepared for Third International Institute of Victimology, Lisbon, 1984.

HOUGH, James Morden, MAYHEW, Path, *Taking Account of Crime: Key Findings from the Second British Crime Survey*, London, Her Majesty's Stationery Office, 1985.

HOUGH, James Morden, MOXON, D., "Dealing with Offenders: Popular Opinions and the Views of Victims", in *Howard Journal*, 24, 3, 1985, pp. 160-175.

HOUGH, James Morden, ROBERTS, Julian, *Attitudes to Punishment: Findings from the British 1996 Crime Survey*, London, Home Office, 1998.

HOYLES, J. Arthur, *Punishment and the Bible*, London, Epworth Press, 1986.

HUDSON, Barbara, *Justice through Punishment: A Critique of the 'Justice Model' of Corrections*, New York, St. Martin's Press, 1987. London, MacMillan, 1987.

HULSMAN, Louk, "Critical Criminology and the Concept of Crime", in *Contemporary Crises*, 10, 1986, pp. 63-80.

HULSMAN, Louk, BERNAT DE CELIS, J., *Peines perdues : le système pénal en question*, Paris, 1982. Translation into Spanish by Sergio POLITOFF, *Sistema penal y seguridad ciudadana: Hacia una alternativa*, preface by Juan BUSTOS RAMÍREZ and Apendix by Sergio POLITOFF, Barcelona, Ariel, 1984.

HUSAK, D., "Why Punish the Deserving?", in *Nous*, 26, 1992, pp. 447-464.

HUSSEY, F., "Just Deserts and Determinate Sentencing: Impact on the Rehabilitation Ideal", in *The Prison Journal*, LIX, 2, fall-winter 1980, pp. 36-47.

IGNATIEFF, Michael, *A Just Messure of Pain: The Penitentiary in the Industrial Revolution 1750-1850*, London, Macmillan, 1978.

"Class Interests and the Penitentiary: A Reply to Rothman", in *The Canadian Criminology Forum*, 5, 1982, p. 66.

"State, Civil Society and Total Institutions: A Critique of Recent Histories of Punishment", in S. COHEN, A. SCULL (eds.), *Social Control and the State*, Oxford, 1983.

ITURMENDI MORALES, José, Introduction to the Spanish translation by Isabel HOYO SIERRA of François OST, *El sistema jurídico entre orden y desorden*, Madrid, Servicio de Publicaciones de la Facultad de Derecho, Universidad Complutense de Madrid, 1997, pp. 11-33.

Preface to *Libro Homenaje a Antón Oneca* (forthcoming).

IVISON, Duncan, "Justifying Punishment in Intercultural Contexts: Whose Norms? Which Values?", in MATRAVERS, Matt (ed.), *Punishment and Political Theory, op. cit.*, pp. 88-108.

JACOBS, James B., *New Perspectives on Prisons and Imprisonment*, Ithaca, NY, Cornell University Press, 1983.

JACOBY, Susan, *Wild Justice: The Evolution of Revenge*, London, Collins, 1985.

JÄGER, "Strafrecht und psychoanalitische Theorie", in *Fest. Henkel*, 1974, pp. 125 ff.

JANUS, Michael G., "Selective Incapacitation: Have We Tried It? Does It Work?", in *Journal of Criminal Justice*, 13, 1985, pp. 117-129.

JAREBORG, N., "What Kind of Criminal Law Do We Want?", in A. SNARE (ed.), *Beware of Punishment*, Oslo, Pax Forlag, 1995, pp. 17-36.

JENSEN, O.C., "Responsibility, Freedom and Punishment", in *Mind*, 75, 1966, pp. 224-238.

JESCHECK, Hans-Heinrich, "Die Krise der Kriminalpolitik", in *Zeitschrift für die gesamte Strafrechtswissenschaft*, 1979.

"Linee direttive del movimiento internazionale di riforma penale", in *L'Indice Penale*, 1979.

JIMÉNEZ DE ASÚA, Luis, "Las penas y las medidas de seguridad (Ponencia al tercer tema del VI Congreso Internacional de Derecho Penal)", in *El Criminalista*, 2nd serie, t. II, Buenos Aires, Ed. V.P. de Zavalia, 1958.

"La recompensa como prevención general – El derecho premial", in *Revista General de Legislación y Jurisprudencia*, t. 125, pp. 5-32 and 353-394.

La ley y el delito, Buenos Aires, Ed. Sudamericana, 6th ed. 1973.

JOHNSON, P., "Bradley and the Nature of Punishment", in Anthony MANSER, Guy STOCK (eds.), *The Philosophy of F.H. Bradley*, Oxford, Clarendon Press, 1984, pp. 101 ff.

JOHNSTON, Norman, SAVITZ, Leonard, WOLFGANG, Marvin E. (eds.), *The Sociology of Punishment and Correction*, New York, Wiley, 1962.

JONES, David Arthur (1946-), *Crime Without Punishment*, Lexington, Mass., Lexington Books, 1979.

KAFKA, Franz, *En la colonia penitenciaria*, Barcelona, Emece Editores S.A., 1976, notes by Klaus WAGENBACH.

KAISER, Gunther, "Was Wissen wir von der Strafe?", in *Fest. Bockelmann*, 1979, pp. 923 ff.

"Capital Punishment in Criminological Perspective", in *Crime Prevention and Criminal Justice Newsletter*, 12-13, 1986, pp. 10-18.

KANT, Immanuel, *Die Metaphisik der Sitten*, Königsberg, 1797; W. Weischedel, Frankfurt am Main, Suhrkamp Verlag, 1982. 10th ed., Frankfurt, 1993.

Eine Vorlesung Kants über Ethik, Berlin, 1924; translation into English, *Lectures on Ethics*, by L. INFIELD, London, Methuen and Co. (reed. 1979); translation into Spanish, *Lecciones de Ética*, by R. RODRÍGUEZ ARAMAYO and C. ROLDÁN PANADERO, introduction and notes by the former, Barcelona, Crítica, 1988.

KARMEN, Andrew, *Crime Victims. An Introduction to Victimology*, Belmont, California, Wadsworth, 1984.

KASACHKOFF, Tziporah (1942-), "The Criteria of Punishment: Some Neglected Considerations", in *Canadian Journal of Philosophy*, 2, 1973, pp. 363-378.

KASKA, G.S., "Wrongdoing and Guilt", in *The Journal of Philosophy*, 1974.

KAUFMAN, A.S., "The Reform Theory of Punishment, in *Ethics*, 1971, 1960, pp. 49-52.

"Anthony Quinton on Punishment", in *Analysis*, 20, 1959, pp. 10-13.

KAUFMANN, Hilde, *Ejecución penal y terapia social*, Buenos Aires, Depalma, 1979.

KELLING, George L., "Police and Communities : The Quiet Revolution", in *Perspectives on Policing*, 1, National Institute of Justice John F. Kennedy School of Government, Harvard University, 1988.

KELSEN, Hans, "Casuality and Retribution in the Evolution of Human Thought", in *Philosophy of Science*, 8, 1941, pp. 533-556; translation into Spanish by A. CALSAMIGLIA in Hans KELSEN, *¿Qué es justicia?*, Barcelona, Ariel, 1982.

KENNEDY, M., "Beyond Incrimination: Some Neglected Aspects of the Theory of Punishment", in William J. CHAMBLISS, Milton MANKOFF (eds.), *Whose Law? What Order?*, New York, 1976.

KENNER, L., "On Blaming", in *Philosophy*, 1967.

KITTRIE, Nicholas N., *The Right to Be Different: Deviance and Enforced Therapy*, Baltimore-London, The John Hopkins Press, 1971.

KLEINIG, John, *Punishment and Desert*, The Hague, Martinus Nijhoff, 1973.

"Criminally Harming Others", in *Criminal Justice Ethics*, 1986, pp. 3-10.

"Punishment and Moral Seriousness", in *Israel Law Review*, 25, 1991, pp. 401-421.

KLUG, Ulrich, "Para una crítica de la filosofía penal de Kant y Hegel", in *Problemas actuales de las Ciencias penales y de la Filosofía del Derecho. Homenaje al profesor L. Jiménez de Asúa*, Buenos Aires, Ed. Pannedille, 1970.

Skeptische Rechtsphilosophie und humanes Strafrecht, Berlin-New York, Springer, 1981.

KNIGGE, G., *Het irrationele van de straf*, Arnhem, Gouda Quint, 1988.

KNOWLES, Dudley, "Punishment and Rights", in Matt MATRAVERS (ed.), *Punishment and Political Theory*, *op. cit.*, pp. 28-48.

KNUDTEN (ed.), *Crime, Criminology and Contemporary Society*, Illinois, 1970.

KOHLER, Michael, *Der Begriff der Strafe*, Heidelberg, R.v. Decker, 1986.

KRAEPELIN, *Vergeltungsstrafe, Rechtsstrafe, Schutzstrafe*, Heidelberg, 1906.

KRAUSE, Karl Christian Friedrich (1781-1832), *Grundlage des Naturrechts oder philosophischer Grundiss des Ideals des Rechts*, Freiburg, Haufe, 2003.

KRIEKEN, R. Van, "Violence, Self-Discipline and Modernity: Beyond the Civilizing Process", in *The Sociological Review*, 37, 1989, pp. 193-218.

LACAN, Jacques, "La metáfora del sujeto", in *Introducción teórica a las funciones del psicoanálisis en criminología*, Buenos Aires, Homo Sapiens, 1978.

LACEY, Nicola, *State Punishment: Political Principles and Community Values*, London-New York, Routledge and Kegan Paul, 1988.

"Penal Practices and Political Theory: An Agenda for Dialogue", in MATRAVERS, Matt (ed.), *Punishment and Political Theory, op. cit.*, pp. 152-165.

LAIRD, J., "The Justification of Punishment", in *The Monist*, 41, 1931, pp. 352-275.

LANDROVE DÍAZ, Gerardo, *Las consecuencias jurídicas del delito*, 3rd ed., Barcelona, Bosch, 1984. 5th ed., Madrid, Tecnos, 2002.

LARDIZABAL, Manuel de, *Discurso sobre las penas*, Introduction by José ANTÓN ONECA, in *Revista de Estudios Penitenciarios*, 174, July-September 1966.

LASSO DE LA VEGA, J., *El dolor y la condición humana en el teatro de Sófocles*, Barcelona, 1971.

LAUREN, Paul Gordon, "Nuevos retos para los derechos humanos. El futuro a la luz del pasado", in *Anuario de Derechos Humanos. Nueva Época*, t. V, 2004, Madrid, Instituto de Derechos Humanos, Facultad de Derecho, Universidad Complutense de Madrid, pp. 369-386; translation into Spanish by Fernando FALCÓN Y TELLA.

LAZARIDIS, S.A., "La rétribution dans la philosophie pénale anglo-saxonne d'aujourd'hui", in *Archives de Philosophie du Droit*, 28, 1983, pp. 91-108.

LEA, John, YOUNG, Jock, *What is to be Done About Law and Oder*, Harmondsworth, 1984.

LECLERCQ, J., "Réflexions sur le droit de punir", in *Estudios de Deusto*, vol. XIII, 1965, pp. 569-487.

LESCH, Heiko H., *La función de la pena*, Cuadernos "Luis Jiménez de Asúa", translation into Spanish by Javier SÁNCHEZ-Vera GÓMEZ-TRELLES, Madrid, Dykinson, 1999.

LÉVY, Thierry, *Le dèsir de punir : essay sur le privilège pénal*, Paris, Fayard, 1979.

Le crime en toute humanité, Paris, B. Grasset, 1984.

LEWIS, C.S., *The Problem of Pain*, Great Britain, 1940, Fontana Books, 1980.

"The Humanitarian Theory of Punishment", in *Res Judicatae*, 6, 1953; and in Leon RADZINOWICZ, M. WOLFGANG (eds.), *Crime and Punishment*, vol. 2, New York, Basic Books, 1971.

LEWIS, H.D., HARVEY, J.W., PAUL, G.A., "The Problem of Guilt", in *Proceedings of the Aristotelian Society*, Suppl. Vol. 31, 1947.

LILLIE, N., "Towards a Biblical Doctrine of Punishment", in *Scottish Journal of Theology*, 21, 1968, pp. 449-461.

LINDBLOM, Ulf, "Smärtbehandling under omprövning", in *Nordisk medisin*, 95, 1980, p. 75.

LIPSON, Albert J., PETERSON, Mark A., *California Justice Under Determinate Sentencing: A Review and Agenda for Research*, Santa Monica, California, Rand Corporation, 1980.

LIPTON, Douglas, MARTINSON, Robert, WILKS, Judith, *The Effectiveness of Correctional Treatment*, New York, Praeger, 1975.

LISLE, J., "The Justification of Punishment", in *International Journal of Ethics*, 25, 1914, pp. 346-359.

LISZT, Franz von, "Die deterministischen Gegner der Zweckstrafe" (1893), in *Strafrechtliche Aufsätze und Vorträge*, 2, 1905, pp. 25 ff.

"Der Zweckgedanke im Strafrecht", in *Strafrechtliche Aufsätze und Vorträge*, Berlin, 1905; 1970 (reed.).

LOCKE, D., "The Many Faces of Punishment", in *Mind*, 72, 1963, pp. 568-572.

LOCKE, John, *Two Treatises on Civil Government* (1690), translation into Spanish by A. LÁZARO ROS, *Ensayo sobre el gobierno*, Madrid, Aguilar, 1969.

LOFTSGORDON, D, "Present-day British Philosophers on Punishment", in *Journal of Philosophy*, 63, 1966, pp. 341-353.

LOMBROSO, Cesare, *L'uomo delinquente in rapporto alla antropologia, alla giurisprudenzia ed alla psichiatria*, Torino, Bocca, 1878.

LÓPEZ CALERA, Nicolás, *¿Es posible un mundo justo? Estudios de Filosofía jurídica y política*, Granada, Universidad de Granada, 2003.

LÓPEZ CALERA, Nicolás (ed.), *La palabra contra el terrorismo*, Granada, 2004.

LÓPEZ REY Y ARROYO, Manuel, *Cuestiones Penológicas*, Tucuman, Editorial Richardet, 1955.

"Some Considerations on the Character and Organization of Prison Labour", in *Journal of Criminal Law*, 1958.

"Les exigences pénales d'aujourd'hui et la politique criminelle contemporaine", in *Revue Internationale de Criminologie et de Police Technique*, vol. XVI, 4, 1962.

LÓS, María, *Communist Ideology, Law and Crime: A Comparative View of the URSS and Poland*, Basingstoke, Macmillan, 1988.

LOWMAN, John, MENZIES, Robert J., PALYS, T.S. (eds.), *Transcarceration: Essays in the Sociology of Social Control*, Aldershot, 1987.

LUZÓN CUESTA, José María, "Responsabilidad civil por delito (Derecho Penal)", in *Enciclopedia Jurídica Básica*, t. IV, Madrid, Civitas, 1995, pp. 5916-5922.

LUZÓN PEÑA, Diego-Manuel, *Medición de la pena y sustitutivos penales*, Madrid, Instituto de Criminología de la Universidad Complutense de Madrid, 1979.

"Prevención general y Psicoanálisis", in *Derecho Penal y Ciencias Sociales*, Barcelona, Ed. Mir, 1982, pp. 149 ff.

LYNCH, J., "Crime in International Perspective", in James Q. WILSON, Joan PETERSILIA (eds.), *Crime*, San Francisco, CA, Institute of Contemporary Studies, 1995, pp. 11-39.

MABBOTT, J.D. (John David) (1898-1988), "Punishment", in *Mind*, 48, 1939, pp. 152-167, re-ed. in H.B. ACTON (ed.), *The Philosophy of Punishment, op. cit.*, pp. 39-54. Also in Stanley F. GRUPP, *Theories of Punishment*, Bloomington, London, Indiana University Press, 1971.

"Professor Flew on Punishment", in *Philosophy*, 30, 1955, pp. 256-265.
"Freewill and Punishment", in H.D. LEWIS (comp.), *Contemporary British Philosophy*, Third Series, London, Allen and Unwin, 1956, pp. 289-309.
MAC BRIDE, Sean (ed.), *Crime and Punishment*, Dublin, Ireland, Ward River Press, 1982.
MACKENZIE, Mary Margaret, *Plato on Punishment*, Berkeley, University of California Press, 1981.
MACKIE, John Leslie, "Morality and the Retributive Emotions", in *Criminal Justice Ethics*, 1982, pp. 3-11.
MacINTYRE, Alasdair, *After Virtue*, Notre Dame, Indiana, 1981.
MACLAGAN, W.G., "Punishment and Retribution", in *Philosophy*, 14, 1939, pp. 281-298.
MADDEN, Edward H., HANDY, Rollo, FARBER, Marvin, *Philosophical Perspectives on Punishment*, Springfield, Ill., Thomas, 1968.
MAKAREWICZ, Julius, *La evolución de la pena*, Madrid, Hijos de Reus ed. 1907.
MÄKELÄ, Klaus, "Om straffens verkningar", in *Eripainos oikeustiede*, 6, 1975, pp. 237-280.
MALAMUD GOTTI, Jaime E., "¿Debe subsistir el Derecho penal liberal?", in *Doctrina Penal*, 16, 1981.
MALLOW, Edward A., *The Ethics of Law Enforcement and Criminal Punishment*, Washington D.C., University Presses of America, 1983.
MANTOVANI, Ferrando, "Pene e misure alternative", in *Rivista Italiana di Diritto e Procedura Penale*, 1977.
MAPELLI CAFFARENA, Borja, TERRADILLOS BASOCO, Juan, *Las consecuencias jurídicas del delito*, 3rd ed., Madrid, Civitas, 1996.
MARCONI, Pio, *La libertà selvaggia: Stato e punizione nel pensiero anarchico*, 1st ed, Venecia, Marsilio, 1979.
MARI, Enrique Eduardo, *La problemática del castigo: el discurso de Jeremy Bentham y Michel Foucault*, 1st ed, Buenos Aires, Hachette, 1983.
MARTIN, R, "On the Logic of Justifying Legal Punishment", in *American Philosophical Quarterly*, 7, 1970, pp. 253-259.
MARTINAGE, Renée, *Punir le crime: la répression judiciaire depuis le Code pénal*, Villenueve d'Ascq, Espace Juridique, 1989.
MARTÍNEZ LAGO, Miguel Ángel, "Infracciones y sanciones tributarias (Derecho Financiero y Tributario)", in *Enciclopedia Jurídica Básica*, t. III, Madrid, Civitas, 1995, pp. 3582-3586.
MARTINSON, R., "The Age of Treatment. Some Implications of the Custody Treatment Dimension", in *Issues in Criminology*, 1966.
"What Works ? – Questions and Answers about Prison Reform", in *The Public Interest*, 35, Spring 1974, pp. 22-54.
MARX, Karl (1838-1883), ENGELS, Frederick, *The Communist Manifesto*, New York, Verso, 1998; New York, Penguin, 2002. Translation into Spanish, *El manifiesto comunista*.

MATHIESEN, Thomas, *The Politics of Abolition. Essays in Political Action Theory*, Scandinavian Studies in Criminology, Oslo-London, Martin Robertson, 1974.

"The Future of Control Systems – the Case of Norway", in D. GARLAND, P. YOUNG (eds.), *The Power to Punish*, London, Heinemann, 1983.

MATRAVERS, Matt (ed.), *Punishment and Political Theory*, Oxford and Portland, Oregon, Hart Publishing, 1999.

"Introduction", in MATRAVERS, Matt (ed.), *Punishment and Political Theory, op. cit.*, pp. 1-10.

"What to Say?: The Communicative Element in Punishment and Moral Theory", in MATRAVERS, Matt (ed.), *Punishment and Political Theory, op. cit.*, pp. 108-124.

MAURACH, Reinhart, *Deutsches Strafrecht: ein Lehrbuch*, Karlsruhe, C.F. Müller, 1954.

McCLOSKEY, H.J., "The Complexity of the Concepts of Punishment", in *Philosophy*, 37, 1962, pp. 307-325.

"A Note on Utilitarian Punishment", in *Mind*, 72, 1963, p. 599.

"A Non-Utilitarian Approach to Punishment", in *Inquiry*, 8, 1965, pp. 249-263.

"Utilitarian and Retributive Punishment", in *Journal of Philosophy*, 64, 1967, pp. 91-110.

McCORKLE, Korn, "Resocialization within Walls", *Readings in Criminology and Penology* (Dressler, ed.), 2nd ed, New York-London, 1972.

McPHERSON, T, "Punishment: Definition and Justification", in *Analysis*, 28, 1967, pp. 21-27.

McTAGGART, J., "Hegel's Theory of Punishment", in *International Journal of Ethics*, 6, 1895, pp. 479-502; also in his *Studies in Hegelian Cosmology*, Cambridge, Cambridge University Press, 1918, chapter 5. Included in Gertrude EZORSKY (comp.), *Philosophical Perspectives on Punishment*, Albany, State University of New York, 1972, pp. 40-55.

MEAD, George Herbert (1863-1931), "The Psychology of Punitive Justice", in *American Journal of Sociology*, 23, 1918, pp. 577-602.

MELOSSI, Dario, PAVARINI, Massimo, *Cárcel y fábrica*, México, Siglo XXI, Nueva Criminología, 1980. Translation into English, *The Prison and the Factory: Origins of the Penitentiary System*, London, Macmillan, 1981.

MENDOZA, "Hacia una posibilidad de un Derecho extra-penal", in *Libro Homenaje al Prof. Jiménez de Asúa*, Buenos Aires, 1964.

MENNINGER, Karl Augustus (1893-), *The Crime of Punishment*, New York, Viking Press, 1968.

MEYER, H., "Kant, Hegel und das Strafrecht", in *Fest. Engisch*, 1969, pp. 54 ff.

MIETHE, Terence, "Public Consensus on Crime Seriousness: Normative Structure or Methodological Artifact?", in *Criminology*, 20, 1982, pp. 515-526.

"Types of Consensus in Public Evaluations of Crime: An Illustration of Strategies for Measuring 'Consensus'", in *Journal of Criminal Law and Criminology*, 75, 1984, pp. 459-473.

MILGRAM, Stanley, "Some Conditions of Obedience and Disobedience to Authority", in *Human Relations*, 18, 1965, pp. 57-75.

Obedience to Authority, New York, Harper and Row, 1974.

MILITELLO, Vincenzo, *Prevenzione generale e commisurazione della pena*, Milano, Giuffrè, 1982.

MILL, John Stuart, *On Liberty*, Everyman's Edition, London, Dent, ed. 1910.

MILLER, Jacques-Alain, "La machine panoptique de Jeremy Bentham", in *Ornicar. Bulletin Périodique du Champ Freudien*, Paris, 3, May 1975.

MILLER, Jonathan (1934-), *The Uses of Pain*, introduction by Peter CADOGAN, London, South Place Ethical Society, 1973.

MILLER, W.A., "A Theory of Punishment", in *Philosophy*, 45, 1970, pp. 307-316.

MINSON, J., *The Genealogy of Morals: Nietzsche, Foucault, Donzelot and the Eccentricity of Ethics*, London, 1985.

MIRANDA, María Jesús, "Bentham en España", in *El Panóptico*, Madrid, Ediciones de La Piqueta, 1979.

MIR PUIG, Santiago, "Fundamento constitucional de la pena y teoría del delito", in *La reforma del Derecho Penal*, Barcelona, Bellaterra, 1980, pp. 107 ff.

Función de la pena y teoría del delito en el Estado social y democrático de Derecho, 2nd ed., Barcelona, Bosch, 1982.

"Funktion der Strafe und die Verbrechenslehre im sozialen und demokratischen Rechtsstaat", in *ZStW*, 95, 1983, pp. 413 ff.

"Función fundamentadora y función limitadora de la prevención general positiva", in *Poder y control*, 1986.

MITGUTSCH, Waltraud, *Punishment*, translation into English by Bisel MUELLER, London, Virago, 1988.

MOBERLY, Walter Hamilton, Sir (1881-), "Some Ambiguities in the Retributive Theory of Punishment", in *Proceedings of the Aristotelian Society*, 25, 1924, pp. 289-304.

The Ethics of Punishment, London, Faber, 1968.

MONACO, Lucio, *Prospettive dell'idea dello 'scopo' nella teoria della pena*, Napoli, Jovene, Publicacion della Facoltà Giuridica dell'Università di Napoli, CCXII, 1984.

MONKKONEN, E.H. (ed.), *Crime and Justice in American History*, Westport, CN, Meckler, 1991.

MONTESQUIEU, *De l'esprit des lois*, Paris, Garnier, 1748.

MONTORO BALLESTEROS, Alberto, "En torno a la idea de delito político", in *Horizontes de la Filosofía del Derecho (Homenaje a Luis García San Miguel)*, 2, Universidad de Alcalá, 2002, pp. 269-294.

MOORE, Mark H., "Public Health and Criminal Justice Approaches to Prevention", in Michael TONRY, David P. FARRINGTON (eds.), *Building a Safer Society: Strategic Approaches to Crime Prevention*, Chicago, University of Chicago Press, 1995, pp. 237-262.

"The Legitimation of Criminal Justice Policies and Practices", in *Perspectives on Crime and Justice: 1996-97 Lecture Series*, Washington, DC, National Institute of Justice, 1997.

MOORE, Mark H., ESTRICH, Susan R., McGILLIS, Daniel, SPELMAN, William, *Dangerous Offenders: The Elusive Target of Justice*, Cambridge, Massachusetts, Harvard University Press, 1984.

MORILLAS CUEVA, Lorenzo, "Prisión y Estado social y democrático de Derecho", in *Revista de la Facultad de Derecho de la Universidad de Granada*, 4, 1987, published in 1990.

Teoría de las consecuencias jurídicas del delito, Madrid, Tecnos, 1991.

MORRIS, A.M., *Women, Crime and Criminal Justice*, Oxford, 1987.

MORRIS, Herbert (1928-), (ed.), *Freedom and Responsibility*, Standford, Standford University Press, 1961.

"Persons and Punishment", in *The Monist*, 52, 1968, pp. 475-501; re-ed. in *On Guilt and Innocence..., op. cit.*, pp. 39-58.

"Guilt and Punishment", in *Personalist*, 52, 1971, pp. 305-321.

On Guilt and Innocence: Essays in Legal Philosophy and Moral Psychology, Berkeley, University of California Press, 1976.

"A Paternalistic Theory of Punishment", in *American Philosophical Quarterly*, 18, 4, 1981, pp. 263-271.

MORRIS, Norval, *The Future of Imprisonment*, Chicago, University of Chicago Press, 1974.

"Punishment, Desert and Rehabilitation", in Hyman GROSS, Andrew von HIRSCH (eds.), *Sentencing*, New York, Oxford University Press, 1981.

Madness and the Criminal Law, Chicago, University of Chicago Press, 1983.

MUNDLE, C.W.K., "Punishment and Desert", in *Philosophical Quarterly*, 4, 1954, pp. 216-228; re-ed. in H.B. ACTON, *The Philosophy of Punishment, op. cit.*, pp. 105-114.

MUÑAGORRI LAGUÍA, Ignacio, *Sanción penal y política criminal. Confrontación con la nueva defensa social*, Madrid, Reus, Biblioteca Jurídica de Autores Españoles y Extranjeros, 1977.

MUÑOZ CONDE, Francisco, "Función de la norma penal y reforma del Derecho penal", in *Nuevo Pensamiento Penal*, October-December, 1973.

"El principio de culpabilidad", *III Jornadas de Profesores de Derecho Penal*, Santiago de Compostela, 1975.

"La resocialización del delincuente, análisis y crítica de un mito", in *Cuadernos de Política Criminal*, 1979; also in *La reforma del Derecho Penal*, Barcelona, Bellaterra, 1980.

MURPHY, Jeffrie G., *Kant: The Philosophy of Right*, London, Macmillan, 1970.

Punishment and Rehabilitation, Belmont, California, Wadsworth, 1973.

"Marxism and Retribution", in *Philosophy and Public Affairs*, 2, 1973, pp. 217-243.

Retribution, Justice and Therapy: Essays in the Philosophy of Law, Dordrecht, Holland – Boston, D. Reidel Pub. Co., 1979.

"Retribution and the State's Interest in Punishment", in J.R. PENNOCK, J.W. CHAPMAN (eds.), *Criminal Justice, Nomos XXVII*, New York University Press, 1985, pp. 156-164.

"Retribution, Moral Education and the Liberal State", in *Criminal Justice Ethics*, 4, 1985, pp. 3-10.

MURPHY, Jeffrie G., HAMPTON, Jean, *Forgiveness and Mercy*, New York, Cambridge, 1989.

NAGIN, David, "Crime Rates, Sanction Levels and Constraints on Prison Population", in *Law and Society Review*, 12, 1978, pp. 341-366.

NAGLER, J., *Die Strafe*, Aalen, Scientia Verlag, 1979.

NARAYAN, U., "Appropiate Responses and Preventive Benefits: Justifying Censure and Hard Treatment in Legal Punishment", in *Oxford Journal of Legal Studies*, 13, 1993, pp. 166-182.

NATIONAL ADVISORY COMMISION ON CRIMINAL JUSTICE STANDARDS AND GOALS, *A National Strategy to Reduce Crime Final Report*, Washington DC, Government Printing Office, 1973.

NAUCKE, Wolfgang, *Tendenzen in der Strafrechtsentwicklung*, Karlsruhe, 1975.

"Generalprävention und Grundrechte der Person", in W. HASSEMER, K. LÜDERSEN, W. NAUCKE, *Hauptprobleme der General-prävention*, Frankfurt am Main, 1979; traslation into Italian, "Prevenzione generale e diritti fondamentali della persona", in *Teoria e prassi della prevenzione generale dei reati*, Bologna, 1980.

"Die Kriminalpolitik des Marburger Programms 1882", in *ZStW*, 94, 1982, pp. 525 ff.

"Le droit penal retributif selon Kant", in *Retribution et Justice Penale, Travaux et Recherches de l'Université de Droit, d'Economie et des Sciences Sociales de Paris*, Paris, P.U.F., 1983.

NAVAKWE, Walter Mutsumi (1940-), *Punishment and Prevention of Crime in Jeremy Bentham's Thought*, 1983, Microform.

NEBLET, W., "The Ethics of Guilt", in *The Journal of Philosophy*, 1974.

NEIER, Aryeh (1937-), *Crime and Punishment: A Radical Solution*, New York, Stein and Day, 1976.

NELKIN, D., "Discipline and Punish: Some Notes on the Margin", in *Howard Journal*, 28, 4, 1989, pp. 245-254.

NEUMANN, Ulfried (1947-), SCHROTH, Ulrich, *Neuere Theorien von Kriminalität und Strafe*, Darmstadt, Wissenschaftliche Buchgesellschaft, 1980.

NEWMAN, G., *Comparative Deviance: Perception and Law in Six Cultures*, New York, Elsevier, 1976.

The Punishment Response, New York, Harper and Row, 1978.

Just and Painful, London, MacMillan, 1983.

NIETZSCHE, Friedrich Wilhelm (1844-1900), "The Genealogy of Morals" (in *The Birth of Tragedy and the Genealogy of Morals)*, New York, 1956; edition in German, 1887.

NILSTUN, Tore, *Aristotle on Freedom and Punishment*, Lund, Studenlitteratu, 19.

NINO, Carlos Santiago, *La definición del delito*, Buenos Aires, Astrea, 1969.

Los límites de la responsabilidad penal: una teoría liberal del delito. Buenos Aires. Astrea. 1980.

"A Consensual Theory of Punishment", in *Philosophy and Public Affairs*, 12, 1983, pp. 289-306.

NORMANDEU, André, "Halte à la croissance des prisons ! ", in *Revue de Droit Penal et de Criminologie*, 1977.

"Le mythe de la réhabilitation", in *Revue de Droit Penale et de Criminologie*, 1978.

NORRIE, Alan William (1953-), *Crime, Reason and History: A Critical Introduction to Criminal Law*, Butterworth, Lexis-Nexis, 2001.

Law, Ideology and Punishmet: Retrieval and Critique to the Liberal Ideal of Criminal Justice, Dordrecht-Boston, Kluwer, 1991.

"T. Hobbes and the Philosophy of Punishment", in *Law and Philosophy*, 3, 2, 1984, pp. 229 ff.

"Albert Speer, Guilt, and The Space Between", in MATRAVERS, Matt (ed.), *Punishment and Political Theory, op. cit.*, pp. 133-152.

NOWAKOWSKI, "Freiheit, Schuld, Vergeltung", in *Fest. Rittler*, 1957, pp. 55 ff.

NOZICK, Robert, *Anarchy, State and Utopia*, Oxford, Basil Blackwell, 1974; translation into Spanish by Rolando TAMAYO, México, F.C.E., 1988.

Philosophical Explanations, Oxford, Clarendon Press, 1981.

NUÑEZ BARBERO, Ruperto, "El sentido actual de las sanciones criminales", in *R. E. P.*, 1971, pp. 1163 ff.

NUVOLONE, Pietro, "Le sanzioni criminali nel pensiero di Enrico Ferri e nel momento storico attuale" in *Revue Penale Suisse*, 1956, pp. 345 ff.

"Il rispetto della persona umana nell'esecuzione della pena", in *Justitia*, 1956.

"El problema de la reeducación del condenado", in *Revista Mexicana de Derecho Penal*, 1966.

OJEDA VELÁZQUEZ, Jorge, *Derecho de ejecución de penas*, México, Porrua, 1984.

OLDENQUIST, Andrew, "The Case for Revenge", in *The Public Interest*, 82, 1986, pp. 72-80.

"An Explanation of Retribution", in *Journal of Philosophy*, 9, 1988, pp. 464-478.

OLESA MUÑIDO, Francisco Felipe, *Las medidas de seguridad*, Barcelona, Bosch, 1951.

OPPENHEIMER, Heinrich, *The Rationale of Punishment*, London, University of London Press, 1913.

ORLAND, Leonard, "From Vengeance to Vengeance: Sentencing Reform and the Demise of Rehabilitation", in *Hofstra Law Review*, 7, 1978, pp. 29-56.

ORWELL, George, *Nineteen Eighty-Four*, New York, Penguin Books, 1949.

O'SHAUGHNESSY, "Forgiveness", in *Philosophy*, 1967.

PACKER, Herbert L., *The Limits of Criminal Sanction*, Standford, Calif., Standford University Press, 1968. Translation into Italian, *I limiti della sanzione penale*, Milano, 1978.

PADOVANI, Tullio, *L'utopia punitiva: il problema delle alternative alla detenzione nella sua dimensione storica*, Milano, Giuffrè, 1981.

PAGE, L., "The Retributive Theory of Punishment", in *Nineteenth Century and After*, 148, 1950, pp. 258-265.

PAGLIARO, Antonio, "Aspetti giuridici della prevenzioni", in *L'Indice Penale*, 1976.

"Prospettive di riforma", in *Pene e misure alternative nell'attuale momento storico. (Convengo di Studio "Enrico di Nicola". Atti)*, 1977, pp. 415 ff.

"La riforma delle sanzioni penali tra teoria e prassi", in *Rivista Italiana*, 1979, pp. 1189 ff.

PANTALEÓN PRIETO, Fernando, "Responsabilidad contractual (Derecho Civil)", in *Enciclopedia Jurídica Básica*, t. IV, Madrid, Civitas, 1995, pp. 5922-5927.

PARADA VÁZQUEZ, J.R., "El poder sancionador de la Administración y la crisis del sistema judicial penal", in *RAP*, 67, 1972.

"Evolución y constitucionalización de las infracciones administrativas", in *PJ*, 2, 1982.

PFEIFFER, Diezmar J., SCHEERER, Sebastian, *Kriminalsoziologie*, Stuttgart, Koh lhammer Urban-Taschenbücher, 1979.

PAIXÂO, Antônio Luiz, *Recuperar ou punir?: como o estado trata o criminoso*, Sâo Paulo, Cortez Editora, Editora Autores Asociados, 1987.

PAREJO ALFONSO, Luciano, "Infracciones y sanciones urbanísticas", in *Enciclopedia Jurídica Básica*, t. III, Madrid, Civitas, 1995, pp. 3585-3589.

PARENT, W.A., "The Whole Life View of Criminal Desert", in *Ethics*, 86, 1976, pp. 350-354.

PASHUKANIS, Eugenii Bronislavovich (1891-1938?), *General Theory of Law and Marxism*, London, Ink Links, 1978.

PAULEY, W.C., "Beccaria and Punishment", in *International Journal of Ethics*, 35, 1924, pp. 404-412.

PERELMAN, Chaïm, *Justice et Raison*, Bruxelles, Presses Universitaires de Bruxelles, 1963. 2nd ed., 1970.

PÉREZ ROYO, Fernando, *Los delitos y las infracciones en materia tributaria*, IEF, 1986.

PERROT, Michelle (ed.), *L'impossible prison*, Paris, Seuil, 1980.

PESET, José Luis (coord.), *Enfermedad y castigo*, Madrid, Consejo Superior de Investigaciones Científicas, Instituto "Arnau de Vilanova", 1984.

PETERSON, Mark A., BRAIKER, Harriet B., *Who Commits Crimes*, Cambridge, Massachussets, Oelgeschlager, Jun and Hain, 1981.

PETERSSON, Ingrid, *Utilitarianism, Responsibility and Punishment: with Special Reference to R.B. Brandt's Defence of Utilitarianism*, Lund, Sweden, Tryckbaren, 1976.

PETROCELLI, "La funzione della pena", in *Scritti in Memoria di E. Massari*, Napoli, 1938.

PETTIFER, Ernst William (1882-1962), *Punishment of Former Days*. Preface by Frank BROOK. New preface by Ronald GREGORY, 1st ed., Wakefield, EP Publishing, 1974.

PETTINICO, G., "Crime and Punishment; America Changes its Mind", in *The Public Perspective*, September-October 1994.

PETTIT, Philip, *Judging Justice*, London, Routledge & Kegan Paul, 1980.

"Habermas on Truth and Justice", in G.H.R. PARKINSON (ed.), *Marx and Marxisms*, Cambridge, Cambridge University Press, 1982.

"Social Holism and Moral Theory", in *Proceedings of the Australian Society*, 86, 1985-1986, pp. 173-197.

"Free Riding and Foul Dealing", in *Journal of Philosophy*, 83, 1986, pp. 361-279.

"Rights, Constraints and Trumps", in *Analysis*, 47, 1987, pp. 8-14.

"The Consequentialist Can Recognise Rights", in *Philosophical Quarterly*, 38, 1988, pp. 42-55.

"The Paradox of Loyalty", in *American Philosophical Quarterly*, 25, 1988, pp. 163-171.

PHILLIPSON, Coleman (1878-), *Three Criminal Law Reformers: Beccaria, Bentham, Romilly*, Montclair, N.J., P. Smith, 1970.

PINATEL, "Le traitement des delinquants", in *Revue de Science Criminelle et de Droit Pénal Comparé*, 1964.

" La prison, peut-elle être transformée en institution de traitement ? ", in *Annales Internationales de Criminologie*, 1969.

PINCOFFS, Edmund L., *The Rationale of Legal Punishment*, New York, Humanities Press, 1966.

PLAMENATZ, J., "Responsibility, Blame and Punishment", in LASLETT, Peter, RUNCIMAN, W.G. (eds.), *Philosophy, Politics and Society*, Third Series, Oxford, Blackwell, 1967, pp. 173-193.

PLATO, *Plato: Five Dialogues*, Indianapolis, Hackett Publishing Co., 1981.

PLATT, Tony, TAKAGI, Paul (eds.), *Punishment and Penal Discipline*, Berkeley, California, 1980.

POSNER, Richard A., "Optimal Sentences for White Collar Criminals", in *American Criminal Law Review*, 17, 1980.

POULANTZAS, Nicos Ar, *State, Power, Socialism*, London, Verso, 1980.

PRICE-LAPEDIS, "Jail Inmates Also Are People Who Need People", in *Federal Probation*, September 1965.

PRIMORATZ, Igor, *Justifying Legal Punishment*, Atlantic Highlands, N.J., Humanities Press International, 1989.

QUINTANO RIPOLLÉS, "Culpabilidad y retribución como premisas de la justicia penal", in *Homenaje al profesor Luis Legaz y Lacambra. Estudios Jurídico-Sociales, Universidad de Santiago de Compostela*, 1950, pp. 1027 ff.

"La evolución del Derecho penal moderno ('contra corriente')", in *Anuario de Derecho Penal y Ciencias Penales*, 1957.

QUINTON, A.M., "On Punishment", in *Analysis*, 14, 1953, pp. 133-142; re-ed. in H.B. ACTON, *The Philosophy of Punishment, op. cit.*

RABIE, Marinus André, *Punishment: an Introduction to the Principles*, 3rd ed., Johanesburg, Lex Patria, 1981 ; 4th ed., Cape Town, Lex Patria, 1985.

RABOSSI, Eduardo A., "Sobre la justificación moral del castigo", in *Problemas actuales de las Ciencias Penales y de la Filosofía del Derecho-Homenaje al profesor L. Jiménez de Asúa*, Buenos Aires, Ed. Pannedille, 1970, pp. 185-202.

"Sobre la justificación moral de las acciones. El tema del castigo", in *Crítica-Revista Hispanoamericana de Filosofía*, IV, 1972, pp. 3-46.

La justificación moral del castigo, Buenos Aires, Astrea, Colección Filosofía y Derecho, 5, 1976.

RADZINOWICZ, Leon, Sir, *Ideology and Crime*, New York, Columbia University Press, 1966.

RAMÍREZ DELGADO, Juan Manuel, *Penología. Estudios de las diversas penas y medidas de seguridad*, México, Porrúa, 1995.

RANULF, Svend (1894-1953), *Moral Indignation and Middle Class Psychology: a Sociological Study*, Copenhagen, Levin & Munksgaard, 1938.

RASHDALL, H., "The Theory of Punishment", in *International Journal of Ethics*, 2, 1981, pp. 20-31.

"Mr. Bradley on Punishment", in *International Journal of Ethics*, 4, 1984, pp. 241-243.

RAWLS, John, "Two Concepts of Rules", in *The Philosophical Review*, 64, 1955, pp. 3-32.

A Theory of Justice, Oxford, Clarendon Press, 1962. Oxford, Oxford University Press, 1971. Cambridge, Massachusetts, The Belknap Press of Harvard University Press, 1971; translation into Spanish by María Dolores GONZÁLEZ SOLER. México, F.C.E, 1978.

La justicia como equidad. Una reformulación. Edited by Erin KELLY, Barcelona, Paidos, 2002.

RAYNOR, Peter, *Social Work, Justice and Control*, Oxford, Basil Blackwell, 1985.

RAZ, Joseph, *The Authority of Law. Essays on Law and Morality*, Oxford, Clarendon Press, 1969; translation into Spanish by Rolando TAMAYO, México, U.N.A.M., 1982.

The Concept of a Legal System, Oxford, Clarendon Press, 1970.

REISS, Albert J., *The Police and the Public*, New Haven, Conn., Yale University Press, 1971.

REYES MONTERREAL, J.M., *Acción y responsabilidad civil derivada de delitos y faltas*, Madrid, 1958.

RICO, J.M., "Le droit de punir", in *Criminologie*, XIX, 1, 1986, pp. 113-140.

RIEFF, Philip (1922-), *The Triumph of the Therapeutic: Uses of Faith After Freud*, Chicago, University of Chicago Press, 1966.

ROBERT, Philippe, "L'utilitarisme, les économistes et la délinquance", in *Archives de Philosophie du Droit*, Sirey, 26, 1981.

ROBERTS, J., "Public Opinion, Crime and Criminal Justice", in *Crime and Justice*, 16, 1992, pp. 99-180.

ROBERTS, J., STALANS, R., *Public Opinion, Crime and Criminal Justice*, Boulder, CO, Westview, 1997.

ROBLES, Gregorio, *Sociología del Derecho*, 2nd ed., Madrid, Civitas, 1997.

Crimen y castigo (Ensayo sobre Durkheim), Madrid, Civitas, 2001.

"Émile Durkheim (1858-1917)", in *Juristas universales*, Madrid, Marcial Pons, 2002.

ROCK, P. (ed.), *The History of Criminology*, Aldershot, Dartmouth, 1994.

RÖDER, Karl David August (1806-1879), *Necesaria reforma del sistema penal español mediante el establecimiento del régimen celular*, translation into Spanish by GYL, Madrid, 1873.

Las doctrinas fundamentales reinantes sobre el delito y la pena, translation into Spanish by F. GINER, Madrid, 1876.

RODIÈRE, Michèle, *L'abolition de la peine de mort*, Paris, Documentation Française, 1987.

RODRÍGUEZ DEVESA, José María, "Tratamiento psiquiátrico en la delincuencia", in *R. E. P.*, 1970, pp. 1121 ff.

RODRÍGUEZ MOURULLO, Gonzalo, "Significado político y fundamento ético de la pena y de la medida de seguridad", in *Revista General de Legilación y Jurisprudencia*, Madrid, Reus, 219, 1965.

"Cara y cruz de las sanciones penales", in *Cuadernos para el Diálogo*, "Delito y Sociedad", XXVIII, December 1971, pp. 46 ff.

Delito y pena en la jurisprudencia constitucional, Madrid, Civitas, 2002.

RODRÍGUEZ-SAÑUDO, Fermín, "Sanciones administrativas (Derecho del Trabajo y de la Seguridad Social)", in *Enciclopedia Jurídica Básica*, IV, Madrid, Civitas, 1995, pp. 6060-6063.

ROOD-PIJPERS, E.B.M., *Mensen over misdaad en straf*, Arnhem, Gouda Quint, 1988.

ROSE, A.M., PRELL, A.E., "Does the Punishment Fit Crime? A Study in Social Validation", in *American Journal of Sociology*, 61, 1955, pp. 247-259.

ROSENBAUM, D.R., *Community Crime Prevention*, Beverly Hills, CA, Sage, 1986.

ROSS, A., *Guilt, Responsibility and Punishment*, London, 1975.

"La finalidad del castigo", in *Homenaje a A.R. Gioja: Derecho, Filosofía y Lenguaje*, Astrea, Buenos Aires, 1976.

ROSS, W.D., "The Ethics of Punishment", in *Journal of Philosophical Studies*, 4, 1929, pp. 205-211.

The Right and the Good, Oxford, Clarendon Press, 1965.

ROSSI, P.H., SIMPSON, J.E., MILLER, J.L., "Beyond Crime Seriousness: Fitting the Punishment to the Crime", in *Journal of Quantitative Criminology*, 1, 1985, pp. 59-90.

ROSSI, P.H., WAITE, E., BOSE, C.E., BERK, R.E., "The Seriousness of Crimes: Normative Structure and Individual Differences", in *American Sociological Review*, 39, 1974, pp. 224-237.

ROTHMAN, D, "Prisons: The Failure Model", in *The Nation*, 21 December 1974.

ROXIN, Claus, *Iniciación al Derecho Penal de hoy*, translation, introdution and notes by MUÑOZ CONDE and LUZÓN PEÑA, Sevilla, 1981.

"Sinn und Grenzen staatlicher Strafe", in *Juristische Schulung. Zeitschrift für Studium und Ausbildung*, pp. 377-387; translation into Spanish, "Sentido y límites de la pena estatal", by LUZÓN PEÑA, in *Problemas básicos del Derecho Penal*, Sevilla, Universidad de Sevilla, 1981.

"Schuld, Prävention und Verantwortlichkeit im Strafrecht", in *Fest. Bockelmann*, 1978, pp. 279 ff. Translation into Spanish, "Culpabilidad, prevención y responsabilidad en Derecho penal", in *Culpabilidad y prevención en Derecho penal,* Madrid, 1981.

RUBINSTEIN, Ariel, *On an Anomaly of the Deterrent Effect of Punishment,* Jerusalem, Hebrew University of Jerusalem, Dept. of Economics, 1979.

RUIZ VADILLO, Enrique, "Responsabilidad civil (art. 20 del Código Penal)", in *Comentarios a la Legislación Penal,* V, vol. 1, Madrid, Edersa, 1985.

RUSCHE, Georg, "Labor Market and Penal Sanctions: Thoughts on the Sociology of Punishment", translation into English, edited in Tony PLATT – Paul TAKAGI (eds.), *Punishment and Penal Discipline,* Berkeley, California, 1980.

RUSCHE, Georg, KIRCHHEIMER, *Punishment and Social Structure,* Preface by Thorsten SELLIN, New York, Russell & Russell, 1968; New York, Columbia University Press, 1939.

RUTHERFORD, Andrew (1940-), *Prisons and the Process of Justice: the Reductionist Challenge,* London, Heinemann, 1984.

RYAN, M, *The Politics of Penal Reform,* London, 1983.

SADE, Marquis of, *Diálogo entre un sacerdote y un moribundo,* Buenos Aires, Argonauta, 1980.

SADURSKI, Wojciech, "Distributive Justice and the Theory of Punishment", in *Oxford Journal of Legal Studies,* 5, 1, 1985, pp. 47 ff.

Giving Desert its Due, Dordrecht, Reidel, 1985.

SAINZ CANTERO, José Antonio, "La sustitución de la pena de privación de libertad", in *Estudios Penales II. La reforma penitenciaria,* Santiago de Compostela, 1978.

SALEILLES, Raymond (1855-1912), *L'individualisation de la peine,* Paris, F. Alcan, 1898, 3rd ed. 1927, introduction by Gabriel TARDE; *The individualization of Punishment,* translation by Rachel SZOLD JASTROW; introduction by Roscoe POUND, Boston, Little Brown, 1911.

SANDEL, Michael, *Liberalism and the Limits of Justice,* Cambridge, Cambridge University Press, 1982.

Liberalism and its Critics, Oxford, Blackwell, 1984.

SARTRE, Jean Paul, *El muro,* preface by Guillermo DE TORRE, Buenos Aires, Losada, 4th ed., 1978.

SCHEDLER, George, *Behaviour Modification and 'Punishment' of the Innocent: Towards a Justification of the Institution of Legal Punishment,* Amsterdam, Grüner, 1977.

SCHMIDHÄUSER, Eberhard, *Vom Sinn der Strafe,* Göttinguen, 1958.

SCHMUR, "The New Penology: Fact or Fiction", in *Journal of Criminal Law,* November-December, 1958.

SCHÖCH, "Das Marburger Programm aus der Sicht der modernen Kriminologie", in *ZStW,* 94, 1982, pp. 864 ff.

SCIMÉ, Salvador Francisco, *Pena y libertad: el fin de la pena como garantía de la libertad,* Buenos Aires, Pensamiento Jurídico Editora, 1986.

SCULL, Andrew, *Decarceration: Community Treatment and the Deviant – A Radical View*, Englewood Cliffs, N.J., Prentice Hall, 1977. Cambridge, Polity Press in Association with B. Blackwell, Oxford, 1984.

"Community Corrections: Panacea, Progress or Pretence?", in GARLAND, David, YOUNG, Peter (eds.), *The Power to Punish*, London Heinemann, 1983.

SECHREST, Lee, WHITE, Susan O., BROWN, Elisabeth D., *The Rehabilitation of Criminal Offenders: Problems and Prospects*, Washington DC, National Academy of Science, 1979.

SELLIN, Thorsten (1896-), "L'effet intimidant de la peine (Etude de Sociologie Criminelle)", in *Rev. Sc. Cr.,* 1960, pp. 579 ff.

Capital Punishment, New York, 1967.

SEN, Amartya Kumar, "Utilitarianism and Welfarism", in *Journal of Philosophy*, 76, 1979, pp. 463-489.

Choice, Welfare and Measurement, Oxford, Blackwell, 1982.

"Poor, Relatively Speaking", in *Oxford Economic Papers*, 1982.

SESSAR, Klaus, "Die Resozialisierung der strafenden Gesellschaft. Gedanken zu einer Tagung der Stuttgarter Gemeinschaft 'Artz und Seelsger'", in *Zeitschrift für die gesamte Strafrechswissenschaft*, 1969.

SHEARING, Clifford D., STENNING, Philip, "From the Panopticum to Disney World: The Development of Discipline", in Anthony DOOB, Edward L. GREENSPAN (eds.), *Perspectives in Criminal Law: Essays in Honour of John Ll. J. Edwards*, Aurora, Canada Law Book, 1984.

SHELEFF, Leon Shaskolsky, "From Restitutive Law to Repressive Law: Durkheim's The Division of Labor in Society Revisited", in *Archives Européenes de Sociologie (European Journal of Sociology)*, 16, 1975, pp. 16-45.

Ultimate Penalties: Capital Punishment, Life Imprisonment, Physical Torture, Columbus, Ohio, 1987.

SHER, George, *Desert*, Princeton, NJ, Princeton University Press, 1987.

SILVELA, Luis, *El Derecho Penal en principios y en la legislación vigente en España*, Madrid, R. Fé, 1903.

SIMON, J., FEELEY, M, "True Crime: The New Penology and the Public Discourse on Crime", in T. BLOMBERG, S. COHEN (eds.), *Punishment and Social Control*, New York, Aldine de Gruyter, 1995.

SINGER, Richard G., *Just Deserts: Sentencing Based on Equality and Desert*, Cambridge, Massachusetts, Ballinger, 1979.

SINGER, Simon I, *Recriminalizing Delinquency*, New York, Cambridge University Press, 1996.

SINISCALCO, Marco, *Depenalizzazione e garanzia*, Bologna, Il Mulino, 1983.

SMART, J.C., "Free Will, Praise and Blame", in *Mind*, 1961.

SMITH, Adam, *The Theory of Moral Sentiments* (1759), Oxford, 1976.

SMITH, D.J, "Less Crime Without More Punishment", in *Edinburgh Law Review*, 3, 1999, pp. 394-316.

SMITH, J.M., "Punishment: A Conceptual Map and a Normative Claim", in *Ethics*, 75, 1964, pp. 285-290.

SMITH, Roger, *Trial by Medicine: Insanity and Responsibility in Victorian Trials*, Edinburgh, Edinburgh University Press, 1981.

SNARE, A. (ed.), *Beware of Punishment*, Oslo, Pax Forlag, 1995.

SOCIETÉ INTERNATIONALE DE DÉFENSE SOCIALE, «Programme Minimum de la Société Internationale de Défense Sociale", in *Cahiers de Défense Sociale*, 1973, pp. 23 ff.

SÓFOCLES, *Antígona*, in Colección Clásicos Inolvidables, Buenos Aires, El Ateneo, 2nd ed. 1950.

SOLARI, Gioele (1872-1952), "Kant e la dottrina penale della retribuzione", in *Rivista di Filosofia*, 20, 1929, pp. 25-58.

SORELL, Tom, *Moral Theory and Capital Punishment*, Oxford, U.K. – New York, USA, B. Blackwell in association with the Open University, 1988.

"Punishment in a Kantian Framework", in Matt MATRAVERS (ed.), *Punishment and Political Theory, op. cit.*, pp. 10-28.

SOTO NIETO, F., *La responsabilidad derivada del ilícito culposo*, Madrid, 1982.

SPIERENBURG, Petrus Cornelis, *The Spectacle of Suffering: Executions and the Evolution of Repression*, Cambridge, Cambridge University Press, 1984.

SPITZER, S., "Notes Toward a Theory of Punishment and Social Change", in *Research in Law and Sociology*, 2, 1979, pp. 207-229.

"Punishment and Social Organisation: A Study of Durkheim's Theory of Evolution", in *Law and Society Review*, 9, 1975, pp. 613-637.

"The Rationalization of Crime Control in Capitalist Society", in S. COHEN, A. SCULL (eds.), *Social Control and the State*, Oxford, 1983.

SPITZER, S., SCULL, A., "Social Control in Historical Perspective", in D. GREENBERG (ed.), *Corrections and Punishments*, Beverly Hills, California, 1977.

SPRIGGE, Timothy L.S., "An Utilitarian Reply to Mr. McCloskey", in *Inquiry*, 1965.

STAWELL, F.J., "Hegel's Theory of Punishment", in *International Journal of Ethics*, 7, 1896-1897, pp. 95-96.

STEFANI, Gaston, LEVASSEUR, G., JAMBU-MERLIN, R., *Criminologie et science pénitentiaire*, 5th ed, Paris, Dalloz, 1982.

STERN, L., "Deserved Punishment, Deserved Harm, Deserved Blame", in *Philosophy*, 45, 1970, pp. 317-329.

STILLMAN, Peter G., "Hegel's Idea of Punishment", in *Journal of the History of Philosophy*, 14, 1976, pp. 169-182.

STINCHCOMBE, Arthur L. (*et al.*), *Crime and Punishment – Changing Attitudes in America*, San Francisco, Jossey-Bass Publishers, 1980.

STRATENWERTH, Günter, "Strafrecht und Sozialtheraphie", in *Festschrift für Bockelmann*, 1979.

STRAWSON, P., "Freedom and Resentment", in *Proceedings of the British Academy*, XLVIII, 1962.

STRONG, E.W., "The Justification of Juridical Punishment", in *Ethics*, 79, 1968, pp. 187-198.

STRUCHKOV, N.A., *Correction of the Convicted: Law, Theory, Practice*, translation into English by Oleg STIEFFELMAN, Moscow, Progress Publishers, 1982.

SUAY RINCON, José, *Sanciones administrativas*, Bolonia, 1989.

SUBRAMANYAM, Karattoluvu Ganapati (1903-), *Can the State Kill its Citizen?* Introduction by S. Mohan KUMARANGALAM, Madras, Madras Law Journal Office, 1969.

SUEIRO, Daniel, *La pena de muerte. Ceremonial. Historia. Procedimientos*, Barcelona, Alianza Editorial, 1974.

SUTHERLAND, Edwin Hardin (1883-1950), *Principles of Criminology*, 4th ed, Chicago, J.B. Lippincott Co. 1947.

SUTHERLAND, *White Collar Crime*, 2nd ed., New York, 1961.

SZABO, D., "Nature et culture, l'inné et l'aquis. Quelques considérations sur la réactualisation du débat et ses incidences sur la criminologie", in *L'Année Sociologique*, 35, 1985, pp. 233-271.

SZUMSKI, Bonnie, HALL, Lynn, BURSELL, Susan (eds.), *The Death Penalty: Opposing Viewpoints*, St. Paul, Minn., Greenhaven Press, 1986.

TALLACK, William (1831-1908), *Penological and Preventive Principles*, New York, Garland Pub. 1984.

TARDE, Gabriel de (1843-1904), *Penal Philosophy*, translation into English by Rapelje HOWELL, preface by Edward LINDSEY and introduction by Robert H. GAULT, Montclair, N.J., Patterson Smith, 1968, c. 1912.

TAYLOR, Ian, *Law and Order: Arguments for Socialism*, London, Macmillan, 1981.

"Against Crime for Socialism", in *Crime and Social Justice*, 18, 1982, pp. 4-15.

TAYLOR, Ian, WALTON, Paul, YOUNG, Jock, *Critical Criminology*, London, Routledge & Kegan Paul, 1975; translation into Spanish, *Criminología Crítica*, México, Siglo XXI, 1977.

The New Criminology: For a Social Theory of Deviance, London, Routledge & Kegan Paul, 1975. Translation into Spanish, *La nueva Criminología. Contribución a una teoría de la conducta desviada*, Buenos Aires, Amorrortu, 1975.

TEN, C.L., *Crime, Guilt, and Punishment: A Philosophical Introduction*, Oxford, Clarendon Press; New York, Oxford University Press, 1987.

"Mr Thompson on the Distribution of Punishment", in *Philosophical Quarterly*, 18, 1967, pp. 253-254.

The Economics of Crime and Punishment; A Conference sponsored by American Enterprise Institute for Public Policy Research, Washington, American Enterprise Institute for Public Policy Research, 1973.

TEZANOS, José Félix, "Los límites de la obediencia. Consideraciones sobre el experimento de Stanley Milgram", in *Sistema*, 12, 1976, pp. 99-114.

THALBERG, I., "Remorse", in *Mind*, 1963.

THOMAS, C.W., CAGE, R., FOSTER, S., "Public Opinion on Criminal Law and Legal Sanctions: An Examination of Two Conceptual Models", in *Journal of Criminal Law and Criminology*, 67, 1976, pp. 110-116.

THOMPSON, D.F., "Retribution and the Distribution of Punishment", in *Philosophical Quarterly*, 16, 1966, pp. 341-353.

TITTLE, C., *Control Balance: Towards a General Theory of Deviance*, Boulder CO, Westview Press, 1995.

TOBY, "Is Punishment Necessary?", in *Journal of Criminal Law*, September, 1964.

TONRY, Michael, ZIMRING, Franklin E. (eds.), *Reform and Punishment: Essays on Criminal Sentencing*, Chicago, University of Chicago Press, 1983.

TREMBLAY, P., "La stabilité de la peine: une perspective anti-évolutionniste", in *Revue Internationale de Criminologie et de Police Technique*, XXXIX, 1, 1986, pp. 31-49.

TWENTIETH-CENTURY FUND TASK FORCE ON CRIMINAL SENTENCING, *Fair and Certain Punishment*, New York, McGraw-Hill, 1976.

TZITZIS, J., "La notion de retribution dans la philosophie politique de T. Hobbes", in *Archives de Philosophie du Droit*, 28, Paris, Sirey, 1983.

UMBREIT, Mark S. (1949-), *Crime and Reconciliation: Creative Options for Victims and Offenders*, Nashville, Abingdon Press, 1985.

VANBERG, Viktor, *Verbrechen, Strafe und Abschreckung: die Theorie der Generalprävention im Lichte der neueren sozialwissenschaftlichen Diskussion*, Tübingen, J.C.B. Mohr, 1982.

VARAUT, Jean-Marc, *Le droit au droit : Pour un libéralisme institutionnel*, Paris, Presses Universitaires de France, 1986.

VASALLI, "Funciones e insuficiencias de la pena", in *Libro Homenaje al Prof. Jiménez de Asúa*, I, Buenos Aires, 1964.

VECCHIO, Giorgio del, *Sobre el fundamento de la justicia penal*, translation into Spanish by Eustaquio GALÁN, Madrid, Reus, 1947.

VERDIER, R. (ed.), *La vengeance*, vol. I, Paris, Cujas, 1980.

VEZZETTI, Hugo, "Locura y delito. La regeneración moral de los argentinos". "Penalidad y moralización para una historia de la locura y la psicología de la Argentina", in *Revista Argentina de Psicología*, 26 and 30.

VON HIRSCH, Andrew, "Prediction of Criminal Conduct and Preventive Confinement of Convicted Persons", in *Buffalo Law Review*, 21, 1972, pp. 717-758.

Doing Justice: The Choice of Punishments, New York, Hill and Wang, 1976.

"Commensurability and Crime Prevention: Evaluating Formal Sentencing Structures and their Rationale", in *Journal of Criminal Law and Criminology*, 74, 1, 1983, pp. 209-248.

Past or Future of Crimes: Deservedness and Dangerousness in the Sentencing of Criminals, New Brunswick, NJ, Rutgers University Press, 1985.

Past and Future Crimes, Manchester, Manchester University Press, 1985.

Censure and Sanctions, Oxford, Clarendon Press, 1993.

"Punishment, Penance and the State: A Reply to Duff", in MATRAVERS, Matt (ed.), *Punishment and Political Theory*, *op. cit.*, pp. 69-83.

VON HIRSCH, Andrew, ASHWORTH, A., "Not Just Deserts: A Response to Braithwaite and Pettit", in *Oxford Journal of Legal Studies*, 13, 1992, pp. 83-96.

(eds.), *Principled Sentencing: Readings on Theory and Policy*, 2nd ed., Oxford, Hart Publishing, 1998.

VON HIRSCH, Andrew, GARLAND, David, WAKEFIELD, A. (eds.), *The Ethics of Situational Crime Prevention*, Oxford, Hart Publishing, 2000.

VON HIRSCH, Andrew, HANRAHAN, K., "Determinate Penalty Systems in America: an Overview", in *Crime and Delinquency*, 27, 1981, pp. 289-316.

VULLIERME, Jean-Louis (1955-), "La fin de la justice pénale", in *Archives de Philosophie du Droit*, 28, 1983, pp. 155-179.

WAISS, J.A., "The Justification of Punishment", in *The Review of Methaphysics*, 1972.

WALKER, Hillary, BEAUMONT, Bill, *Probation Work : Critical Theory and Socialist Practice*, Oxford, Basil Blackwell, 1981.

WALKER, Nigel, *Sentencing in a Rational Society*, Harmondsworth, Penguin, 1972.

Punishment, Danger and Stigma: The Morality of Criminal Justice, Oxford, Basil Blackwell, 1980. Totowa, New Jersey, Barnes and Noble Books, 1980.

Sentencing: Theory, Law and Practice, London, Butterworths, 1985.

WALKER, Nigel, HOUGH, Mike (eds.), *Public Attitudes to Sentencing: Surveys from Five Countries*, Aldershot, Gower, 1988.

WALKER, Nigel, MARSH, C., "Do Sentences Affect Public Disapproval?", in *British Journal of Criminology*, 24, 1, 1984, p. 27.

WALTERS, Gary C., CRUSEL, Joane, *Punishment*, San Francisco, W.H. Freeman, 1977.

WALTERS, R.H., CHEYNE, J.A., BANKS, R.K. (eds.), *Punishment*, Harmondsworth, 1972.

WASIK, Martin, VON HIRSCH, Andrew, "Non-Custodial Penalties and the Principles of Desert", in *Criminal Law Review*, 1988, pp. 555-572.

WASSERSTROM, Richard A., "Some Problems on the Definition and Justification of Punishment", in A. GOLDMA, J. KIM (eds.), *Values and Morals*, Dordrecht, Reidel, 1978.

"Punishment", in *Philosophy and Social Issues*, Notre Dame, Notre Dame University Press, 1980, pp. 112-151.

"Why Punish the Guilty", in *Princeton University Magazine*, 20, 1984, pp. 14-19.

WEBER, Max (1864-1920), *Economy and Society* (1920), eds. G. ROTH, G. WITTICH, 2 vols., Berkeley, Ca., 1978.

WEIHOFEN, H., "Retribution is Obsolete", in *Nomos III: Responsibility*, ed. by C.J. FRIEDRICH, Liberal Arts Press, New York, 1960, pp. 116-127.

WELZEL, Hans (1904-), *Das deutsche Strafrecht: eine systematische Darstellung*, Berlin, de Gruyter, 1969.

Abhanlungen zum Strafrecht und zur Rechtsphilosophie, Berlin-New York, de Gruyter, 1975.

WESTERMARCK, E.A., "The Essence of Revenge", in *Mind*, 7, 1898, pp. 289-310.

WHEELER, Stanton, "Socialization in Correctional Communities", in *American Sociological Review*, 1961.

Controlling Delinquents, New York, 1968.

WHITELEY, C.H., "Nowell-Smith on Retribution and Responsibility", in *Mind*, 57, 1948, pp. 230-231.

"On Retribution", in *Philosophy*, 31, 1956, pp. 154-157.

WIENER, M. (ed.), *Humanitarianism or Control? A Symposium on Aspects of Nineteenth Century Social Reform in Britain and America*, Rice University Studies, 67, 1981, 1.

"The March of Penal Progress?", in *The Journal of British Studies*, 26, 1987, pp. 83-96.

WILSON, James Q., *Thinking About Crime*, New York, Random House, 1975. New York, Basic Books, 1983.

WILSON, James Q., HERRNSTEIN, R.J., *Crime and Human Nature*, New York, Simon and Schuster, 1986.

WILSON, Paul R., "What is Deviant Language?", in Paul R. WILSON, John BRAITHWAITE (eds.), *Two Faces of Deviance: Crimes of the Powerless and Powerful*, Brisbane, University of Queensland Press, 1978.

WILSON, Paul R., BROWN, J.W., *Crime and the Community*, Brisbane, University of Queensland Press, 1973.

WINCH, P., "Ethical Reward and Punishment", in *Ethics and Action*, London, Routledge and Kegal Paul, 1972, pp. 210 ff.

WINDLESHAM, Lord, *Politics, Punishment and Populism*, New York, Oxford University Press, 1998.

WOLFGANG, Marvin E., FIGLIO, Robert M., TRACEY, Paul E., SINGER, Simon I., *The National Survey of Crime Severity*, Washington, DC, US Government Printing Office, 1985.

WOOTTON, Barbara (1897-), *Crime and the Criminal Law: Reflections of a Magistrate and Social Scientist*, 2nd ed., London, Stevens, 1981.

WRIGHT, Martin, *Making Good: Prisons, Punishment, and Beyond*, Introduction by Barbara Wootton, London, Burnett Books, 1982.

WRIGHT, Martin, GALAWAY, Burt (eds.), *Mediation and Criminal Justice: Victims, Offenders and Community*, London, Sage, 1989.

WÜRTENBERGER, T., "La doctrine de Franz von Liszt de la culpabilité et de la responsabilité pénale", in *Travaux du Colloque de Philosophie Penale (12-21January 1959)*, Paris, Dalloz, 1961.

YEAGER, M.G., "Unemployment and Imprisonment", in *Journal of Criminal Law and Criminology*, 70, 1979, pp. 585-588.

YOUNG, J., "Working-class Criminology", in Ian TAYLOR, *et al.* (eds.), *Critical Criminology*, London, Routledge & Kegan Paul, 1975.

ZEMAN, T., *Order, Crime and Punishment: The American Criminological Tradition*, Ph.D. diss. University of California (Santa Cruz, June, 1981).

ZIEGENHABEN, Eduard A. (1935-), *Victims, Crime and Social Control*, New York, Praeger Publisher, 1977.

ZILBOORG, Gregory (1890-1959), *The Psychology of the Criminal Act and Punishment*, New York, Harcourt, Brace, 1954; London, Hogarth Press, 1955; New York, Greenwood Press, 1968.

ZIMRING, Franklin E., "Making the Punishment Fit the Crime: A Consumer's Guide to Sentencing Reform", in *The Hastings Center Report*, 6, 1976, pp. 13-17.

ZIMRING, Franklin E., HAWKINS, Gordon J., *Deterrence; the Legal Threat in Crime Control,* preface by James VORENBERG, Chicago, University of Chicago Press, 1973.

La utilidad del castigo, México, Editores Asociados S.A., 1977.

Capital Punishment and the American Agenda, Cambridge-New York, Cambridge University Press, 1986.

"Dangerousness and Criminal Justice", in *Michigan Law Review,* 85, 1987, pp. 481-509.

ZIPF, Hans, "Alteraciones dogmáticas en los fines de la pena de la prevención especial y de la prevención general", in *Estudios jurídicos sobre la reforma penal,* Córdoba, 1987.

ZUGALDIA ESPINAR, José Miguel, "La prevención penal en la individualización judicial de la pena", in *Anuario de Derecho Penal y Ciencias Penales,* 1981.

INDEX